Aho-Girl

\\'ahô͵gərl\\ *Japanese, noun.*
A clueless girl.

4 | **Hiroyuk**

FEH...

CHARACTER PROFILES

AHO-GIRL's Cast of Characters

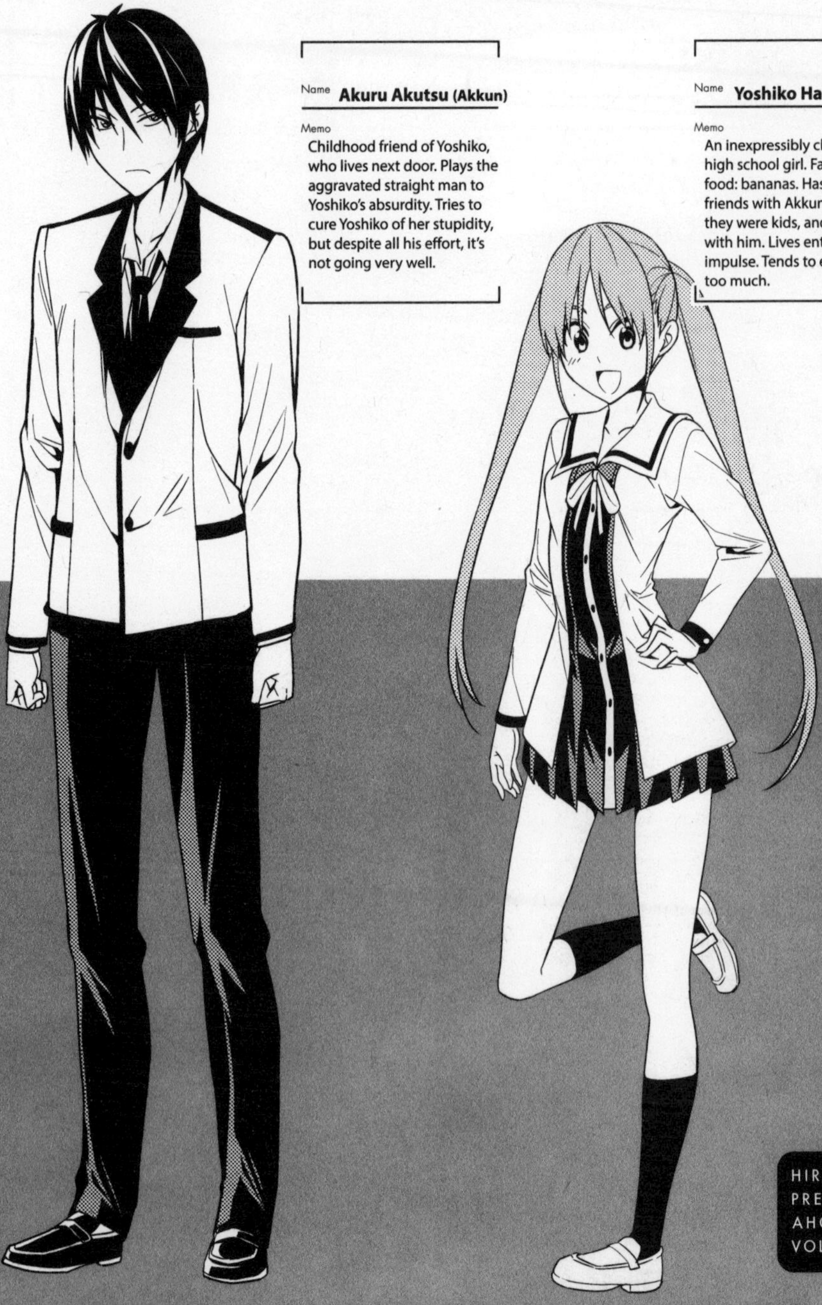

Name **Akuru Akutsu (Akkun)**

Memo

Childhood friend of Yoshiko, who lives next door. Plays the aggravated straight man to Yoshiko's absurdity. Tries to cure Yoshiko of her stupidity, but despite all his effort, it's not going very well.

Name **Yoshiko Hanabatake**

Memo

An inexpressibly clueless high school girl. Favorite food: bananas. Has been friends with Akkun since they were kids, and is in love with him. Lives entirely by impulse. Tends to enjoy life too much.

HIROYUKI PRESENTS AHO-GIRL VOLUME.4

Name **Sayaka Sumino**

Memo

Yoshiko's friend. She's a very kind girl. She knows her kindness lands her in all sorts of trouble, yet she remains kind. Worries about being boring.

Name **Ryuichi Kurosaki**

Memo

An unfortunate hooligan who knows nothing of human kindness and therefore was easily won over by Yoshiko. Seems to want to be friends with Akkun, but there's not much hope for that.

Name **Head Monitor**

Memo

An upperclassman at Yoshiko's school. Has fallen head over heels for Akkun and begun to stray from the moral path, but she doesn't realize it. G cup.

Name **Yoshie Hanabatake**

Memo

Yoshiko's mother. While she does worry about Yoshiko, she's far more worried about her own sunset years. Will use any means necessary to fix Yoshiko up with Akkun.

Name **Ruri Akutsu**

Memo

While her brother Akkun is an overachiever, Ruri's not quite so fortunate. She is constantly dismayed by her terrible grades. Perhaps the day will come when all her hard work pays off. Hates Yoshiko.

Name **Atsuko Oshieda**

Memo

Homeroom teacher for Yoshiko and Akkun's class. Teaches math. She is passionate about education, but has a tendency to treat things far too seriously. Has always attended all-girls schools, and so has no romantic experience.

Name **Dog**

Memo

A ridiculously big dog Yoshiko found at the park. Started out vicious, but once vanquished by Yoshiko, has become docile. Is quite clever and tries to stop Yoshiko from her wilder impulses.

Name **Kids from the Park**

Memo Yoshiko's play friends. These three kids include two very serious, grown-up boys concerned by Yoshiko's idiocy, and a girl named Nozomi who idolizes her. Can often be found playing at the park.

AHO-GIRL CONTENTS

AHO-GIRL

4

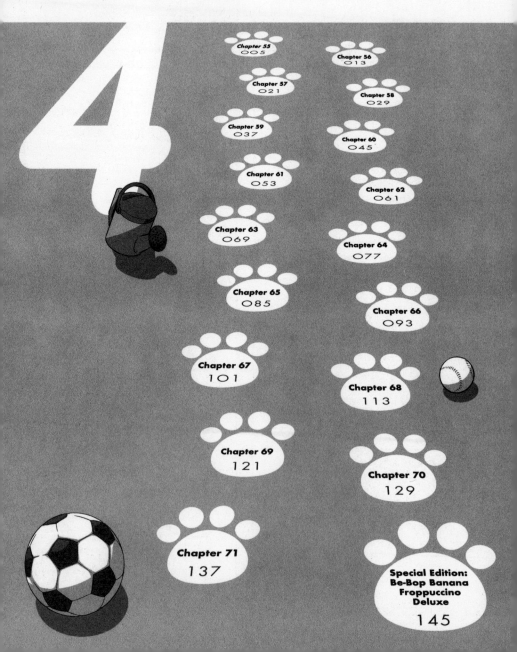

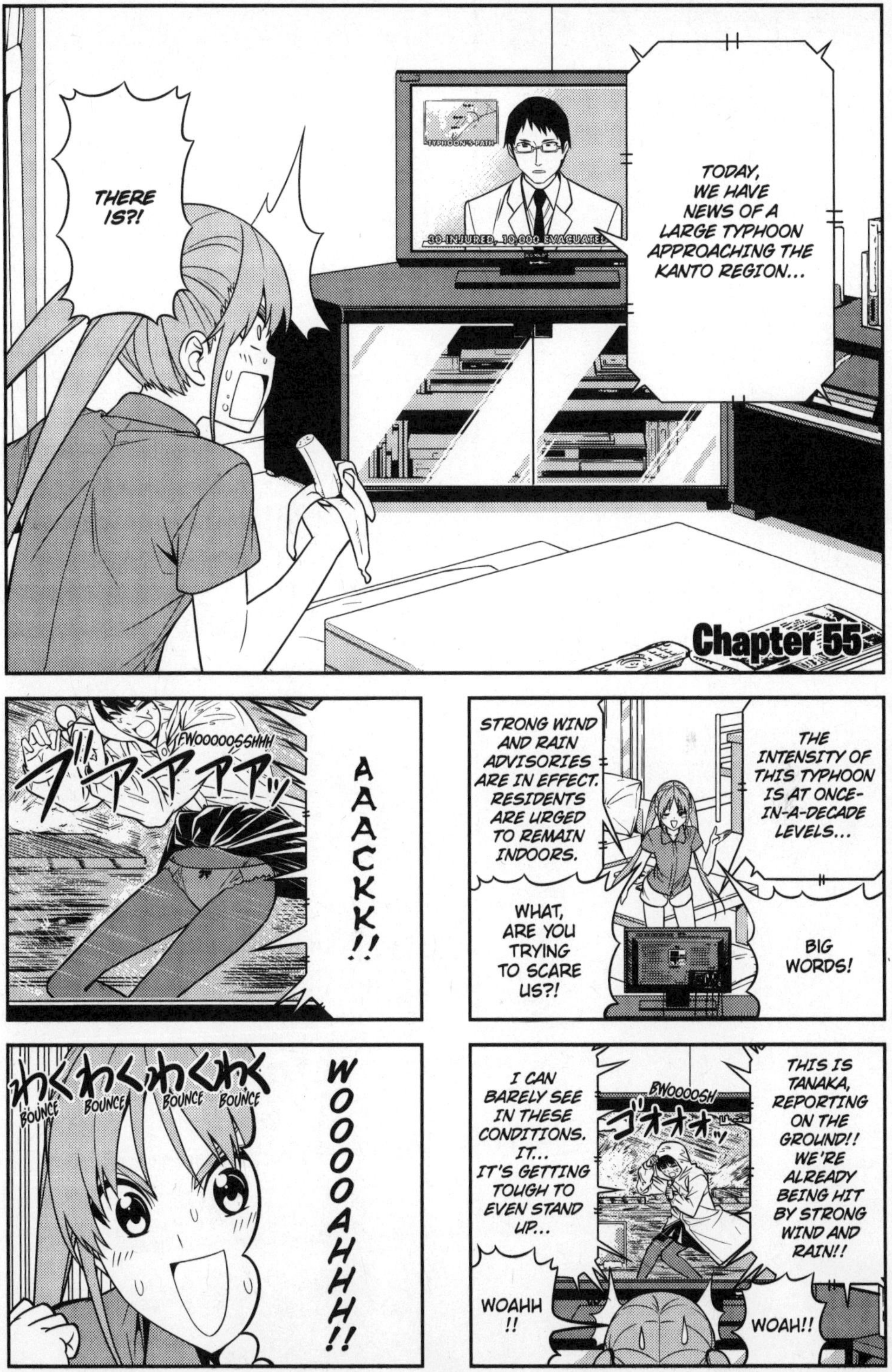
TODAY, WE HAVE NEWS OF A LARGE TYPHOON APPROACHING THE KANTO REGION...
TYPHOON'S PATH
30 INJURED, 10,000 EVACUATED
THERE IS?!
Chapter 55
THE INTENSITY OF THIS TYPHOON IS AT ONCE-IN-A-DECADE LEVELS...
STRONG WIND AND RAIN ADVISORIES ARE IN EFFECT. RESIDENTS ARE URGED TO REMAIN INDOORS.
BIG WORDS!
WHAT, ARE YOU TRYING TO SCARE US?!
AAACKK!!
ブァァァァッ
FWOOOOOSSHHH
THIS IS TANAKA, REPORTING ON THE GROUND!! WE'RE ALREADY BEING HIT BY STRONG WIND AND RAIN!!
ゴオオオッ
BWOOOOSH
I CAN BARELY SEE IN THESE CONDITIONS. IT... IT'S GETTING TOUGH TO EVEN STAND UP...
WOAH!!
WOAHH !!
WOOOOOAHHHH!!
わくわくわくわく
BOUNCE BOUNCE BOUNCE BOUNCE

Start Running

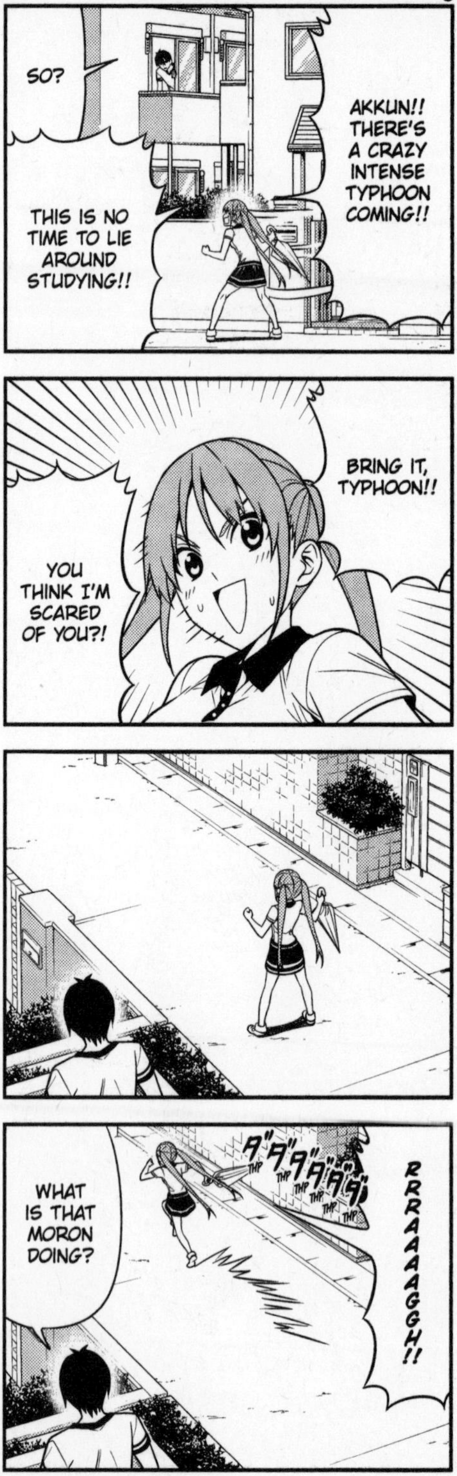
AKKUN!! THERE'S A CRAZY INTENSE TYPHOON COMING!!
THIS IS NO TIME TO LIE AROUND STUDYING!!
SO?
BRING IT, TYPHOON!!
YOU THINK I'M SCARED OF YOU?!
RRRAAAAAGGH!!
THP ダダダダダダ THP THP THP THP THP
WHAT IS THAT MORON DOING?

She Caught Sayaka-chan

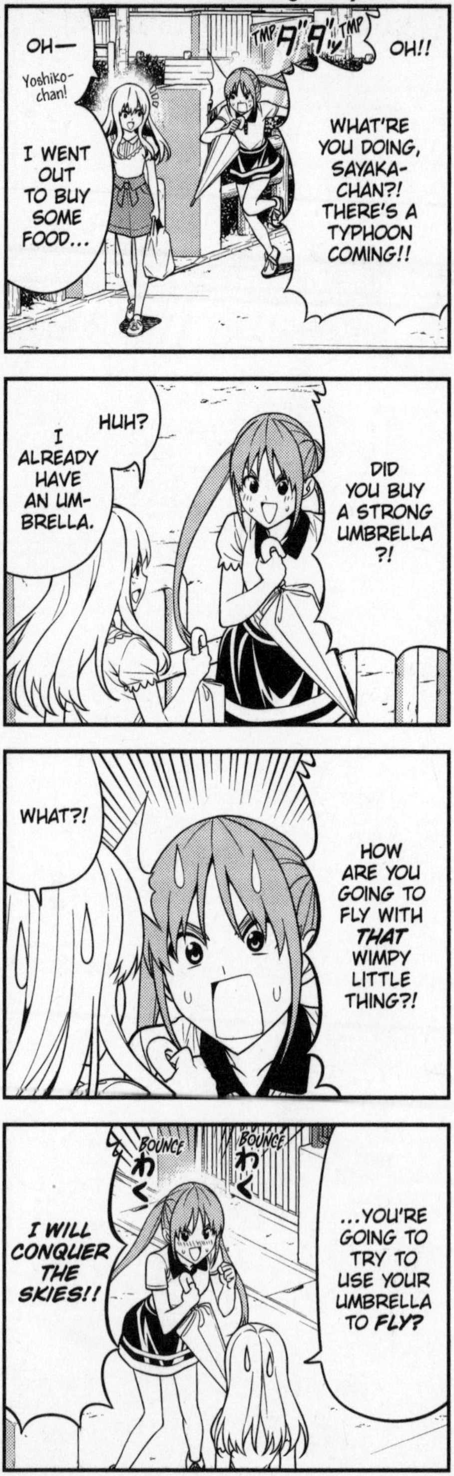
OH!!
TMP ダダッ TMP
WHAT'RE YOU DOING, SAYAKA-CHAN?! THERE'S A TYPHOON COMING!!
OH—
Yoshiko-chan!
I WENT OUT TO BUY SOME FOOD...
DID YOU BUY A STRONG UMBRELLA?!
HUH?
I ALREADY HAVE AN UM-BRELLA.
HOW ARE YOU GOING TO FLY WITH *THAT* WIMPY LITTLE THING?!
WHAT?!
...YOU'RE GOING TO TRY TO USE YOUR UMBRELLA TO *FLY*?
BOUNCE わく BOUNCE わく
I WILL CONQUER THE SKIES!!

The Beginning

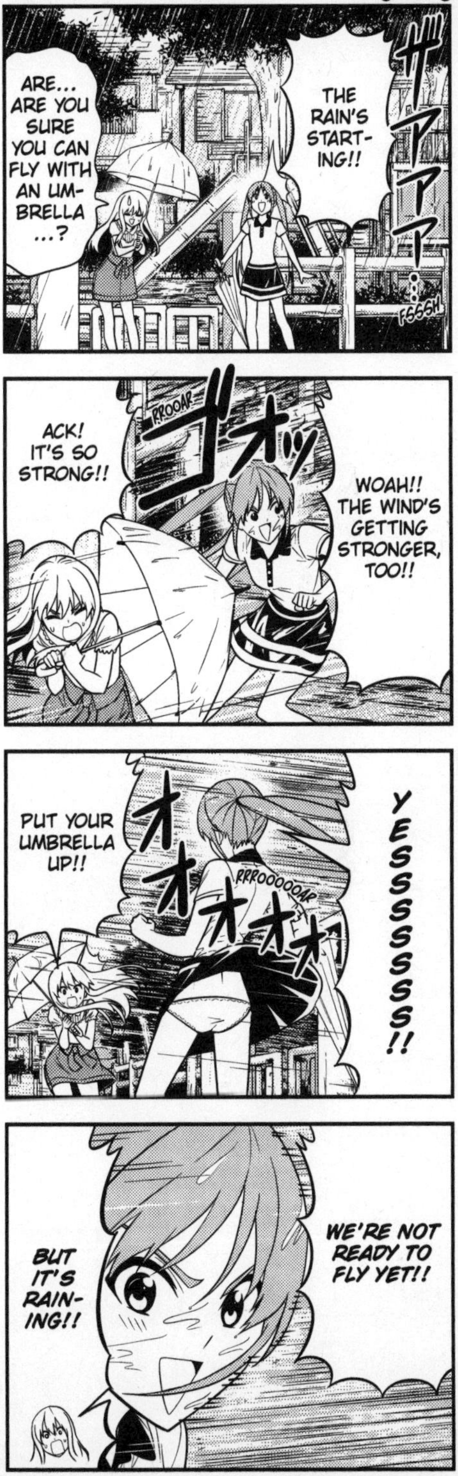
ザアアア…
FSSSH
THE RAIN'S START-ING!!
ARE... ARE YOU SURE YOU CAN FLY WITH AN UM-BRELLA ...?
ゴオッ
RRROOAR
WOAH!! THE WIND'S GETTING STRONGER, TOO!!
ACK! IT'S SO STRONG!!
YESSSSSSS!!
オオオオオ
RRROOOOOAR
PUT YOUR UMBRELLA UP!!
WE'RE NOT READY TO FLY YET!!
BUT IT'S RAIN-ING!!

First Round Elimination

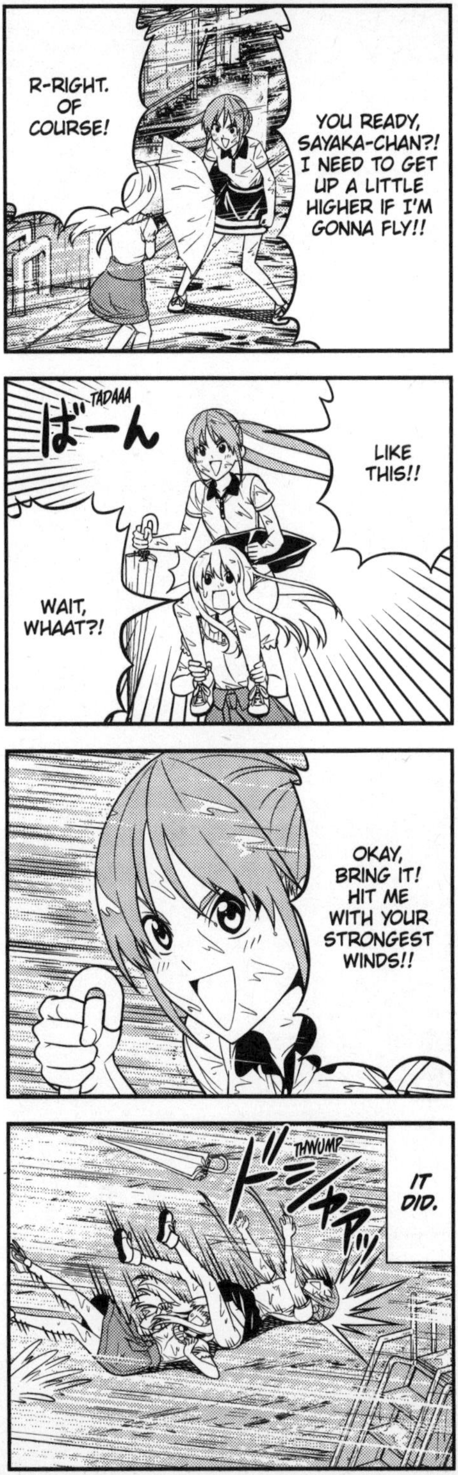
YOU READY, SAYAKA-CHAN?! I NEED TO GET UP A LITTLE HIGHER IF I'M GONNA FLY!!
R-RIGHT. OF COURSE!
ばーん
TADAAA
LIKE THIS!!
WAIT, WHAAT?!
OKAY, BRING IT! HIT ME WITH YOUR STRONGEST WINDS!!
IT DID.
ドシャアッ
THWUMP

It's a Natural Reaction When You Get Cold

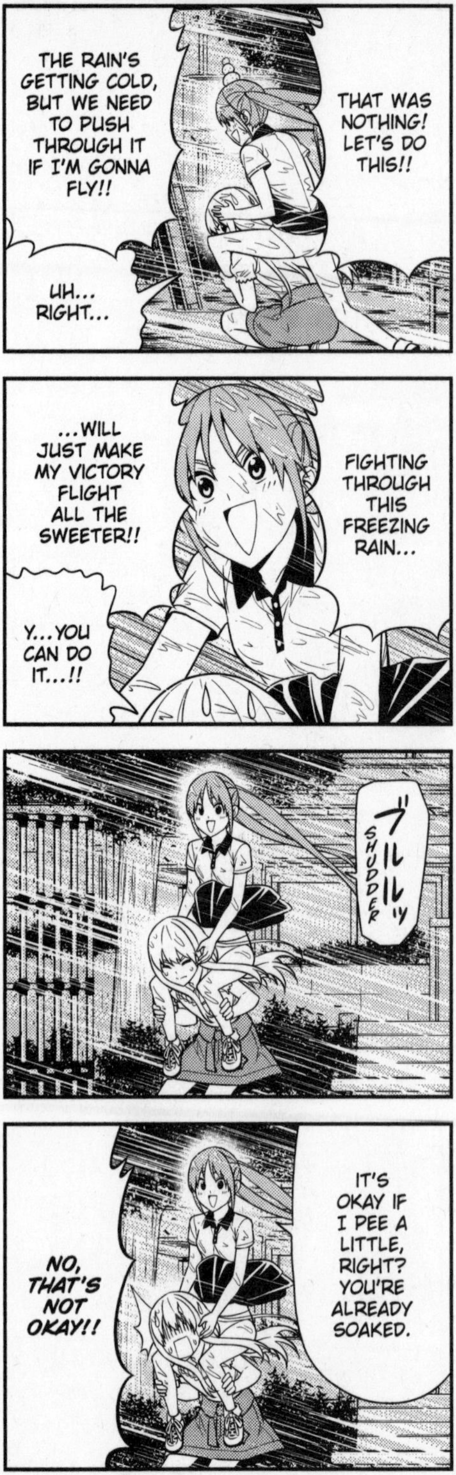

THAT WAS NOTHING! LET'S DO THIS!!
THE RAIN'S GETTING COLD, BUT WE NEED TO PUSH THROUGH IT IF I'M GONNA FLY!!
UH... RIGHT...
FIGHTING THROUGH THIS FREEZING RAIN...
...WILL JUST MAKE MY VICTORY FLIGHT ALL THE SWEETER!!
Y...YOU CAN DO IT...!!
ブルルッ SHUDDER
IT'S OKAY IF I PEE A LITTLE, RIGHT? YOU'RE ALREADY SOAKED.
NO, THAT'S NOT OKAY!!

That Just Happened on TV

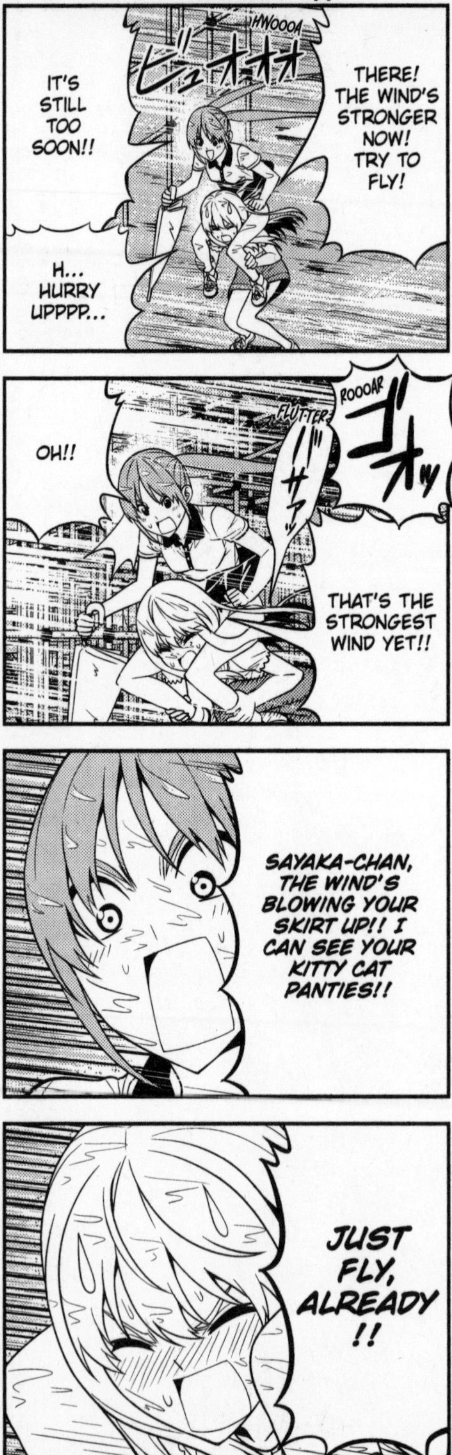

ビュオオオ HWOOOA
THERE! THE WIND'S STRONGER NOW! TRY TO FLY!
IT'S STILL TOO SOON!!
H... HURRY UPPPP...
ゴオッ ROOOAR
バサアッ FLUTTER
OH!!
THAT'S THE STRONGEST WIND YET!!
SAYAKA-CHAN, THE WIND'S BLOWING YOUR SKIRT UP!! I CAN SEE YOUR KITTY CAT PANTIES!!
JUST FLY, ALREADY!!

Hold on Tight and Go for It!

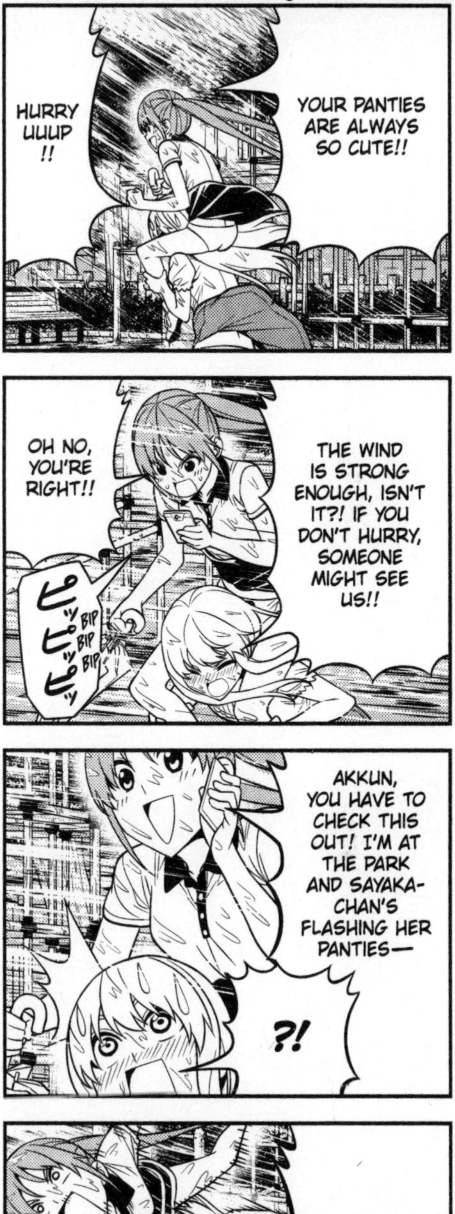
YOUR PANTIES ARE ALWAYS SO CUTE!!
HURRY UUUP !!
THE WIND IS STRONG ENOUGH, ISN'T IT?! IF YOU DON'T HURRY, SOMEONE MIGHT SEE US!!
OH NO, YOU'RE RIGHT!!
ピッピッピッ
BIP BIP BIP
AKKUN, YOU HAVE TO CHECK THIS OUT! I'M AT THE PARK AND SAYAKA-CHAN'S FLASHING HER PANTIES—
?!
TAKE THAAAAT !!
RRAAGH
WOOAH!

Yoshiko-chan! You're Flyyying!

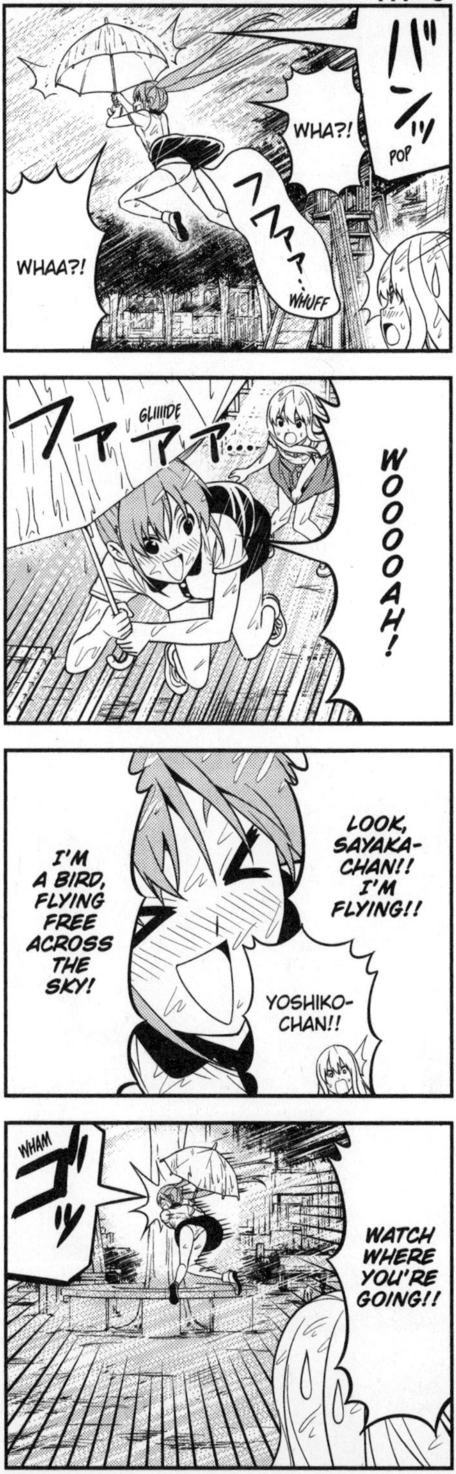
バンッ
POP
WHA?!
フワァァ…
WHUFF
WHAA?!
ファアア…
GLIIIIDE
WOOOOOAH!
LOOK, SAYAKA-CHAN!! I'M FLYING!!
I'M A BIRD, FLYING FREE ACROSS THE SKY!
YOSHIKO-CHAN!!
ゴッ
WHAM
WATCH WHERE YOU'RE GOING!!

Uncontainable Excitement

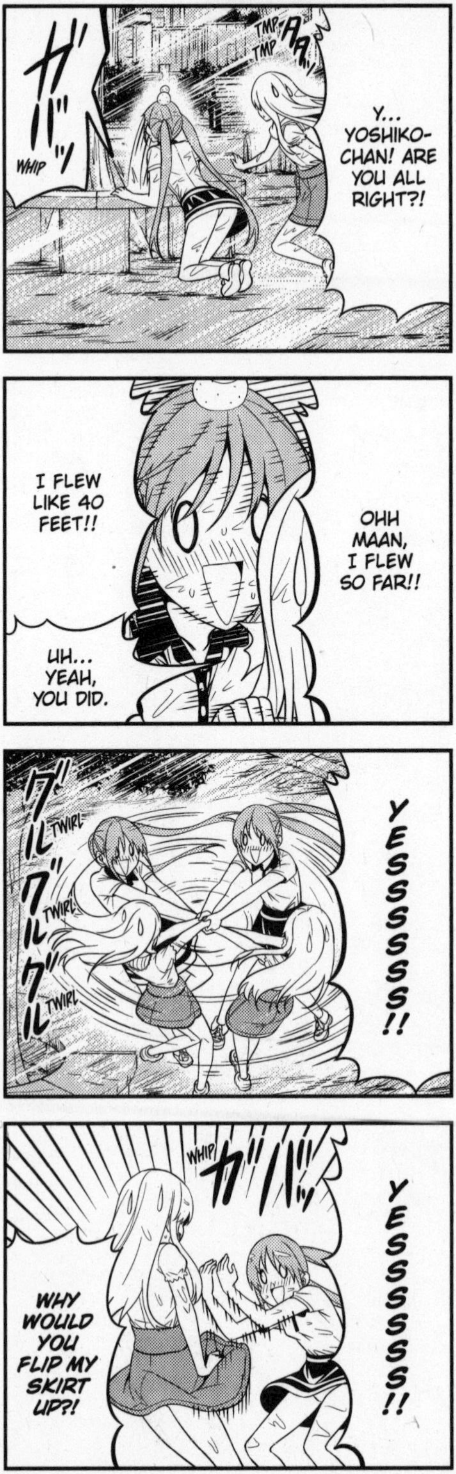
TMP TMP
AA
Y... YOSHIKO-CHAN! ARE YOU ALL RIGHT?!
ガバッ
WHIP
OHH MAAN, I FLEW SO FAR!!
I FLEW LIKE 40 FEET!!
UH... YEAH, YOU DID.
YESSSSSS!!
TWIRL
TWIRL
TWIRL
グルグル
YESSSSSS!!
WHIP
ガバッ
WHY WOULD YOU FLIP MY SKIRT UP?!

Perfect Pose

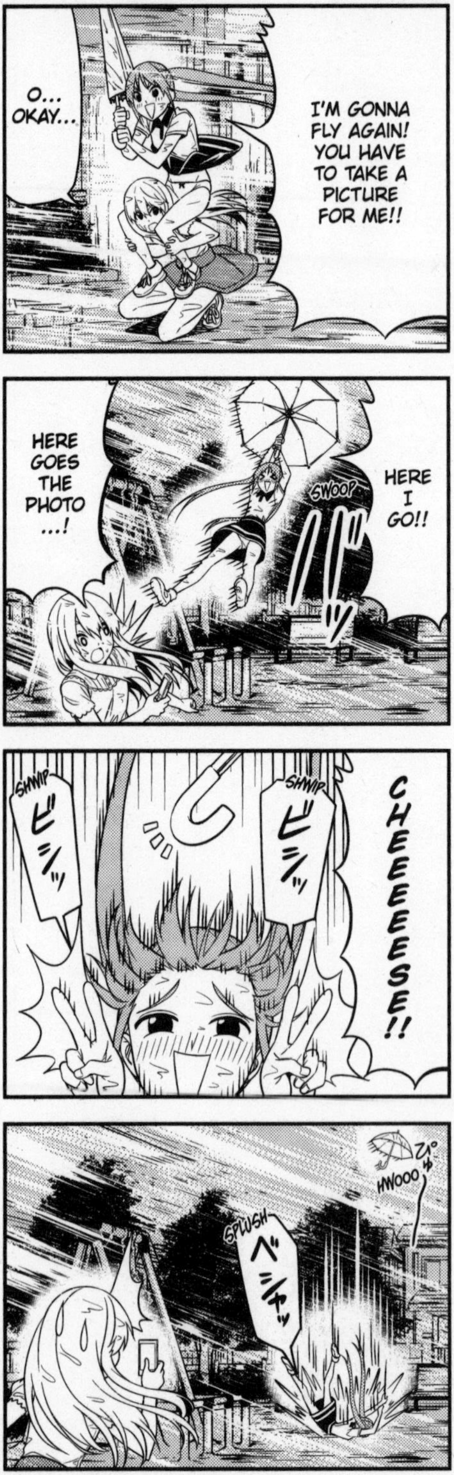
I'M GONNA FLY AGAIN! YOU HAVE TO TAKE A PICTURE FOR ME!!
O... OKAY...
HERE I GO!!
SWOOP
バッ
HERE GOES THE PHOTO ...!
CHEEEEEESE!!
SHWIP
ビシッ
SHWIP
ビシッ
ぴゅー
HWOOO
SPLUSH
べシャッ

So Happy

THE TY-PHOON DE-PARTS ...

AHHH...! I'LL SEE YOU AGAIN... NEXT YEAR... TYPHOON...

I DON'T LIKE HOW SATISFIED SHE LOOKS ...

(Ah! Ah! Arashiii! Game Center)

Aho-Girl

\\'ahô‚gərl\\ *Japanese, noun.*
A clueless girl.

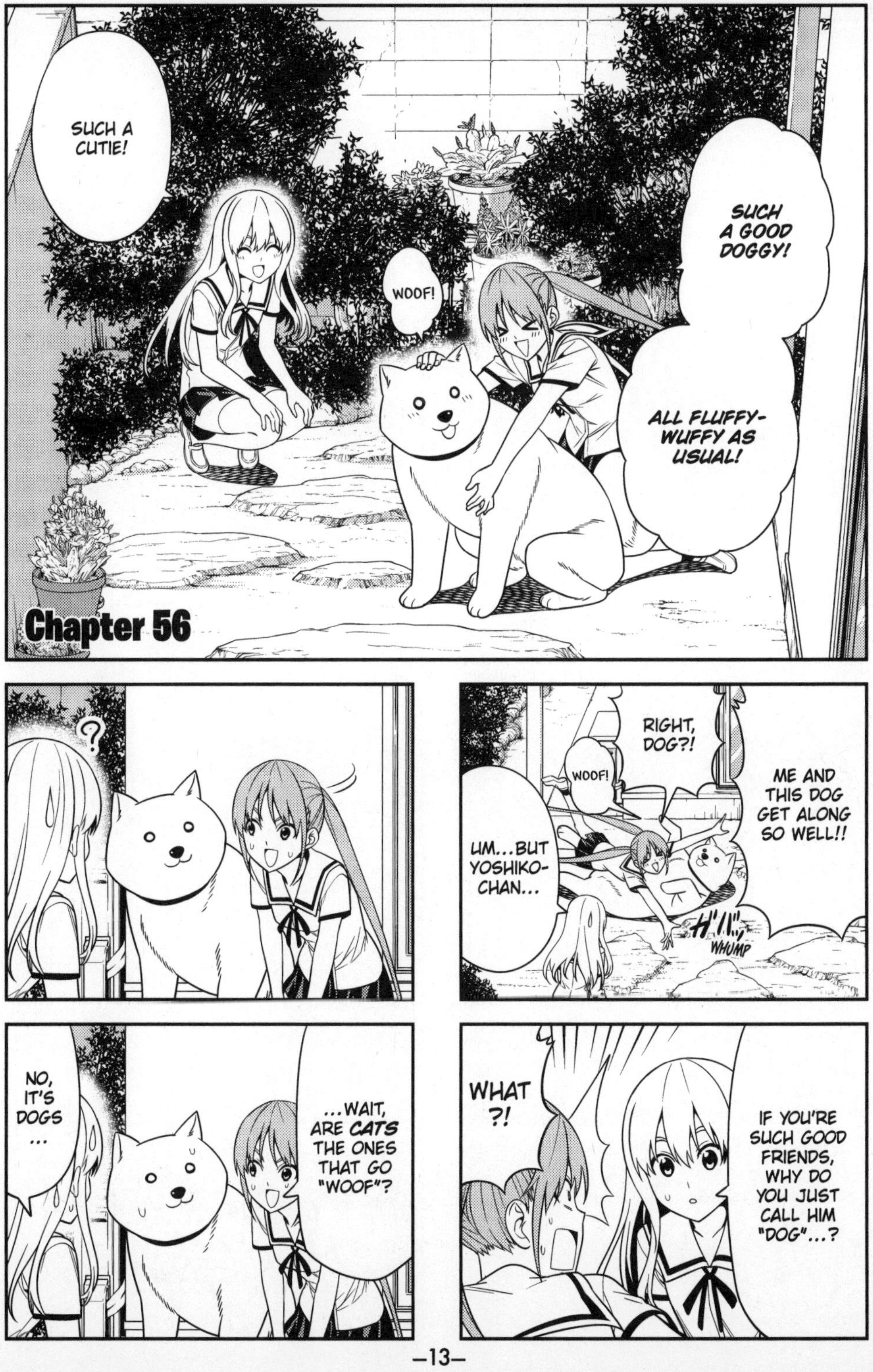
SUCH A GOOD DOGGY!
ALL FLUFFY-WUFFY AS USUAL!
WOOF!
SUCH A CUTIE!
Chapter 56
ME AND THIS DOG GET ALONG SO WELL!!
RIGHT, DOG?!
WOOF!
UM...BUT YOSHIKO-CHAN...
WHUMP
?
IF YOU'RE SUCH GOOD FRIENDS, WHY DO YOU JUST CALL HIM "DOG"...?
WHAT ?!
...WAIT, ARE *CATS* THE ONES THAT GO "WOOF"?
NO, IT'S DOGS ...

Sayaka's Leveling up Her Straight Man Skills!

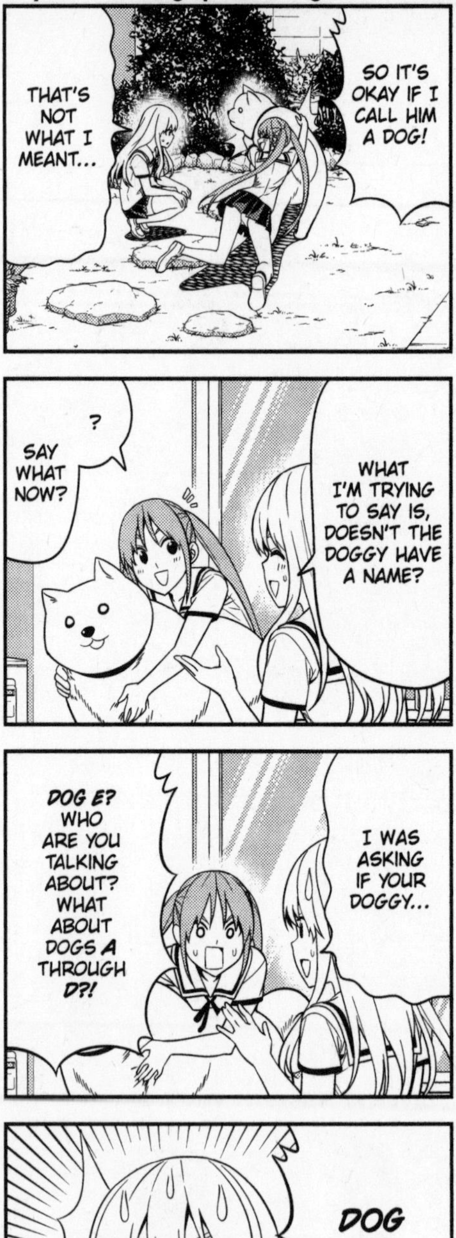
SO IT'S OKAY IF I CALL HIM A DOG!
THAT'S NOT WHAT I MEANT...
WHAT I'M TRYING TO SAY IS, DOESN'T THE DOGGY HAVE A NAME?
? SAY WHAT NOW?
I WAS ASKING IF YOUR DOGGY...
DOG E? WHO ARE YOU TALKING ABOUT? WHAT ABOUT DOGS A THROUGH D?!
DOG E?!

How to Achieve Peace

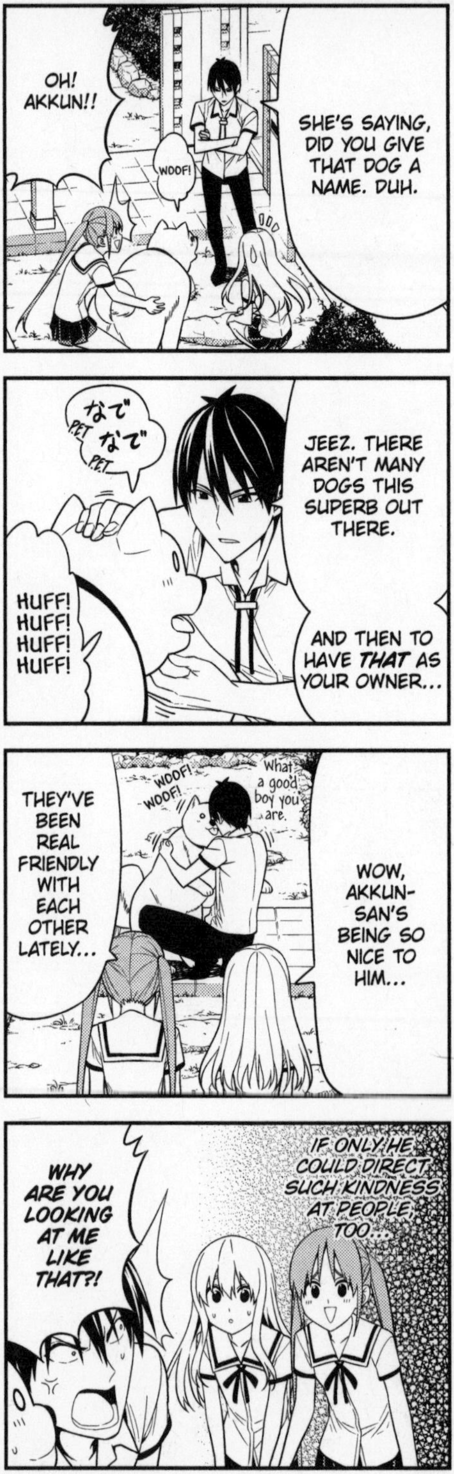
SHE'S SAYING, DID YOU GIVE THAT DOG A NAME. DUH.
WOOF!
OH! AKKUN!!
JEEZ. THERE AREN'T MANY DOGS THIS SUPERB OUT THERE.
AND THEN TO HAVE THAT AS YOUR OWNER...
なで PET なで PET
HUFF! HUFF! HUFF! HUFF!
WOW, AKKUN-SAN'S BEING SO NICE TO HIM...
What a good boy you are.
WOOF! WOOF!
THEY'VE BEEN REAL FRIENDLY WITH EACH OTHER LATELY...
IF ONLY HE COULD DIRECT SUCH KINDNESS AT PEOPLE, TOO...
WHY ARE YOU LOOKING AT ME LIKE THAT?!

So Freakin' Cool

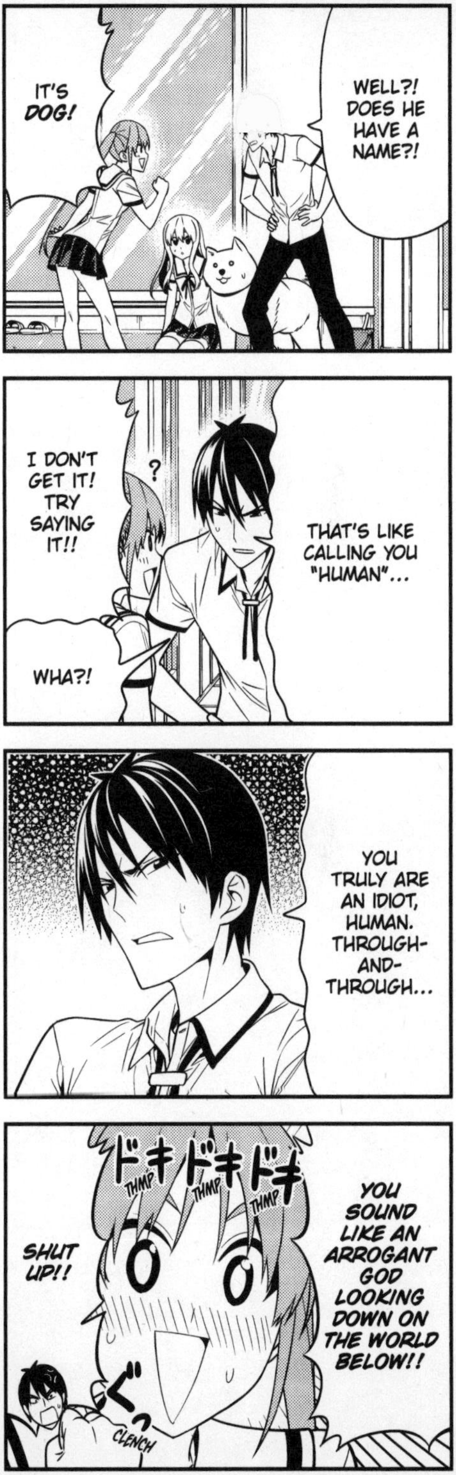
WELL?! DOES HE HAVE A NAME?!
IT'S DOG!
THAT'S LIKE CALLING YOU "HUMAN"...
I DON'T GET IT! TRY SAYING IT!!
?
WHA?!
YOU TRULY ARE AN IDIOT, HUMAN. THROUGH-AND-THROUGH...
ドキドキドキ
THMP THMP THMP
YOU SOUND LIKE AN ARROGANT GOD LOOKING DOWN ON THE WORLD BELOW!!
SHUT UP!!
ぐっ
CLENCH

The Mystery Deepens

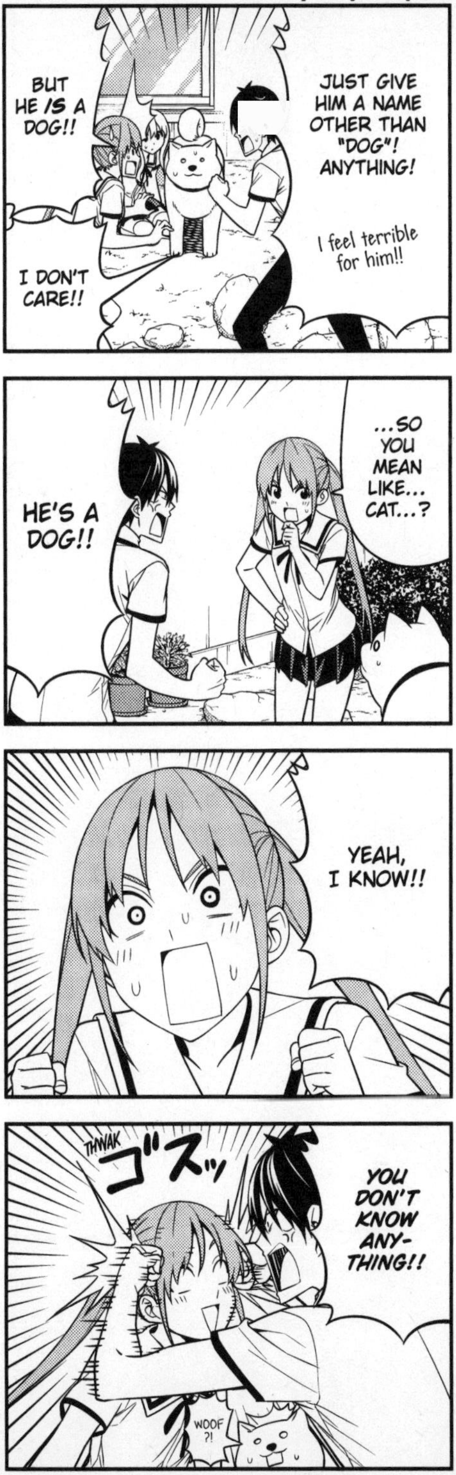
JUST GIVE HIM A NAME OTHER THAN "DOG"! ANYTHING!
I feel terrible for him!!
BUT HE IS A DOG!!
I DON'T CARE!!
...SO YOU MEAN LIKE... CAT...?
HE'S A DOG!!
YEAH, I KNOW!!
ゴスッ
THWAK
YOU DON'T KNOW ANYTHING!!
WOOF?!

DING DING DING!

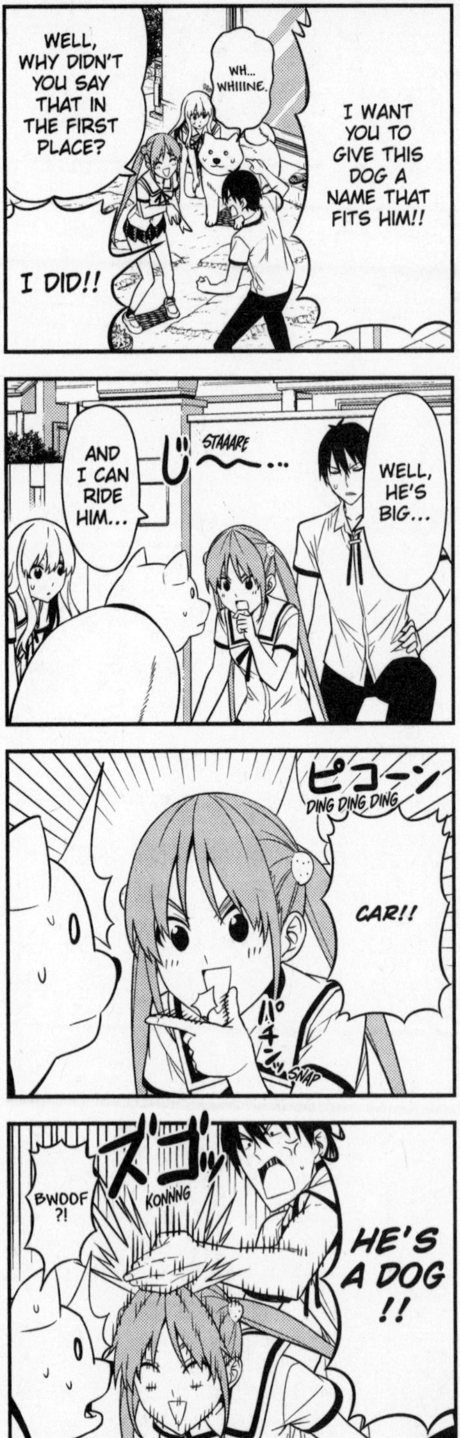
I WANT YOU TO GIVE THIS DOG A NAME THAT FITS HIM!!
WH... WHIIINE.
WELL, WHY DIDN'T YOU SAY THAT IN THE FIRST PLACE?
I DID!!
WELL, HE'S BIG...
じ〜… STAAARE
AND I CAN RIDE HIM...
ピコーン DING DING DING
CAR!!
パチンッ SNAP
HE'S A DOG!!
ズゴッ KONNNG
BWOOF?!

After Akkun's Favorite Director

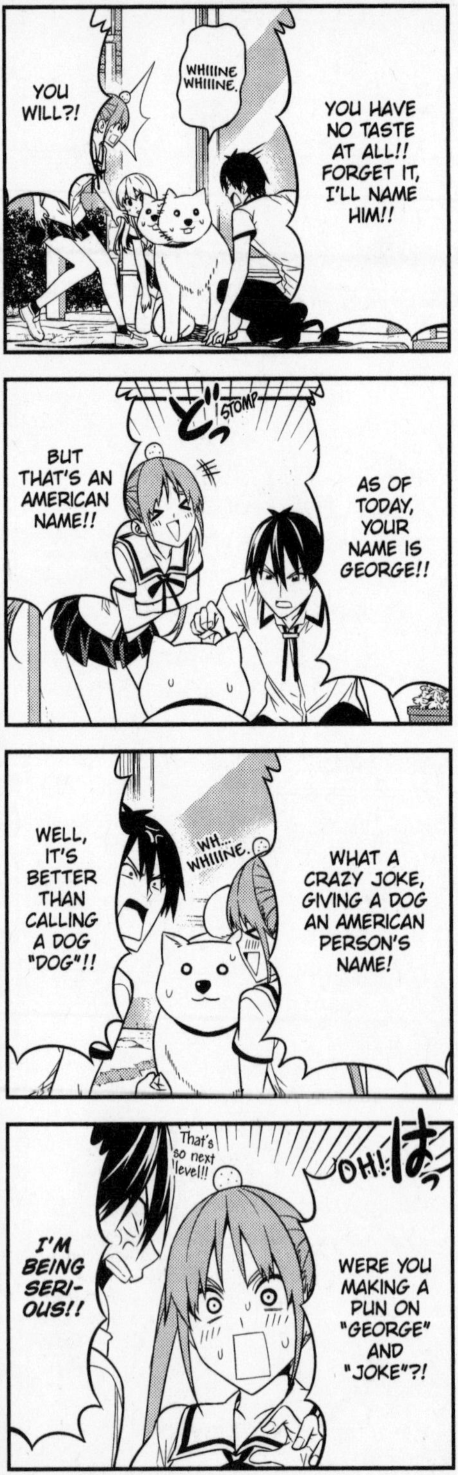
YOU HAVE NO TASTE AT ALL!! FORGET IT, I'LL NAME HIM!!
WHIIINE WHIIINE.
YOU WILL?!
AS OF TODAY, YOUR NAME IS GEORGE!!
どっ STOMP
BUT THAT'S AN AMERICAN NAME!!
WHAT A CRAZY JOKE, GIVING A DOG AN AMERICAN PERSON'S NAME!
WH... WHIIINE.
WELL, IT'S BETTER THAN CALLING A DOG "DOG"!!
はっ OH!
WERE YOU MAKING A PUN ON "GEORGE" AND "JOKE"?!
That's so next level!!!
I'M BEING SERI-OUS!!

Heated Debate

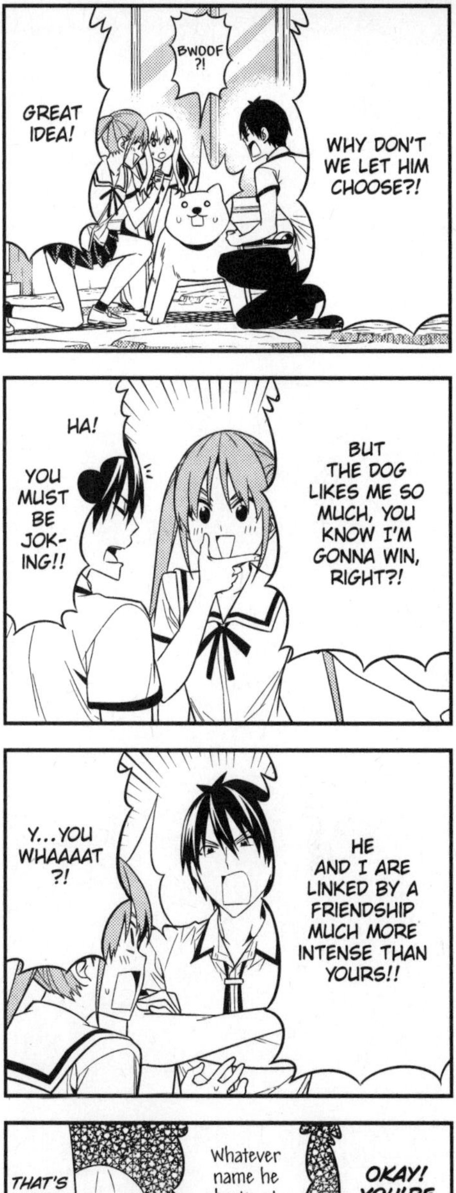
WHY DON'T WE LET HIM CHOOSE?!
BWOOF ?!
GREAT IDEA!
BUT THE DOG LIKES ME SO MUCH, YOU KNOW I'M GONNA WIN, RIGHT?!
HA!
YOU MUST BE JOK-ING!!
HE AND I ARE LINKED BY A FRIENDSHIP MUCH MORE INTENSE THAN YOURS!!
Y...YOU WHAAAAT ?!
OKAY! YOU'RE ON!
Whatever name he barks at wins!
THAT'S SO MUCH PRES-SURE ...
ダラ PLIP
ダラ PLIP

His Choice

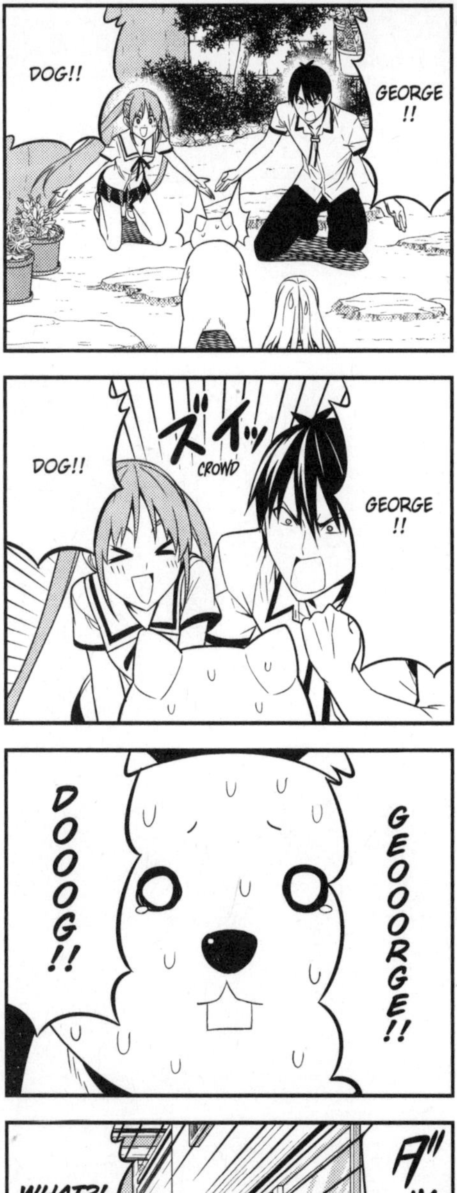
GEORGE !!
DOG!!
GEORGE !!
ズイッ CROWD
DOG!!
GEOOORGE!!
DOOOOG!!
ダッ BOLT
WHAT?!
Are we playing chase?!

The Distant Howl of Love

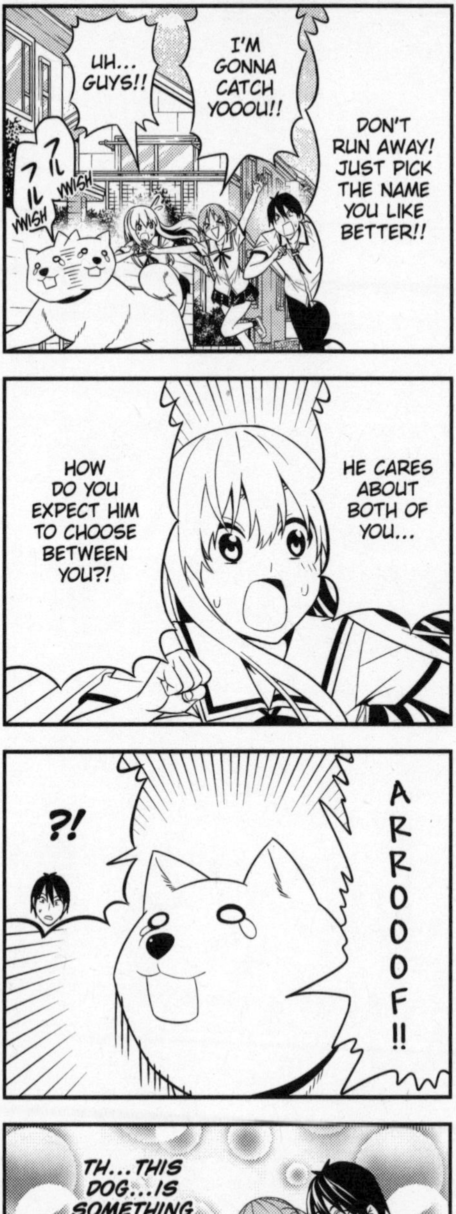
DON'T RUN AWAY! JUST PICK THE NAME YOU LIKE BETTER!!
I'M GONNA CATCH YOOOU!!
UH... GUYS!!
フル VWISH
フル VWISH
HE CARES ABOUT BOTH OF YOU...
HOW DO YOU EXPECT HIM TO CHOOSE BETWEEN YOU?!
ARROOOOF!!
?!
TH...THIS DOG...IS SOMETHING ELSE...

Fighting Is Stupid

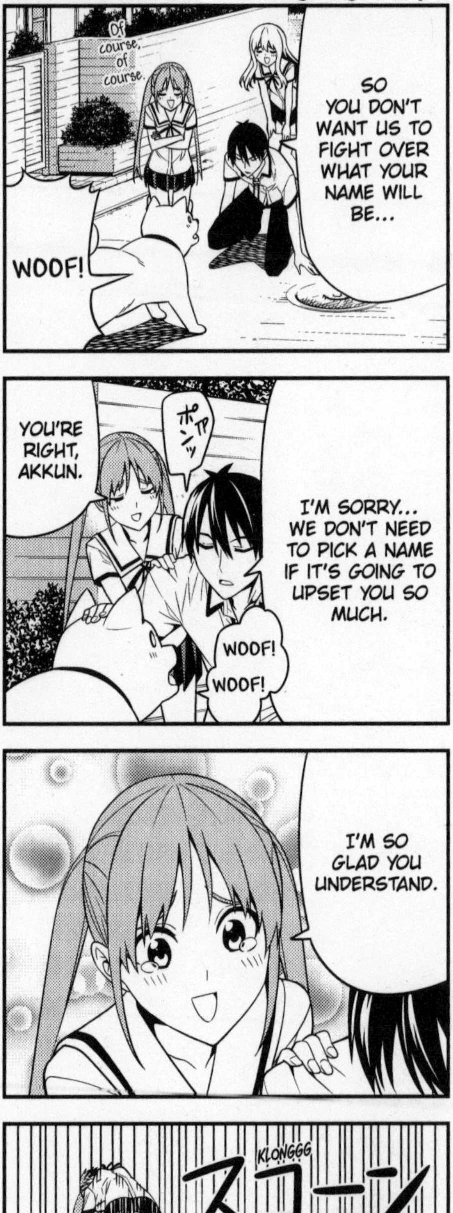
SO YOU DON'T WANT US TO FIGHT OVER WHAT YOUR NAME WILL BE...
Of course, of course.
WOOF!
I'M SORRY... WE DON'T NEED TO PICK A NAME IF IT'S GOING TO UPSET YOU SO MUCH.
ポンッ TP
YOU'RE RIGHT, AKKUN.
WOOF!
WOOF!
I'M SO GLAD YOU UNDERSTAND.
スコーン KLONGGG

The Fighting Will Never End

THIS ONLY STARTED BECAUSE *YOU* DECIDED TO BE WEIRD AND CALL HIM "DOG"!!
IT'S NOT WEIRD, THOUGH!
あわあわ
FLUSTER FLUSTER
WHY DON'T YOU TRY BEING SOMEONE'S DOG, THEN!!
THIS... IS REALLY TOUGH ON YOU...
WHIIIINE.
THAT WOULD BE GREAT!!
IT WOULD NOT!!

(Nyan to Wonderful)

Aho-Girl

\\'ahô͵gərl\\ *Japanese, noun.*
A clueless girl.

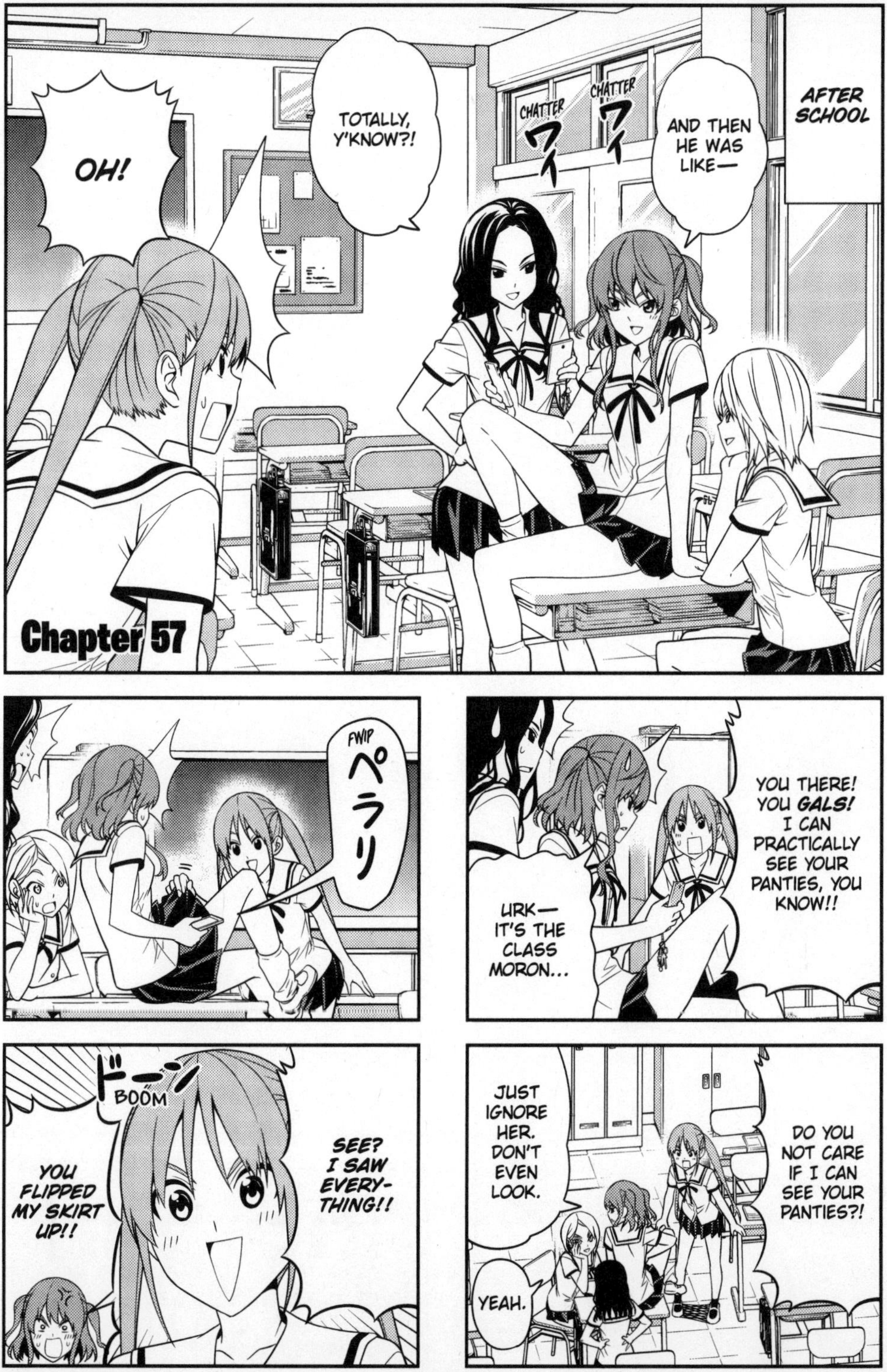
AFTER SCHOOL
AND THEN HE WAS LIKE—
CHATTER ワイ
CHATTER ワイ
TOTALLY, Y'KNOW?!
OH!
Chapter 57
YOU THERE! YOU GALS! I CAN PRACTICALLY SEE YOUR PANTIES, YOU KNOW!!
URK— IT'S THE CLASS MORON...
FWIP ペラリ
DO YOU NOT CARE IF I CAN SEE YOUR PANTIES?!
JUST IGNORE HER. DON'T EVEN LOOK.
YEAH.
ドーン BOOM
SEE? I SAW EVERY-THING!!
YOU FLIPPED MY SKIRT UP!!

Prejudice

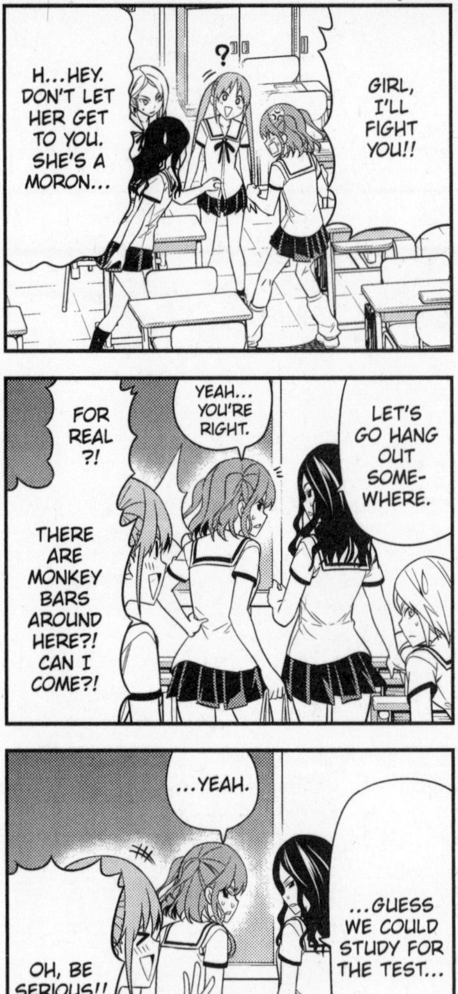
GIRL, I'LL FIGHT YOU!!
?
H...HEY. DON'T LET HER GET TO YOU. SHE'S A MORON...
LET'S GO HANG OUT SOME-WHERE.
YEAH... YOU'RE RIGHT.
FOR REAL?!
THERE ARE MONKEY BARS AROUND HERE?! CAN I COME?!
...GUESS WE COULD STUDY FOR THE TEST...
(She's lying.)
...YEAH.
OH, BE SERIOUS!!
Hilarious!
GALS LIKE YOU DON'T STUDY! EVERYONE KNOWS THAT!!
YOU MAKING FUN OF US?!

This Is How You Make Friends

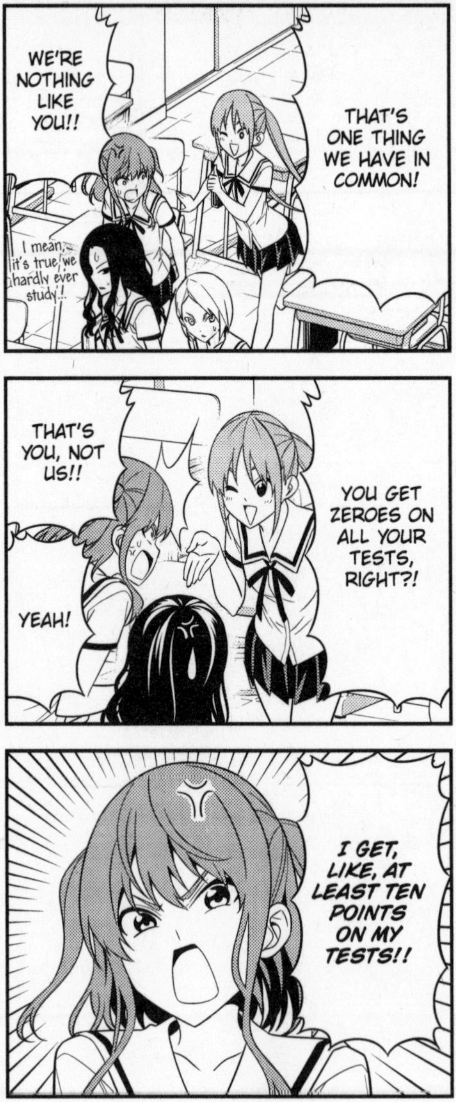
THAT'S ONE THING WE HAVE IN COMMON!
WE'RE NOTHING LIKE YOU!!
I mean, it's true, we hardly ever study!
YOU GET ZEROES ON ALL YOUR TESTS, RIGHT?!
THAT'S YOU, NOT US!!
YEAH!
I GET, LIKE, AT LEAST TEN POINTS ON MY TESTS!!
SEE?! YOU'RE AN IDIOT!!
仲間!
KINDRED SPIRITS
I JUST HATE STUDYING, THAT'S ALL!!
ぐっ
NICE

Terminator

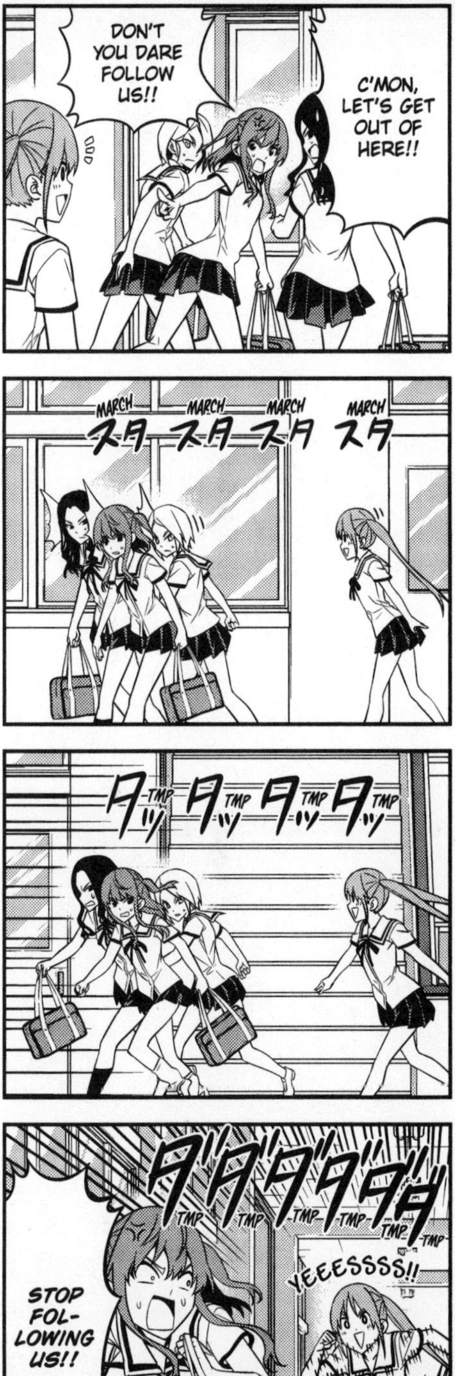
C'MON, LET'S GET OUT OF HERE!!
DON'T YOU DARE FOLLOW US!!
MARCH
MARCH
MARCH
MARCH
TMP
TMP
TMP
TMP
TMP
TMP
TMP
TMP
TMP
TMP
YEEESSSS!!
STOP FOL-LOWING US!!

You Say Such Cool Stuff

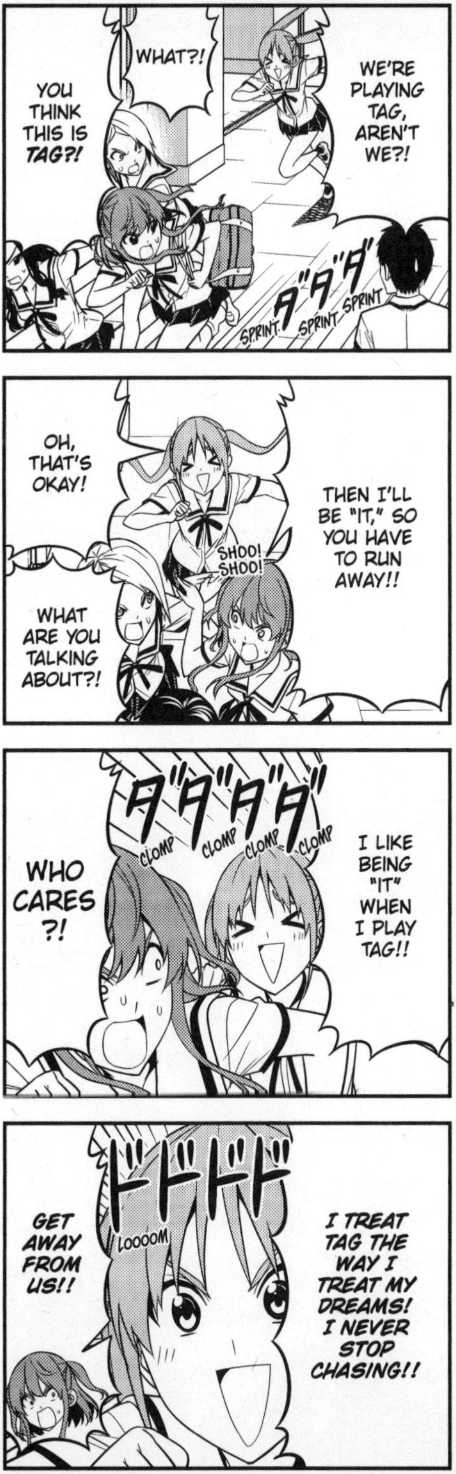
WE'RE PLAYING TAG, AREN'T WE?!
WHAT?!
YOU THINK THIS IS *TAG?!*
SPRINT
SPRINT
SPRINT
THEN I'LL BE "IT," SO YOU HAVE TO RUN AWAY!!
OH, THAT'S OKAY!
SHOO! SHOO!
WHAT ARE YOU TALKING ABOUT?!
I LIKE BEING "IT" WHEN I PLAY TAG!!
CLOMP
CLOMP
CLOMP
CLOMP
WHO CARES ?!
I TREAT TAG THE WAY I TREAT MY DREAMS! I NEVER STOP CHASING!!
LOOOOM
GET AWAY FROM US!!

She's Also Hiding It for Her

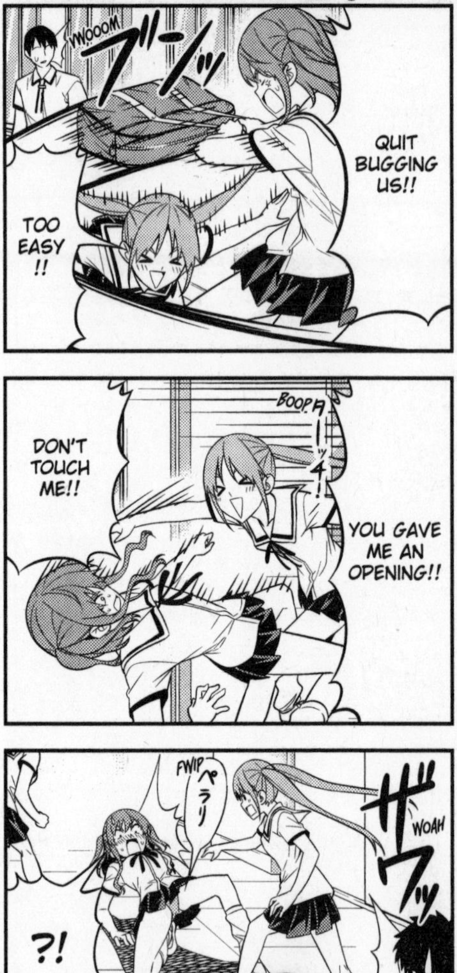
YWOOOM
ブーンッ
QUIT BUGGING US!!
TOO EASY !!
BOOP
ター ッ!
YOU GAVE ME AN OPENING!!
DON'T TOUCH ME!!
ザワッ
WOAH
ペラリ
FWIP
?!
BOOP
ター ッ!
ANOTHER OPENING !!
I WILL KILL YOU!!
スパーン!
SWAT

What Choice Do You Have?

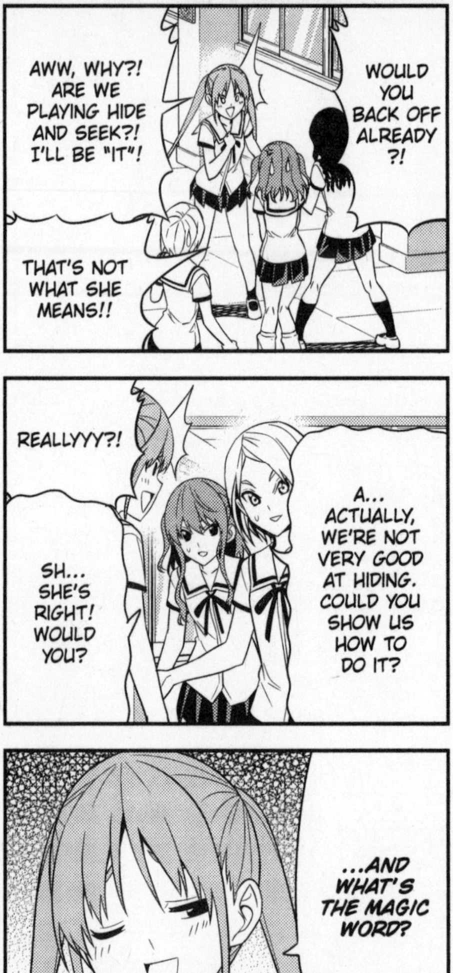
WOULD YOU BACK OFF ALREADY ?!
AWW, WHY?! ARE WE PLAYING HIDE AND SEEK?! I'LL BE "IT"!
THAT'S NOT WHAT SHE MEANS!!
A... ACTUALLY, WE'RE NOT VERY GOOD AT HIDING. COULD YOU SHOW US HOW TO DO IT?
REALLYYY?!
SH... SHE'S RIGHT! WOULD YOU?
...AND WHAT'S THE MAGIC WORD?
YWOOSH
PRETTY PLEASE !!
サッ
HUP
HOW CAN I SAY NO!!

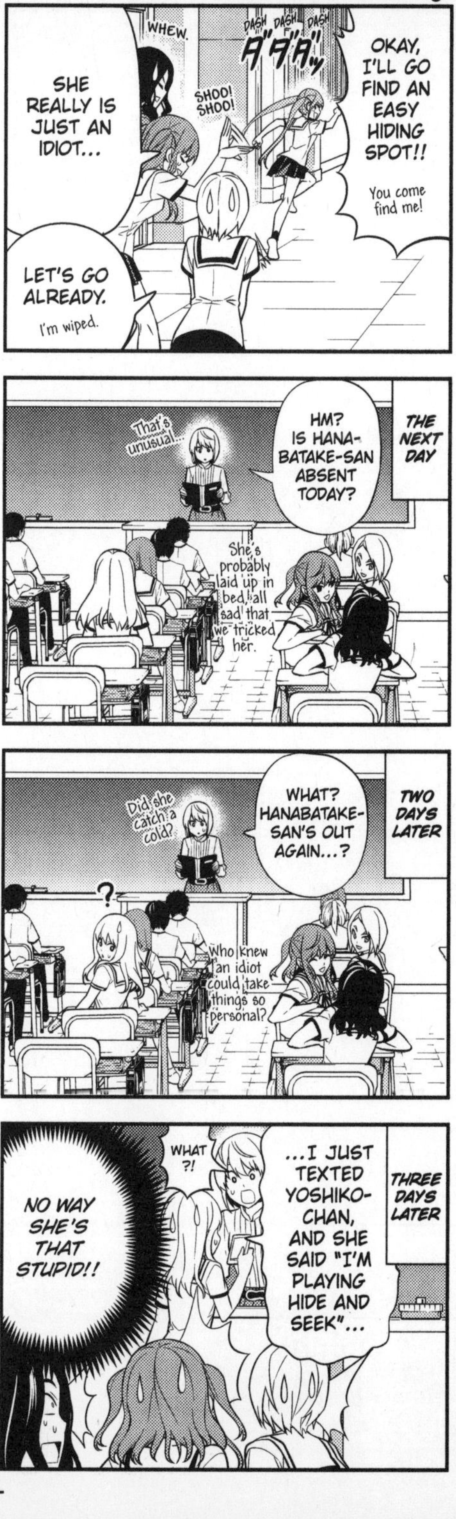
OKAY, I'LL GO FIND AN EASY HIDING SPOT!!
You come find me!
DASH DASH DASH
SHOO! SHOO!
WHEW.
SHE REALLY IS JUST AN IDIOT...
LET'S GO ALREADY.
I'm wiped.
THE NEXT DAY
HM? IS HANA-BATAKE-SAN ABSENT TODAY?
That's unusual.
She's probably laid up in bed, all sad that we tricked her.
TWO DAYS LATER
WHAT? HANABATAKE-SAN'S OUT AGAIN...?
Did she catch a cold?
?
Who knew an idiot could take things so personal?
THREE DAYS LATER
...I JUST TEXTED YOSHIKO-CHAN, AND SHE SAID "I'M PLAYING HIDE AND SEEK"...
WHAT ?!
NO WAY SHE'S THAT STUPID!!

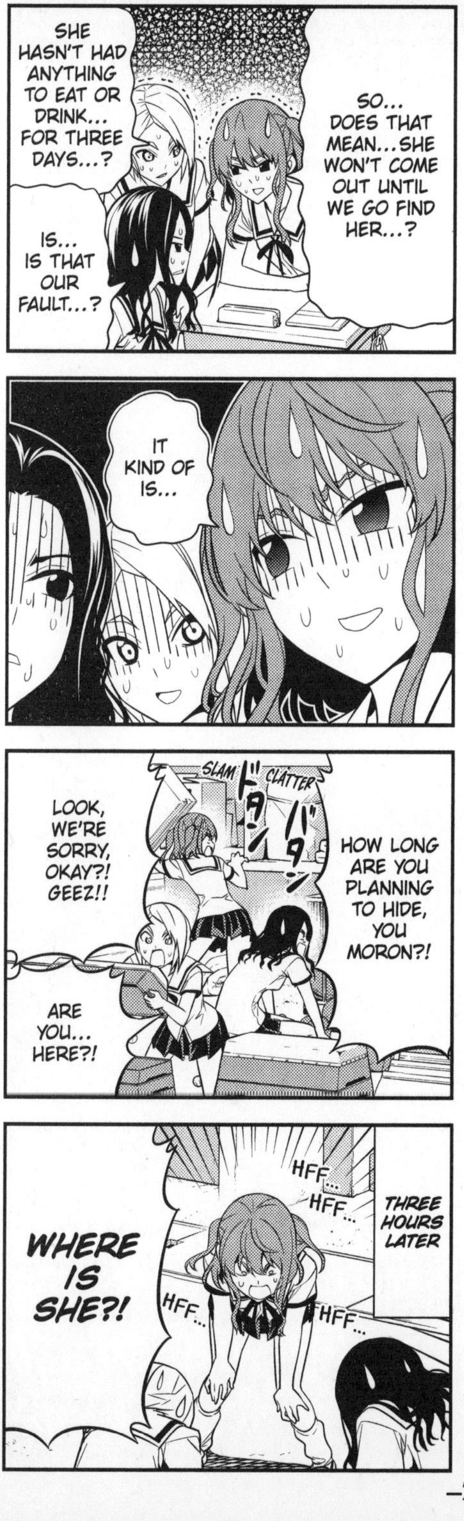
SO... DOES THAT MEAN...SHE WON'T COME OUT UNTIL WE GO FIND HER...?
SHE HASN'T HAD ANYTHING TO EAT OR DRINK... FOR THREE DAYS...?
IS... IS THAT OUR FAULT...?
IT KIND OF IS...
SLAM CLATTER
HOW LONG ARE YOU PLANNING TO HIDE, YOU MORON?!
LOOK, WE'RE SORRY, OKAY?! GEEZ!!
ARE YOU... HERE?!
THREE HOURS LATER
HFF... HFF...
WHERE IS SHE?!
HFF... HFF...

Found You!

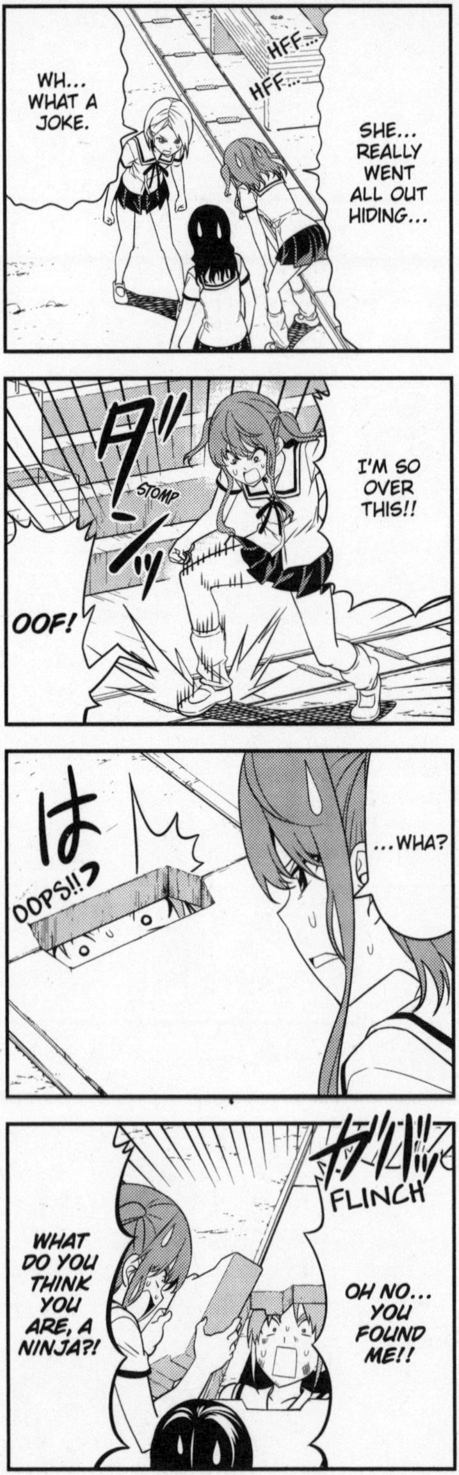
HFF... HFF...
SHE... REALLY WENT ALL OUT HIDING...
WH... WHAT A JOKE.
I'M SO OVER THIS!!
ダンッ
STOMP
OOF!
...WHA?
はっ
OOPS!!
ガバッ
FLINCH
OH NO... YOU FOUND ME!!
WHAT DO YOU THINK YOU ARE, A NINJA?!

I Made a Friend

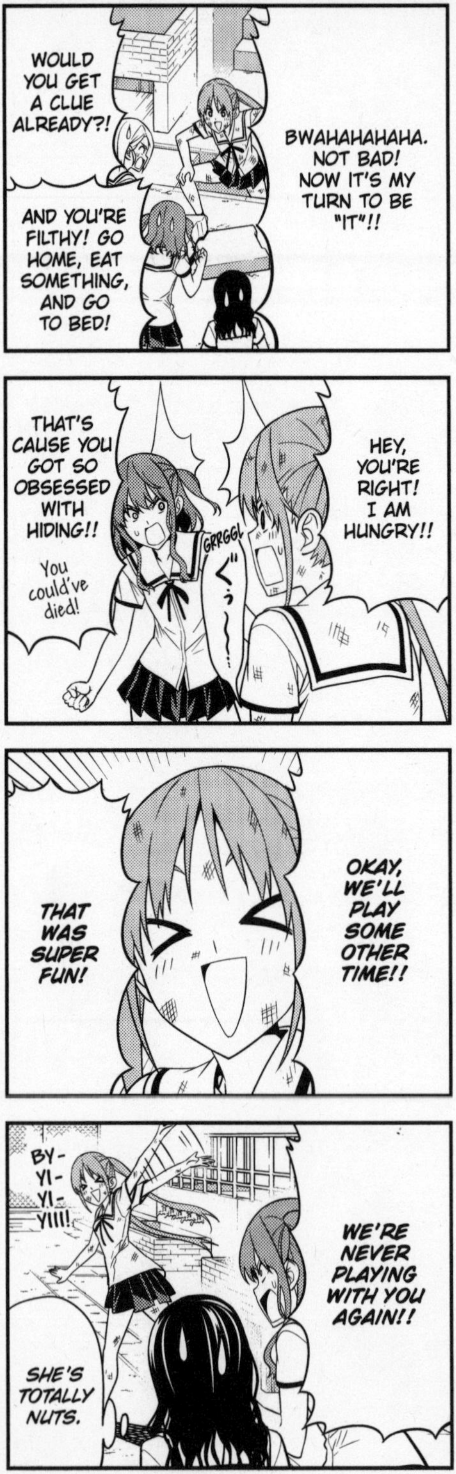
BWAHAHAHAHA. NOT BAD! NOW IT'S MY TURN TO BE "IT"!!
WOULD YOU GET A CLUE ALREADY?!
AND YOU'RE FILTHY! GO HOME, EAT SOMETHING, AND GO TO BED!
HEY, YOU'RE RIGHT! I AM HUNGRY!!
GRRGGL
ぐぅ～
THAT'S CAUSE YOU GOT SO OBSESSED WITH HIDING!!
You could've died!
OKAY, WE'LL PLAY SOME OTHER TIME!!
THAT WAS SUPER FUN!
WE'RE NEVER PLAYING WITH YOU AGAIN!!
BY-YI-YI-YIII!
SHE'S TOTALLY NUTS.

This Has Happened Before

THE THREE DAYS YOSHIKO WAS HIDING
SKRITCH
SKRITCH
SKRITCH
NO IDEA WHO IT IS, BUT SOME-WHERE—
SOME-ONE MUST BE PLAYING HIDE AND SEEK WITH YOSHIKO...
...I WIN!!
HE GOT A LOT OF STUDYING DONE

Aho-Girl

\\'ahô¸gərl\\ *Japanese, noun*.
A clueless girl.

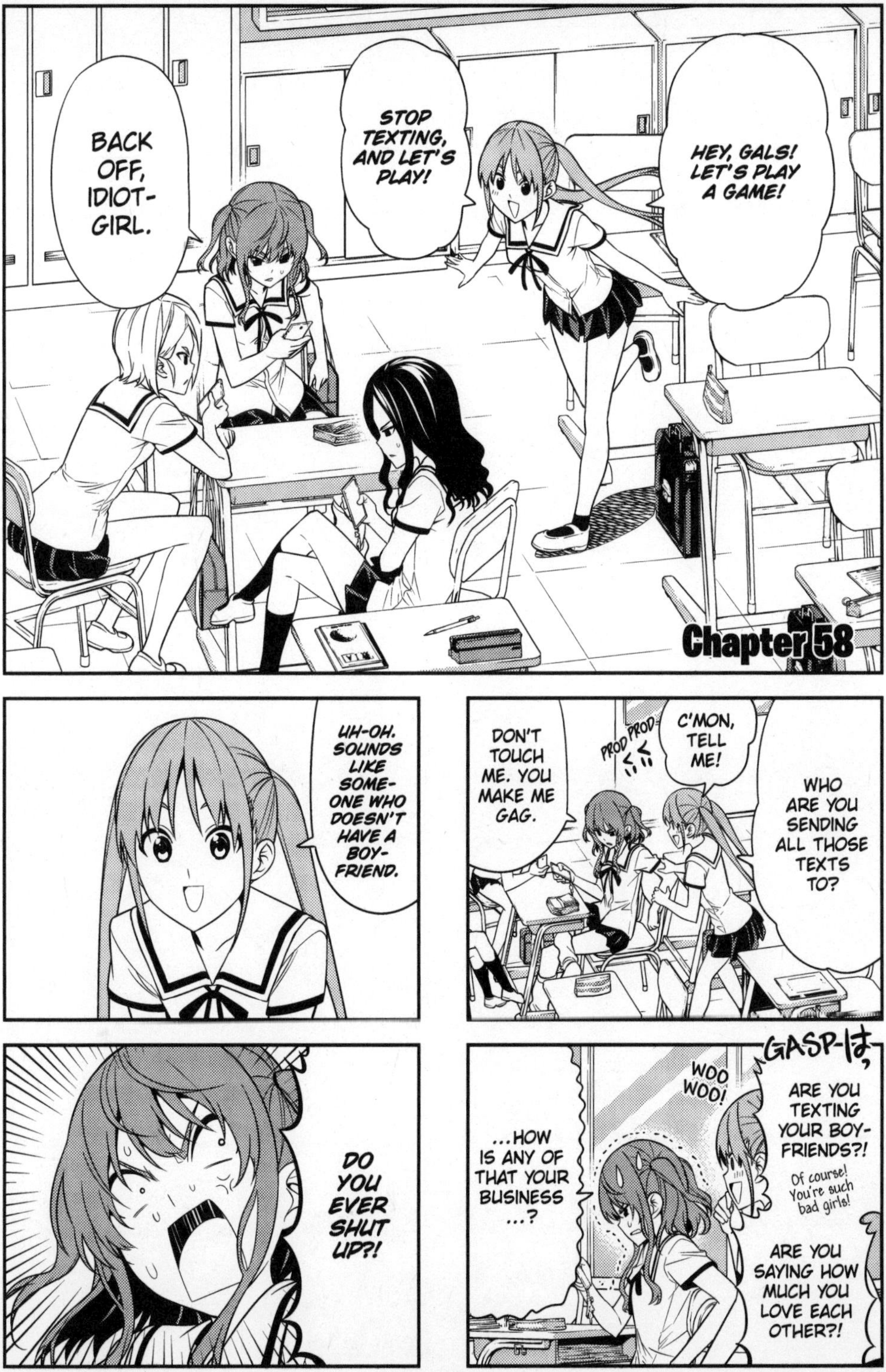
HEY, GALS! LET'S PLAY A GAME!
STOP TEXTING, AND LET'S PLAY!
BACK OFF, IDIOT-GIRL.
Chapter 58
C'MON, TELL ME!
WHO ARE YOU SENDING ALL THOSE TEXTS TO?
PROD PROD
DON'T TOUCH ME. YOU MAKE ME GAG.
UH-OH. SOUNDS LIKE SOME-ONE WHO DOESN'T HAVE A BOY-FRIEND.
GASP
WOO WOO!
ARE YOU TEXTING YOUR BOY-FRIENDS?!
Of course! You're such bad girls!
ARE YOU SAYING HOW MUCH YOU LOVE EACH OTHER?!
...HOW IS ANY OF THAT YOUR BUSINESS ...?
DO YOU EVER SHUT UP?!

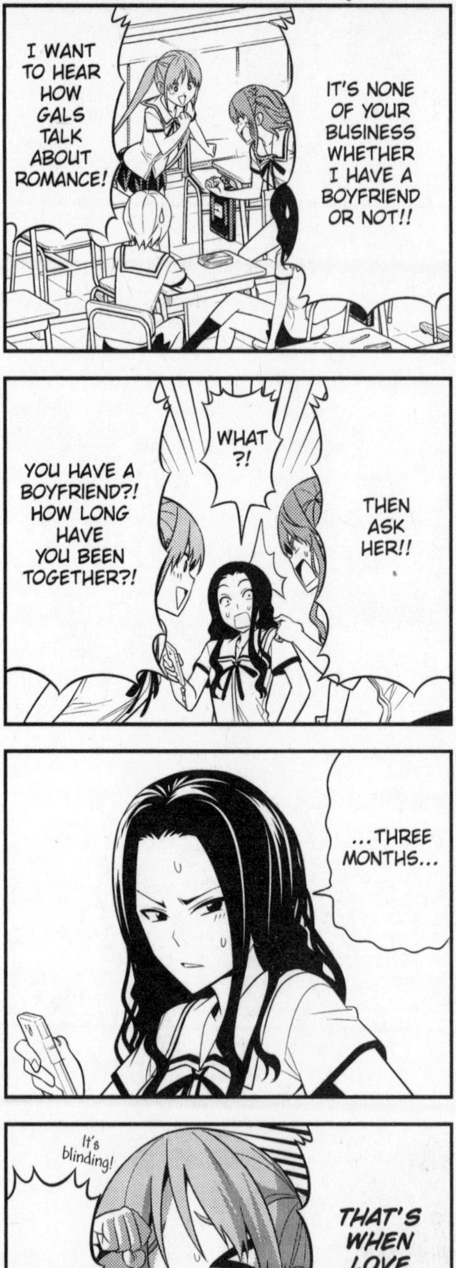
IT'S NONE OF YOUR BUSINESS WHETHER I HAVE A BOYFRIEND OR NOT!!
I WANT TO HEAR HOW GALS TALK ABOUT ROMANCE!
WHAT ?!
THEN ASK HER!!
YOU HAVE A BOYFRIEND?! HOW LONG HAVE YOU BEEN TOGETHER?!
...THREE MONTHS...
THAT'S WHEN LOVE SHINES BRIGHT-EST!!
It's blinding!
C... CUT IT OUT!!

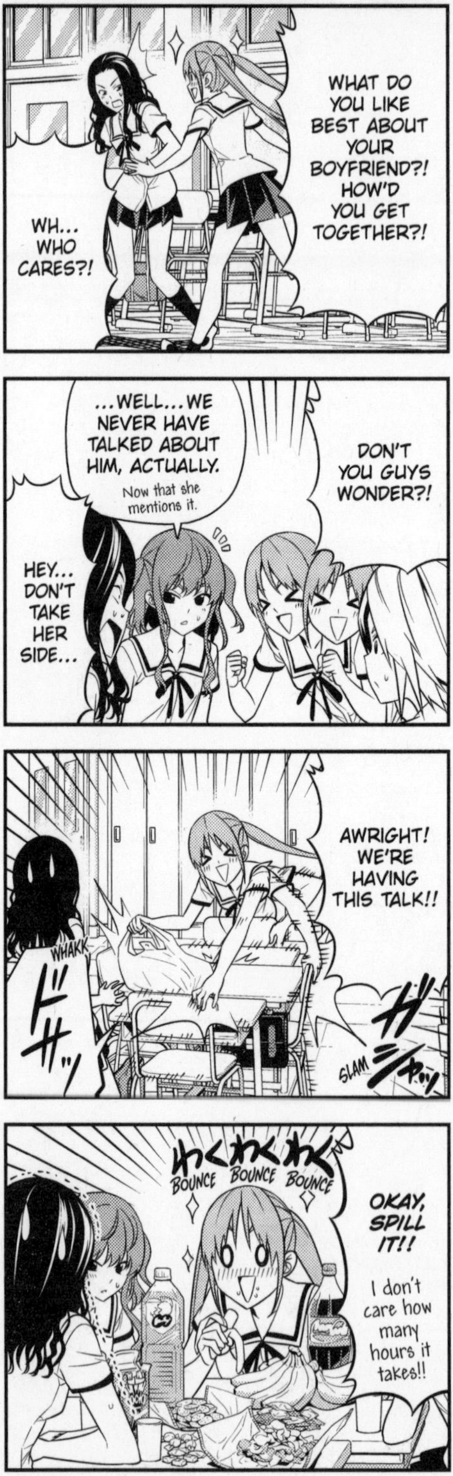
WHAT DO YOU LIKE BEST ABOUT YOUR BOYFRIEND?! HOW'D YOU GET TOGETHER?!
WH... WHO CARES?!
DON'T YOU GUYS WONDER?!
...WELL...WE NEVER HAVE TALKED ABOUT HIM, ACTUALLY.
Now that she mentions it.
HEY... DON'T TAKE HER SIDE...
AWRIGHT! WE'RE HAVING THIS TALK!!
ガシャッ
SLAM
WHAKK
ドサッ
わくわくわく
BOUNCE BOUNCE BOUNCE
OKAY, SPILL IT!!
I don't care how many hours it takes!!

Thanks for That!

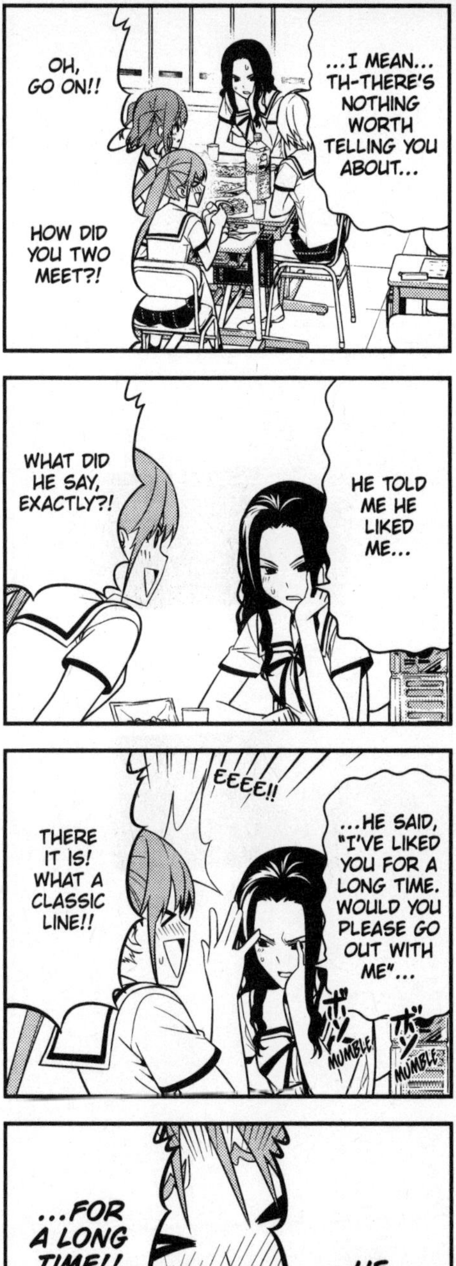

...I MEAN... TH-THERE'S NOTHING WORTH TELLING YOU ABOUT...
OH, GO ON!!
HOW DID YOU TWO MEET?!
HE TOLD ME HE LIKED ME...
WHAT DID HE SAY, EXACTLY?!
...HE SAID, "I'VE LIKED YOU FOR A LONG TIME. WOULD YOU PLEASE GO OUT WITH ME"...
EEEE!!
THERE IT IS! WHAT A CLASSIC LINE!!
MUMBLE
MUMBLE
HE LIKED YOU...
...FOR A LONG TIME!!
SHE'S ENJOYING THIS WAY TOO MUCH...

Well That's No Good

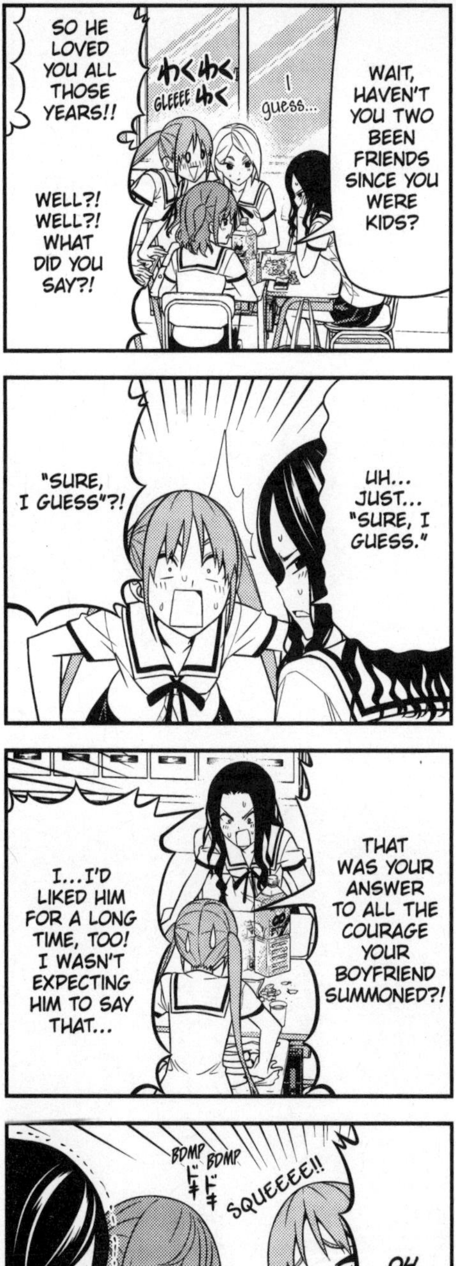

WAIT, HAVEN'T YOU TWO BEEN FRIENDS SINCE YOU WERE KIDS?
I guess...
わくわく
GLEEEE
わく
SO HE LOVED YOU ALL THOSE YEARS!!
WELL?! WELL?! WHAT DID YOU SAY?!
UH... JUST... "SURE, I GUESS."
"SURE, I GUESS"?!
THAT WAS YOUR ANSWER TO ALL THE COURAGE YOUR BOYFRIEND SUMMONED?!
I...I'D LIKED HIM FOR A LONG TIME, TOO! I WASN'T EXPECTING HIM TO SAY THAT...
OH, THAT'S ADORABLE!!
SQUEEEEE!!
BDMP BDMP

Seriously, That's No Good

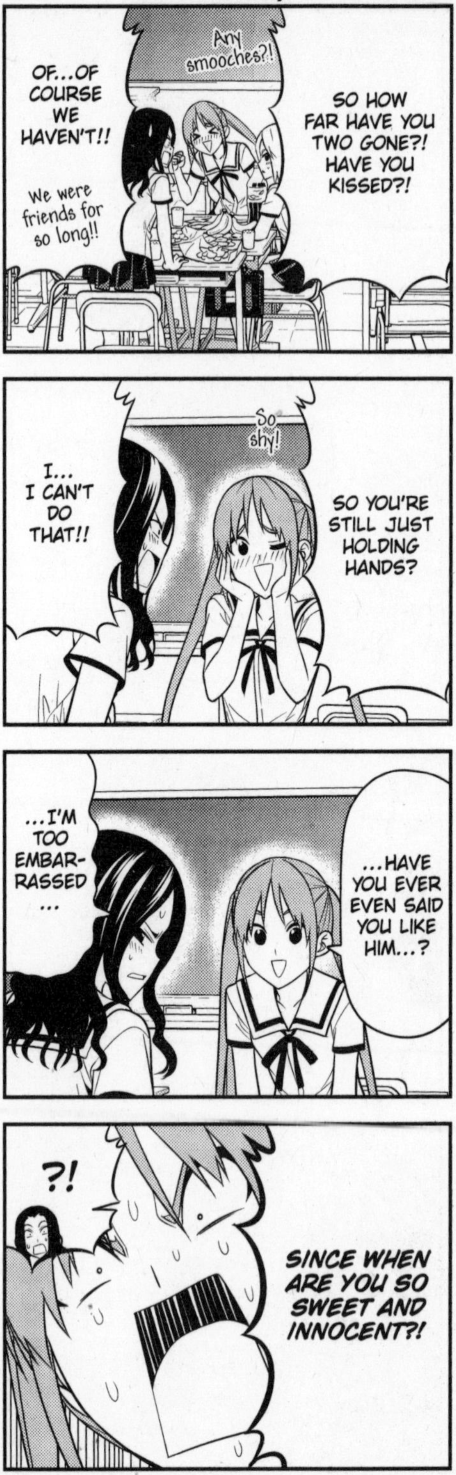
SO HOW FAR HAVE YOU TWO GONE?! HAVE YOU KISSED?!
Any smooches?!
OF...OF COURSE WE HAVEN'T!!
We were friends for so long!!
SO YOU'RE STILL JUST HOLDING HANDS?
So shy!
I... I CAN'T DO THAT!!
...HAVE YOU EVER EVEN SAID YOU LIKE HIM...?
...I'M TOO EMBARRASSED...
SINCE WHEN ARE YOU SO SWEET AND INNOCENT?!
?!

You Have to Tell Him

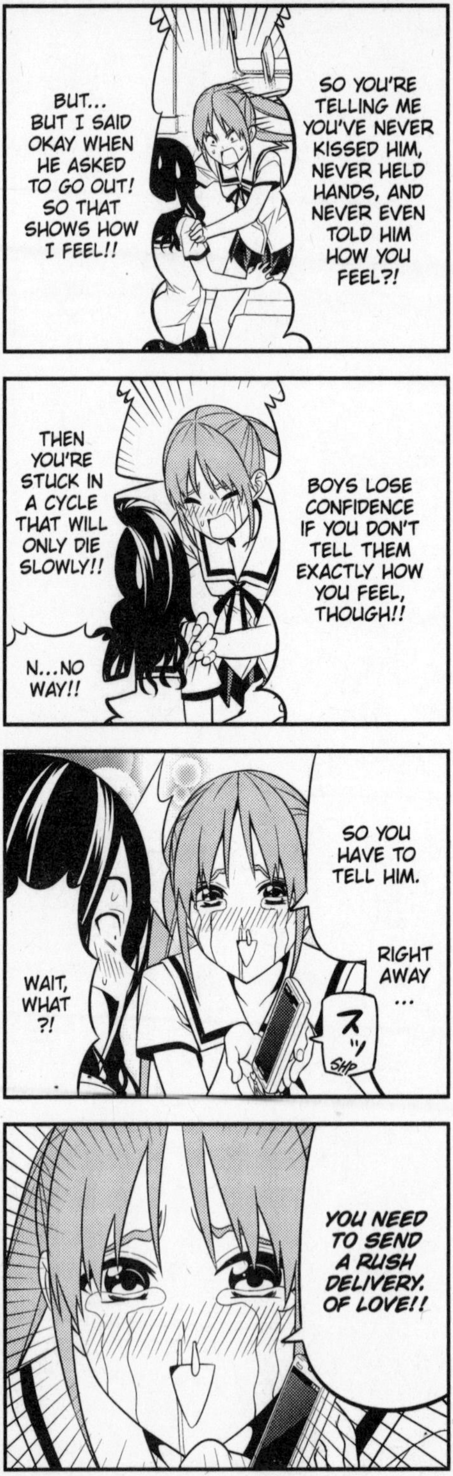
SO YOU'RE TELLING ME YOU'VE NEVER KISSED HIM, NEVER HELD HANDS, AND NEVER EVEN TOLD HIM HOW YOU FEEL?!
BUT... BUT I SAID OKAY WHEN HE ASKED TO GO OUT! SO THAT SHOWS HOW I FEEL!!
BOYS LOSE CONFIDENCE IF YOU DON'T TELL THEM EXACTLY HOW YOU FEEL, THOUGH!!
THEN YOU'RE STUCK IN A CYCLE THAT WILL ONLY DIE SLOWLY!!
N...NO WAY!!
SO YOU HAVE TO TELL HIM.
RIGHT AWAY...
スッ
SHP
WAIT, WHAT?!
YOU NEED TO SEND A RUSH DELIVERY. OF LOVE!!

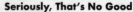

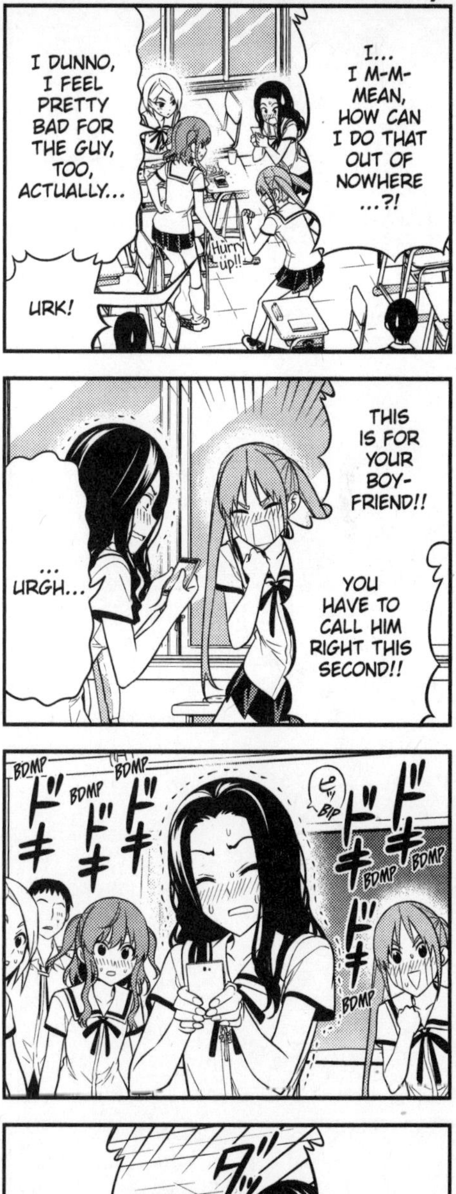
I... I M-M-MEAN, HOW CAN I DO THAT OUT OF NOWHERE...?!
I DUNNO, I FEEL PRETTY BAD FOR THE GUY, TOO, ACTUALLY...
Hurry up!!
URK!
THIS IS FOR YOUR BOY-FRIEND!!
YOU HAVE TO CALL HIM RIGHT THIS SECOND!!
...URGH...
ドキ BDMP
ドキ BDMP
ピッ BIP
ドキ BDMP
ドキ BDMP
ドキ BDMP
ドキ BDMP
HEY! THERE'S NO REASON I HAVE TO DO THIS HERE!!
ダッ DASH
AWW!!

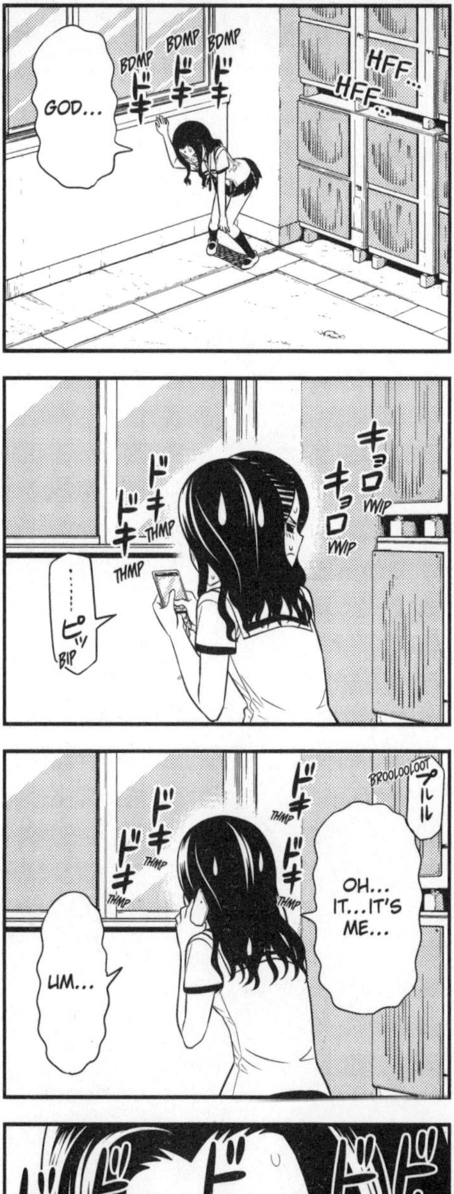
HFF... HFF...
ドキ BDMP
ドキ BDMP
ドキ BDMP
GOD...
キョロ VWIP
キョロ VWIP
ドキ THMP
ドキ THMP
......ピッ BIP
プル BROOLOOLOOT
ドキ THMP
ドキ THMP
ドキ THMP
ドキ THMP
OH... IT...IT'S ME...
UM...
ドキ BDMP
ドキ BDMP
ドキ BDMP
ドキ BDMP
ドキ BDMP
I WAS JUST...

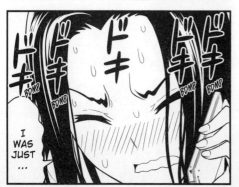

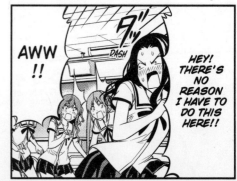

Can You Hear Me Now?

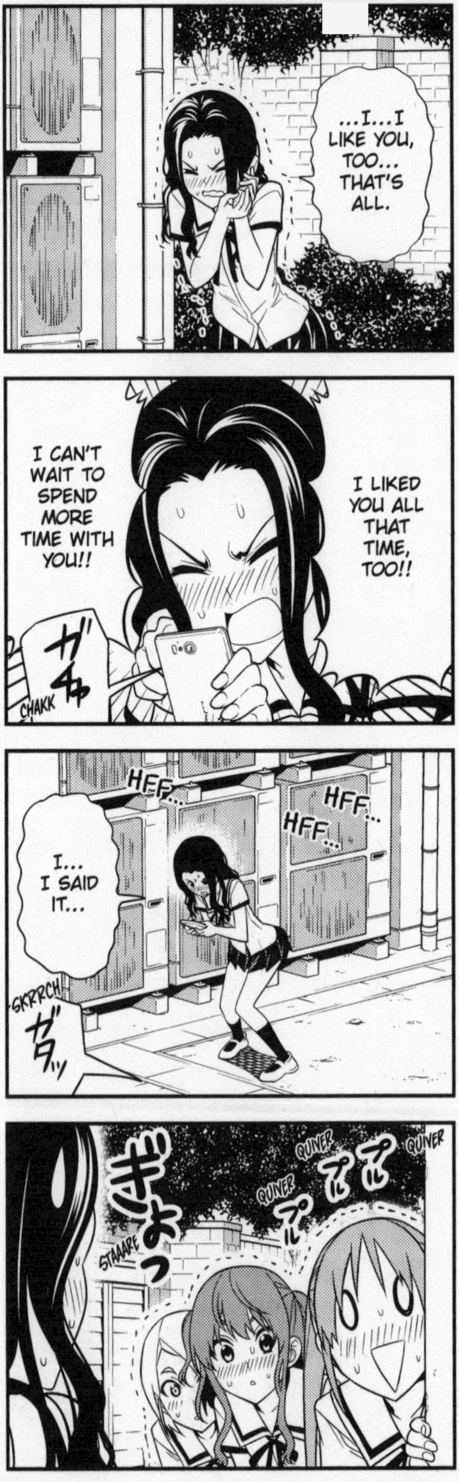

...I...I LIKE YOU, TOO... THAT'S ALL.
I LIKED YOU ALL THAT TIME, TOO!!
I CAN'T WAIT TO SPEND MORE TIME WITH YOU!!
CHAKK
HFF...
HFF...
HFF...
I... I SAID IT...
SKRRCH
QUIVER
QUIVER
QUIVER
プルプル
ぎょっ
STAAARE

Wishing You a Happy Life Together

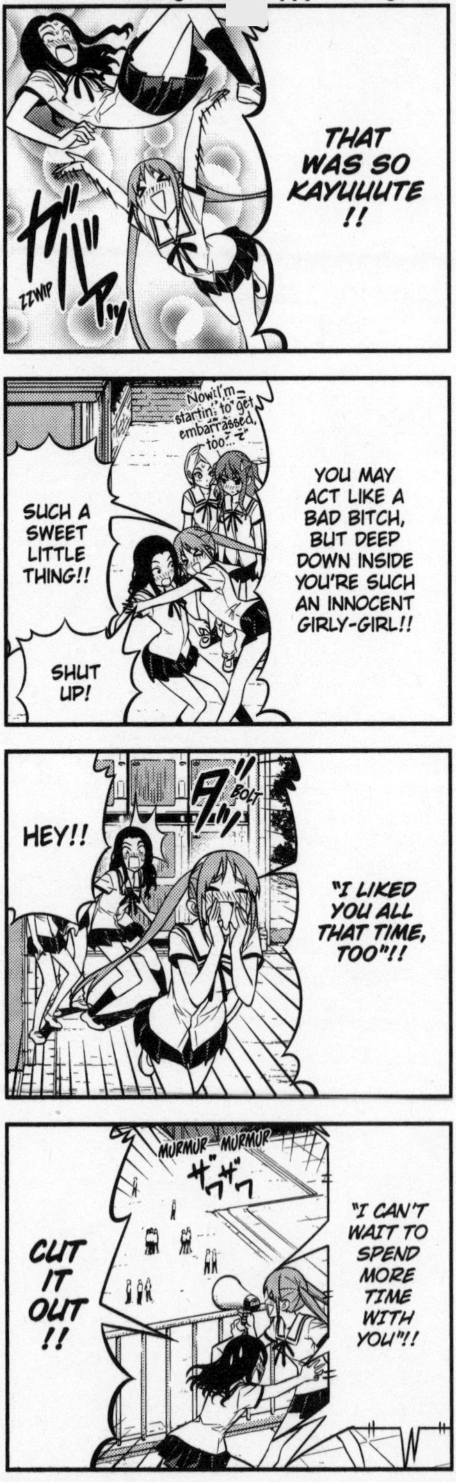

THAT WAS SO KAYUUUTE !!
ZZWIP
YOU MAY ACT LIKE A BAD BITCH, BUT DEEP DOWN INSIDE YOU'RE SUCH AN INNOCENT GIRLY-GIRL!!
Now I'm startin' to get embarrassed, too...
SUCH A SWEET LITTLE THING!!
SHUT UP!
"I LIKED YOU ALL THAT TIME, TOO"!!
BOLT
HEY!!
"I CAN'T WAIT TO SPEND MORE TIME WITH YOU"!!
MURMUR MURMUR
CUT IT OUT !!

I'm Blushing

GEEZ ...
THAT MORON...
HFF...
HFF...
STILL ...
YOU REALLY ARE IN LOVE, HUH...?
PLEASE JUST STOP!!

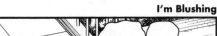

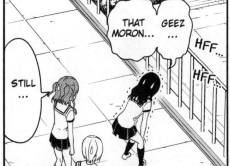

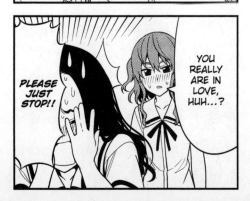

(Aobee, Kisuke,)

Aho-Girl

\\'ahô͵gərl\\ *Japanese, noun.*
A clueless girl.

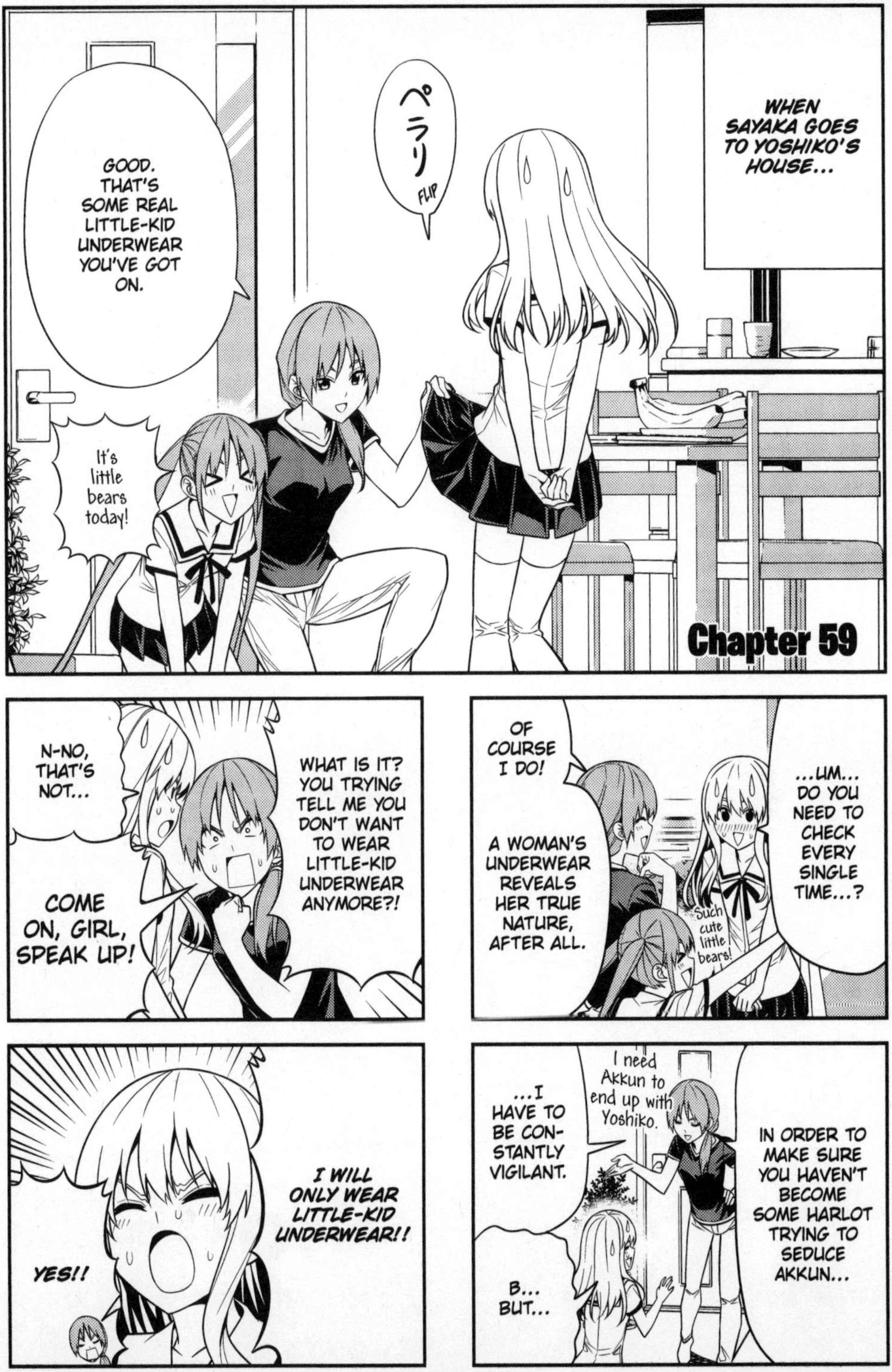
WHEN SAYAKA GOES TO YOSHIKO'S HOUSE...
ペラリ
FLIP
GOOD. THAT'S SOME REAL LITTLE-KID UNDERWEAR YOU'VE GOT ON.
It's little bears today!
Chapter 59
...UM... DO YOU NEED TO CHECK EVERY SINGLE TIME...?
OF COURSE I DO!
A WOMAN'S UNDERWEAR REVEALS HER TRUE NATURE, AFTER ALL.
Such cute little bears!
WHAT IS IT? YOU TRYING TELL ME YOU DON'T WANT TO WEAR LITTLE-KID UNDERWEAR ANYMORE?!
N-NO, THAT'S NOT...
COME ON, GIRL, SPEAK UP!
IN ORDER TO MAKE SURE YOU HAVEN'T BECOME SOME HARLOT TRYING TO SEDUCE AKKUN...
I need Akkun to end up with Yoshiko.
...I HAVE TO BE CONSTANTLY VIGILANT.
B... BUT...
I WILL ONLY WEAR LITTLE-KID UNDERWEAR!!
YES!!

The Real—Really Real—

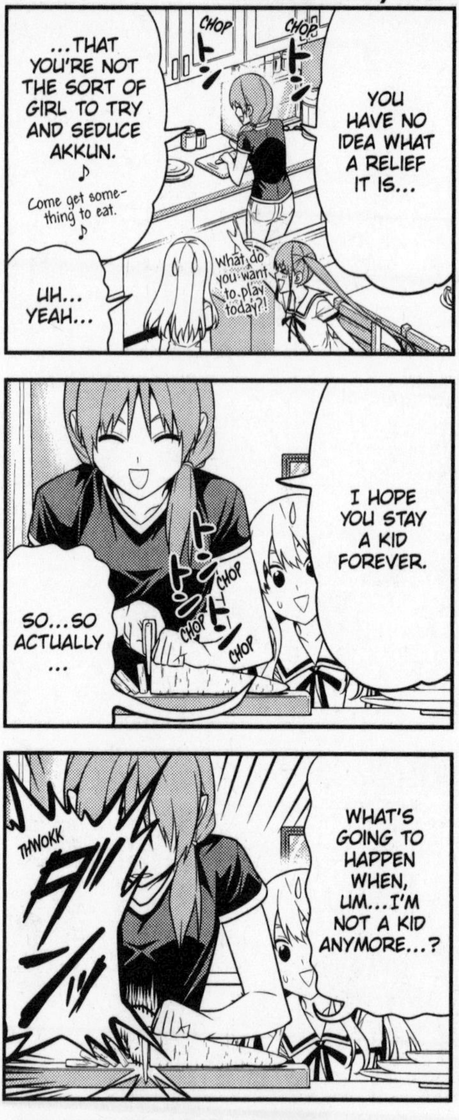
YOU HAVE NO IDEA WHAT A RELIEF IT IS...
CHOP
CHOP
...THAT YOU'RE NOT THE SORT OF GIRL TO TRY AND SEDUCE AKKUN. ♪
Come get something to eat. ♪
What do you want to play today?!
UH... YEAH...
I HOPE YOU STAY A KID FOREVER.
CHOP
CHOP
CHOP
CHOP
SO...SO ACTUALLY ...
WHAT'S GOING TO HAPPEN WHEN, UM...I'M NOT A KID ANYMORE...?
THWOKK
OH NO, LOOK AT THAT. I SLICED RIGHT THROUGH THE CUTTING BOARD...
BUM BUM BUM
TREMBLE
TREMBLE
TREMBLE

A Rebellious Age

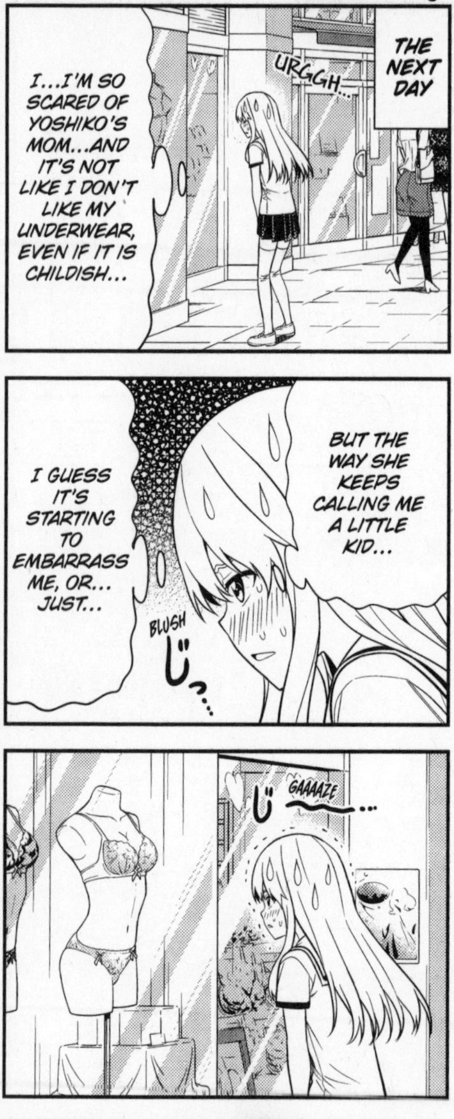
THE NEXT DAY
URGGH...
I...I'M SO SCARED OF YOSHIKO'S MOM...AND IT'S NOT LIKE I DON'T LIKE MY UNDERWEAR, EVEN IF IT IS CHILDISH...
BUT THE WAY SHE KEEPS CALLING ME A LITTLE KID...
I GUESS IT'S STARTING TO EMBARRASS ME, OR... JUST...
BLUSH
GAAAAZE
...IT MAKES ME WANT TO SPREAD MY WINGS A LITTLE!!
Thank you for shopping with us!

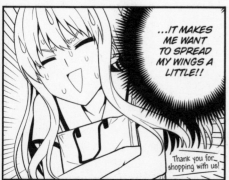

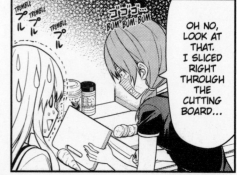

The Worst Kind of Luck

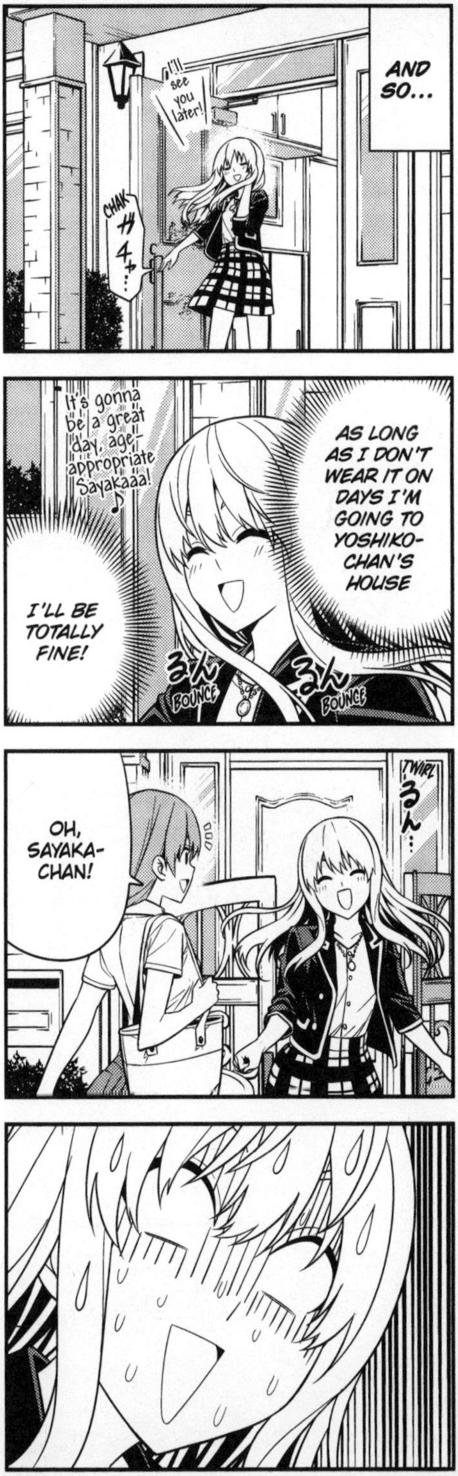

AND SO...
I'll see you later!
CHAK
AS LONG AS I DON'T WEAR IT ON DAYS I'M GOING TO YOSHIKO-CHAN'S HOUSE
It's gonna be a great day, age-appropriate Sayakaaa! ♪
I'LL BE TOTALLY FINE!
BOUNCE
BOUNCE
TWIRL
OH, SAYAKA-CHAN!

You've Betrayed Me

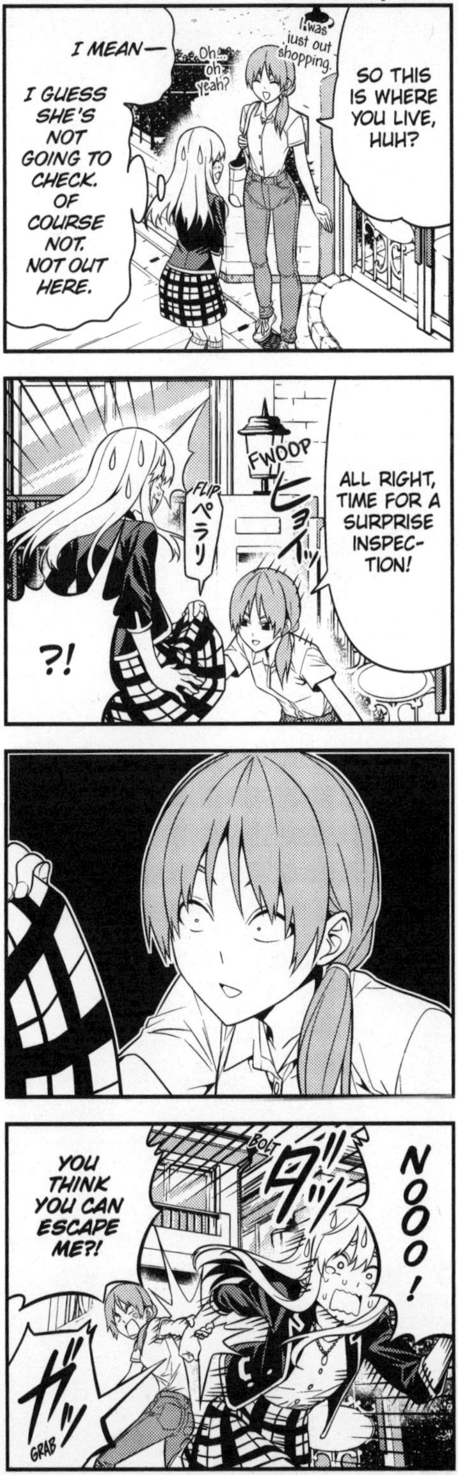

SO THIS IS WHERE YOU LIVE, HUH?
I was just out shopping.
Oh... oh yeah?
I MEAN— I GUESS SHE'S NOT GOING TO CHECK. OF COURSE NOT. NOT OUT HERE.
ALL RIGHT, TIME FOR A SURPRISE INSPECTION!
FWOOP
FLIP
?!
NOOOO!
BOLT
YOU THINK YOU CAN ESCAPE ME?!
GRAB

A Meager Act of Resistance

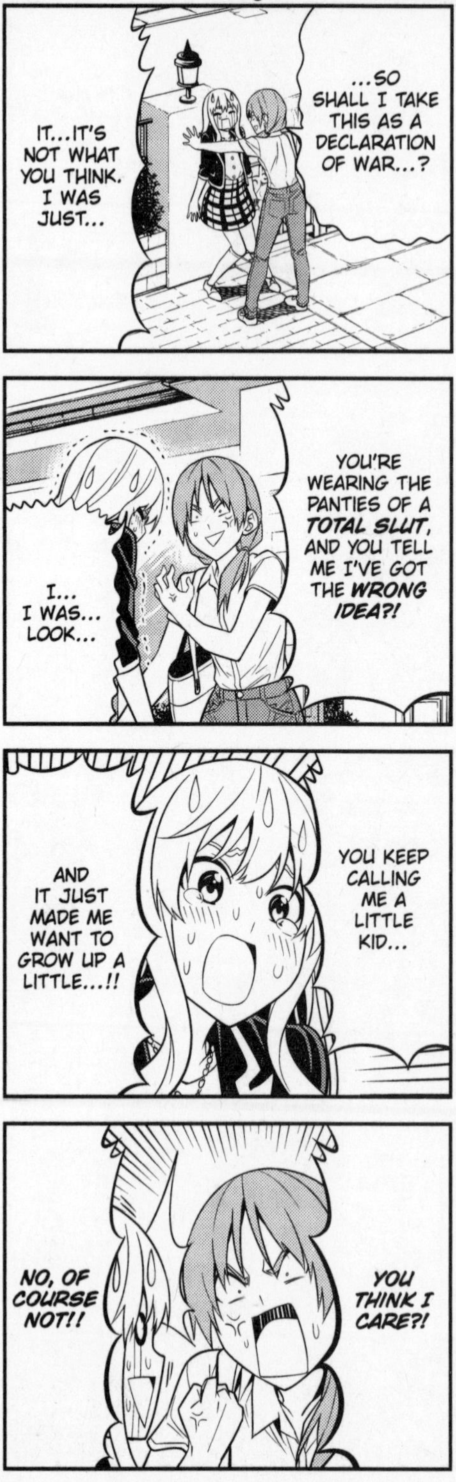
...SO SHALL I TAKE THIS AS A DECLARATION OF WAR...?
IT...IT'S NOT WHAT YOU THINK. I WAS JUST...
YOU'RE WEARING THE PANTIES OF A ***TOTAL SLUT***, AND YOU TELL ME I'VE GOT THE ***WRONG IDEA?!***
I... I WAS... LOOK...
YOU KEEP CALLING ME A LITTLE KID...
AND IT JUST MADE ME WANT TO GROW UP A LITTLE...!!
YOU THINK I CARE?!
NO, OF COURSE NOT!!

Sure Death: The Professional

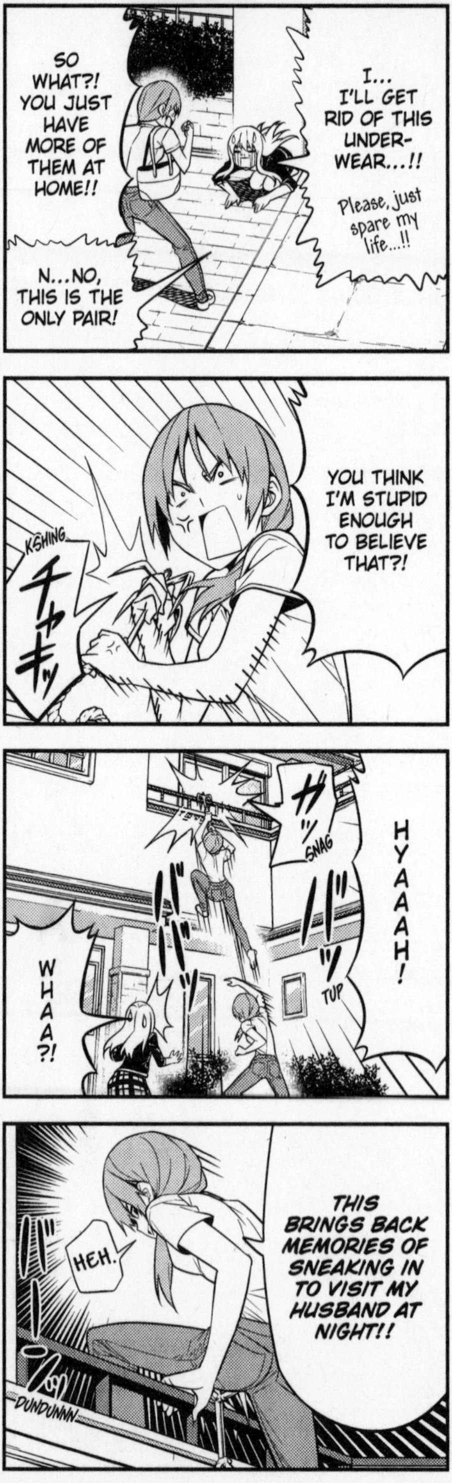
I... I'LL GET RID OF THIS UNDER-WEAR...!!
Please, just spare my life...!!
SO WHAT?! YOU JUST HAVE MORE OF THEM AT HOME!!
N...NO, THIS IS THE ONLY PAIR!
YOU THINK I'M STUPID ENOUGH TO BELIEVE THAT?!
KSHING
チャキッ
HYAAAAH!
ガッ
SNAG
TUP
WHAAA?!
THIS BRINGS BACK MEMORIES OF SNEAKING IN TO VISIT MY HUSBAND AT NIGHT!!
HEH.
DUNDUNNN

The Way to Tell

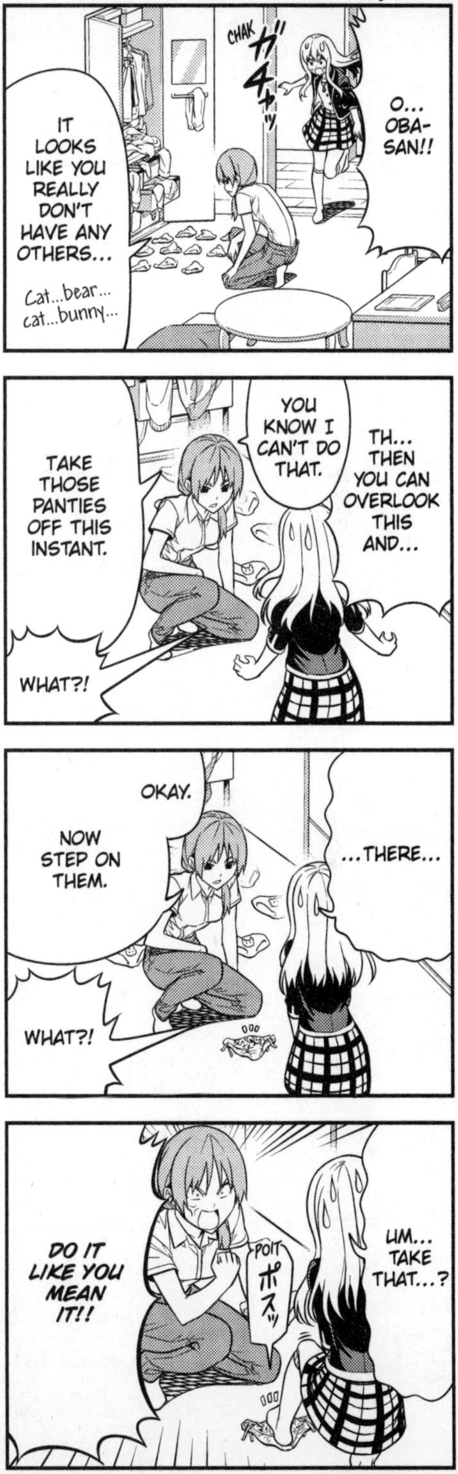

CHAK
O... OBA-SAN!!
IT LOOKS LIKE YOU REALLY DON'T HAVE ANY OTHERS...
Cat...bear... cat...bunny...
TH... THEN YOU CAN OVERLOOK THIS AND...
YOU KNOW I CAN'T DO THAT.
TAKE THOSE PANTIES OFF THIS INSTANT.
WHAT?!
...THERE...
OKAY.
NOW STEP ON THEM.
WHAT?!
UM... TAKE THAT...?
POIT
DO IT LIKE YOU MEAN IT!!

A Fine Debauch

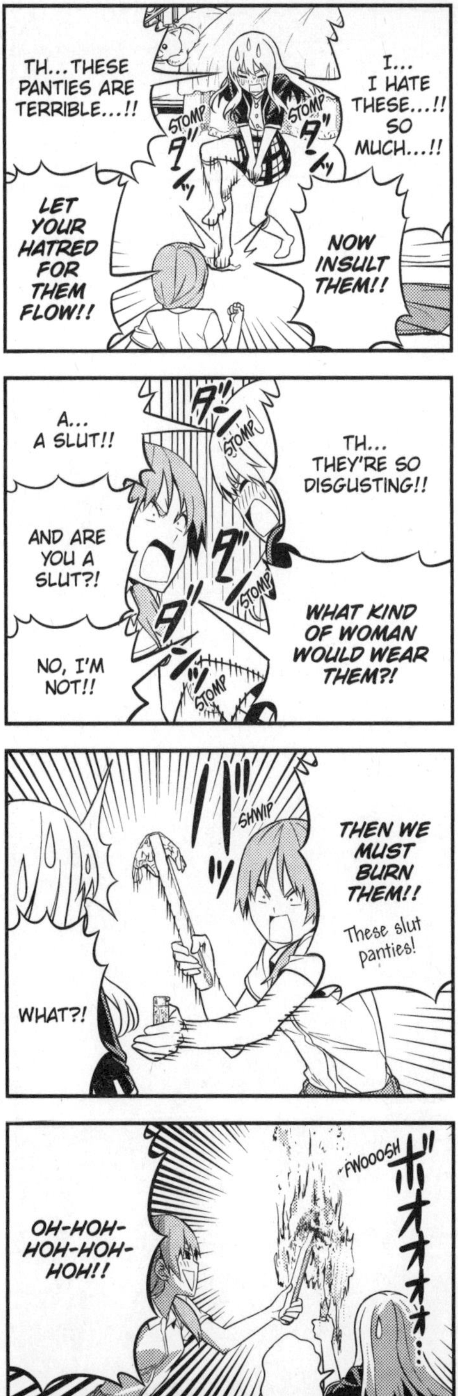

I... I HATE THESE...!! SO MUCH...!!
STOMP
STOMP
TH...THESE PANTIES ARE TERRIBLE...!!
NOW INSULT THEM!!
LET YOUR HATRED FOR THEM FLOW!!
TH... THEY'RE SO DISGUSTING!!
STOMP
STOMP
STOMP
A... A SLUT!!
AND ARE YOU A SLUT?!
WHAT KIND OF WOMAN WOULD WEAR THEM?!
NO, I'M NOT!!
THEN WE MUST BURN THEM!!
These slut panties!
SHWIP
WHAT?!
FWOOOSH
OH-HOH-HOH-HOH-HOH!!
...

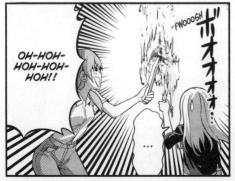

A Gentler Side

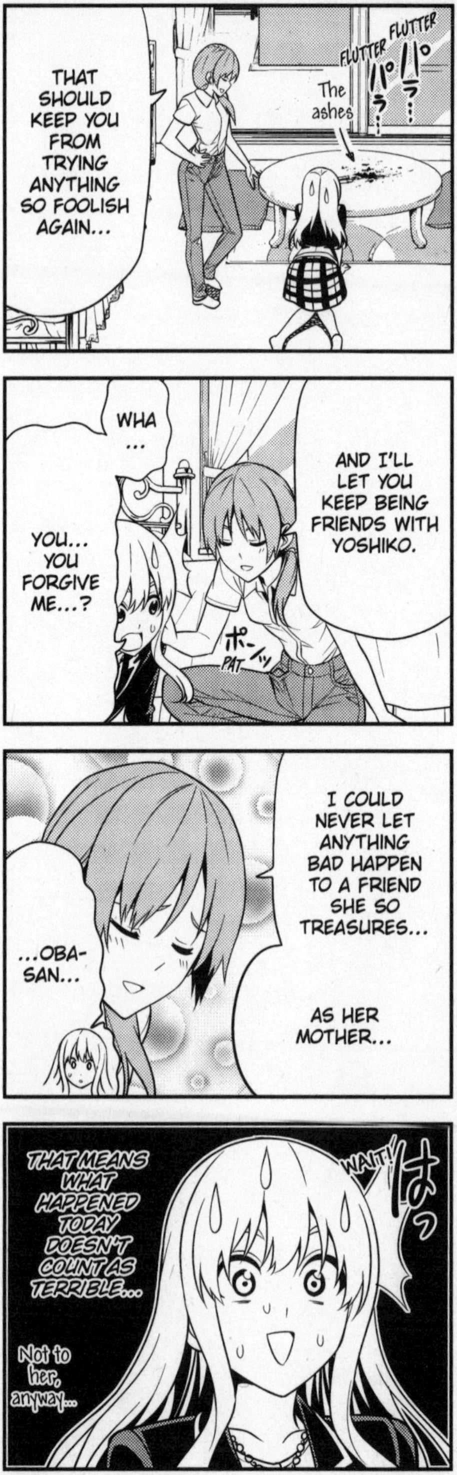
FLUTTER FLUTTER
パラ パラ…
The ashes
THAT SHOULD KEEP YOU FROM TRYING ANYTHING SO FOOLISH AGAIN…
AND I'LL LET YOU KEEP BEING FRIENDS WITH YOSHIKO.
WHA…
YOU… YOU FORGIVE ME…?
ポーンッ PAT
I COULD NEVER LET ANYTHING BAD HAPPEN TO A FRIEND SHE SO TREASURES…
AS HER MOTHER…
…OBA-SAN…
はっ WAIT!
THAT MEANS WHAT HAPPENED TODAY DOESN'T COUNT AS TERRIBLE…
Not to her, anyway…

Duty Fulfilled

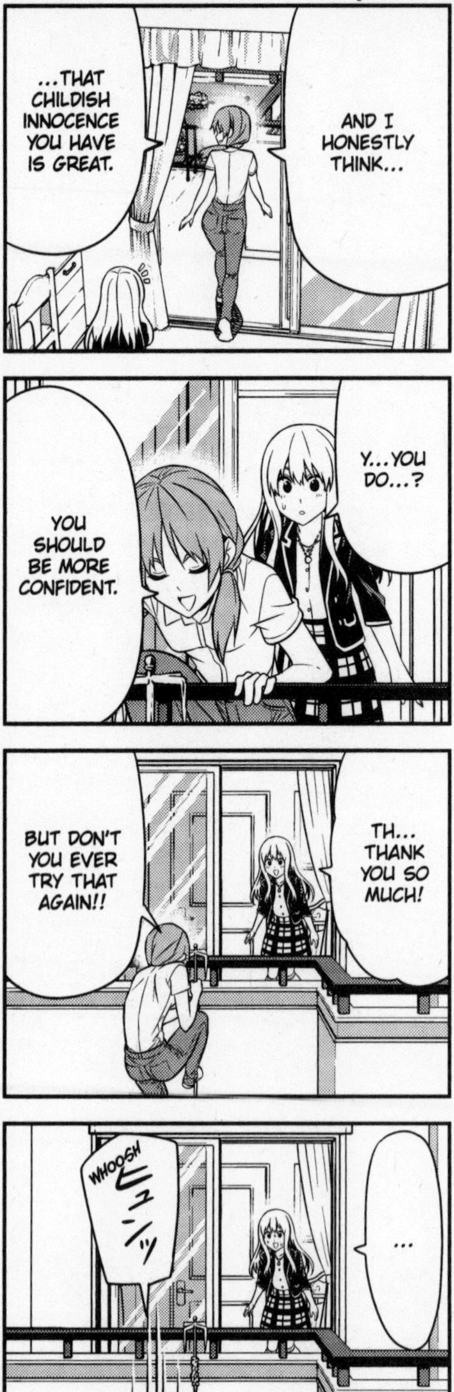
AND I HONESTLY THINK…
…THAT CHILDISH INNOCENCE YOU HAVE IS GREAT.
Y…YOU DO…?
YOU SHOULD BE MORE CONFIDENT.
TH… THANK YOU SO MUCH!
BUT DON'T YOU EVER TRY THAT AGAIN!!
…
WHOOSH ヒュンッ

Well, of Course You Would

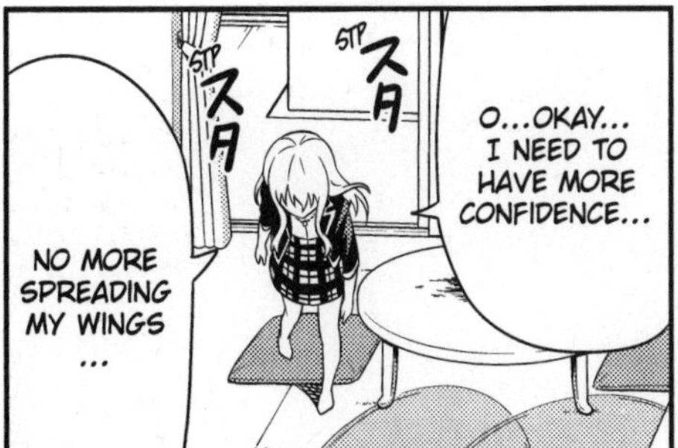
O...OKAY... I NEED TO HAVE MORE CONFIDENCE...
STP スタ
STP スタ
NO MORE SPREADING MY WINGS ...

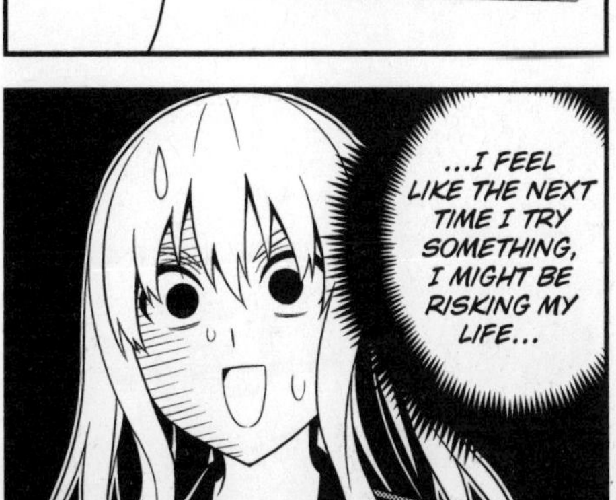
...I FEEL LIKE THE NEXT TIME I TRY SOMETHING, I MIGHT BE RISKING MY LIFE...

(Love potion number)

Aho-Girl

\\'ahô͵gərl\\ *Japanese, noun.*
A clueless girl.

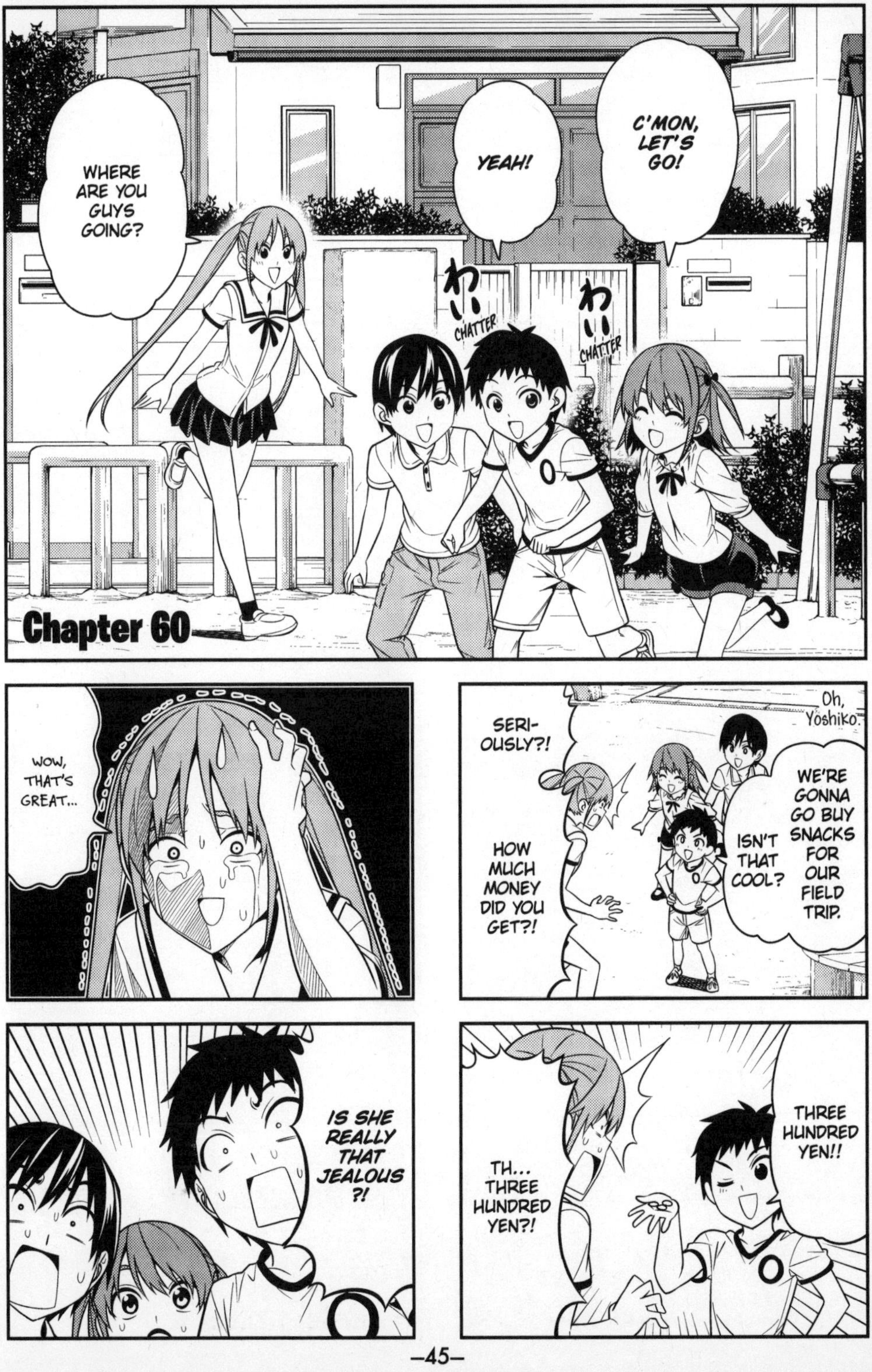
C'MON, LET'S GO!
YEAH!
WHERE ARE YOU GUYS GOING?
わい CHATTER
わい CHATTER
Chapter 60
Oh, Yoshiko.
WE'RE GONNA GO BUY SNACKS FOR OUR FIELD TRIP.
ISN'T THAT COOL?
SERI-OUSLY?!
HOW MUCH MONEY DID YOU GET?!
WOW, THAT'S GREAT...
THREE HUNDRED YEN!!
TH... THREE HUNDRED YEN?!
IS SHE REALLY THAT JEALOUS?!

High Schoolers Don't Have That Kind of Cash

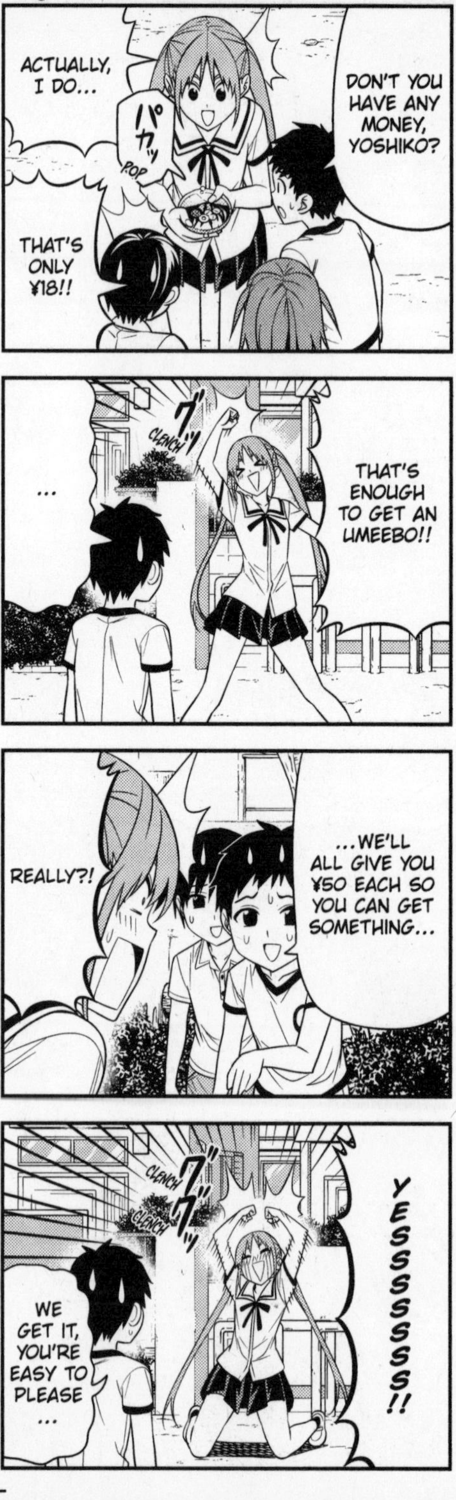
DON'T YOU HAVE ANY MONEY, YOSHIKO?
ACTUALLY, I DO...
パカッ
POP
THAT'S ONLY ¥18!!
THAT'S ENOUGH TO GET AN UMEEBO!!
グッ
CLENCH
...
...WE'LL ALL GIVE YOU ¥50 EACH SO YOU CAN GET SOMETHING...
REALLY?!
YESSSSSS!!
グッ
CLENCH
グッ
CLENCH
WE GET IT, YOU'RE EASY TO PLEASE...

I'm Not Sure How to Say This

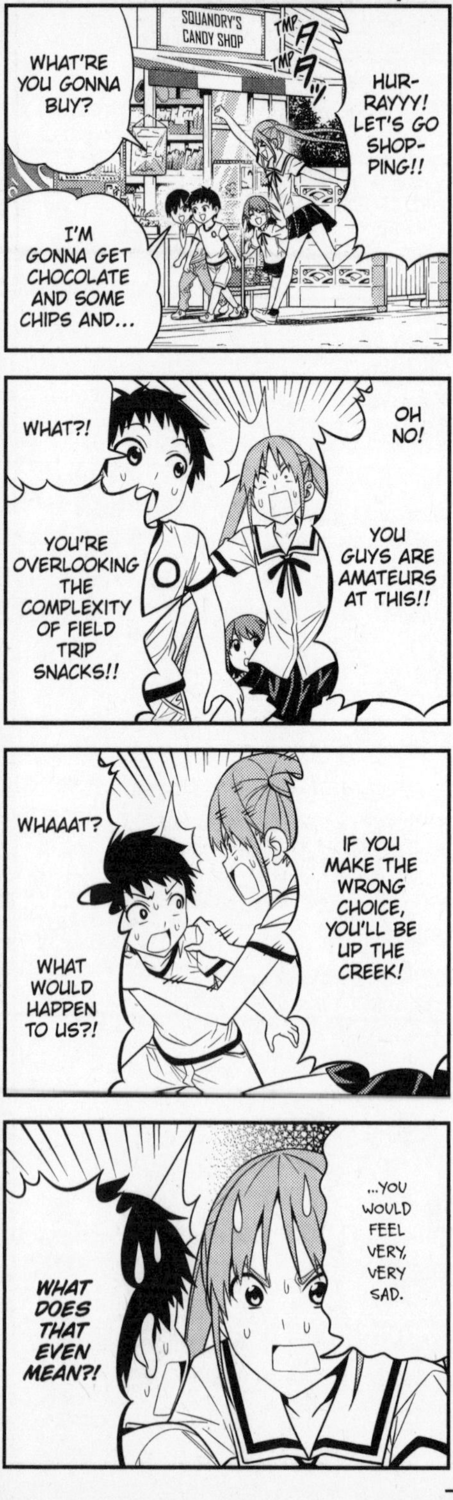
HURRAYYY! LET'S GO SHOPPING!!
TMP TMP
タタッ
SQUANDRY'S CANDY SHOP
WHAT'RE YOU GONNA BUY?
I'M GONNA GET CHOCOLATE AND SOME CHIPS AND...
OH NO!
YOU GUYS ARE AMATEURS AT THIS!!
WHAT?!
YOU'RE OVERLOOKING THE COMPLEXITY OF FIELD TRIP SNACKS!!
IF YOU MAKE THE WRONG CHOICE, YOU'LL BE UP THE CREEK!
WHAAAT?
WHAT WOULD HAPPEN TO US?!
...YOU WOULD FEEL VERY, VERY SAD.
WHAT DOES THAT EVEN MEAN?!

Logical Analysis

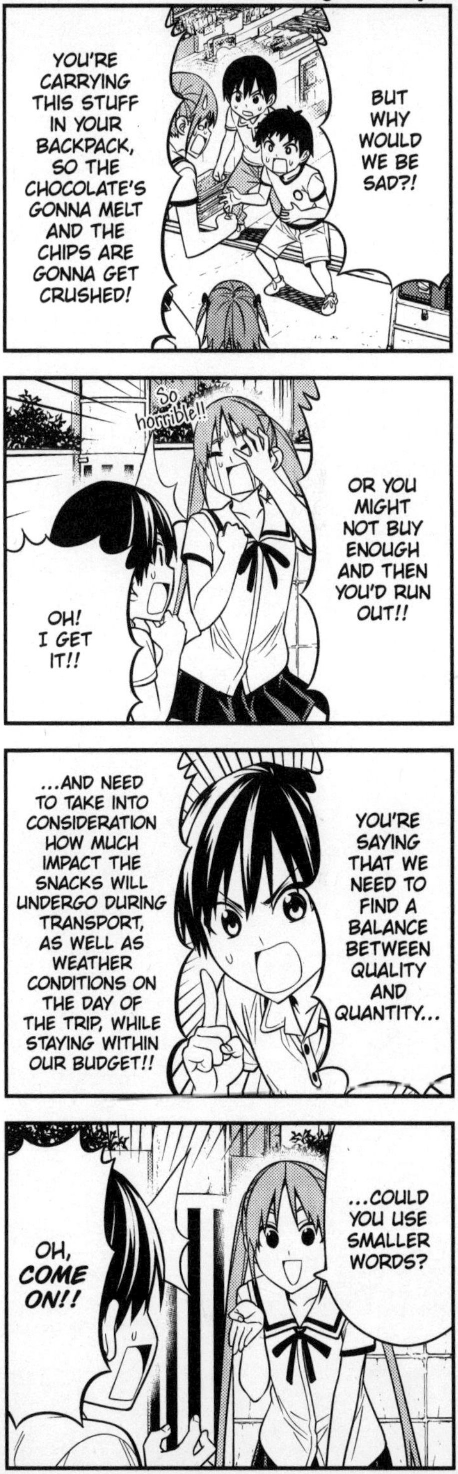
BUT WHY WOULD WE BE SAD?!
YOU'RE CARRYING THIS STUFF IN YOUR BACKPACK, SO THE CHOCOLATE'S GONNA MELT AND THE CHIPS ARE GONNA GET CRUSHED!
So horrible!!
OR YOU MIGHT NOT BUY ENOUGH AND THEN YOU'D RUN OUT!!
OH! I GET IT!!
YOU'RE SAYING THAT WE NEED TO FIND A BALANCE BETWEEN QUALITY AND QUANTITY...
...AND NEED TO TAKE INTO CONSIDERATION HOW MUCH IMPACT THE SNACKS WILL UNDERGO DURING TRANSPORT, AS WELL AS WEATHER CONDITIONS ON THE DAY OF THE TRIP, WHILE STAYING WITHIN OUR BUDGET!!
...COULD YOU USE SMALLER WORDS?
OH, COME ON!!

A Sleazy Candy Shop

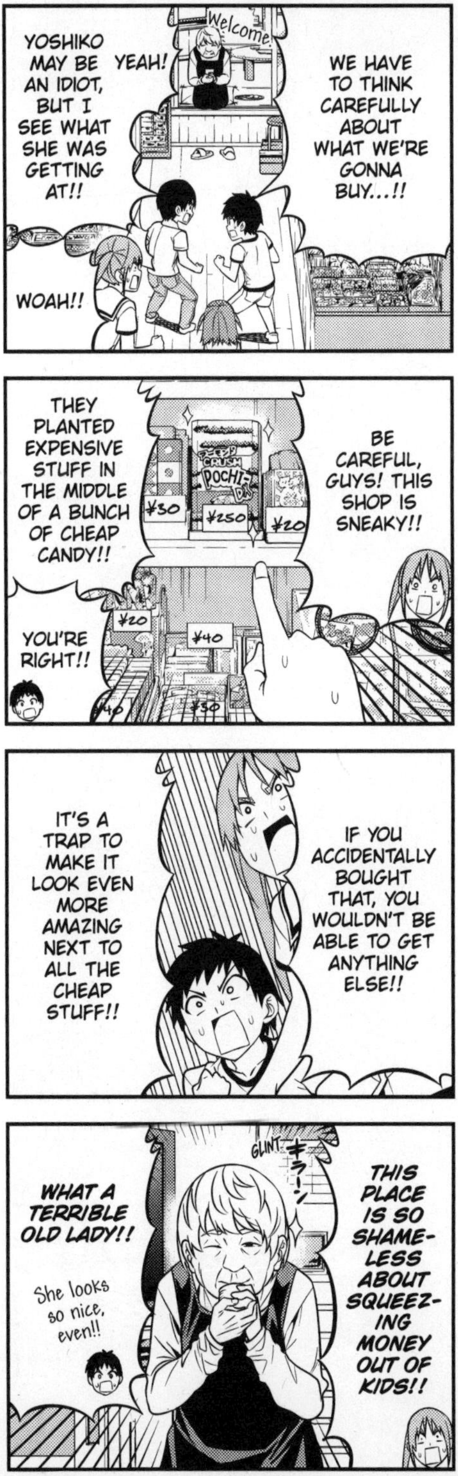
Welcome
WE HAVE TO THINK CAREFULLY ABOUT WHAT WE'RE GONNA BUY...!!
YEAH!
YOSHIKO MAY BE AN IDIOT, BUT I SEE WHAT SHE WAS GETTING AT!!
WOAH!!
BE CAREFUL, GUYS! THIS SHOP IS SNEAKY!!
CRUSH
POCHI-DA
¥30
¥250
¥20
THEY PLANTED EXPENSIVE STUFF IN THE MIDDLE OF A BUNCH OF CHEAP CANDY!!
¥20
¥40
¥40
¥30
YOU'RE RIGHT!!
IF YOU ACCIDENTALLY BOUGHT THAT, YOU WOULDN'T BE ABLE TO GET ANYTHING ELSE!!
IT'S A TRAP TO MAKE IT LOOK EVEN MORE AMAZING NEXT TO ALL THE CHEAP STUFF!!
GLINT
THIS PLACE IS SO SHAMELESS ABOUT SQUEEZING MONEY OUT OF KIDS!!
WHAT A TERRIBLE OLD LADY!!
She looks so nice, even!!

Turn Aside Temptation

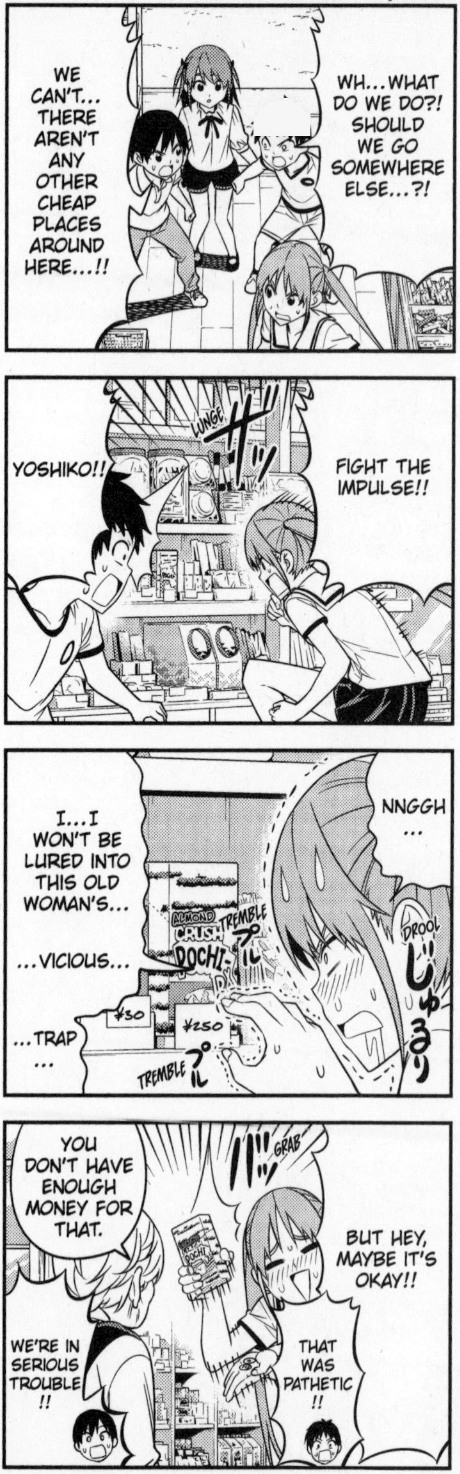
WH...WHAT DO WE DO?! SHOULD WE GO SOMEWHERE ELSE...?!
WE CAN'T... THERE AREN'T ANY OTHER CHEAP PLACES AROUND HERE...!!
FIGHT THE IMPULSE!!
LUNGE
YOSHIKO!!
NNGGH ...
DROOL
TREMBLE
I...I WON'T BE LURED INTO THIS OLD WOMAN'S...
...VICIOUS...
ALMOND CRUSH POCHI-D
¥30
¥250
...TRAP ...
TREMBLE
GRAB
BUT HEY, MAYBE IT'S OKAY!!
YOU DON'T HAVE ENOUGH MONEY FOR THAT.
THAT WAS PATHETIC !!
WE'RE IN SERIOUS TROUBLE !!

An Unexpected Development

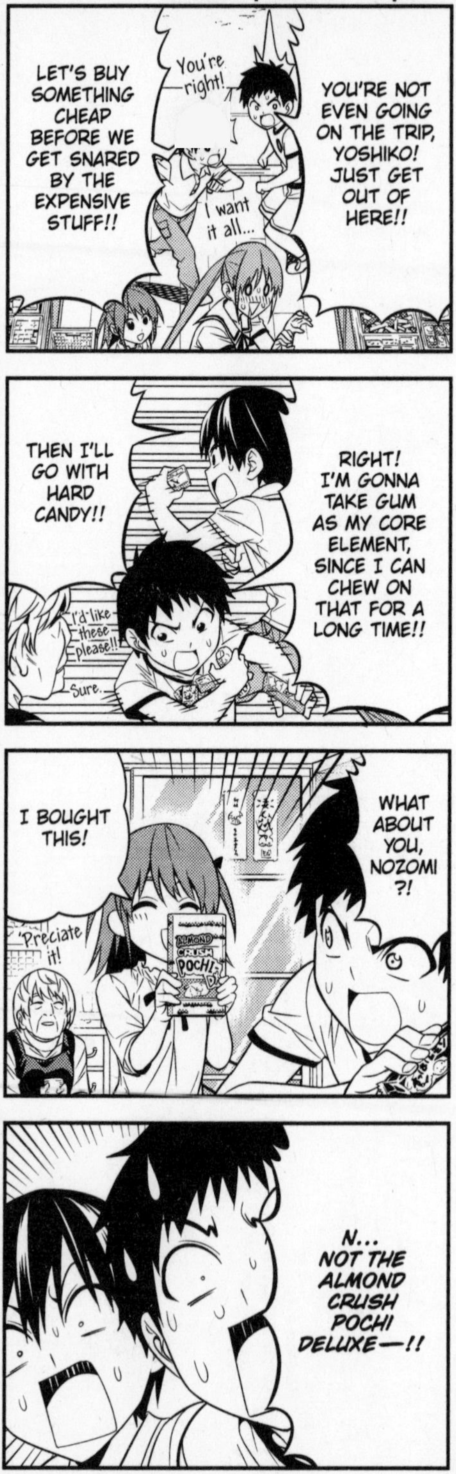
YOU'RE NOT EVEN GOING ON THE TRIP, YOSHIKO! JUST GET OUT OF HERE!!
You're right!
I want it all...
LET'S BUY SOMETHING CHEAP BEFORE WE GET SNARED BY THE EXPENSIVE STUFF!!
RIGHT! I'M GONNA TAKE GUM AS MY CORE ELEMENT, SINCE I CAN CHEW ON THAT FOR A LONG TIME!!
THEN I'LL GO WITH HARD CANDY!!
I'd like these please!!
Sure.
WHAT ABOUT YOU, NOZOMI ?!
I BOUGHT THIS!
ALMOND CRUSH POCHI-D
'Preciate it!
N... NOT THE ALMOND CRUSH POCHI DELUXE—!!

An Unexpected Theory

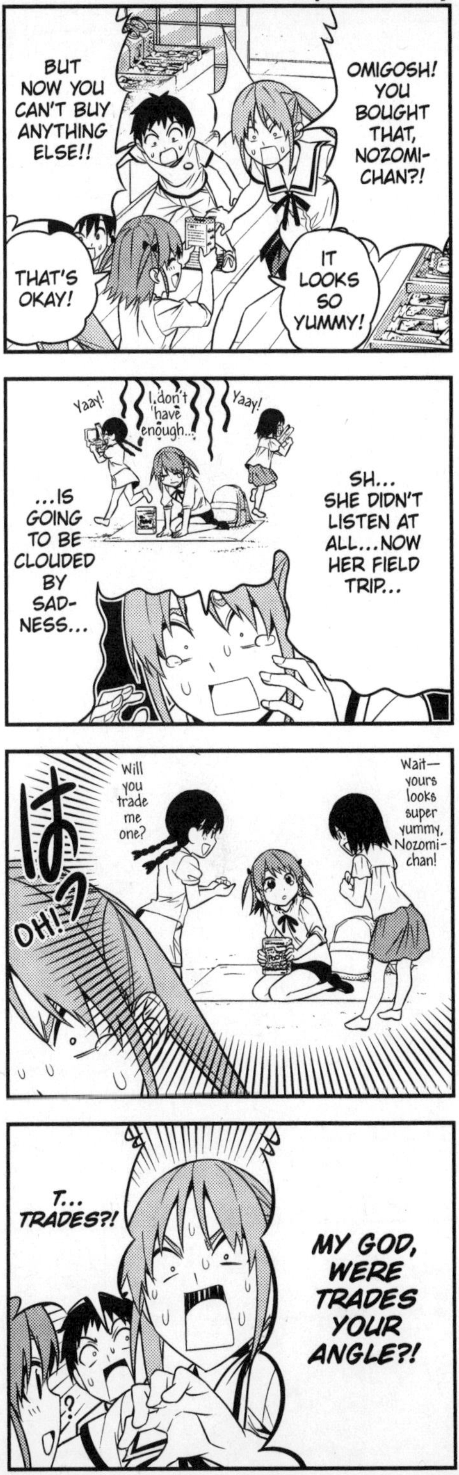
OMIGOSH! YOU BOUGHT THAT, NOZOMI-CHAN?!
BUT NOW YOU CAN'T BUY ANYTHING ELSE!!
IT LOOKS SO YUMMY!
THAT'S OKAY!
SH... SHE DIDN'T LISTEN AT ALL...NOW HER FIELD TRIP...
...IS GOING TO BE CLOUDED BY SAD-NESS...
Yaay!
I don't have enough...
Yaay!
Wait—yours looks super yummy, Nozomi-chan!
Will you trade me one?
はっ
OH!?
T... TRADES?!
MY GOD, WERE TRADES YOUR ANGLE?!

Almond Crwhatever...I'm calling it ACP

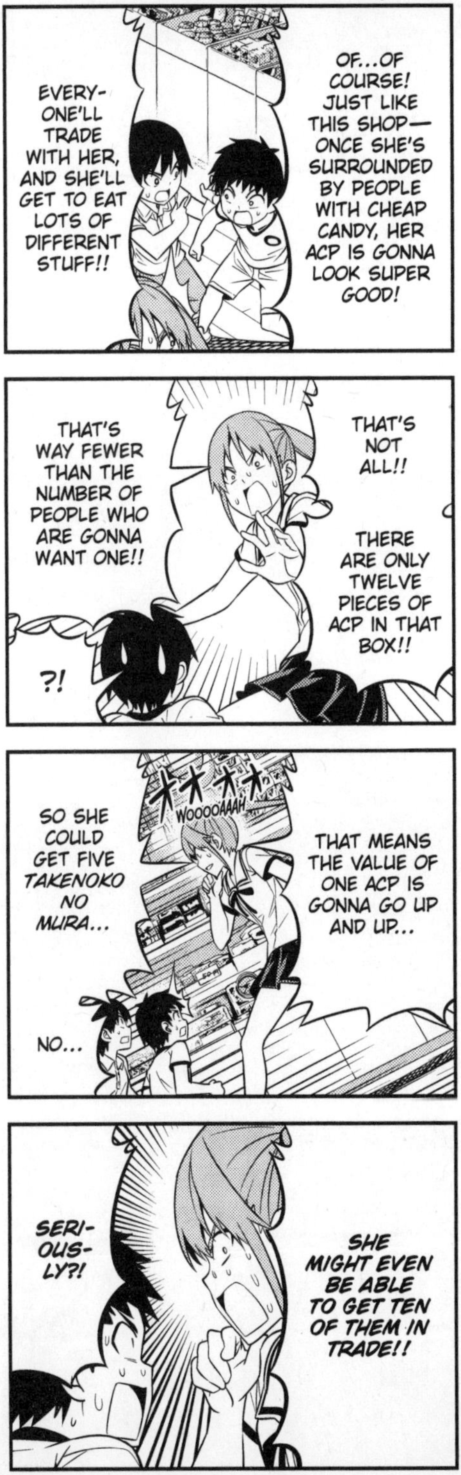
OF...OF COURSE! JUST LIKE THIS SHOP—ONCE SHE'S SURROUNDED BY PEOPLE WITH CHEAP CANDY, HER ACP IS GONNA LOOK SUPER GOOD!
EVERY-ONE'LL TRADE WITH HER, AND SHE'LL GET TO EAT LOTS OF DIFFERENT STUFF!!
THAT'S NOT ALL!!
THERE ARE ONLY TWELVE PIECES OF ACP IN THAT BOX!!
THAT'S WAY FEWER THAN THE NUMBER OF PEOPLE WHO ARE GONNA WANT ONE!!
?!
WOOOOAAAH
THAT MEANS THE VALUE OF ONE ACP IS GONNA GO UP AND UP...
SO SHE COULD GET FIVE *TAKENOKO NO MURA*...
NO...
SHE MIGHT EVEN BE ABLE TO GET TEN OF THEM IN TRADE!!
SERI-OUSLY?!

The Game Is Lost

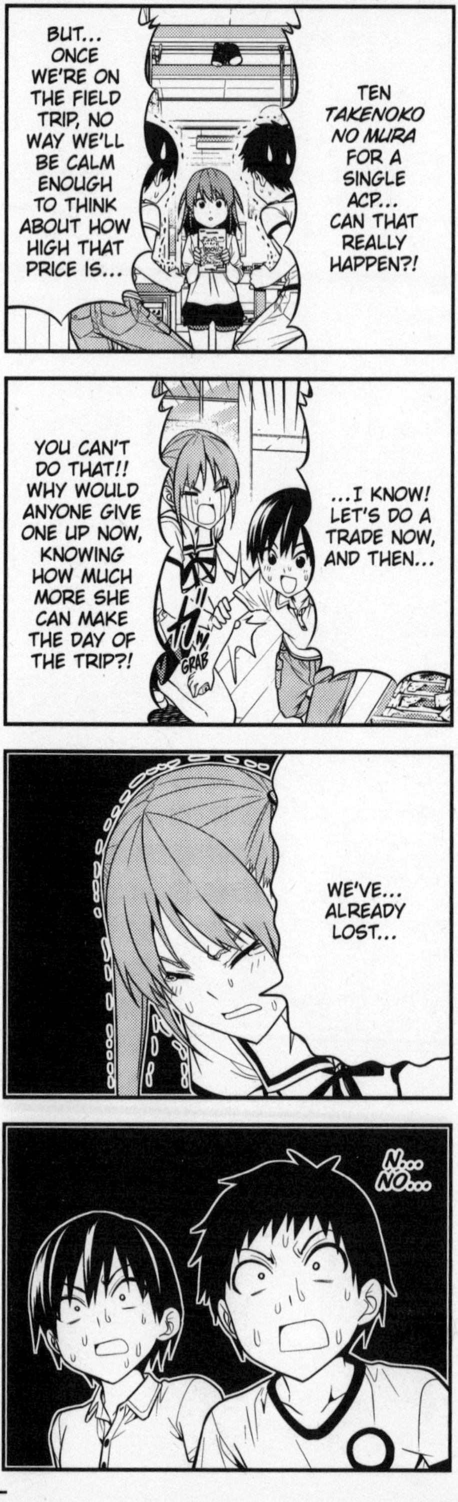
TEN TAKENOKO NO MURA FOR A SINGLE ACP... CAN THAT REALLY HAPPEN?!
BUT... ONCE WE'RE ON THE FIELD TRIP, NO WAY WE'LL BE CALM ENOUGH TO THINK ABOUT HOW HIGH THAT PRICE IS...
...I KNOW! LET'S DO A TRADE NOW, AND THEN...
YOU CAN'T DO THAT!! WHY WOULD ANYONE GIVE ONE UP NOW, KNOWING HOW MUCH MORE SHE CAN MAKE THE DAY OF THE TRIP?!
GRAB
WE'VE... ALREADY LOST...
N... NO...

What an Angel

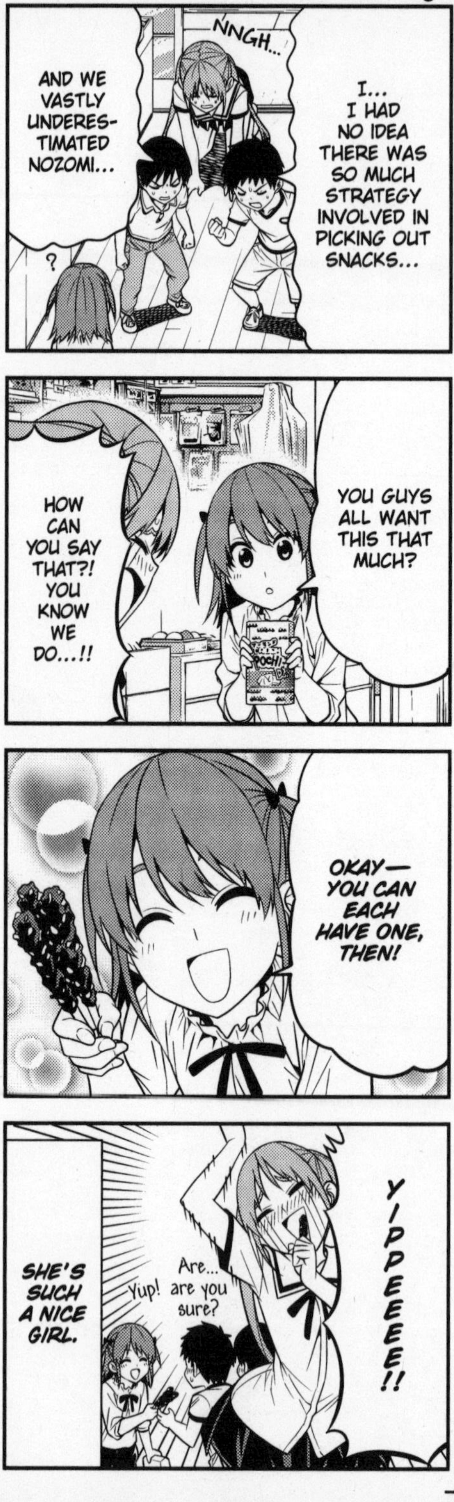
NNGH...
I... I HAD NO IDEA THERE WAS SO MUCH STRATEGY INVOLVED IN PICKING OUT SNACKS...
AND WE VASTLY UNDERES-TIMATED NOZOMI...
?
YOU GUYS ALL WANT THIS THAT MUCH?
HOW CAN YOU SAY THAT?! YOU KNOW WE DO...!!
OKAY— YOU CAN EACH HAVE ONE, THEN!
YIPPEEEE!!
Are... are you sure?
Yup!
SHE'S SUCH A NICE GIRL.

Breaker of Bonds

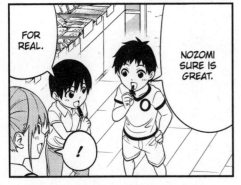

NOZOMI SURE IS GREAT.
FOR REAL.
!
HEY, NOZOMI-CHAN! I BET YOU HAVE A CRUSH ON ONE OF THEM!
HEY! CUT THAT OUT!!

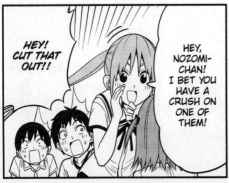

(Chocolate chocolate chocolate is my)

Aho-Girl

\'ahô,gərl\ *Japanese, noun*.

A clueless girl.

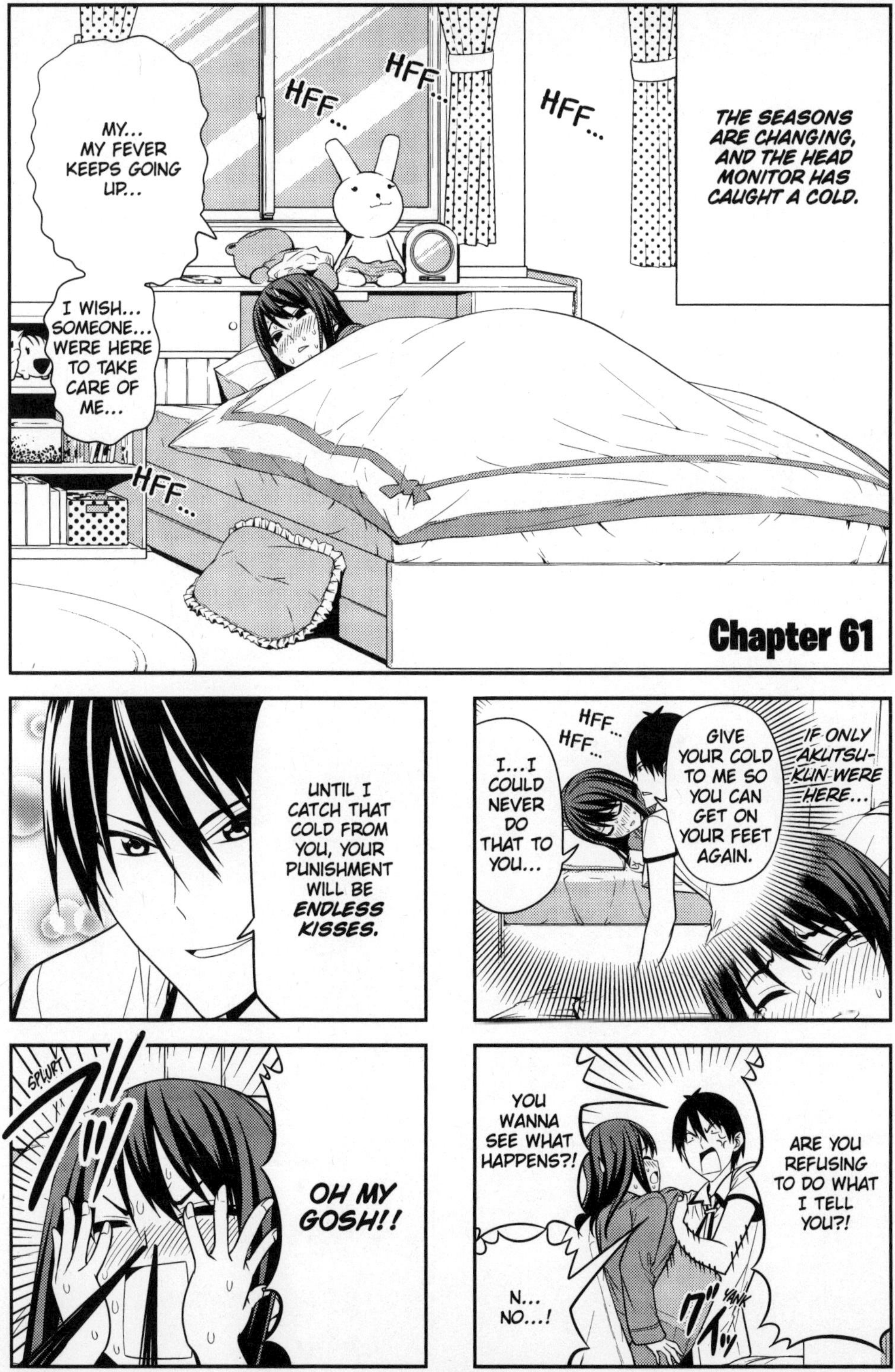
THE SEASONS ARE CHANGING, AND THE HEAD MONITOR HAS CAUGHT A COLD.
HFF...
HFF...
HFF...
MY... MY FEVER KEEPS GOING UP...
I WISH... SOMEONE... WERE HERE TO TAKE CARE OF ME...
HFF...
Chapter 61
IF ONLY AKUTSU-KUN WERE HERE...
GIVE YOUR COLD TO ME SO YOU CAN GET ON YOUR FEET AGAIN.
HFF... HFF...
I...I COULD NEVER DO THAT TO YOU...
UNTIL I CATCH THAT COLD FROM YOU, YOUR PUNISHMENT WILL BE ENDLESS KISSES.
ARE YOU REFUSING TO DO WHAT I TELL YOU?!
YOU WANNA SEE WHAT HAPPENS?!
YANK
N... NO...!
SPLURT
OH MY GOSH!!

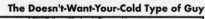

The Doesn't-Want-Your-Cold Type of Guy

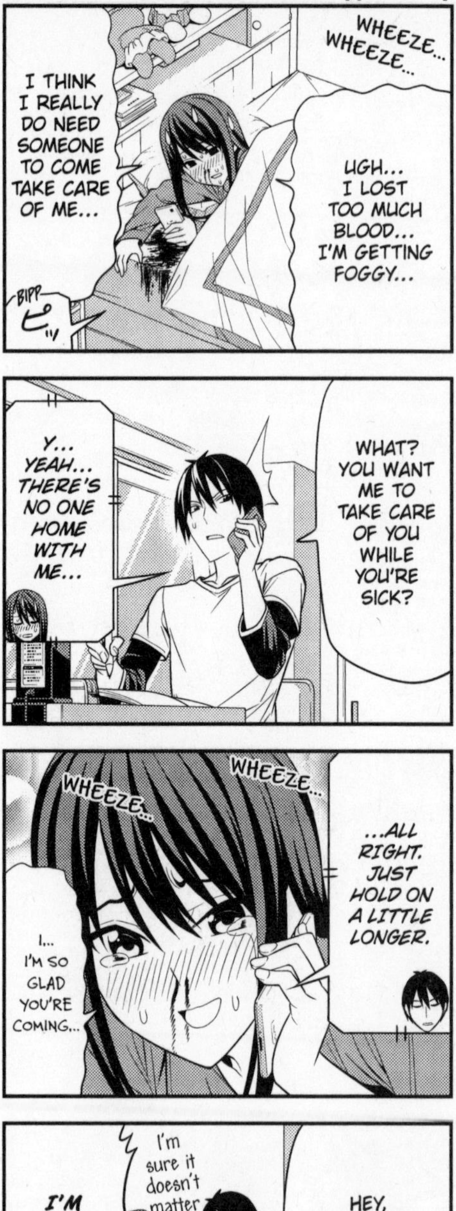
WHEEZE... WHEEZE...
UGH... I LOST TOO MUCH BLOOD... I'M GETTING FOGGY...
I THINK I REALLY DO NEED SOMEONE TO COME TAKE CARE OF ME...
BIPP ピッ
WHAT? YOU WANT ME TO TAKE CARE OF YOU WHILE YOU'RE SICK?
Y... YEAH... THERE'S NO ONE HOME WITH ME...
WHEEZE...
WHEEZE...
...ALL RIGHT. JUST HOLD ON A LITTLE LONGER.
I... I'M SO GLAD YOU'RE COMING...
HEY, YOSHIKO. THE HEAD MONITOR WANTS YOU TO GO TAKE CARE OF HER WHILE SHE'S SICK.
I'm sure it doesn't matter who goes.
I'M ON MY WAY!!

Serious Business

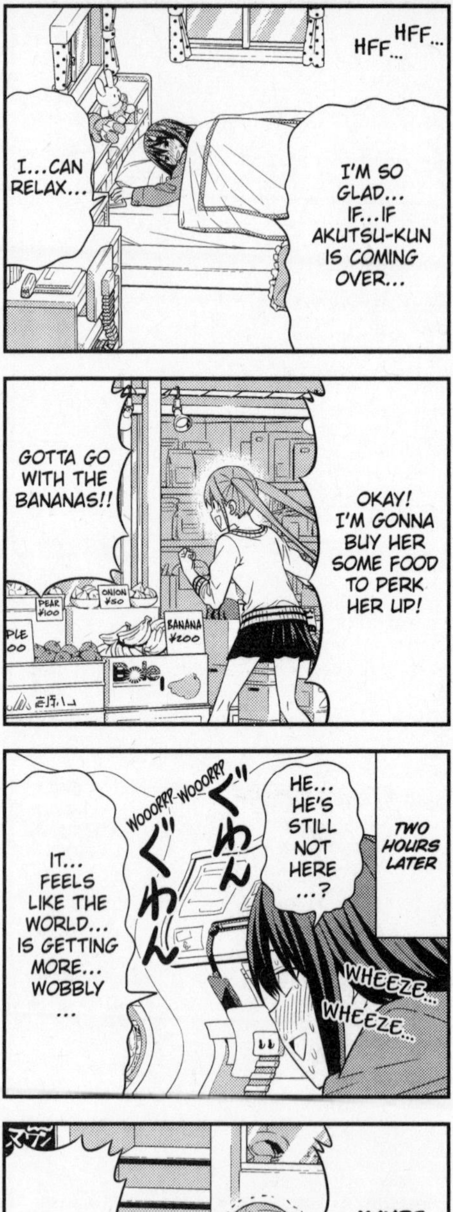
HFF... HFF...
I'M SO GLAD... IF...IF AKUTSU-KUN IS COMING OVER...
I...CAN RELAX...
OKAY! I'M GONNA BUY HER SOME FOOD TO PERK HER UP!
GOTTA GO WITH THE BANANAS!!
ONION ¥50
PEAR ¥100
BANANA ¥200
TWO HOURS LATER
HE... HE'S STILL NOT HERE ...?
WOOORRP-WOOORRP ぐわん ぐわん
IT... FEELS LIKE THE WORLD... IS GETTING MORE... WOBBLY ...
WHEEZE...
WHEEZE...
MAYBE THESE BANANAS ARE BETTER!!
BUT THESE ARE SO MUCH GLOSS-IER...!!
For two whole hours...
Then again...

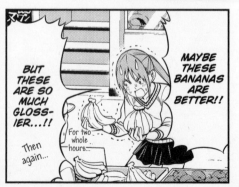

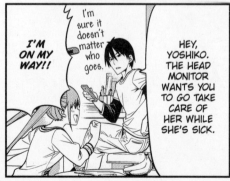

Optical Illusion

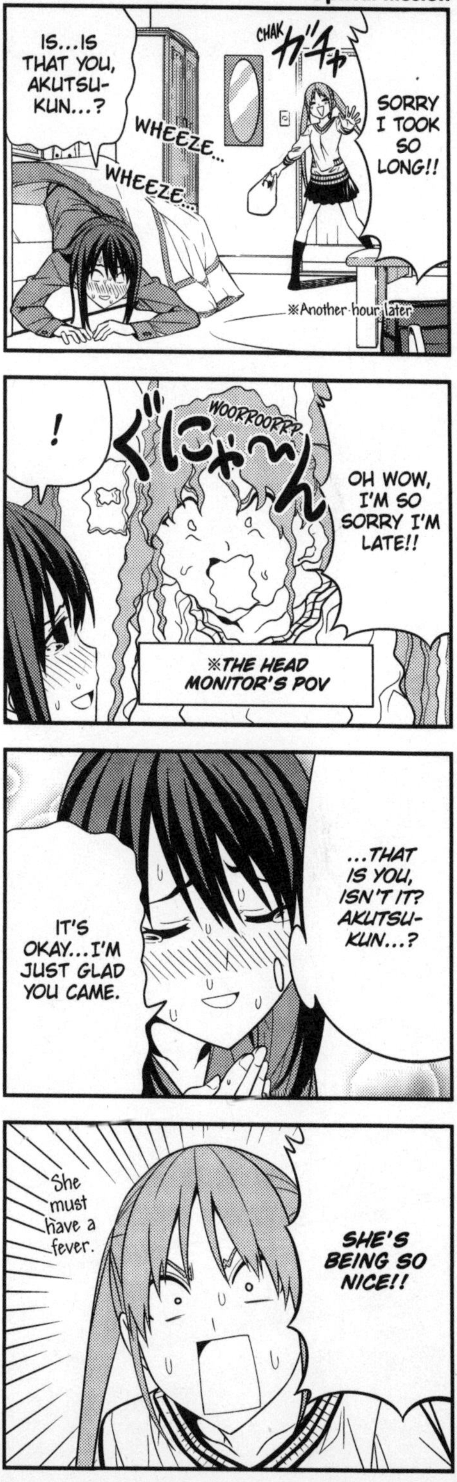
ガチャ
CHAK
SORRY I TOOK SO LONG!!
IS...IS THAT YOU, AKUTSU-KUN...?
WHEEZE...
WHEEZE...
※Another hour later
WOORROORRP
ぐにゃ～ん
OH WOW, I'M SO SORRY I'M LATE!!
!
※THE HEAD MONITOR'S POV
...THAT IS YOU, ISN'T IT? AKUTSU-KUN...?
IT'S OKAY...I'M JUST GLAD YOU CAME.
SHE'S BEING SO NICE!!
She must have a fever.

Quite Bashful

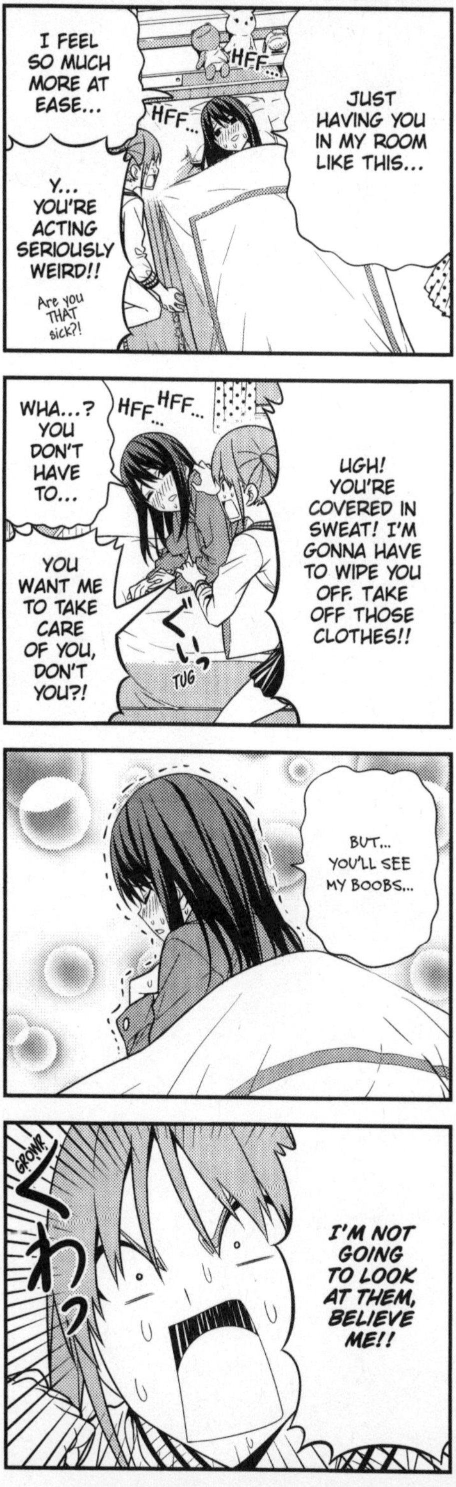
JUST HAVING YOU IN MY ROOM LIKE THIS...
I FEEL SO MUCH MORE AT EASE...
HFF...
HFF...
Y... YOU'RE ACTING SERIOUSLY WEIRD!!
Are you THAT sick?!
UGH! YOU'RE COVERED IN SWEAT! I'M GONNA HAVE TO WIPE YOU OFF. TAKE OFF THOSE CLOTHES!!
HFF... HFF...
WHA...? YOU DON'T HAVE TO...
YOU WANT ME TO TAKE CARE OF YOU, DON'T YOU?!
ぐいっ
TUG
BUT... YOU'LL SEE MY BOOBS...
I'M NOT GOING TO LOOK AT THEM, BELIEVE ME!!
くわっ
GROWR

This Was Your Plan All Along

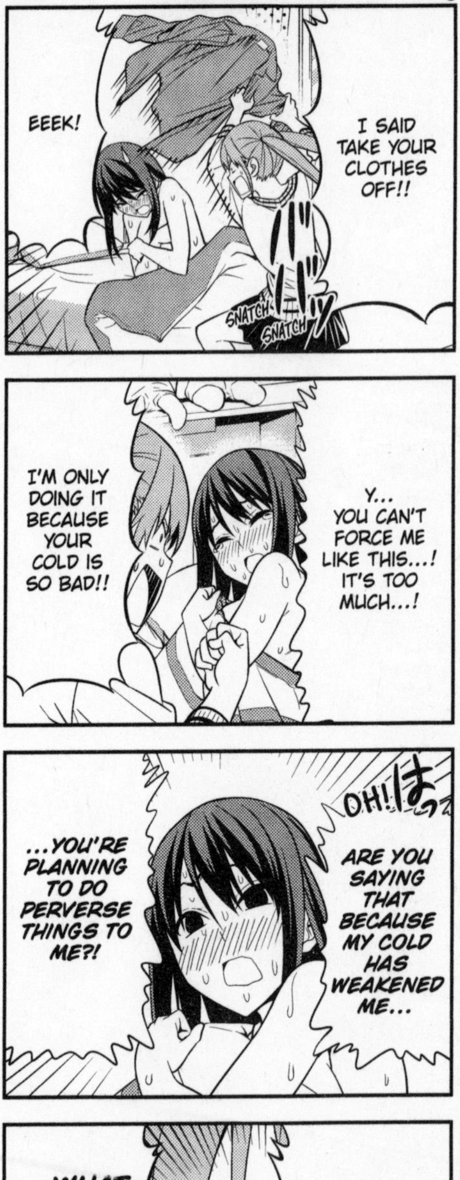
I SAID TAKE YOUR CLOTHES OFF!!
EEEK!
SNATCH
SNATCH
Y... YOU CAN'T FORCE ME LIKE THIS...! IT'S TOO MUCH...!
I'M ONLY DOING IT BECAUSE YOUR COLD IS SO BAD!!
OH! はっ
ARE YOU SAYING THAT BECAUSE MY COLD HAS WEAKENED ME...
...YOU'RE PLANNING TO DO PERVERSE THINGS TO ME?!
I HAVE NO IDEA...
...WHAT YOU'RE TALKING ABOUT!!

Shove It

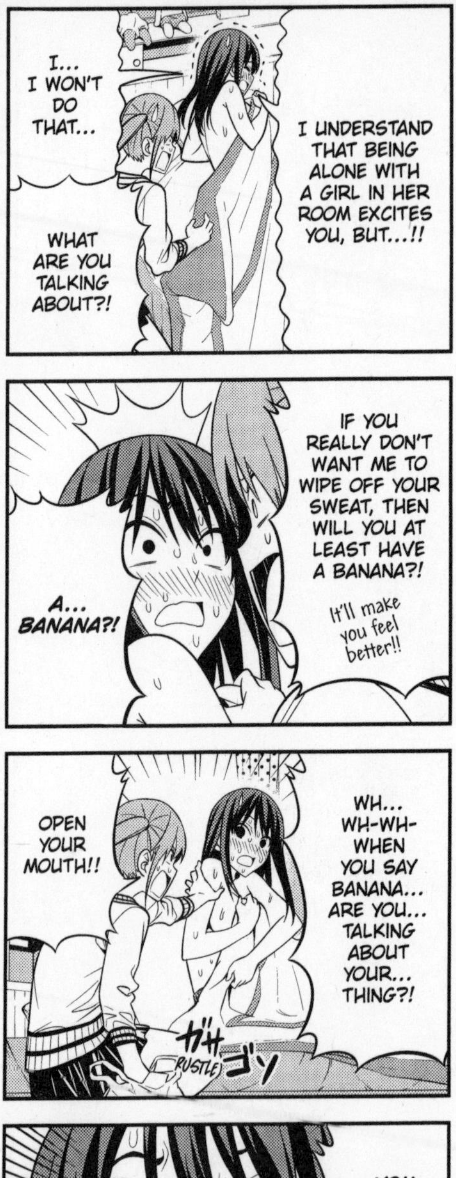
I UNDERSTAND THAT BEING ALONE WITH A GIRL IN HER ROOM EXCITES YOU, BUT...!!
I... I WON'T DO THAT...
WHAT ARE YOU TALKING ABOUT?!
IF YOU REALLY DON'T WANT ME TO WIPE OFF YOUR SWEAT, THEN WILL YOU AT LEAST HAVE A BANANA?!
It'll make you feel better!!
A... BANANA?!
WH... WH-WH-WHEN YOU SAY BANANA... ARE YOU... TALKING ABOUT YOUR... THING?!
OPEN YOUR MOUTH!!
ガサゴソ
RUSTLE
YOU WANT TO PUT IT IN MY MOUTH?!
WHERE ELSE WOULD I PUT IT?!

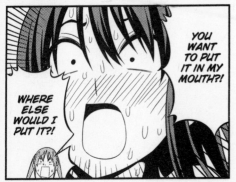

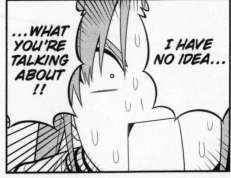

Rivalry

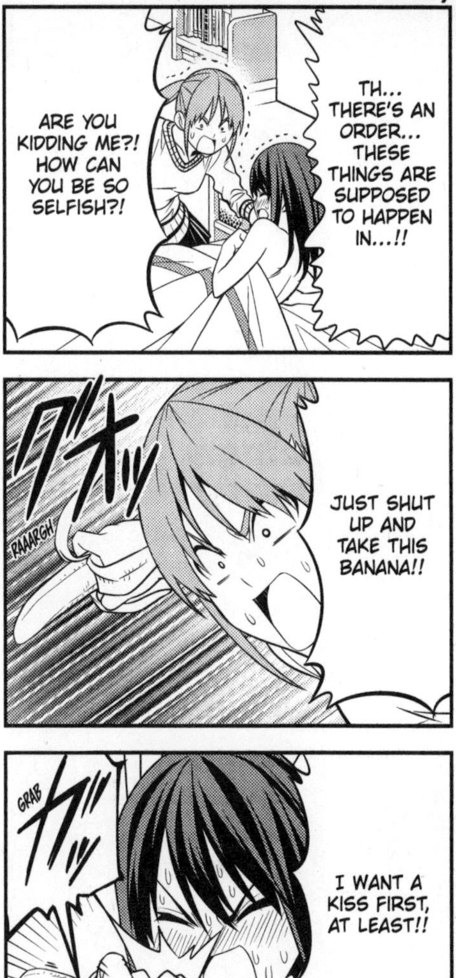
TH... THERE'S AN ORDER... THESE THINGS ARE SUPPOSED TO HAPPEN IN...!!
ARE YOU KIDDING ME?! HOW CAN YOU BE SO SELFISH?!
グオッ
RAAARGH
JUST SHUT UP AND TAKE THIS BANANA!!
ガッ
GRAB
I WANT A KISS FIRST, AT LEAST!!
グググググ
GRRRKKK
I DON'T WANT YOUR BANANA TO BE THE FIRST THING THAT EVER TOUCHES MY LIPS!!
H... HOW CAN YOU STILL BE THIS STRONG?!

Don't Make Me Say It

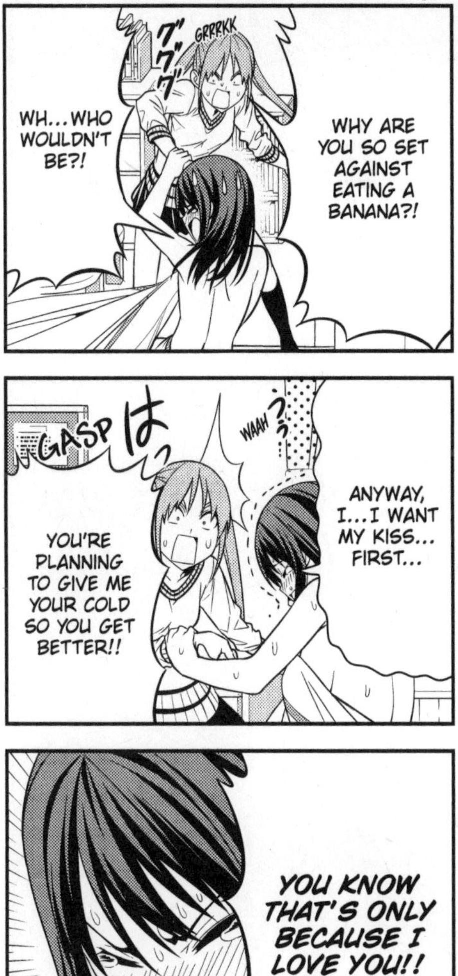
WHY ARE YOU SO SET AGAINST EATING A BANANA?!
グググ
GRRRKK
WH...WHO WOULDN'T BE?!
ANYWAY, I...I WANT MY KISS... FIRST...
WAAH
GASP は
YOU'RE PLANNING TO GIVE ME YOUR COLD SO YOU GET BETTER!!
YOU KNOW THAT'S ONLY BECAUSE I LOVE YOU!!
WHAT THE HELL?!

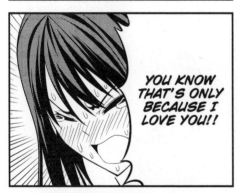

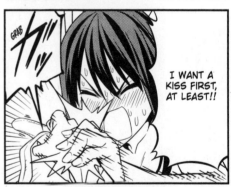

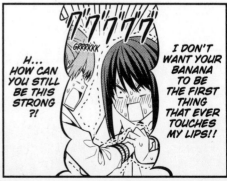

What a Jerk!

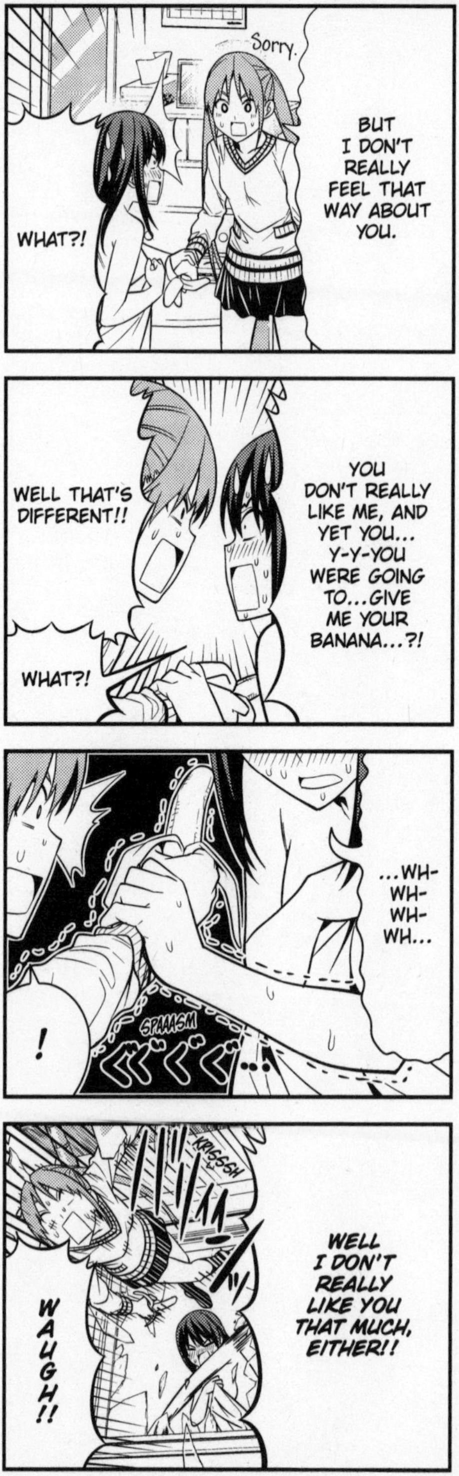
Sorry.
BUT I DON'T REALLY FEEL THAT WAY ABOUT YOU.
WHAT?!
YOU DON'T REALLY LIKE ME, AND YET YOU... Y-Y-YOU WERE GOING TO...GIVE ME YOUR BANANA...?!
WELL THAT'S DIFFERENT!!
WHAT?!
...WH- WH- WH- WH...
SPAAASM
ぐぐぐ...
!
KRISSSH
WELL I DON'T REALLY LIKE YOU THAT MUCH, EITHER!!
WAUGH!!

All Clear

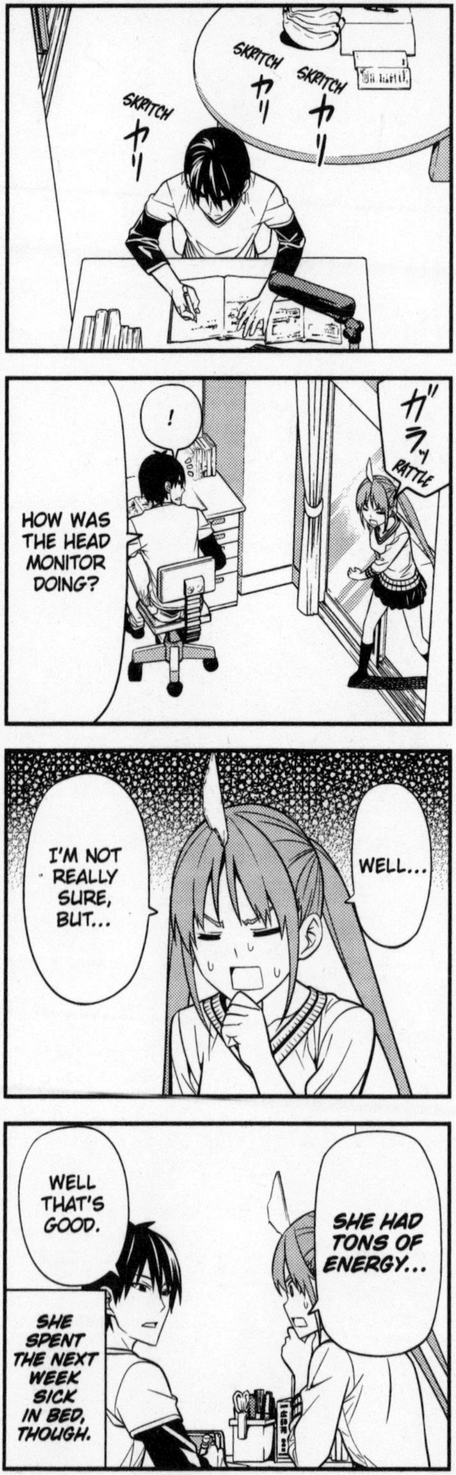
SKRITCH
カリ
SKRITCH
カリ
SKRITCH
カリ
ガラッ
RATTLE
!
HOW WAS THE HEAD MONITOR DOING?
WELL...
I'M NOT REALLY SURE, BUT...
SHE HAD TONS OF ENERGY...
WELL THAT'S GOOD.
SHE SPENT THE NEXT WEEK SICK IN BED, THOUGH.

There Is No Cure

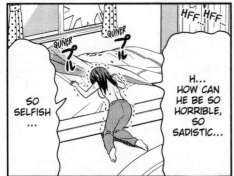

HFF... HFF...
QUIVER
プル
QUIVER
プル
H... HOW CAN HE BE SO HORRIBLE, SO SADISTIC...
SO SELFISH...
...AND YET... I LOVE HIM...
SHE IS GRAVELY ILL.

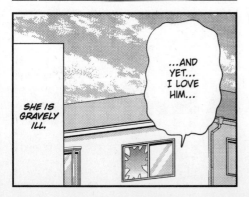

(Priority one: sleep. Priority two:)

Aho-Girl

\'ahô,gərl\ *Japanese, noun*.

A clueless girl.

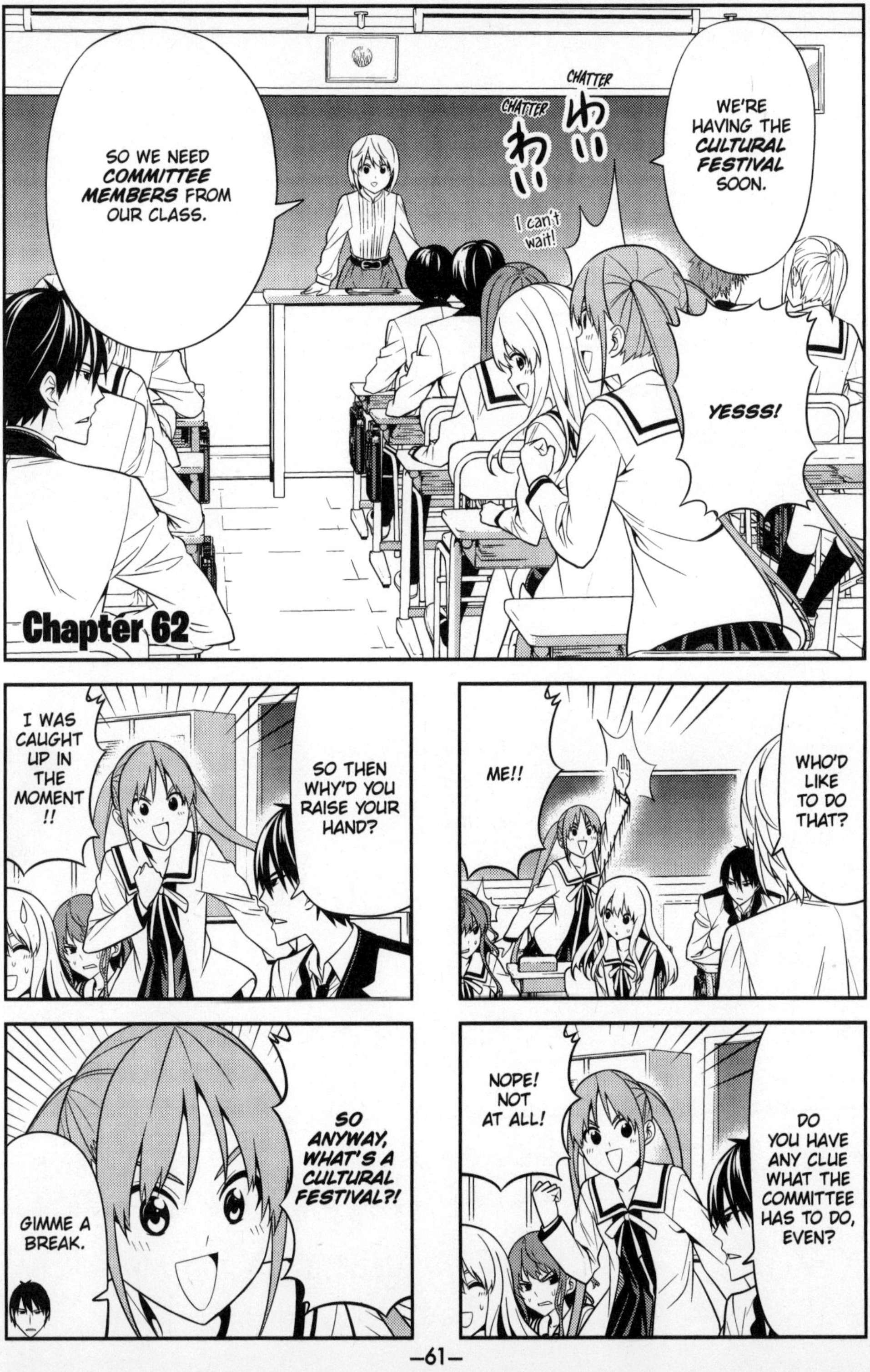
WE'RE HAVING THE CULTURAL FESTIVAL SOON.
CHATTER
わい
CHATTER
わい
I can't wait!
SO WE NEED COMMITTEE MEMBERS FROM OUR CLASS.
YESSS!
Chapter 62
WHO'D LIKE TO DO THAT?
ME!!
SO THEN WHY'D YOU RAISE YOUR HAND?
I WAS CAUGHT UP IN THE MOMENT!!
DO YOU HAVE ANY CLUE WHAT THE COMMITTEE HAS TO DO, EVEN?
NOPE! NOT AT ALL!
SO ANYWAY, WHAT'S A CULTURAL FESTIVAL?!
GIMME A BREAK.

She Probably Just Doesn't Understand

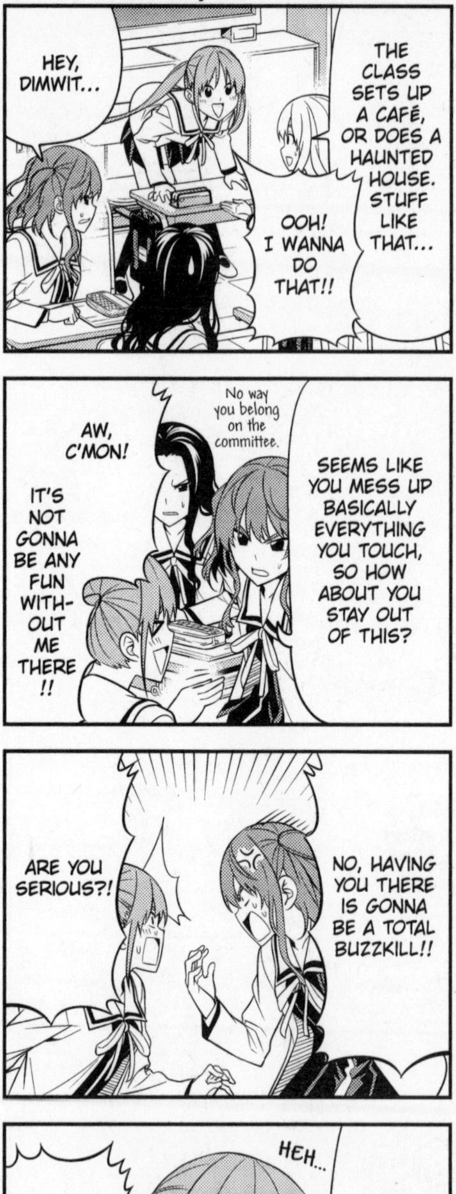
THE CLASS SETS UP A CAFÉ, OR DOES A HAUNTED HOUSE. STUFF LIKE THAT...
OOH! I WANNA DO THAT!!
HEY, DIMWIT...
SEEMS LIKE YOU MESS UP BASICALLY EVERYTHING YOU TOUCH, SO HOW ABOUT YOU STAY OUT OF THIS?
No way you belong on the committee.
AW, C'MON!
IT'S NOT GONNA BE ANY FUN WITHOUT ME THERE!!
NO, HAVING YOU THERE IS GONNA BE A TOTAL BUZZKILL!!
ARE YOU SERIOUS?!
HEH...
NO, AFTER ALL YOU'RE NEW TO ALL THIS...
LOOK WHO'S TALKING!!

Stoic

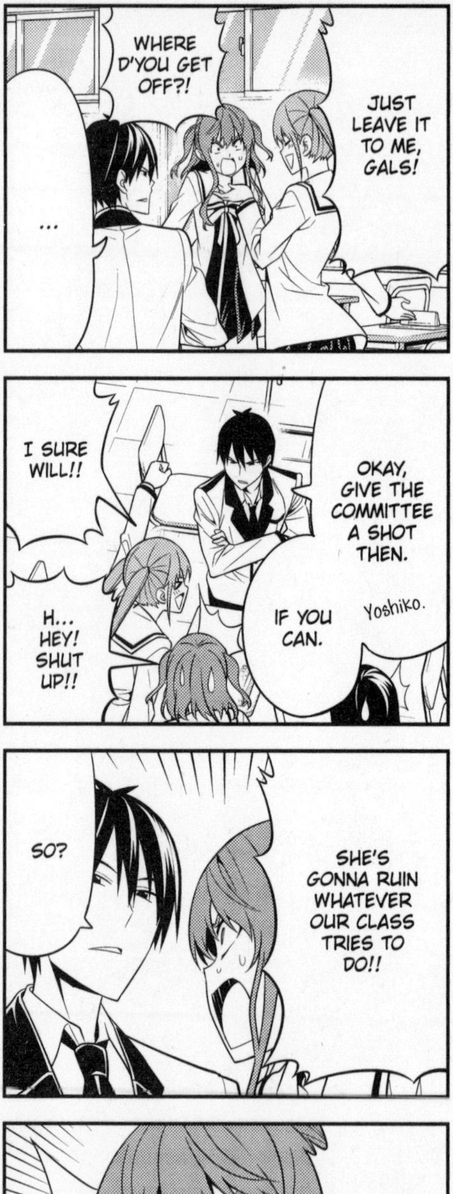
JUST LEAVE IT TO ME, GALS!
WHERE D'YOU GET OFF?!
...
OKAY, GIVE THE COMMITTEE A SHOT THEN.
Yoshiko.
IF YOU CAN.
I SURE WILL!!
H... HEY! SHUT UP!!
SHE'S GONNA RUIN WHATEVER OUR CLASS TRIES TO DO!!
SO?
WHAT DO YOU MEAN, "SO"?!

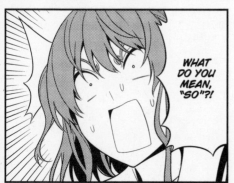

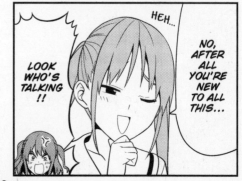

Stoked

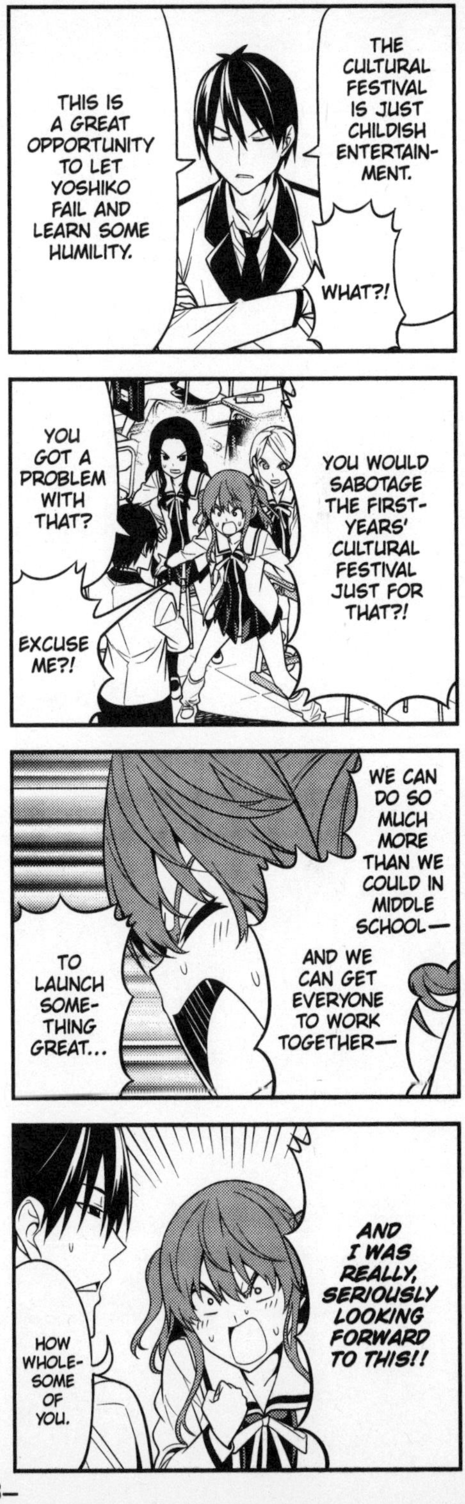
THE CULTURAL FESTIVAL IS JUST CHILDISH ENTERTAINMENT.
THIS IS A GREAT OPPORTUNITY TO LET YOSHIKO FAIL AND LEARN SOME HUMILITY.
WHAT?!
YOU WOULD SABOTAGE THE FIRST-YEARS' CULTURAL FESTIVAL JUST FOR THAT?!
YOU GOT A PROBLEM WITH THAT?
EXCUSE ME?!
WE CAN DO SO MUCH MORE THAN WE COULD IN MIDDLE SCHOOL—
AND WE CAN GET EVERYONE TO WORK TOGETHER—
TO LAUNCH SOMETHING GREAT...
AND I WAS REALLY, SERIOUSLY LOOKING FORWARD TO THIS!!
HOW WHOLESOME OF YOU.

Cold-blooded Animal

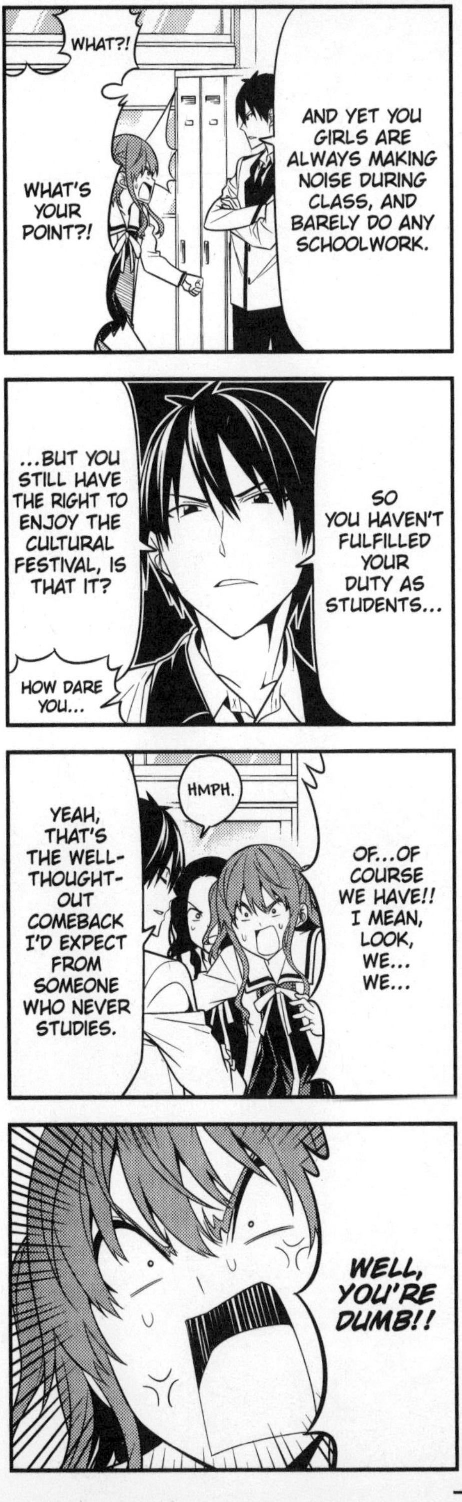
AND YET YOU GIRLS ARE ALWAYS MAKING NOISE DURING CLASS, AND BARELY DO ANY SCHOOLWORK.
WHAT?!
WHAT'S YOUR POINT?!
SO YOU HAVEN'T FULFILLED YOUR DUTY AS STUDENTS...
...BUT YOU STILL HAVE THE RIGHT TO ENJOY THE CULTURAL FESTIVAL, IS THAT IT?
HOW DARE YOU...
OF...OF COURSE WE HAVE!! I MEAN, LOOK, WE... WE...
HMPH.
YEAH, THAT'S THE WELL-THOUGHT-OUT COMEBACK I'D EXPECT FROM SOMEONE WHO NEVER STUDIES.
WELL, YOU'RE DUMB!!

Well, It's True

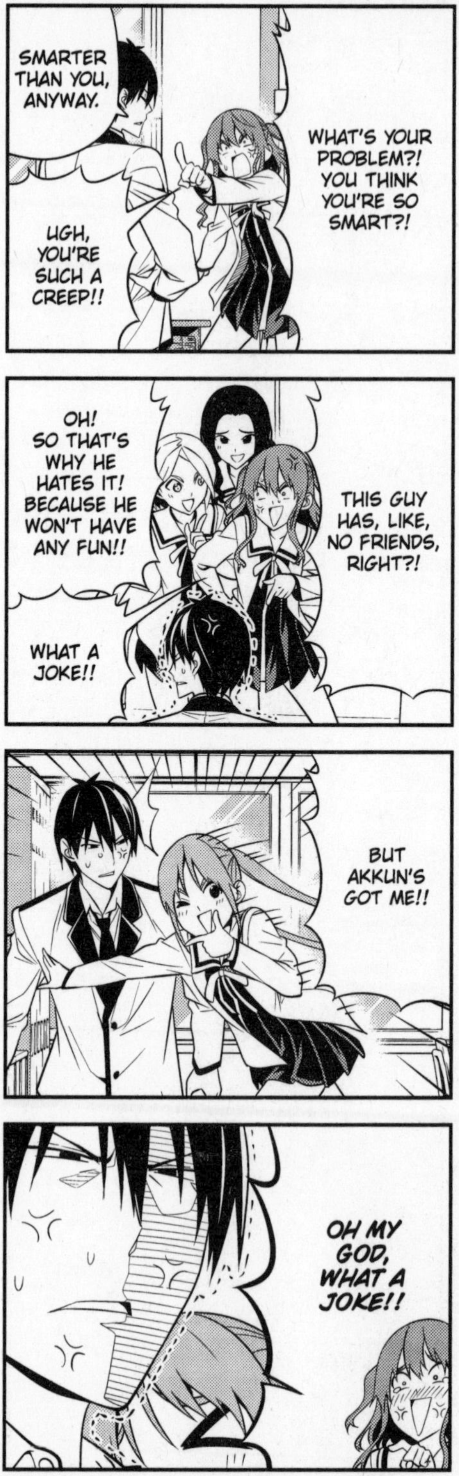
WHAT'S YOUR PROBLEM?! YOU THINK YOU'RE SO SMART?!
SMARTER THAN YOU, ANYWAY.
UGH, YOU'RE SUCH A CREEP!!
THIS GUY HAS, LIKE, NO FRIENDS, RIGHT?!
OH! SO THAT'S WHY HE HATES IT! BECAUSE HE WON'T HAVE ANY FUN!!
WHAT A JOKE!!
BUT AKKUN'S GOT ME!!
OH MY GOD, WHAT A JOKE!!

We're Not Getting Anywhere

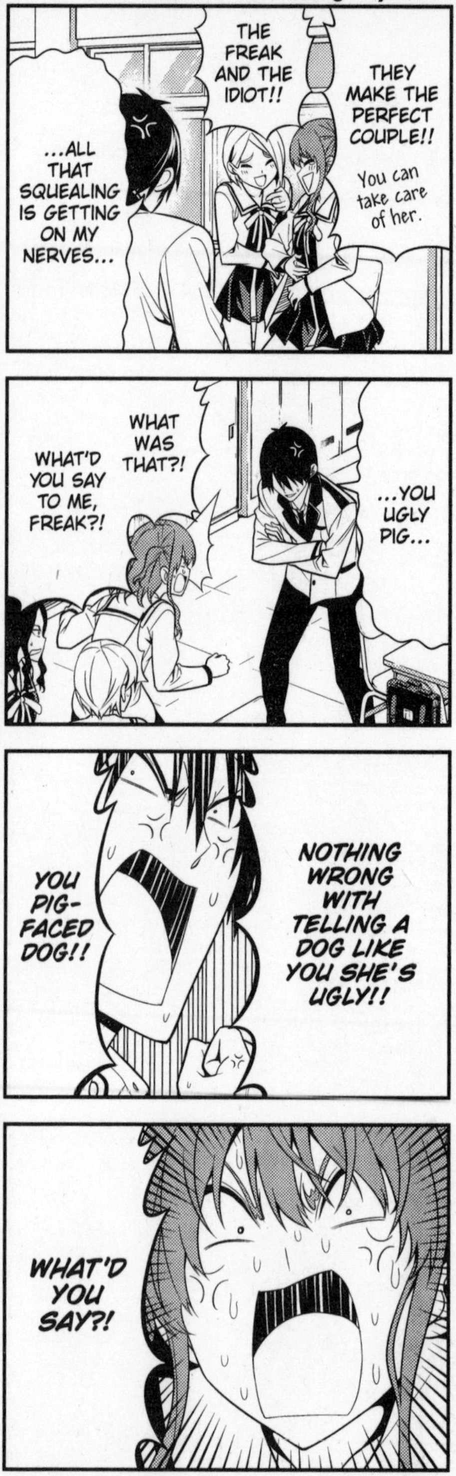
THE FREAK AND THE IDIOT!!
THEY MAKE THE PERFECT COUPLE!!
You can take care of her.
...ALL THAT SQUEALING IS GETTING ON MY NERVES...
...YOU UGLY PIG...
WHAT WAS THAT?!
WHAT'D YOU SAY TO ME, FREAK?!
NOTHING WRONG WITH TELLING A DOG LIKE YOU SHE'S UGLY!!
YOU PIG-FACED DOG!!
WHAT'D YOU SAY?!

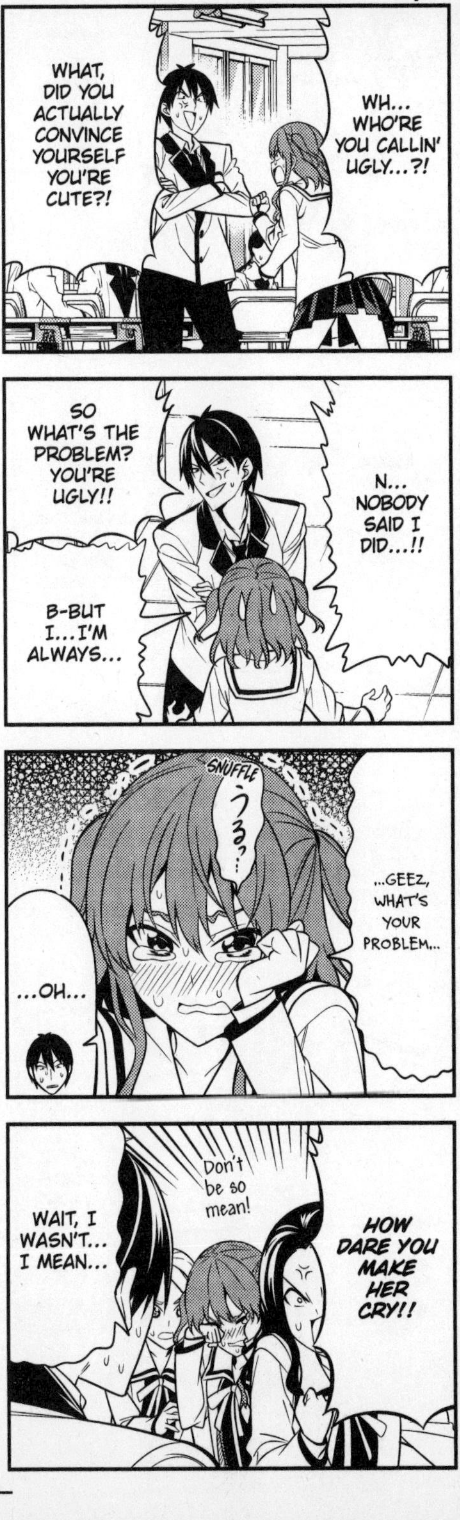
WH... WHO'RE YOU CALLIN' UGLY...?!
WHAT, DID YOU ACTUALLY CONVINCE YOURSELF YOU'RE CUTE?!
N... NOBODY SAID I DID...!!
SO WHAT'S THE PROBLEM? YOU'RE UGLY!!
B-BUT I...I'M ALWAYS...
SNUFFLE
うるっ...
...GEEZ, WHAT'S YOUR PROBLEM...
...OH...
HOW DARE YOU MAKE HER CRY!!
Don't be so mean!
WAIT, I WASN'T... I MEAN...

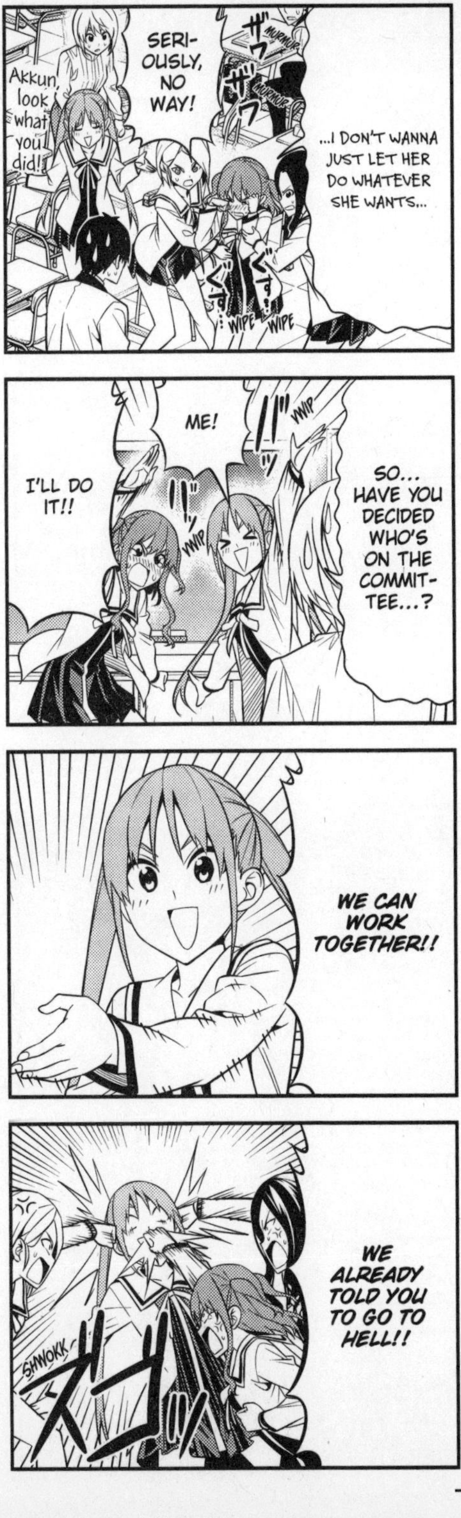
...I DON'T WANNA JUST LET HER DO WHATEVER SHE WANTS...
ザワ MURMUR
ザワ MURMUR
SERI-OUSLY, NO WAY!
Akkun, look what you did!!
ぐすっ WIPE
ぐすっ WIPE
SO... HAVE YOU DECIDED WHO'S ON THE COMMIT-TEE...?
バッ WHIP
ME!
I'LL DO IT!!
バッ WHIP
WE CAN WORK TOGETHER!!
WE ALREADY TOLD YOU TO GO TO HELL!!
SHWOKK
ズゴッ

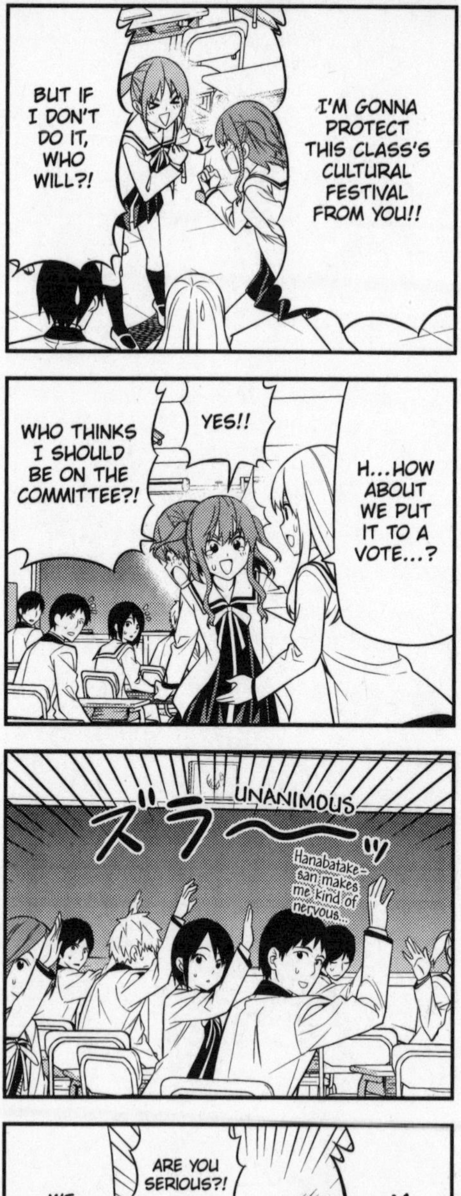
I'M GONNA PROTECT THIS CLASS'S CULTURAL FESTIVAL FROM YOU!!
BUT IF I DON'T DO IT, WHO WILL?!
H...HOW ABOUT WE PUT IT TO A VOTE...?
YES!!
WHO THINKS I SHOULD BE ON THE COMMITTEE?!
UNANIMOUS
ズラ〜〜ッ
Hanabatake-san makes me kind of nervous...
YESSSSSS!!
ARE YOU SERIOUS?!
WE SHOULD'VE JUST VOTED IN THE FIRST PLACE...

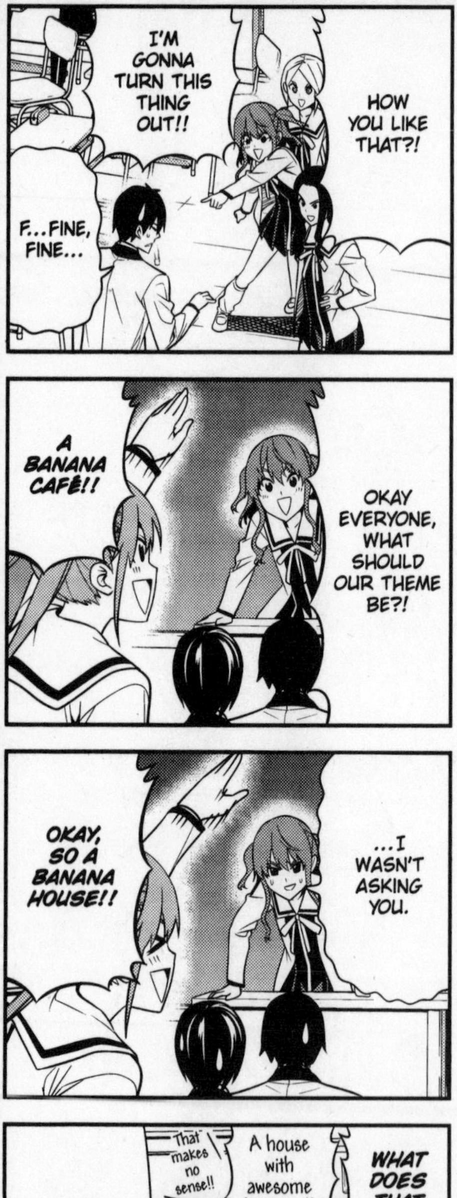
HOW YOU LIKE THAT?!
I'M GONNA TURN THIS THING OUT!!
F...FINE, FINE...
OKAY EVERYONE, WHAT SHOULD OUR THEME BE?!
A BANANA CAFÉ!!
...I WASN'T ASKING YOU.
OKAY, SO A BANANA HOUSE!!
WHAT DOES THAT EVEN MEAN?!
A house with awesome bananas!!
That makes no sense!!
YOSHIKO WAS GOING TO BE A PROBLEM EITHER WAY.

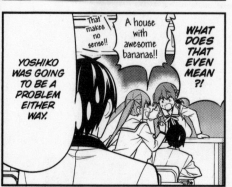

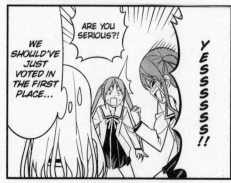

Horrifying

BANANA CAFÉ
Welcome!
Banana
BANANA HOUSE
Welcome home, madam!
Madam!

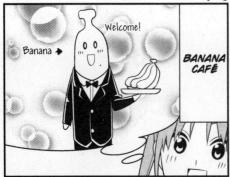

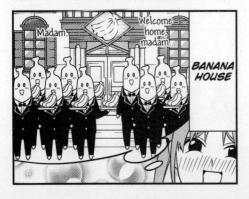

(Pure LOVE Academy: Maiden Heart)

Aho-Girl

\\'ahô͵gərl\\ *Japanese, noun.*
A clueless girl.

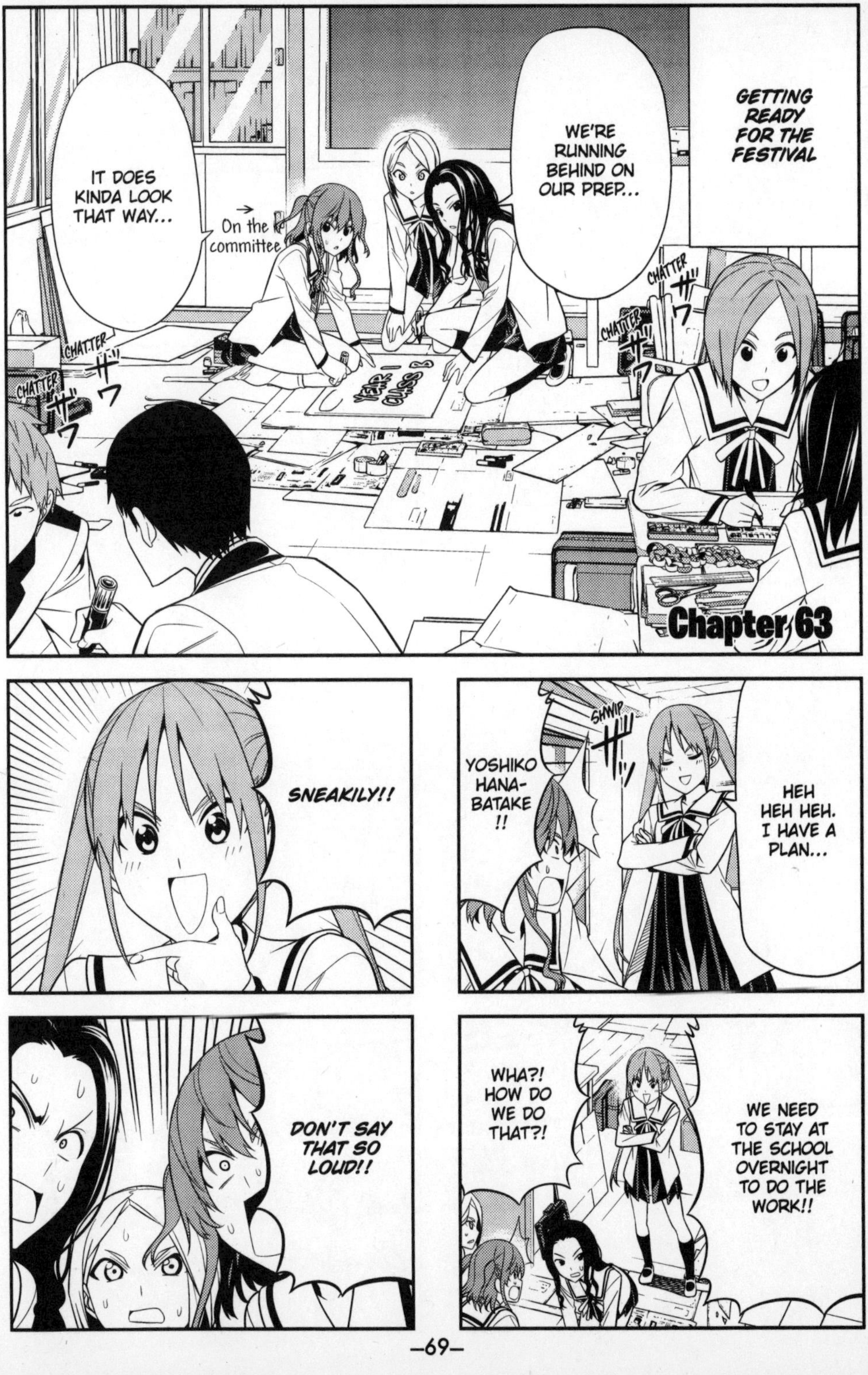
GETTING READY FOR THE FESTIVAL
WE'RE RUNNING BEHIND ON OUR PREP...
CHATTER
CHATTER
IT DOES KINDA LOOK THAT WAY...
→ On the committee
CHATTER
CHATTER
Chapter 63
HEH HEH HEH. I HAVE A PLAN...
SHWIP
YOSHIKO HANA-BATAKE !!
SNEAKILY!!
WE NEED TO STAY AT THE SCHOOL OVERNIGHT TO DO THE WORK!!
WHA?! HOW DO WE DO THAT?!
DON'T SAY THAT SO LOUD!!

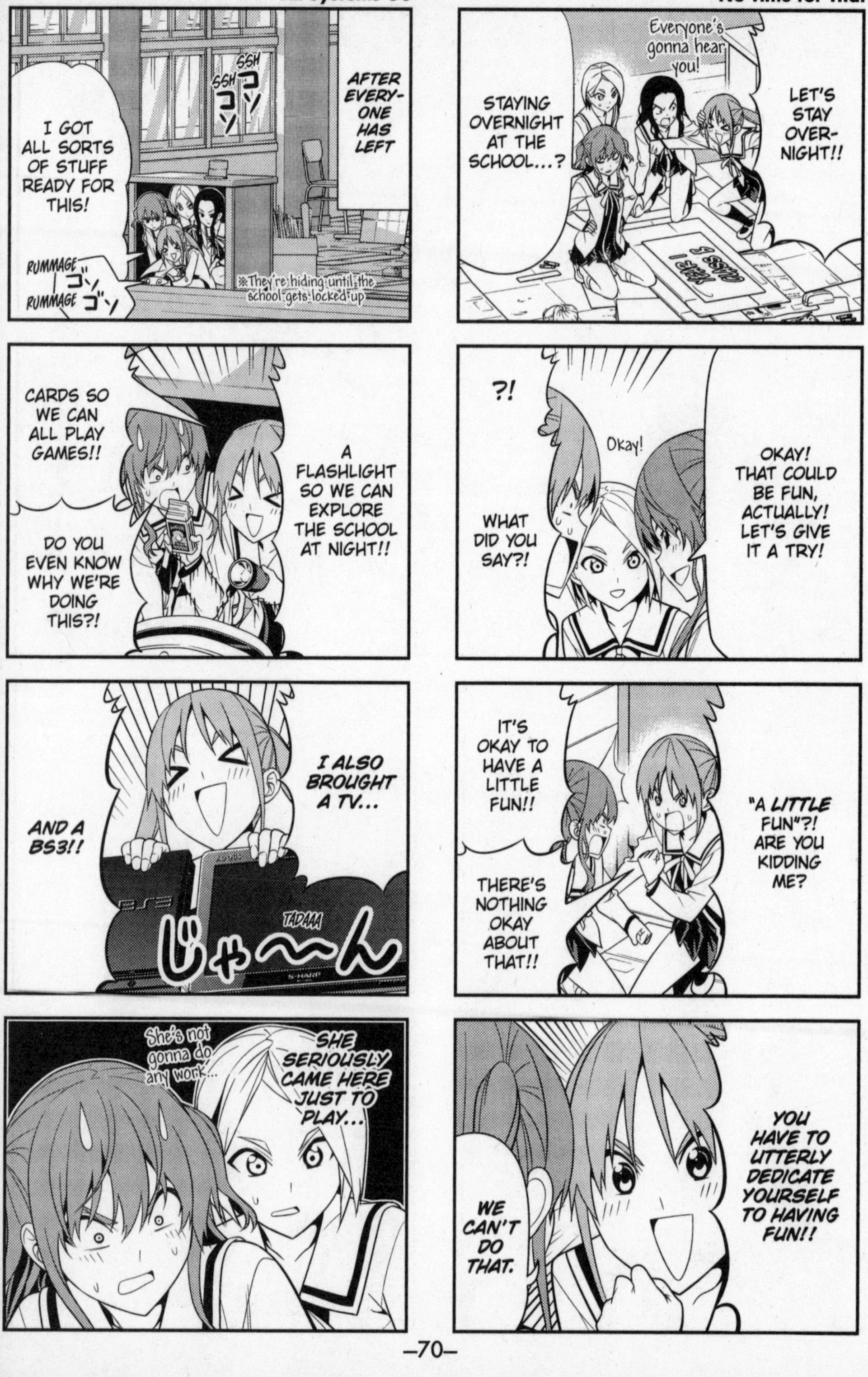
LET'S STAY OVER-NIGHT!!
Everyone's gonna hear you!
STAYING OVERNIGHT AT THE SCHOOL...?
OKAY! THAT COULD BE FUN, ACTUALLY! LET'S GIVE IT A TRY!
Okay!
?!
WHAT DID YOU SAY?!
IT'S OKAY TO HAVE A LITTLE FUN!!
"A LITTLE FUN"?! ARE YOU KIDDING ME?
THERE'S NOTHING OKAY ABOUT THAT!!
YOU HAVE TO UTTERLY DEDICATE YOURSELF TO HAVING FUN!!
WE CAN'T DO THAT.
AFTER EVERYONE HAS LEFT
SSH コソ
SSH コソ
I GOT ALL SORTS OF STUFF READY FOR THIS!
RUMMAGE ゴソ
RUMMAGE ゴソ
※They're hiding until the school gets locked up
A FLASHLIGHT SO WE CAN EXPLORE THE SCHOOL AT NIGHT!!
CARDS SO WE CAN ALL PLAY GAMES!!
DO YOU EVEN KNOW WHY WE'RE DOING THIS?!
I ALSO BROUGHT A TV...
AND A BS3!!
TADAAA
じゃ～ん
SHE SERIOUSLY CAME HERE JUST TO PLAY...
She's not gonna do any work...

Really?!

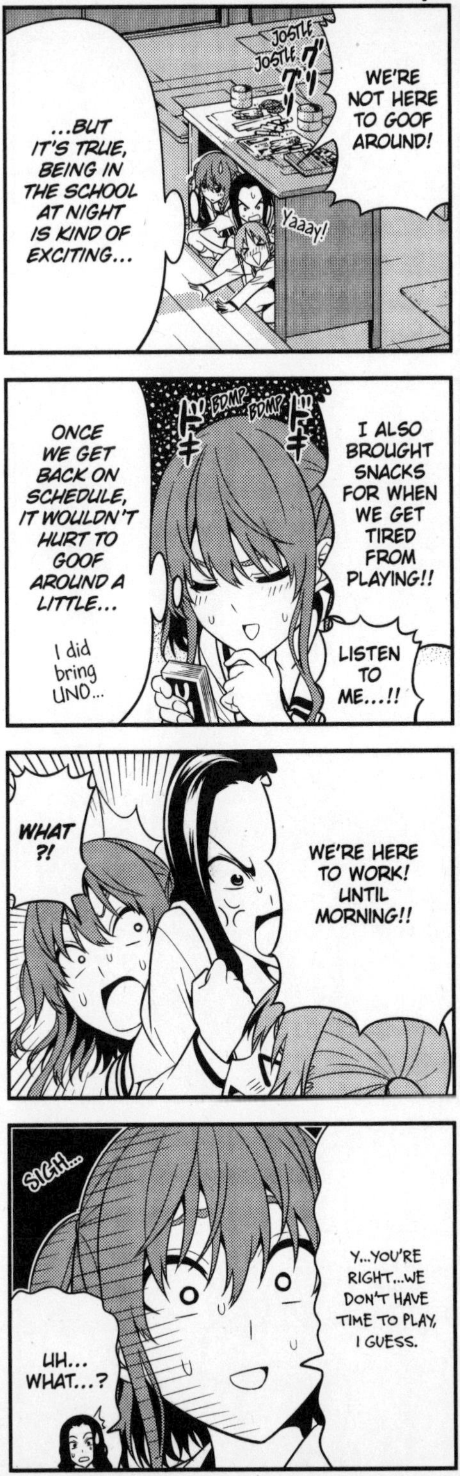
JOSTLE JOSTLE
WE'RE NOT HERE TO GOOF AROUND!
Yaaay!
...BUT IT'S TRUE, BEING IN THE SCHOOL AT NIGHT IS KIND OF EXCITING...
I ALSO BROUGHT SNACKS FOR WHEN WE GET TIRED FROM PLAYING!!
BDMP BDMP
ONCE WE GET BACK ON SCHEDULE, IT WOULDN'T HURT TO GOOF AROUND A LITTLE...
LISTEN TO ME...!!
I did bring UNO...
WE'RE HERE TO WORK! UNTIL MORNING!!
WHAT?!
Y...YOU'RE RIGHT...WE DON'T HAVE TIME TO PLAY, I GUESS.
UH... WHAT...?
SIGH...

Seriously, We Don't Have Time for That

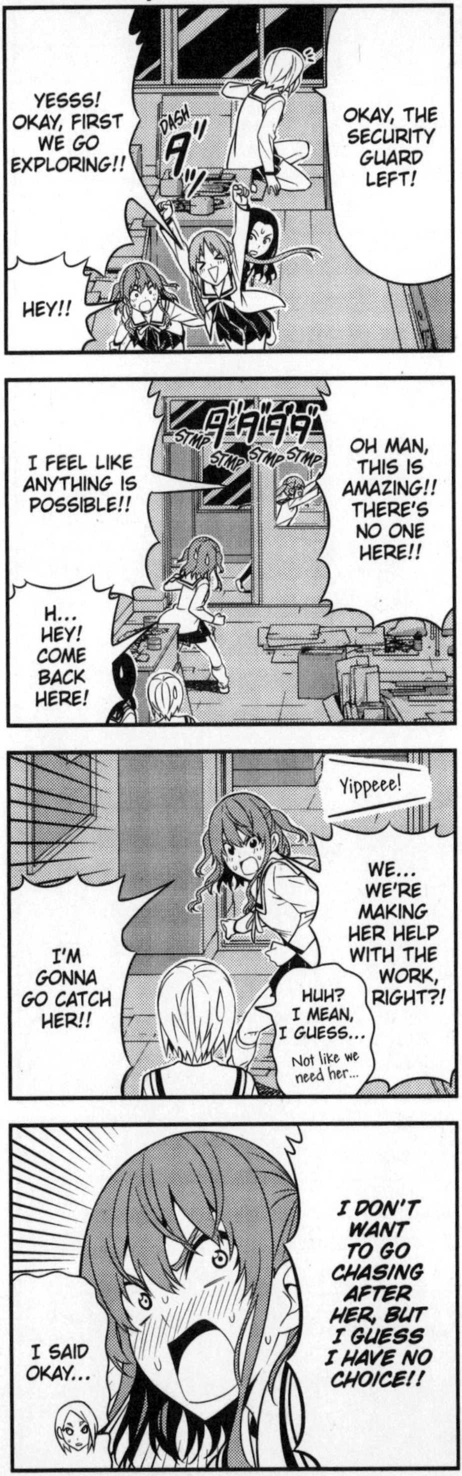
OKAY, THE SECURITY GUARD LEFT!
DASH
YESSS! OKAY, FIRST WE GO EXPLORING!!
HEY!!
OH MAN, THIS IS AMAZING!! THERE'S NO ONE HERE!!
STMP STMP STMP STMP
I FEEL LIKE ANYTHING IS POSSIBLE!!
H... HEY! COME BACK HERE!
Yippeee!
WE... WE'RE MAKING HER HELP WITH THE WORK, RIGHT?!
HUH? I MEAN, I GUESS...
Not like we need her...
I'M GONNA GO CATCH HER!!
I DON'T WANT TO GO CHASING AFTER HER, BUT I GUESS I HAVE NO CHOICE!!
I SAID OKAY...

Abundant Curiosity

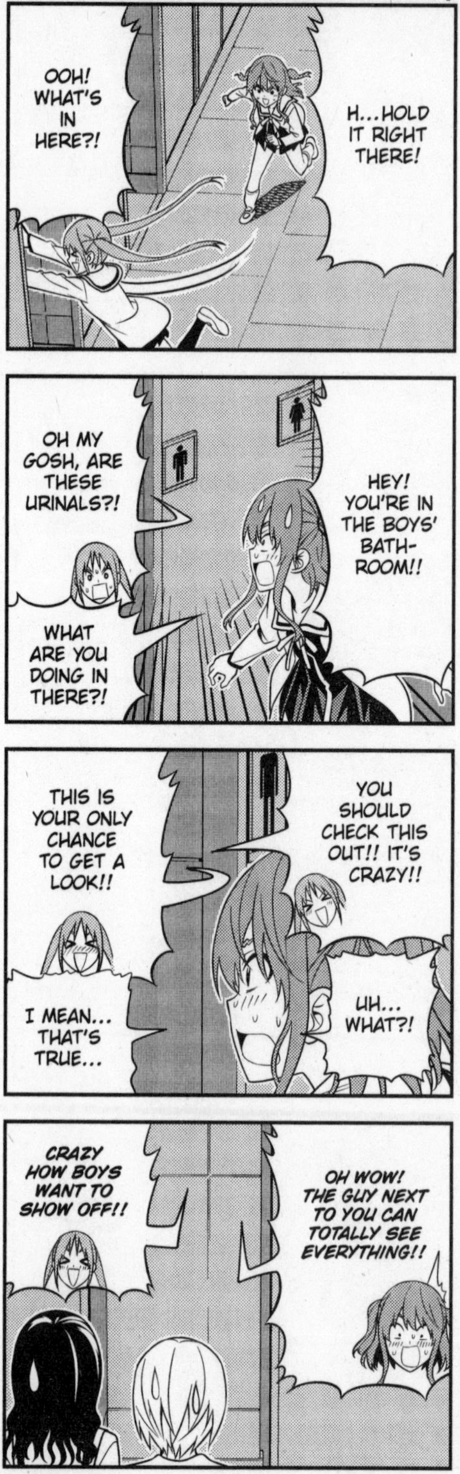
H...HOLD IT RIGHT THERE!
OOH! WHAT'S IN HERE?!
HEY! YOU'RE IN THE BOYS' BATH-ROOM!!
OH MY GOSH, ARE THESE URINALS?!
WHAT ARE YOU DOING IN THERE?!
YOU SHOULD CHECK THIS OUT!! IT'S CRAZY!!
THIS IS YOUR ONLY CHANCE TO GET A LOOK!!
UH... WHAT?!
I MEAN... THAT'S TRUE...
OH WOW! THE GUY NEXT TO YOU CAN TOTALLY SEE EVERYTHING!!
CRAZY HOW BOYS WANT TO SHOW OFF!!

Which One Is It?

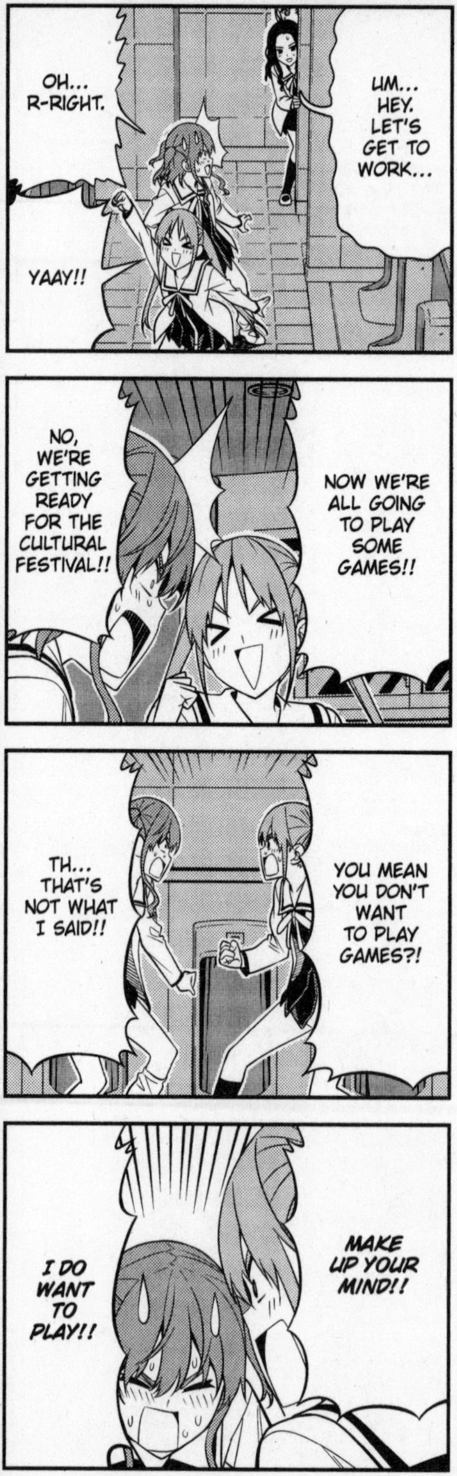
UM... HEY. LET'S GET TO WORK...
OH... R-RIGHT.
YAAY!!
NOW WE'RE ALL GOING TO PLAY SOME GAMES!!
NO, WE'RE GETTING READY FOR THE CULTURAL FESTIVAL!!
YOU MEAN YOU DON'T WANT TO PLAY GAMES?!
TH... THAT'S NOT WHAT I SAID!!
MAKE UP YOUR MIND!!
I DO WANT TO PLAY!!

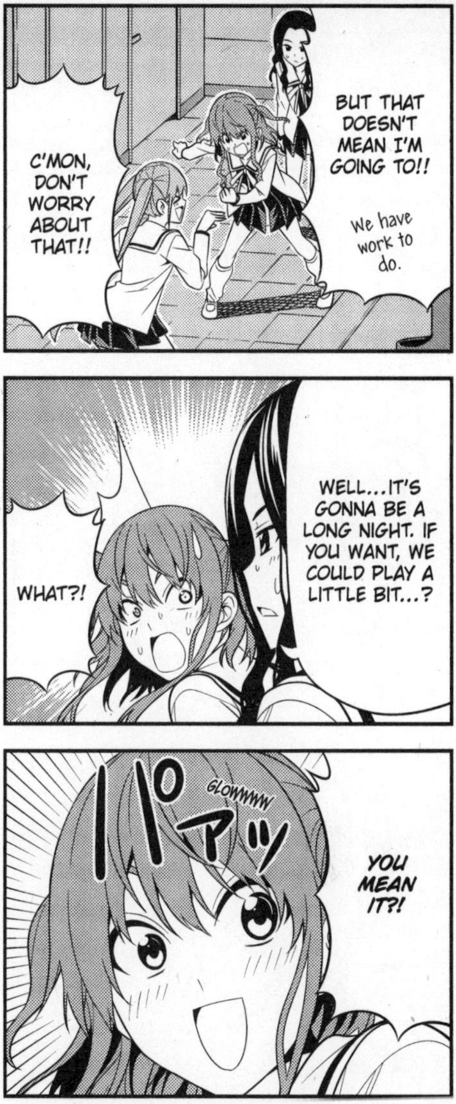
BUT THAT DOESN'T MEAN I'M GOING TO!!
We have work to do.
C'MON, DON'T WORRY ABOUT THAT!!
WELL...IT'S GONNA BE A LONG NIGHT. IF YOU WANT, WE COULD PLAY A LITTLE BIT...?
WHAT?!
パァッ
GLOWWWW
YOU MEAN IT?!
UH... SURE...
Okay, just for a little while then!!
タタタッ
STMP STMP STMP
Ha ha ha!!
I'VE NEVER SEEN SUCH A HUGE SMILE ON HER FACE...

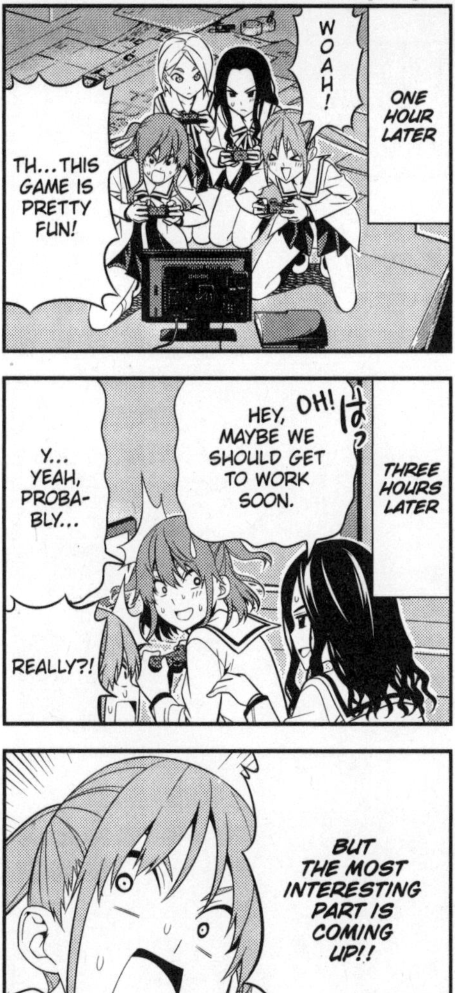
ONE HOUR LATER
WOAH!
TH...THIS GAME IS PRETTY FUN!
THREE HOURS LATER
はっ
OH!
HEY, MAYBE WE SHOULD GET TO WORK SOON.
Y... YEAH, PROBA-BLY...
REALLY?!
BUT THE MOST INTERESTING PART IS COMING UP!!
W...WE'LL GET TO THE WORK AFTER THIS, FOR SURE!
UM... OKAY...

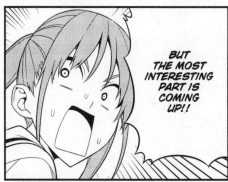

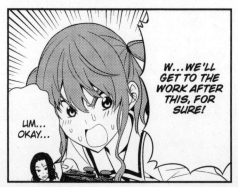

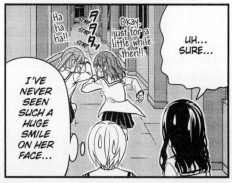

Earnest Plea

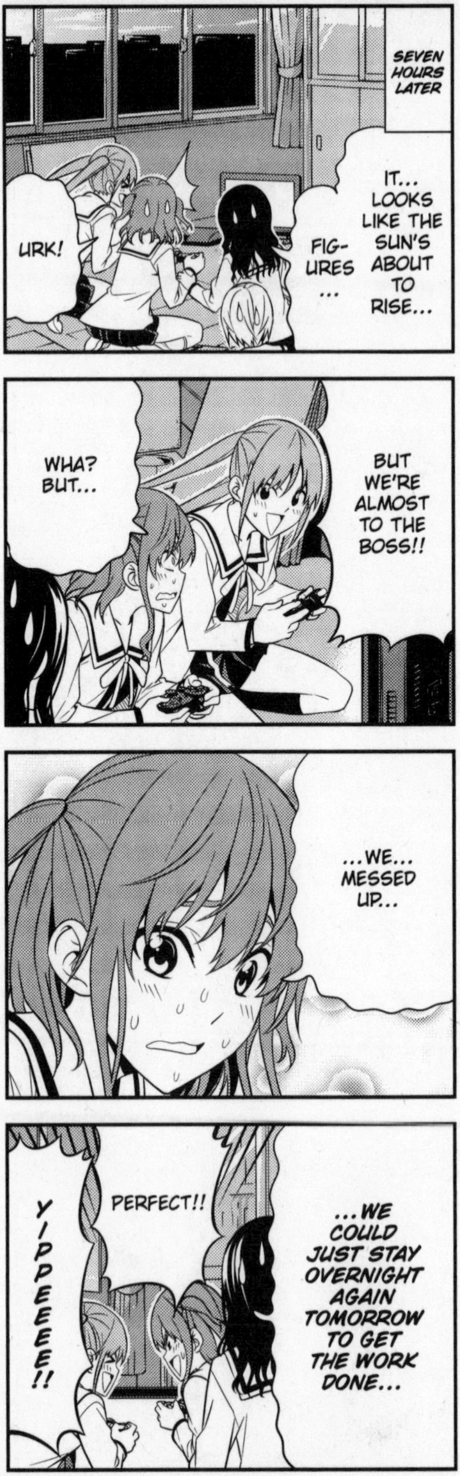
SEVEN HOURS LATER
IT... LOOKS LIKE THE SUN'S ABOUT TO RISE...
FIG-URES...
URK!
BUT WE'RE ALMOST TO THE BOSS!!
WHA? BUT...
...WE... MESSED UP...
...WE COULD JUST STAY OVERNIGHT AGAIN TOMORROW TO GET THE WORK DONE...
PERFECT!!
YIPPEEEE!!

The Morning After

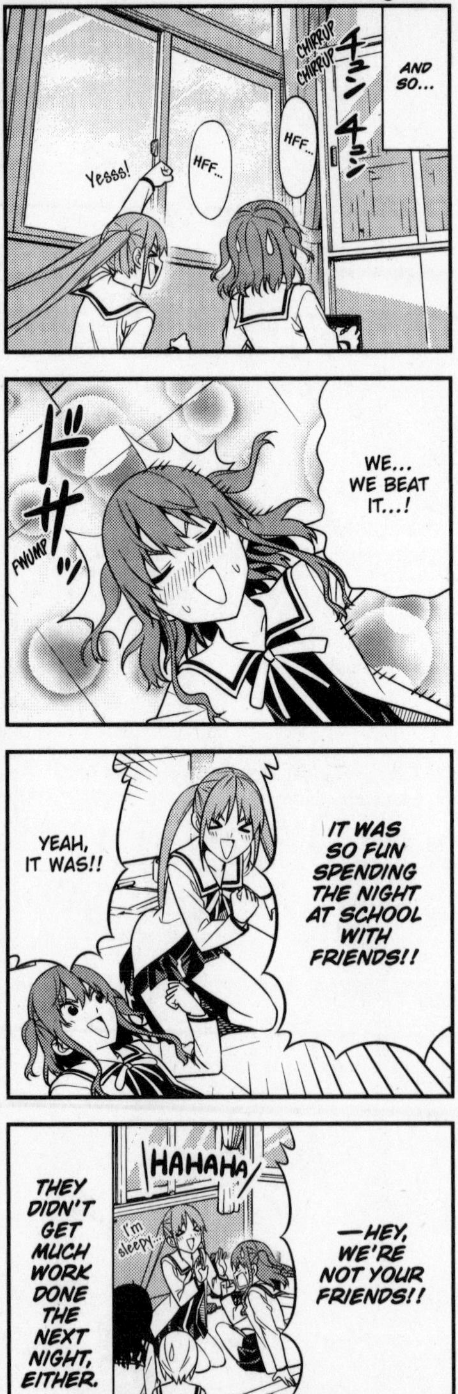
AND SO...
チュン チュン
CHIRRUP CHIRRUP
HFF...
HFF...
Yesss!
WE... WE BEAT IT...!
ドサッ
FWUMP
IT WAS SO FUN SPENDING THE NIGHT AT SCHOOL WITH FRIENDS!!
YEAH, IT WAS!!
—HEY, WE'RE NOT YOUR FRIENDS!!
HAHAHA
I'm sleepy...
THEY DIDN'T GET MUCH WORK DONE THE NEXT NIGHT, EITHER.

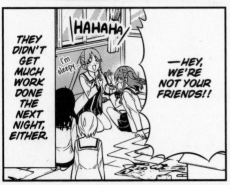

One Hour Isn't Enough

TMP スタ
TMP スタ
...THERE'S ONE THING I LEARNED FROM ALL THIS...
IT'S SO HARD TO PUT A VIDEO GAME DOWN...!!
...IT SO IS.

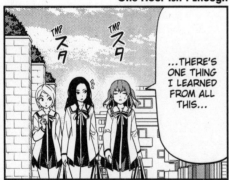

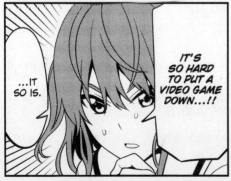

Aho-Girl

\\'ahô͵gərl\\ *Japanese, noun.*
A clueless girl.

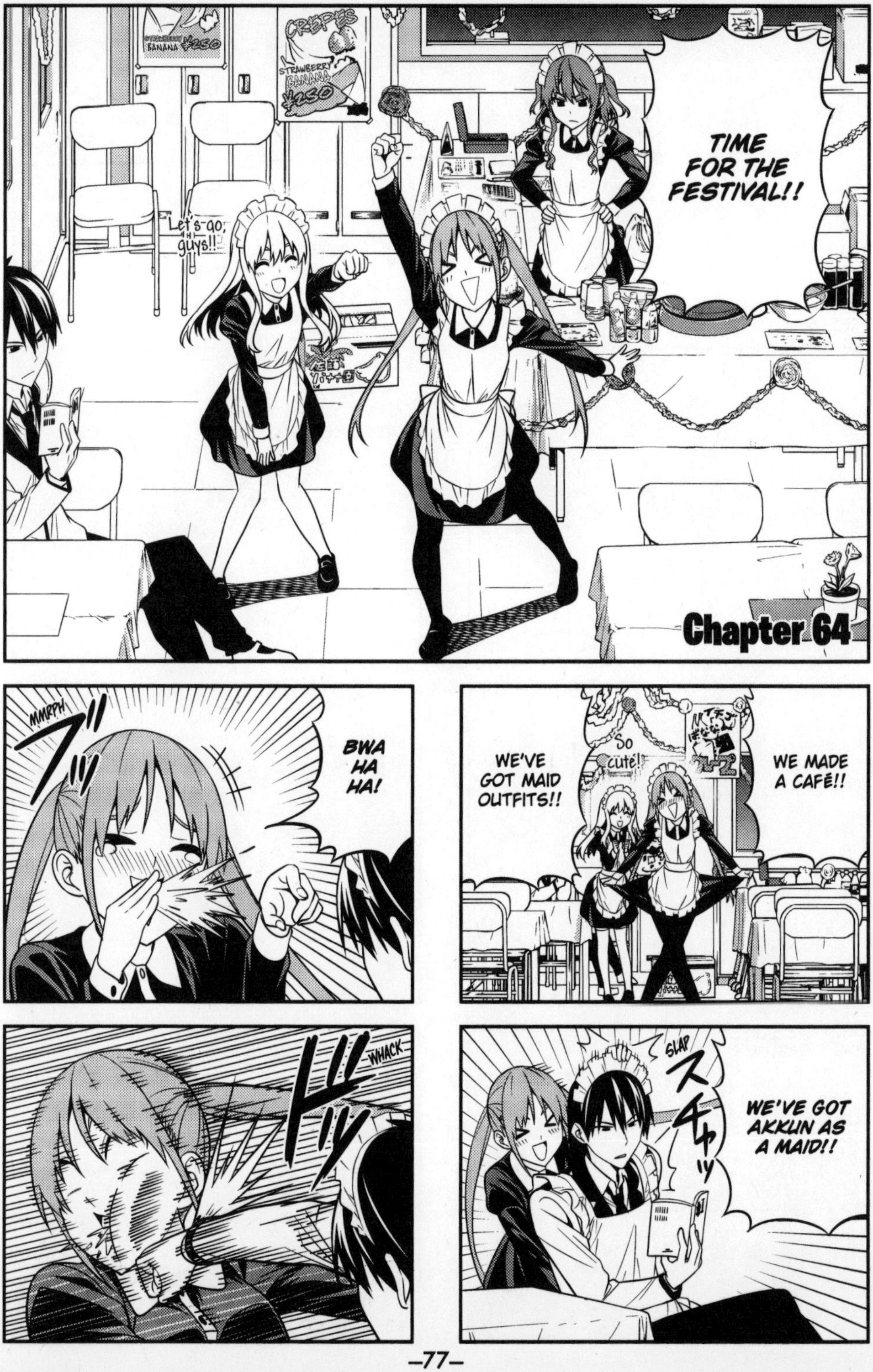
TIME FOR THE FESTIVAL!!
Let's go, guys!!
CREPES
STRAWBERRY BANANA ¥250
Chapter 64
WE MADE A CAFÉ!!
So cute!
WE'VE GOT MAID OUTFITS!!
SLAP
WE'VE GOT AKKUN AS A MAID!!
MMRPH
BWA HA HA!
WHACK

Ingredient of the Day

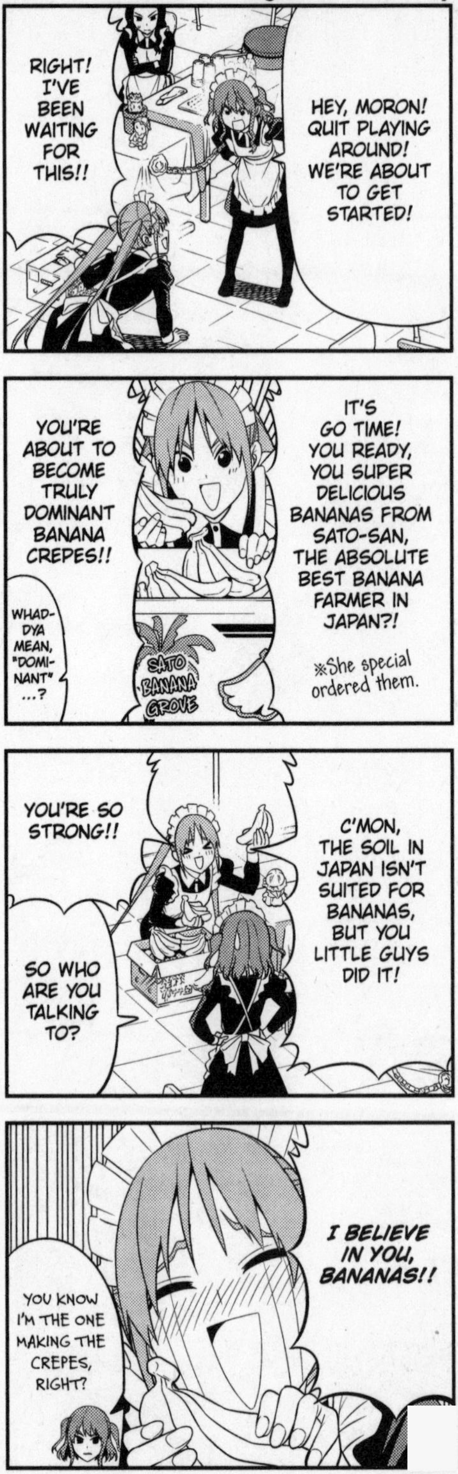
HEY, MORON! QUIT PLAYING AROUND! WE'RE ABOUT TO GET STARTED!
RIGHT! I'VE BEEN WAITING FOR THIS!!
IT'S GO TIME! YOU READY, YOU SUPER DELICIOUS BANANAS FROM SATO-SAN, THE ABSOLUTE BEST BANANA FARMER IN JAPAN?!
※She special ordered them.
YOU'RE ABOUT TO BECOME TRULY DOMINANT BANANA CREPES!!
SATO BANANA GROVE
WHADDYA MEAN, "DOMINANT"...?
C'MON, THE SOIL IN JAPAN ISN'T SUITED FOR BANANAS, BUT YOU LITTLE GUYS DID IT!
YOU'RE SO STRONG!!
SO WHO ARE YOU TALKING TO?
I BELIEVE IN YOU, BANANAS!!
YOU KNOW I'M THE ONE MAKING THE CREPES, RIGHT?

When They Get a Break

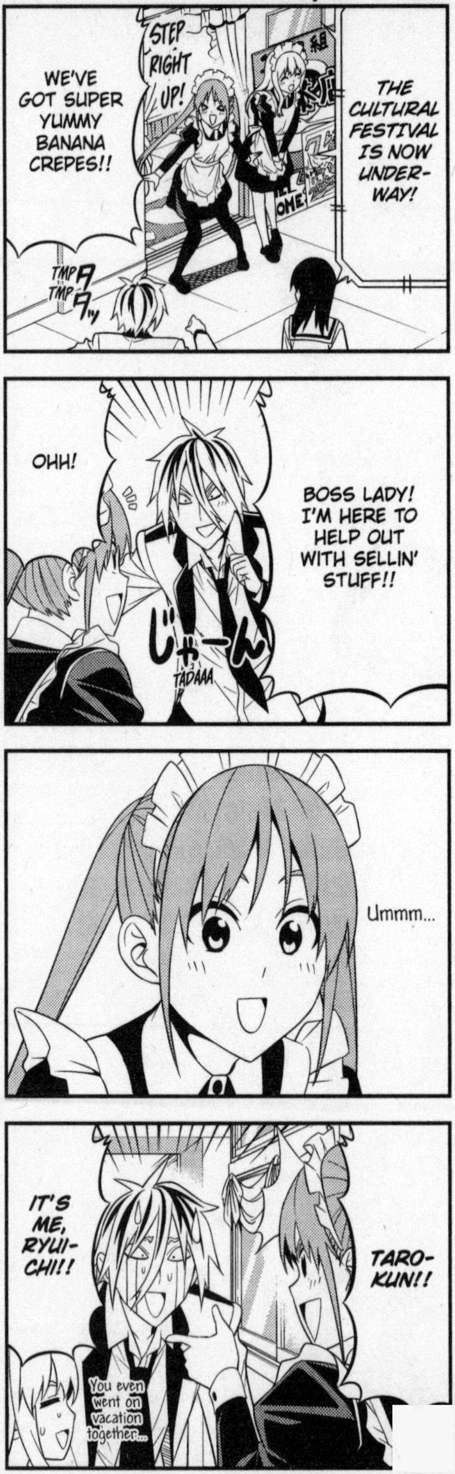
THE CULTURAL FESTIVAL IS NOW UNDERWAY!
STEP RIGHT UP!
WE'VE GOT SUPER YUMMY BANANA CREPES!!
TMP TMP
BOSS LADY! I'M HERE TO HELP OUT WITH SELLIN' STUFF!!
OHH!
じゃーん
TADAAA
Ummm...
TARO-KUN!!
IT'S ME, RYUICHI!!
You even went on vacation together...

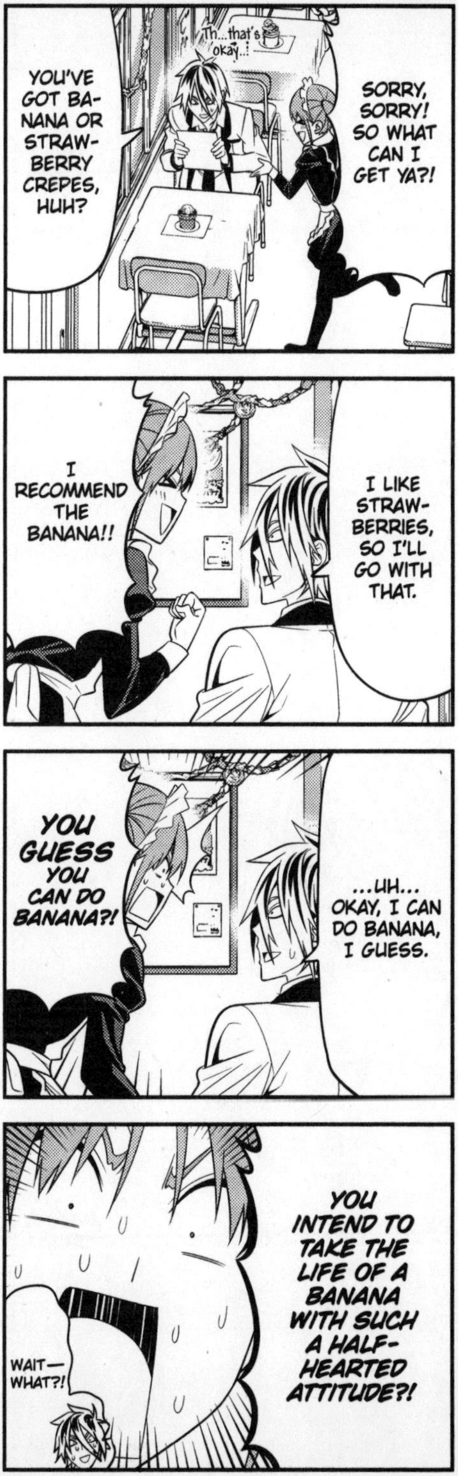
SORRY, SORRY! SO WHAT CAN I GET YA?!
Th...that's okay..!
YOU'VE GOT BANANA OR STRAWBERRY CREPES, HUH?
I LIKE STRAWBERRIES, SO I'LL GO WITH THAT.
I RECOMMEND THE BANANA!!
...UH... OKAY, I CAN DO BANANA, I GUESS.
YOU GUESS YOU CAN DO BANANA?!
YOU INTEND TO TAKE THE LIFE OF A BANANA WITH SUCH A HALF-HEARTED ATTITUDE?!
WAIT— WHAT?!

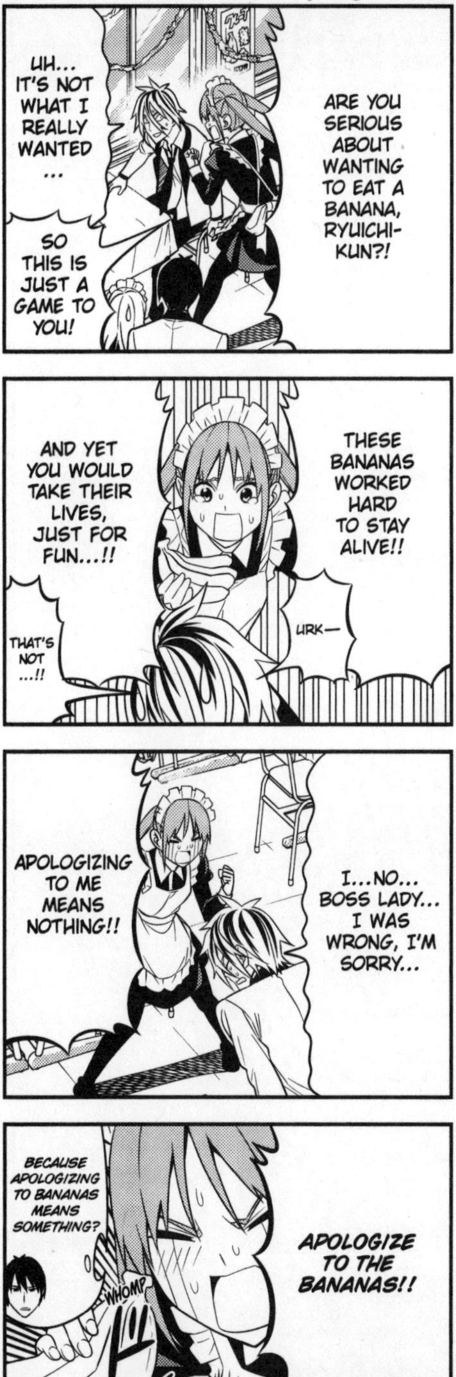
ARE YOU SERIOUS ABOUT WANTING TO EAT A BANANA, RYUICHI-KUN?!
UH... IT'S NOT WHAT I REALLY WANTED ...
SO THIS IS JUST A GAME TO YOU!
THESE BANANAS WORKED HARD TO STAY ALIVE!!
AND YET YOU WOULD TAKE THEIR LIVES, JUST FOR FUN...!!
URK—
THAT'S NOT ...!!
I...NO... BOSS LADY... I WAS WRONG, I'M SORRY...
APOLOGIZING TO ME MEANS NOTHING!!
APOLOGIZE TO THE BANANAS!!
WHOMP
BECAUSE APOLOGIZING TO BANANAS MEANS SOMETHING?

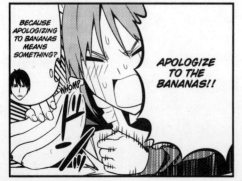

Tearful...

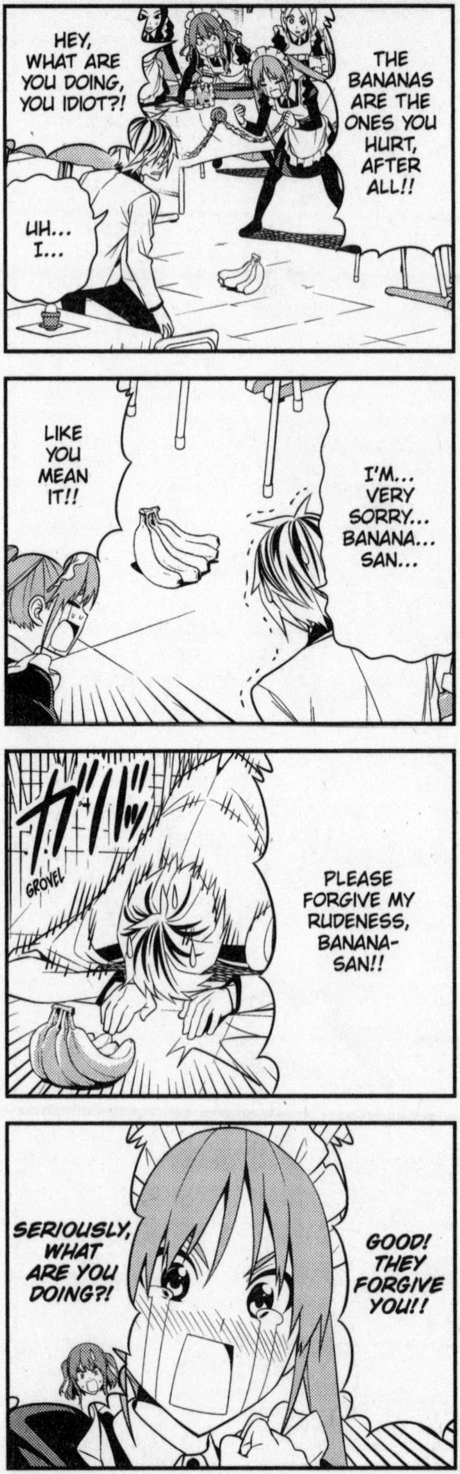
THE BANANAS ARE THE ONES YOU HURT, AFTER ALL!!
HEY, WHAT ARE YOU DOING, YOU IDIOT?!
UH... I...
I'M... VERY SORRY... BANANA... SAN...
LIKE YOU MEAN IT!!
ガバッ
GROVEL
PLEASE FORGIVE MY RUDENESS, BANANA-SAN!!
GOOD! THEY FORGIVE YOU!!
SERIOUSLY, WHAT ARE YOU DOING?!

Voice for the Voiceless

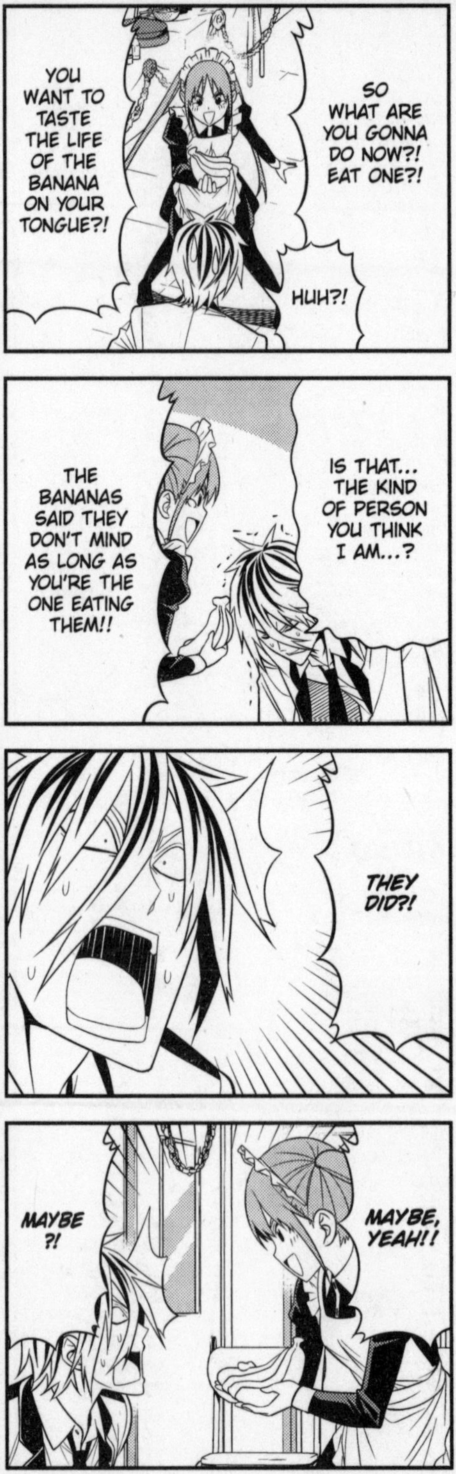
SO WHAT ARE YOU GONNA DO NOW?! EAT ONE?!
YOU WANT TO TASTE THE LIFE OF THE BANANA ON YOUR TONGUE?!
HUH?!
IS THAT... THE KIND OF PERSON YOU THINK I AM...?
THE BANANAS SAID THEY DON'T MIND AS LONG AS YOU'RE THE ONE EATING THEM!!
THEY DID?!
MAYBE, YEAH!!
MAYBE ?!

The First Taste

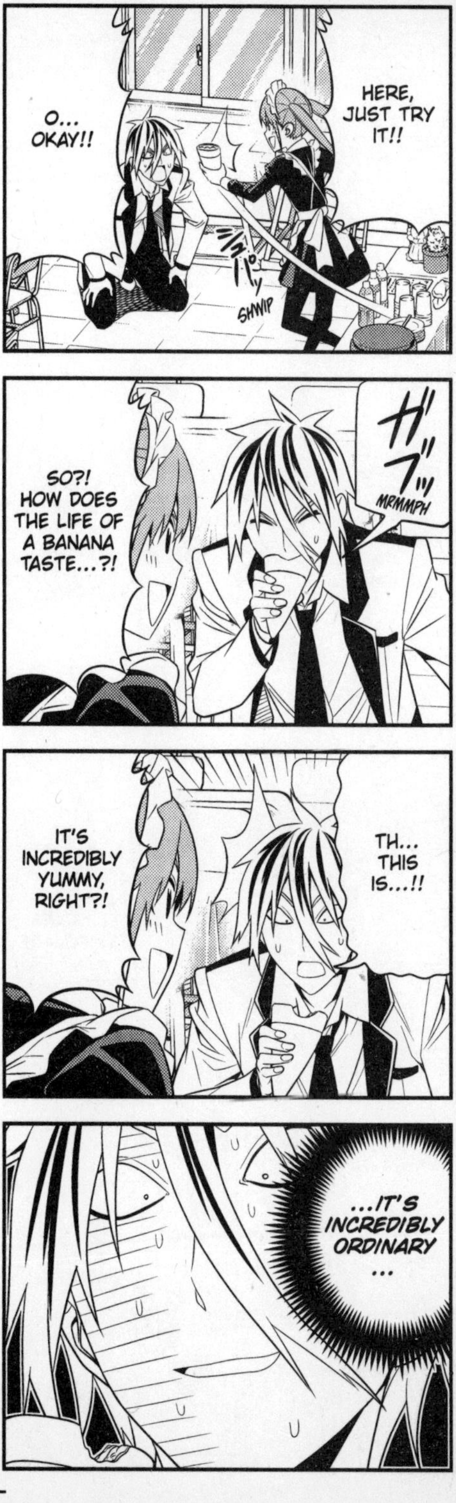
HERE, JUST TRY IT!!
O... OKAY!!
SHWIP
MRMMPH
SO?! HOW DOES THE LIFE OF A BANANA TASTE...?!
TH... THIS IS...!!
IT'S INCREDIBLY YUMMY, RIGHT?!
...IT'S INCREDIBLY ORDINARY ...

Ryuichi's Choice

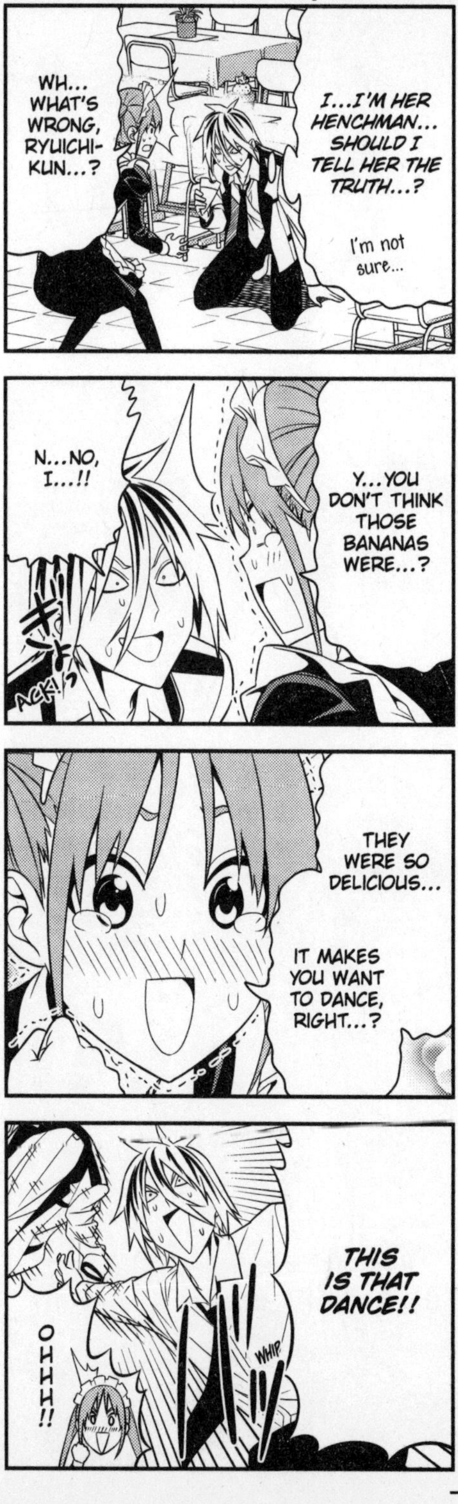
I...I'M HER HENCHMAN... SHOULD I TELL HER THE TRUTH...?
I'm not sure...
WH... WHAT'S WRONG, RYUICHI-KUN...?
Y...YOU DON'T THINK THOSE BANANAS WERE...?
N...NO, I...!!
ACK!
THEY WERE SO DELICIOUS...
IT MAKES YOU WANT TO DANCE, RIGHT...?
THIS IS THAT DANCE!!
WHIP
OHHH!!

You're the Grown-up, Ryuichi-kun

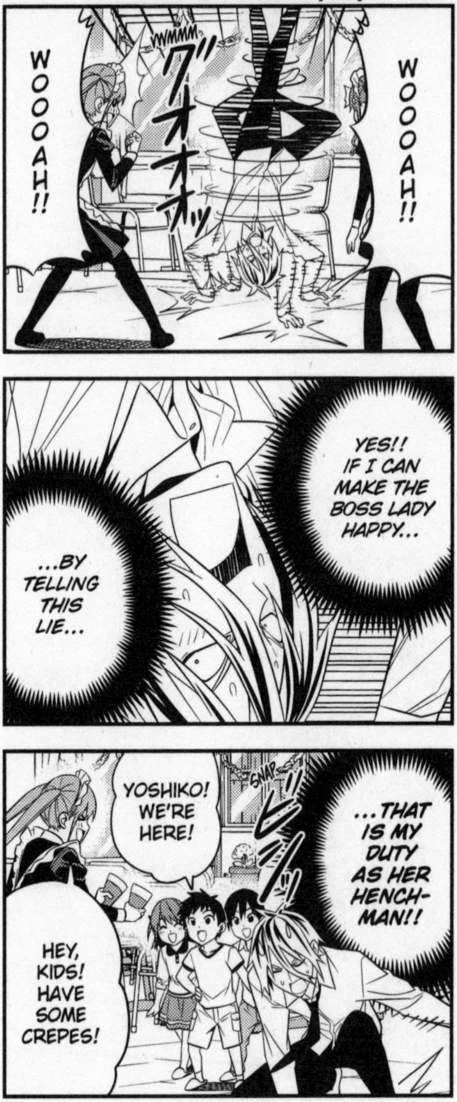
WOOOAH!!
VWMMM
グオオオッ
WOOOAH!!
YES!! IF I CAN MAKE THE BOSS LADY HAPPY...
...BY TELLING THIS LIE...
SNAP
...THAT IS MY DUTY AS HER HENCH-MAN!!
YOSHIKO! WE'RE HERE!
HEY, KIDS! HAVE SOME CREPES!
THEY'RE SO YUMMY IT MAKES YOU WANT TO DANCE, RIGHT?!
HUH? IT'S PRETTY ORDINARY ...
HOW DARE YOU?!

Yoshiko's Opinion of Ryuichi

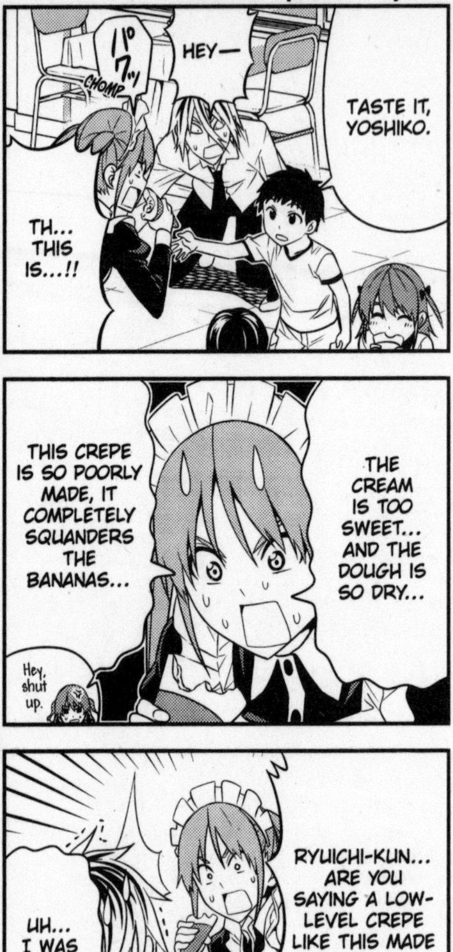
TASTE IT, YOSHIKO.
HEY—
パクッ
CHOMP
TH... THIS IS...!!
THE CREAM IS TOO SWEET... AND THE DOUGH IS SO DRY...
THIS CREPE IS SO POORLY MADE, IT COMPLETELY SQUANDERS THE BANANAS...
Hey, shut up.
RYUICHI-KUN... ARE YOU SAYING A LOW-LEVEL CREPE LIKE THIS MADE YOU WANT TO DANCE...?
UH... I WAS JUST...
THAT'S KINDA FUNNY!!
You're my flunky all right!
SERI-OUSLY?!

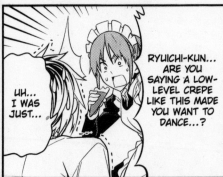

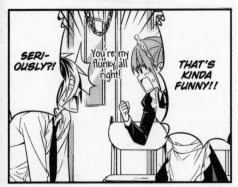

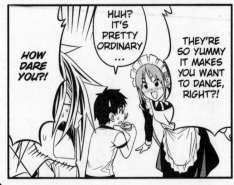

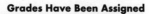

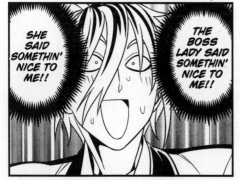

Grades Have Been Assigned

THE BOSS LADY SAID SOMETHIN' NICE TO ME!!
SHE SAID SOMETHIN' NICE TO ME!!
HURRAAAAAAY!!
THAT GOON IS SO WEIRD...

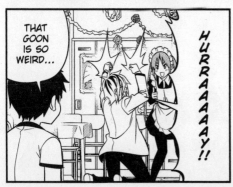

Aho-Girl

\\'ahô,gərl\\ *Japanese, noun.*
A clueless girl.

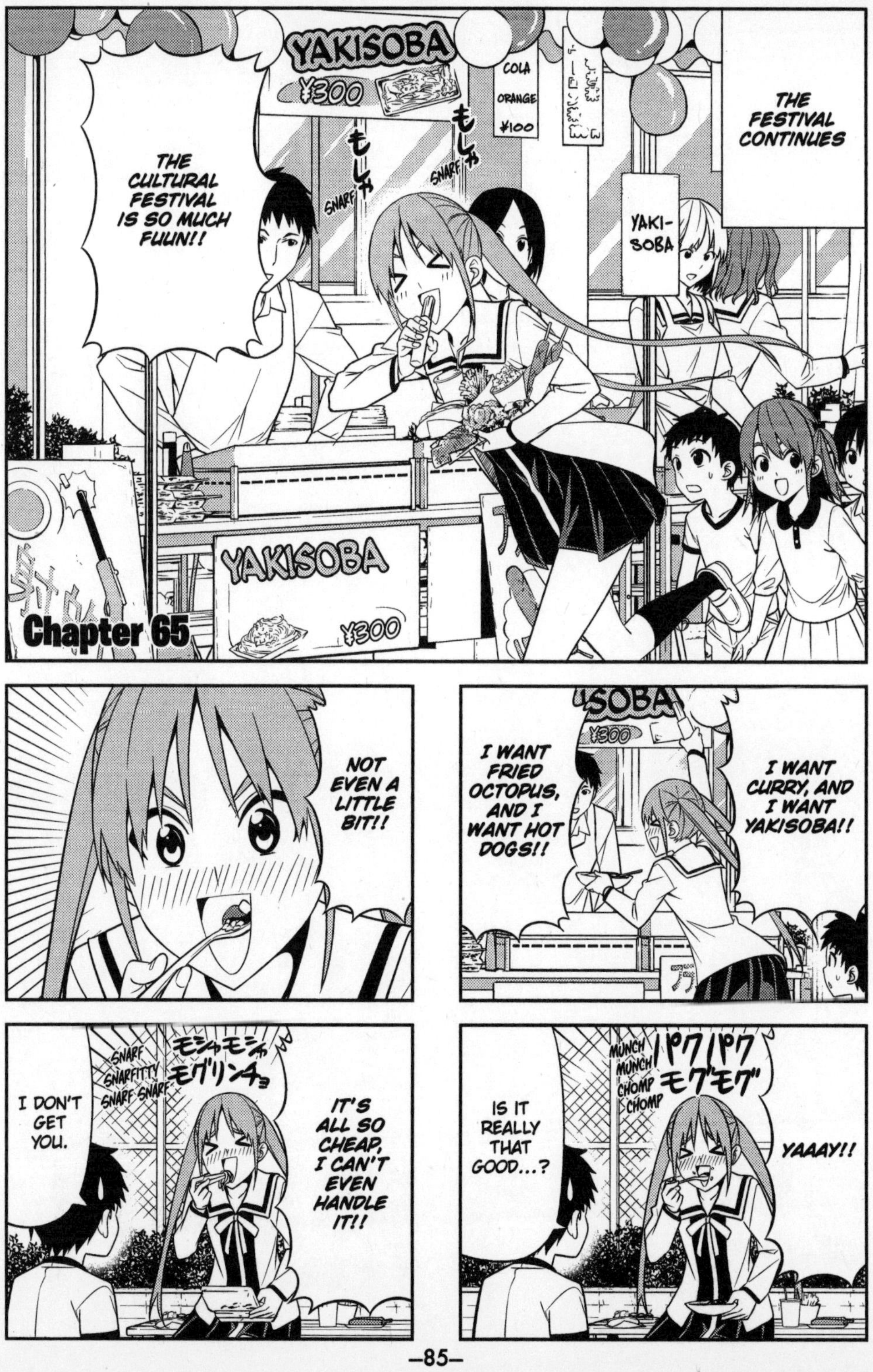
THE FESTIVAL CONTINUES
YAKI-SOBA
COLA ORANGE ¥100
YAKISOBA
¥300
もしゃ
SNARF
もしゃ
SNARF
THE CULTURAL FESTIVAL IS SO MUCH FUUN!!
YAKISOBA ¥300
Chapter 65
I WANT CURRY, AND I WANT YAKISOBA!!
I WANT FRIED OCTOPUS, AND I WANT HOT DOGS!!
NOT EVEN A LITTLE BIT!!
YAAAY!!
パクパク モグモグ
MUNCH MUNCH CHOMP CHOMP
IS IT REALLY THAT GOOD...?
IT'S ALL SO CHEAP, I CAN'T EVEN HANDLE IT!!
モシャモシャ モグリンチョ
SNARF SNARFITTY SNARF SNARF
I DON'T GET YOU.

Spotted by Yoshiko

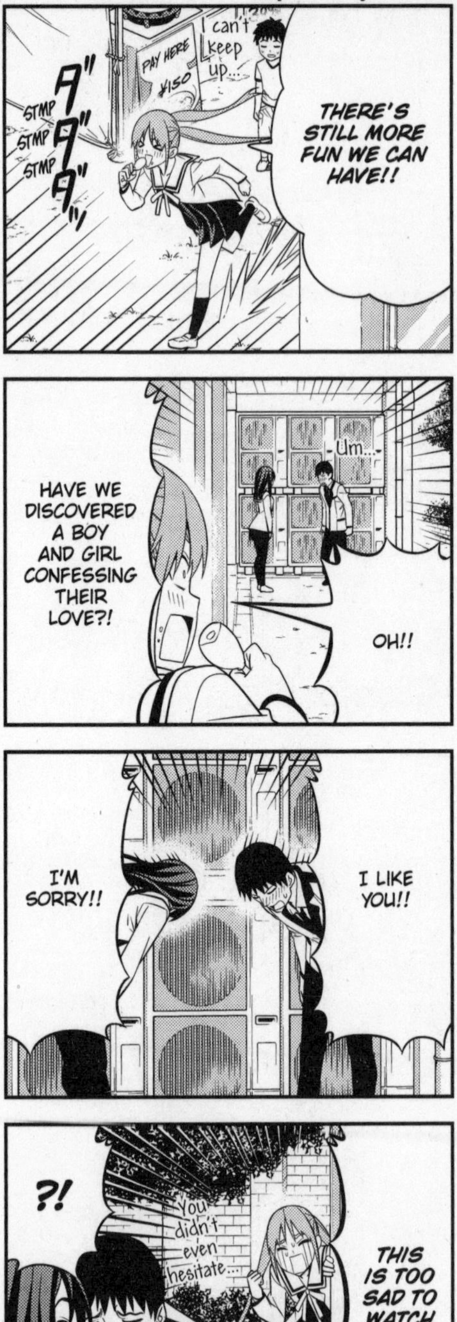
THERE'S STILL MORE FUN WE CAN HAVE!!
I can't keep up...
PAY HERE ¥150
STMP STMP STMP
Um...
HAVE WE DISCOVERED A BOY AND GIRL CONFESSING THEIR LOVE?!
OH!!
I LIKE YOU!!
I'M SORRY!!
THIS IS TOO SAD TO WATCH ...!!
You didn't even hesitate...
?!

Natural Endowments

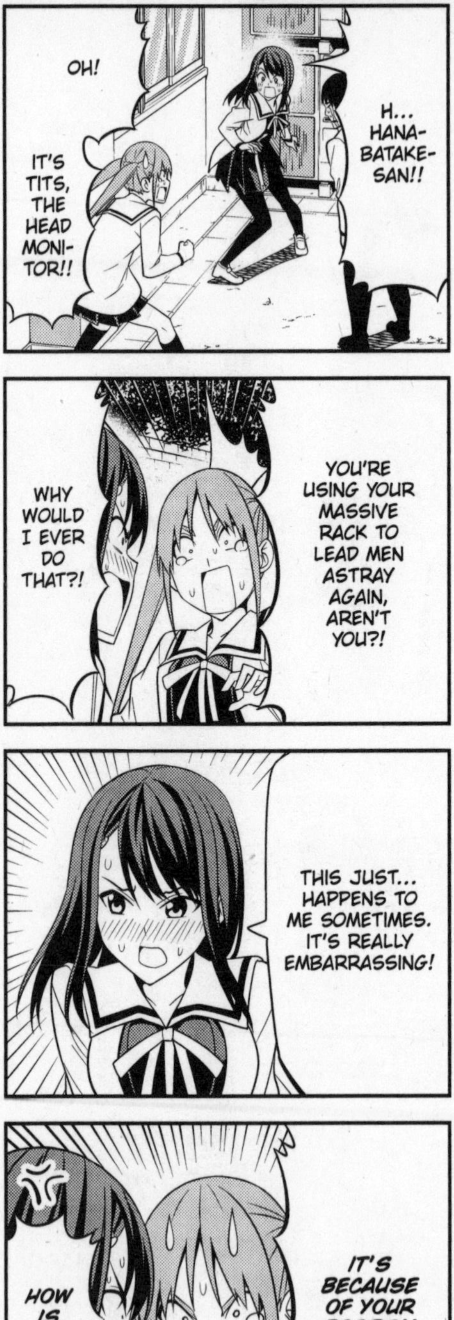
H... HANA-BATAKE-SAN!!
OH!
IT'S TITS, THE HEAD MONI-TOR!!
YOU'RE USING YOUR MASSIVE RACK TO LEAD MEN ASTRAY AGAIN, AREN'T YOU?!
WHY WOULD I EVER DO THAT?!
THIS JUST... HAPPENS TO ME SOMETIMES. IT'S REALLY EMBARRASSING!
IT'S BECAUSE OF YOUR BOOBS!!
HOW IS THAT MY FAULT ?!

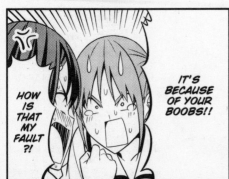

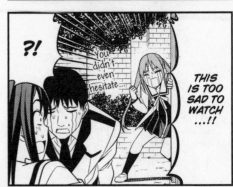

But Head Monitor...I Love You...

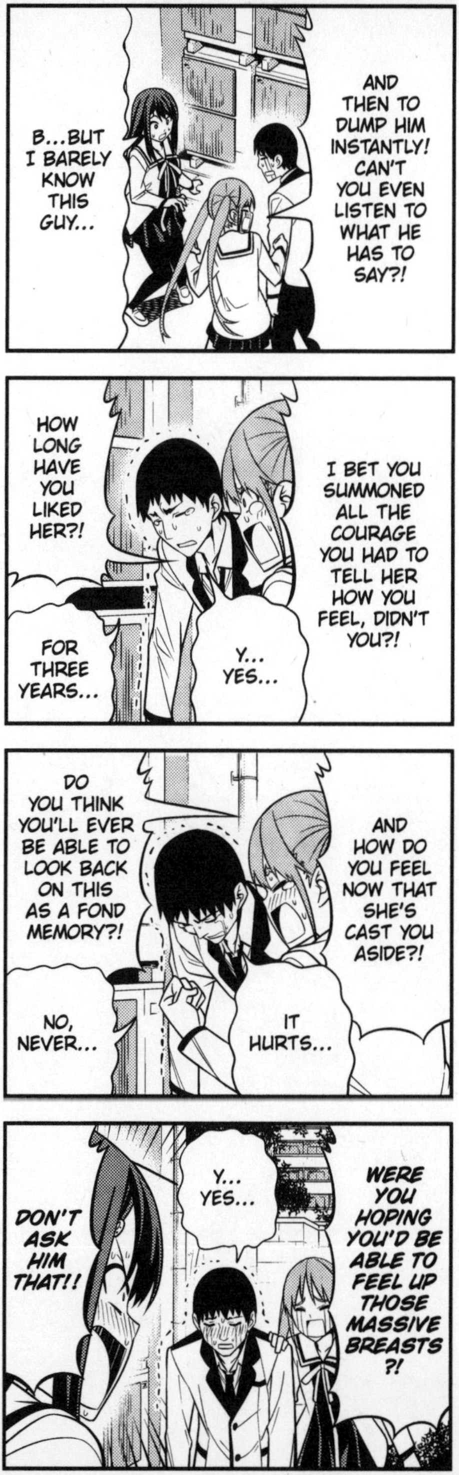
AND THEN TO DUMP HIM INSTANTLY! CAN'T YOU EVEN LISTEN TO WHAT HE HAS TO SAY?!
B...BUT I BARELY KNOW THIS GUY...
I BET YOU SUMMONED ALL THE COURAGE YOU HAD TO TELL HER HOW YOU FEEL, DIDN'T YOU?!
Y... YES...
HOW LONG HAVE YOU LIKED HER?!
FOR THREE YEARS...
AND HOW DO YOU FEEL NOW THAT SHE'S CAST YOU ASIDE?!
IT HURTS...
DO YOU THINK YOU'LL EVER BE ABLE TO LOOK BACK ON THIS AS A FOND MEMORY?!
NO, NEVER...
WERE YOU HOPING YOU'D BE ABLE TO FEEL UP THOSE MASSIVE BREASTS?!
Y... YES...
DON'T ASK HIM THAT!!

In That Case

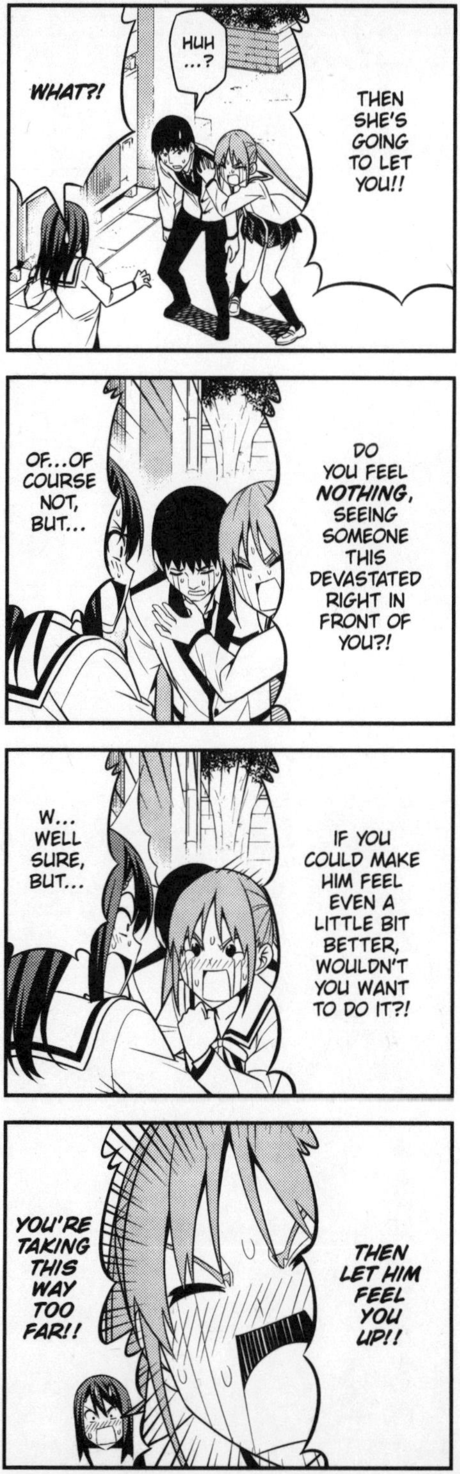
THEN SHE'S GOING TO LET YOU!!
HUH ...?
WHAT?!
DO YOU FEEL NOTHING, SEEING SOMEONE THIS DEVASTATED RIGHT IN FRONT OF YOU?!
OF...OF COURSE NOT, BUT...
IF YOU COULD MAKE HIM FEEL EVEN A LITTLE BIT BETTER, WOULDN'T YOU WANT TO DO IT?!
W... WELL SURE, BUT...
THEN LET HIM FEEL YOU UP!!
YOU'RE TAKING THIS WAY TOO FAR!!

The Very Image

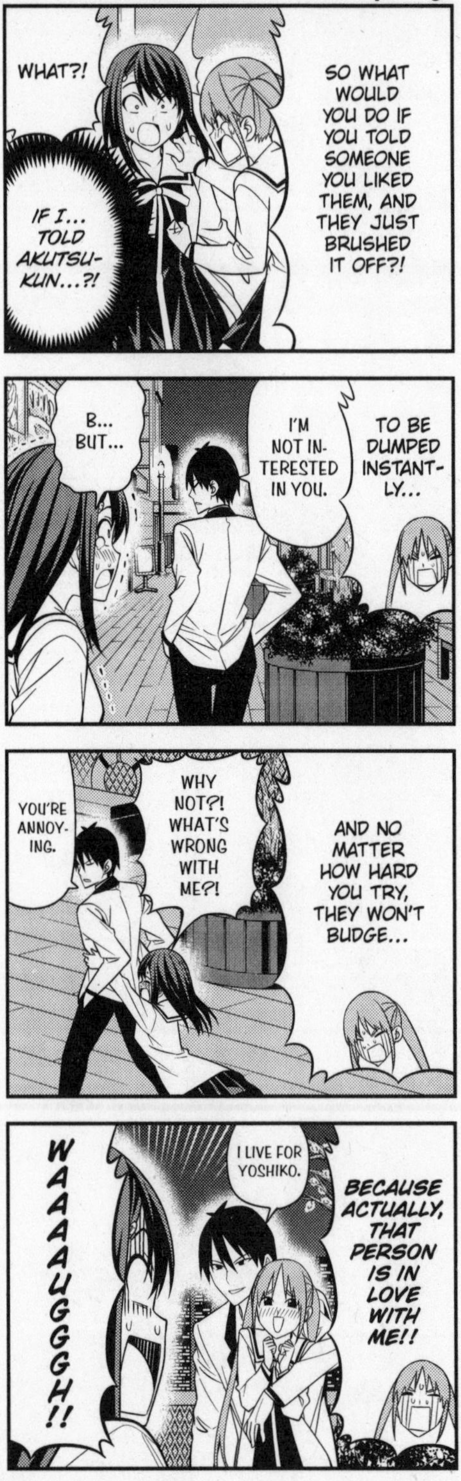
SO WHAT WOULD YOU DO IF YOU TOLD SOMEONE YOU LIKED THEM, AND THEY JUST BRUSHED IT OFF?!
WHAT?!
IF I... TOLD AKUTSU-KUN...?!
TO BE DUMPED INSTANT-LY...
I'M NOT IN-TERESTED IN YOU.
B... BUT...
AND NO MATTER HOW HARD YOU TRY, THEY WON'T BUDGE...
WHY NOT?! WHAT'S WRONG WITH ME?!
YOU'RE ANNOY-ING.
BECAUSE ACTUALLY, THAT PERSON IS IN LOVE WITH ME!!
I LIVE FOR YOSHIKO.
WAAAAAUGGGH!!

Astounding Power of Imagination

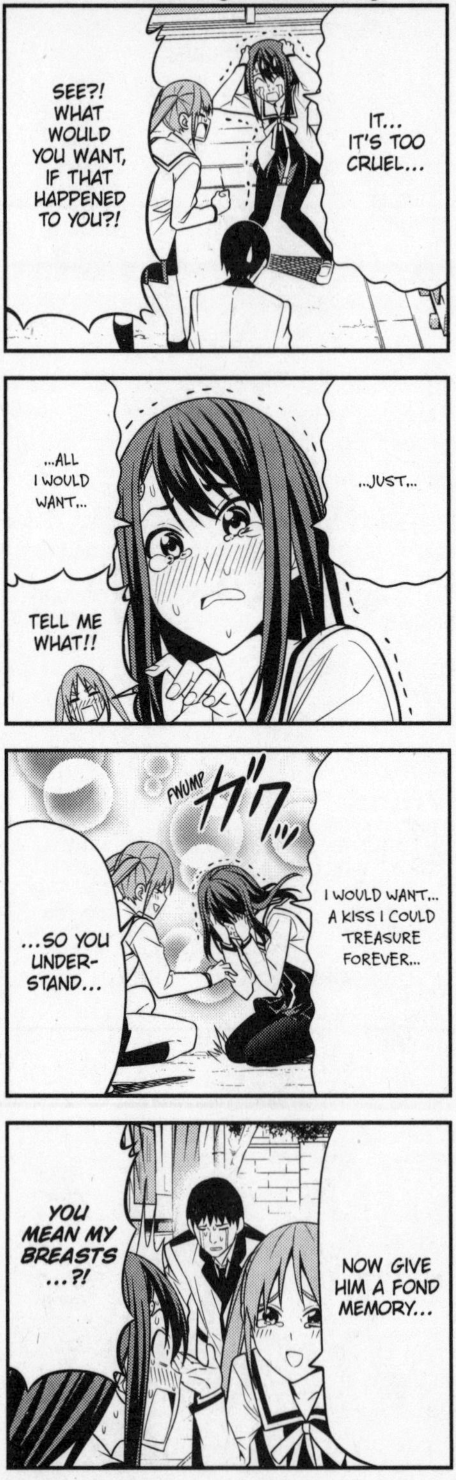
IT... IT'S TOO CRUEL...
SEE?! WHAT WOULD YOU WANT, IF THAT HAPPENED TO YOU?!
...JUST...
...ALL I WOULD WANT...
TELL ME WHAT!!
I WOULD WANT... A KISS I COULD TREASURE FOREVER...
FWUMP
...SO YOU UNDER-STAND...
NOW GIVE HIM A FOND MEMORY...
YOU MEAN MY BREASTS...?!

A Manful Decision

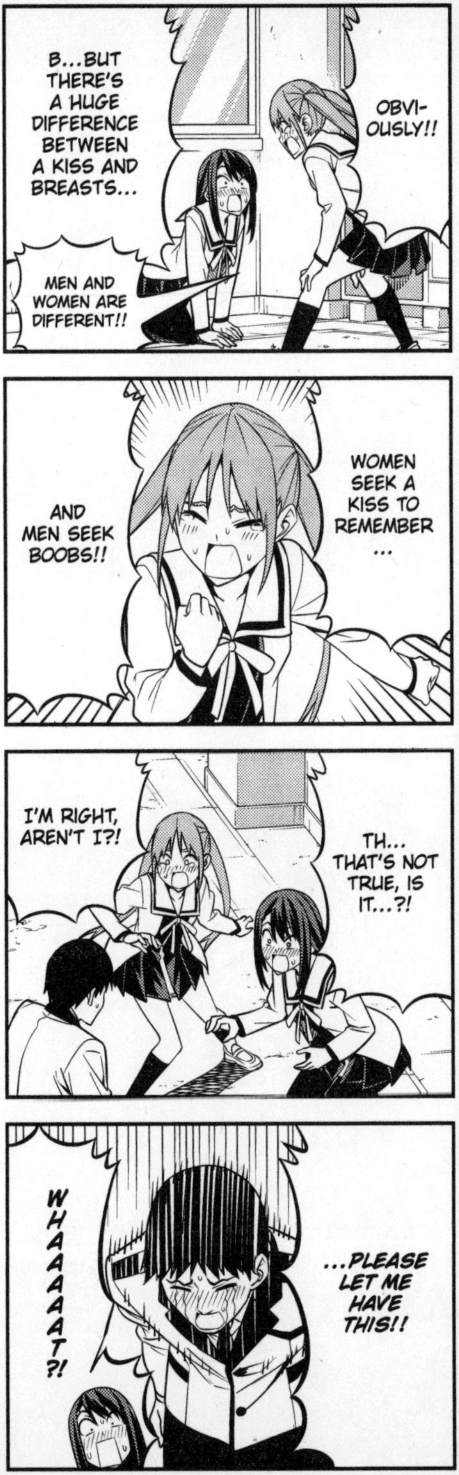
OBVI-OUSLY!!
B...BUT THERE'S A HUGE DIFFERENCE BETWEEN A KISS AND BREASTS...
MEN AND WOMEN ARE DIFFERENT!!
WOMEN SEEK A KISS TO REMEMBER ...
AND MEN SEEK BOOBS!!
TH... THAT'S NOT TRUE, IS IT...?!
I'M RIGHT, AREN'T I?!
...PLEASE LET ME HAVE THIS!!
WHAAAAAAAT?!

Grab Her and We'll Talk This out

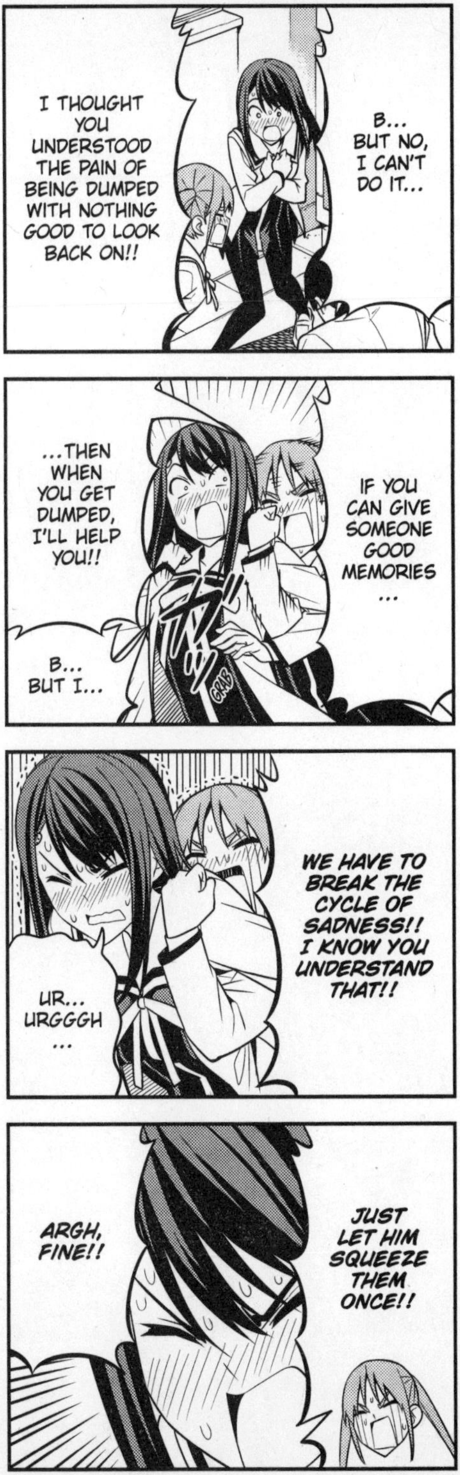
B... BUT NO, I CAN'T DO IT...
I THOUGHT YOU UNDERSTOOD THE PAIN OF BEING DUMPED WITH NOTHING GOOD TO LOOK BACK ON!!
IF YOU CAN GIVE SOMEONE GOOD MEMORIES ...
...THEN WHEN YOU GET DUMPED, I'LL HELP YOU!!
GRAB
B... BUT I...
WE HAVE TO BREAK THE CYCLE OF SADNESS!! I KNOW YOU UNDERSTAND THAT!!
UR... URGGGH ...
JUST LET HIM SQUEEZE THEM ONCE!!
ARGH, FINE!!

Just Looking for a Quiet Place to Study

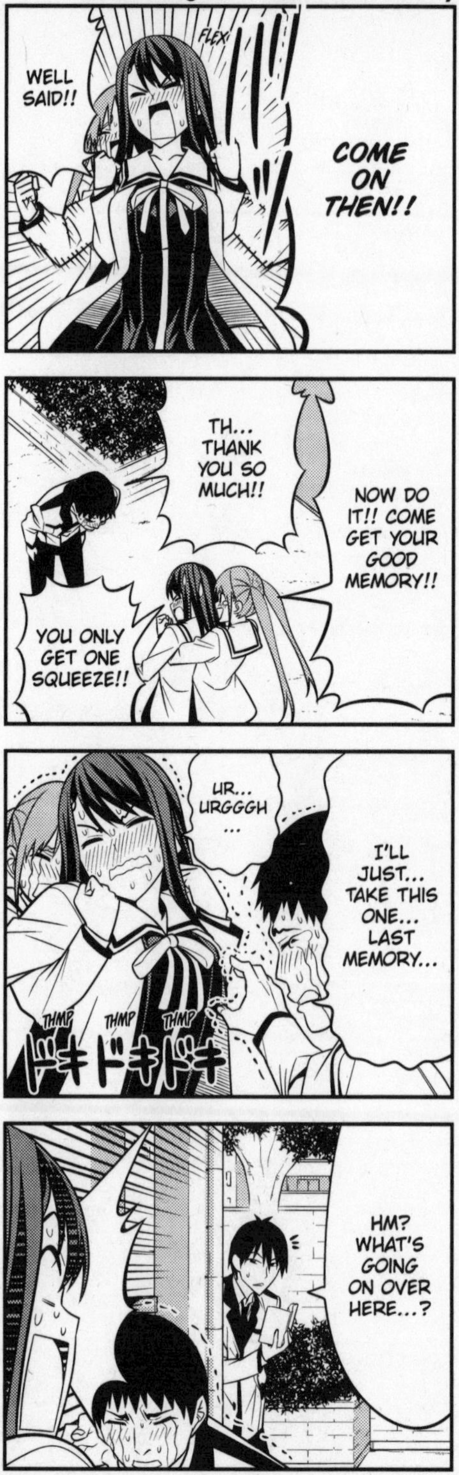
FLEX!
WELL SAID!!
COME ON THEN!!
TH... THANK YOU SO MUCH!!
NOW DO IT!! COME GET YOUR GOOD MEMORY!!
YOU ONLY GET ONE SQUEEZE!!
UR... URGGGH ...
I'LL JUST... TAKE THIS ONE... LAST MEMORY...
THMP THMP THMP
ドキドキドキ
HM? WHAT'S GOING ON OVER HERE...?

Hurricanrana

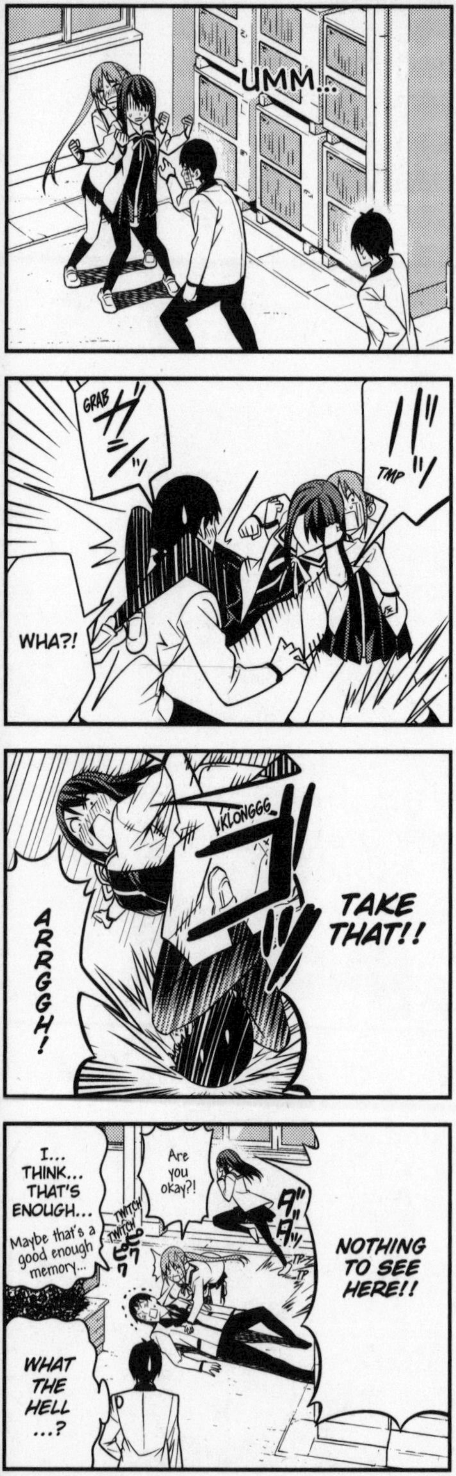
UMM...
GRAB
TMP
WHA?!
KLONGGG
TAKE THAT!!
ARRGGH!
NOTHING TO SEE HERE!!
Are you okay?!
I... THINK... THAT'S ENOUGH...
TWITCH TWITCH
Maybe that's a good enough memory...
WHAT THE HELL ...?

What a Terrible Rule

HFF...
HFF...
HFF...
S... STILL...
DOES THIS MEAN THE NEXT TIME SOMEONE TELLS ME THEY LIKE ME...
...I HAVE TO LET THEM FEEL ME UP...?
IT DOES NOT.

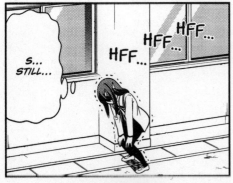

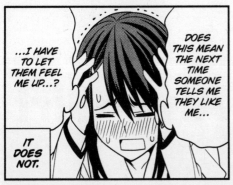

Aho-Girl

\\'ahô͵gərl\\ *Japanese, noun.*
A clueless girl.

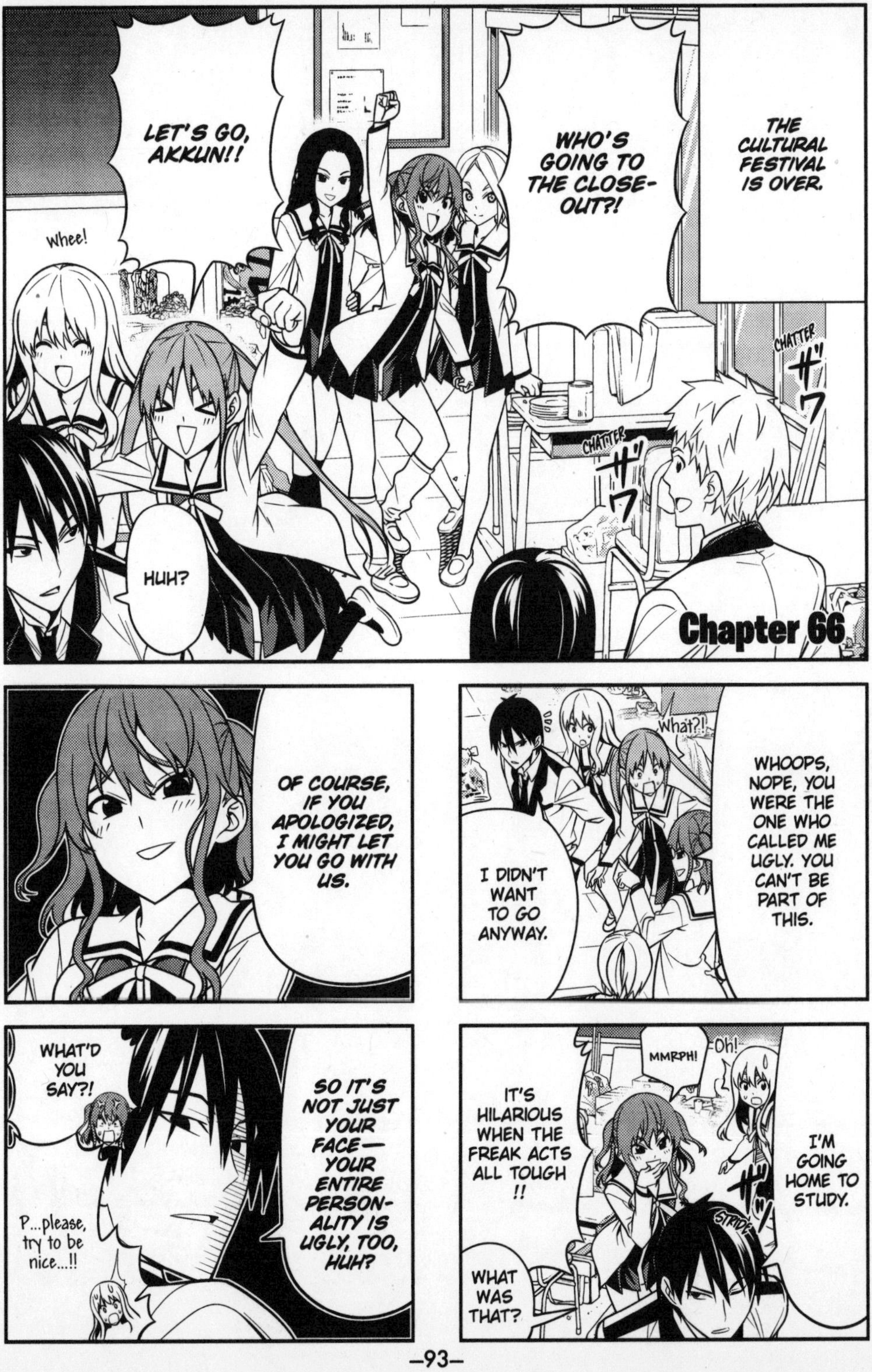
THE CULTURAL FESTIVAL IS OVER.
WHO'S GOING TO THE CLOSE-OUT?!
LET'S GO, AKKUN!!
Whee!
CHATTER
CHATTER
HUH?
Chapter 66
WHOOPS, NOPE, YOU WERE THE ONE WHO CALLED ME UGLY. YOU CAN'T BE PART OF THIS.
What?!
I DIDN'T WANT TO GO ANYWAY.
OF COURSE, IF YOU APOLOGIZED, I MIGHT LET YOU GO WITH US.
Oh!
MMRPH!
I'M GOING HOME TO STUDY.
STRIDE
IT'S HILARIOUS WHEN THE FREAK ACTS ALL TOUGH!!
WHAT WAS THAT?
SO IT'S NOT JUST YOUR FACE—YOUR ENTIRE PERSONALITY IS UGLY, TOO, HUH?
WHAT'D YOU SAY?!
P...please, try to be nice...!!

There Are

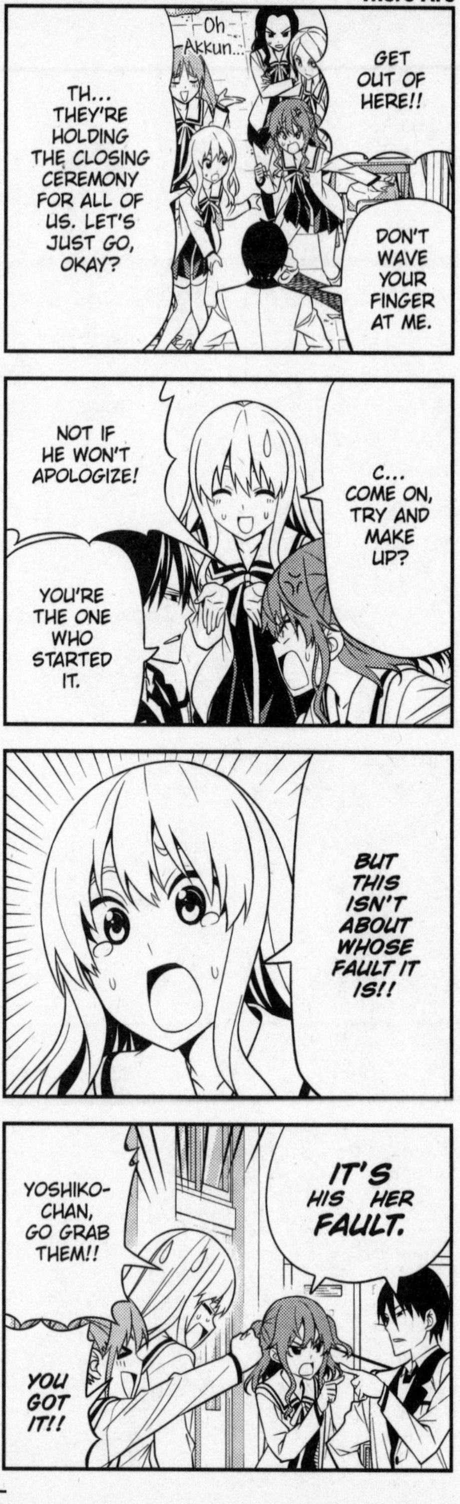
GET OUT OF HERE!!
Oh Akkun...
TH... THEY'RE HOLDING THE CLOSING CEREMONY FOR ALL OF US. LET'S JUST GO, OKAY?
DON'T WAVE YOUR FINGER AT ME.
C... COME ON, TRY AND MAKE UP?
NOT IF HE WON'T APOLOGIZE!
YOU'RE THE ONE WHO STARTED IT.
BUT THIS ISN'T ABOUT WHOSE FAULT IT IS!!
IT'S HIS HER FAULT.
YOSHIKO-CHAN, GO GRAB THEM!!
YOU GOT IT!!

What a Chilly Vibe

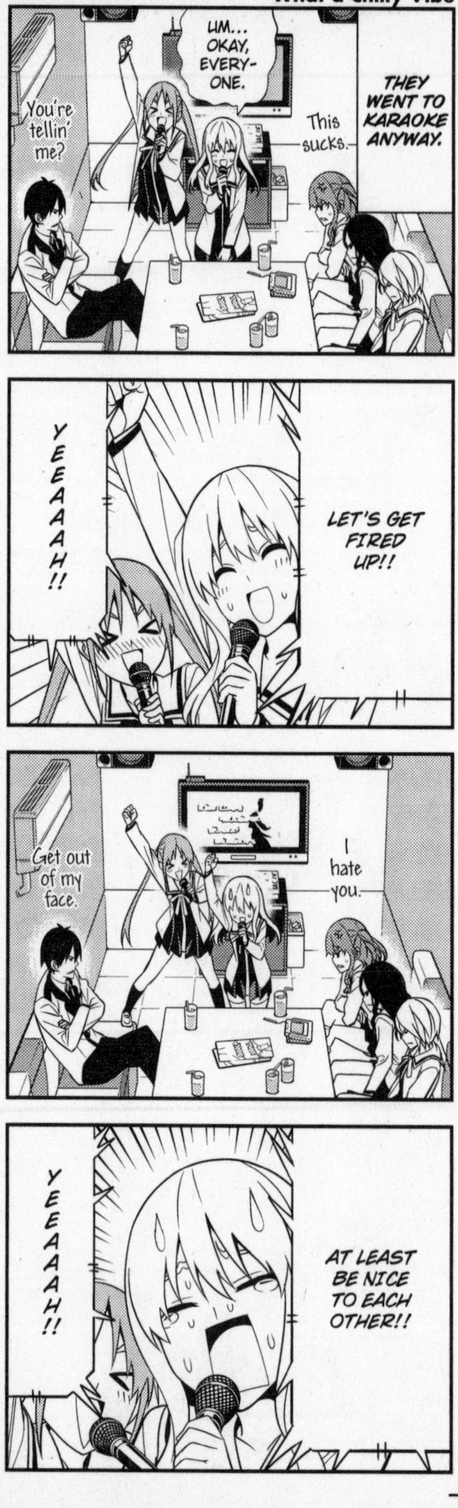
THEY WENT TO KARAOKE ANYWAY.
UM... OKAY, EVERYONE.
This sucks.
You're tellin' me?
LET'S GET FIRED UP!!
YEEAAAAH!!
I hate you.
Get out of my face.
AT LEAST BE NICE TO EACH OTHER!!
YEEAAAAH!!

Sayaka's Transformation

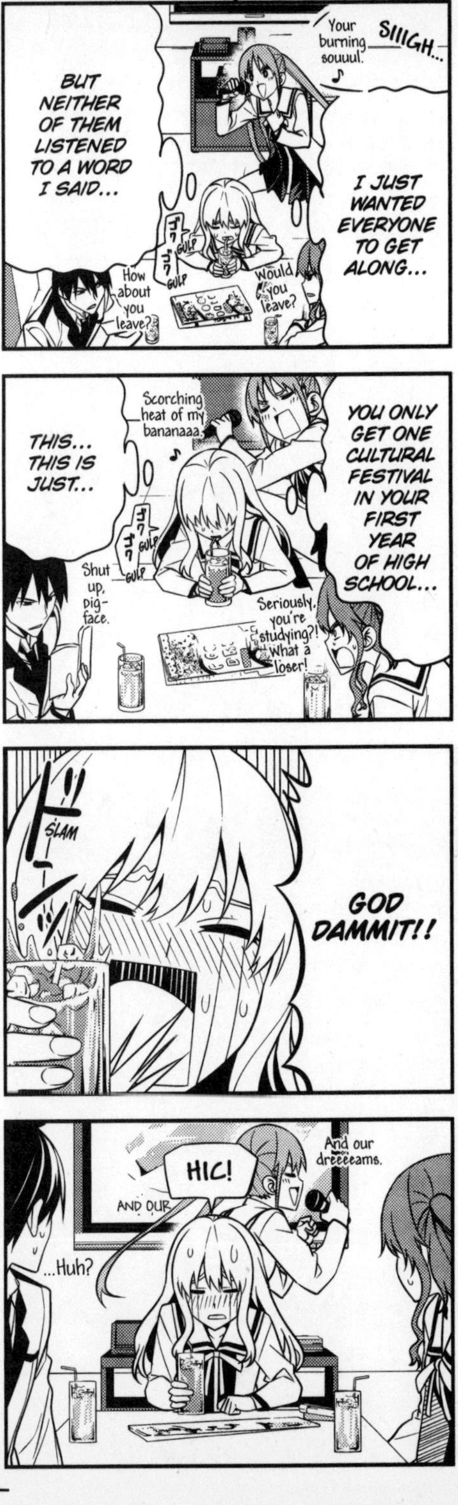
SIIIGH...
Your burning souuul. ♪
I JUST WANTED EVERYONE TO GET ALONG...
BUT NEITHER OF THEM LISTENED TO A WORD I SAID...
Would you leave?
GULP
GULP
How about you leave?
YOU ONLY GET ONE CULTURAL FESTIVAL IN YOUR FIRST YEAR OF HIGH SCHOOL...
Scorching heat of my bananaaa. ♪
THIS... THIS IS JUST...
GULP
GULP
Seriously, you're studying?! What a loser!
Shut up, pig-face.
GOD DAMMIT!!
SLAM
And our dreeeeams.
HIC!
AND OUR
...Huh?

Super Sayaka Appears on the Scene

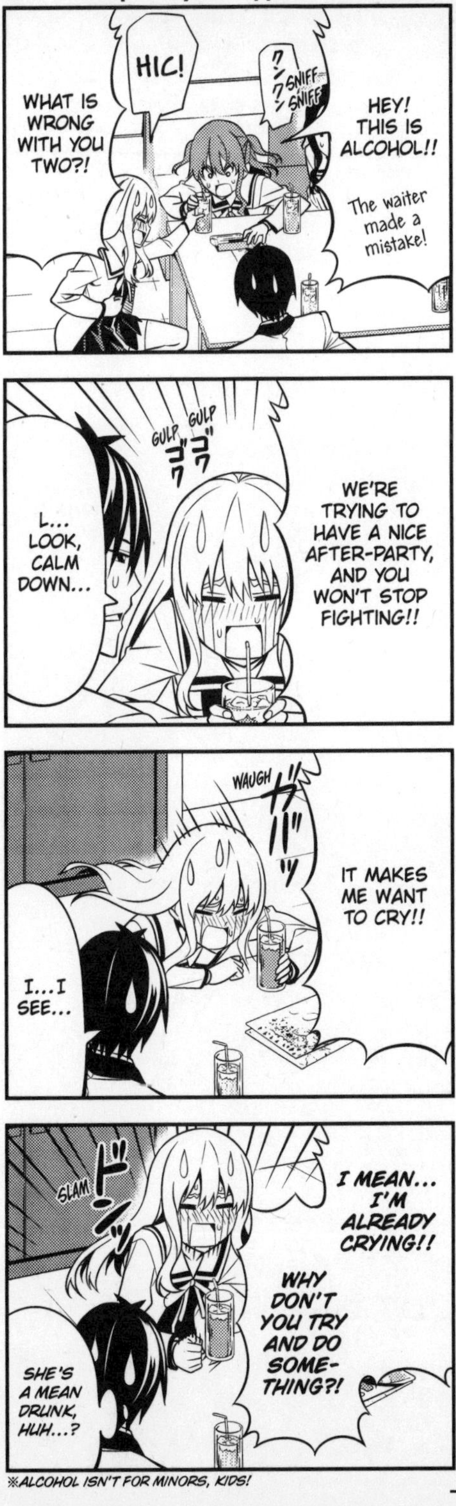
HEY! THIS IS ALCOHOL!!
The waiter made a mistake!
SNIFF SNIFF
HIC!
WHAT IS WRONG WITH YOU TWO?!
WE'RE TRYING TO HAVE A NICE AFTER-PARTY, AND YOU WON'T STOP FIGHTING!!
GULP GULP
L... LOOK, CALM DOWN...
IT MAKES ME WANT TO CRY!!
WAUGH
I...I SEE...
I MEAN... I'M ALREADY CRYING!!
WHY DON'T YOU TRY AND DO SOME-THING?!
SLAM
SHE'S A MEAN DRUNK, HUH...?

※ALCOHOL ISN'T FOR MINORS, KIDS!

So You Know What You're Doing!

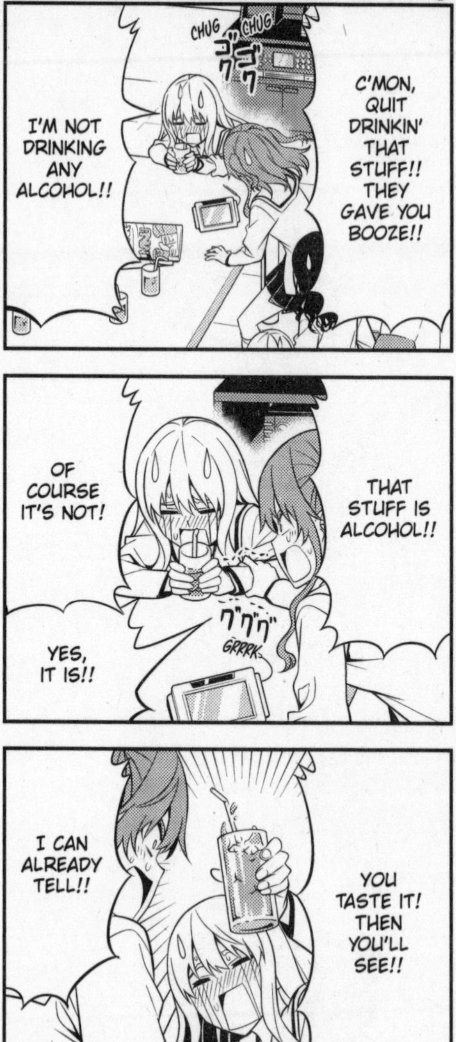
C'MON, QUIT DRINKIN' THAT STUFF!! THEY GAVE YOU BOOZE!!
CHUG CHUG
I'M NOT DRINKING ANY ALCOHOL!!
THAT STUFF IS ALCOHOL!!
OF COURSE IT'S NOT!
GRRRK
YES, IT IS!!
YOU TASTE IT! THEN YOU'LL SEE!!
I CAN ALREADY TELL!!
OH, SO NOW YOU DON'T WANT MY BOOZE, EITHER?!
SLAM

You Admitted It!

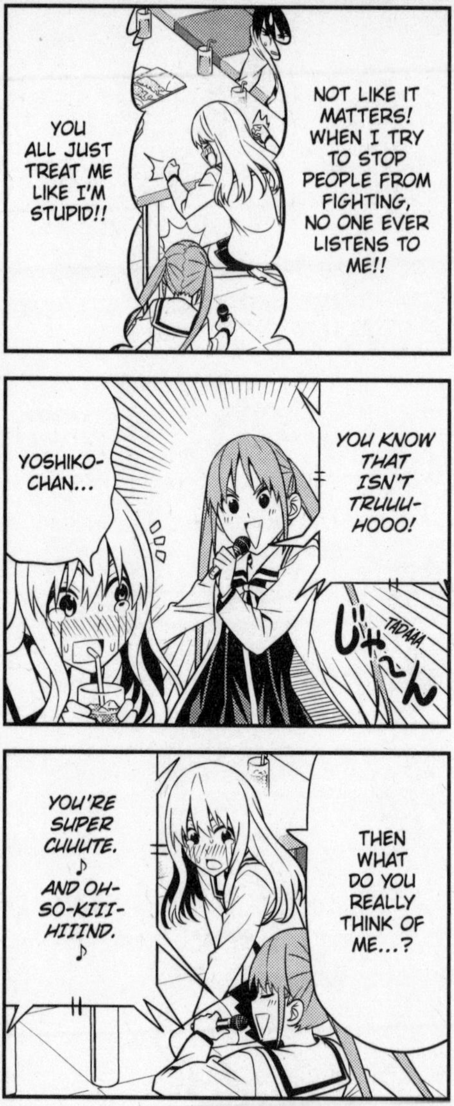
NOT LIKE IT MATTERS! WHEN I TRY TO STOP PEOPLE FROM FIGHTING, NO ONE EVER LISTENS TO ME!!
YOU ALL JUST TREAT ME LIKE I'M STUPID!!
YOU KNOW THAT ISN'T TRUUU-HOOO!
TADAAA
YOSHIKO-CHAN...
THEN WHAT DO YOU REALLY THINK OF ME...?
YOU'RE SUPER CUUUTE. ♪ AND OH-SO-KIIII-HIIIND. ♪
WITH TEENY TINY LITTLE BOOBS. ♪
That's the best part! ♪
WAAAAAH!!

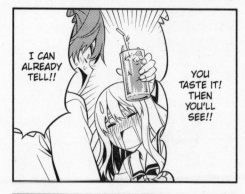

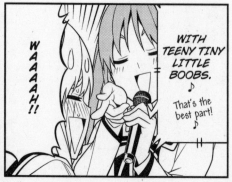

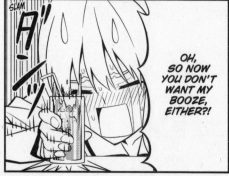

All Men Are Like That

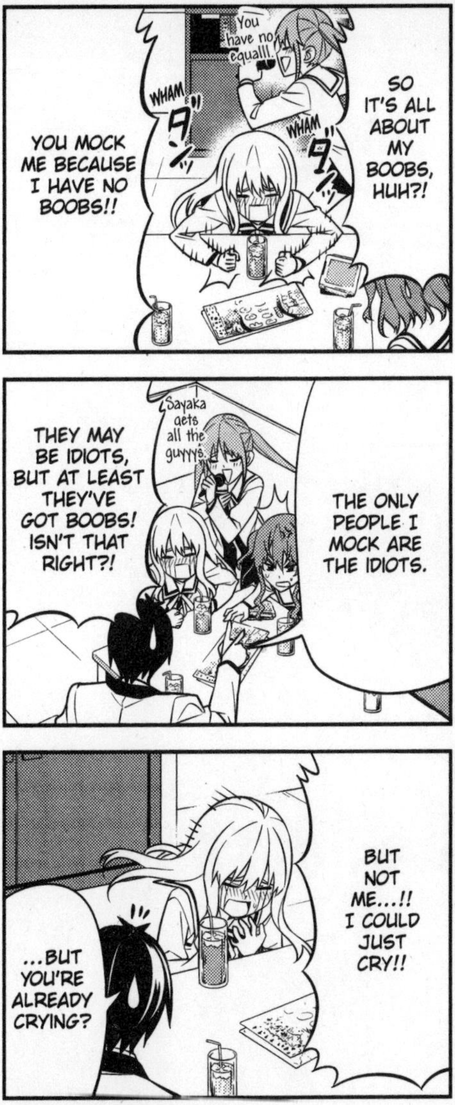
You have no equal!!
SO IT'S ALL ABOUT MY BOOBS, HUH?!
WHAM
WHAM
YOU MOCK ME BECAUSE I HAVE NO BOOBS!!
THE ONLY PEOPLE I MOCK ARE THE IDIOTS.
Sayaka gets all the guyyys.
THEY MAY BE IDIOTS, BUT AT LEAST THEY'VE GOT BOOBS! ISN'T THAT RIGHT?!
BUT NOT ME...!! I COULD JUST CRY!!
...BUT YOU'RE ALREADY CRYING?
OH, SO THAT'S THE PART YOU HAVE A PROBLEM WITH?!
SLAM
I HAVE NO IDEA WHAT TO DO HERE.

Super Sayaka #2

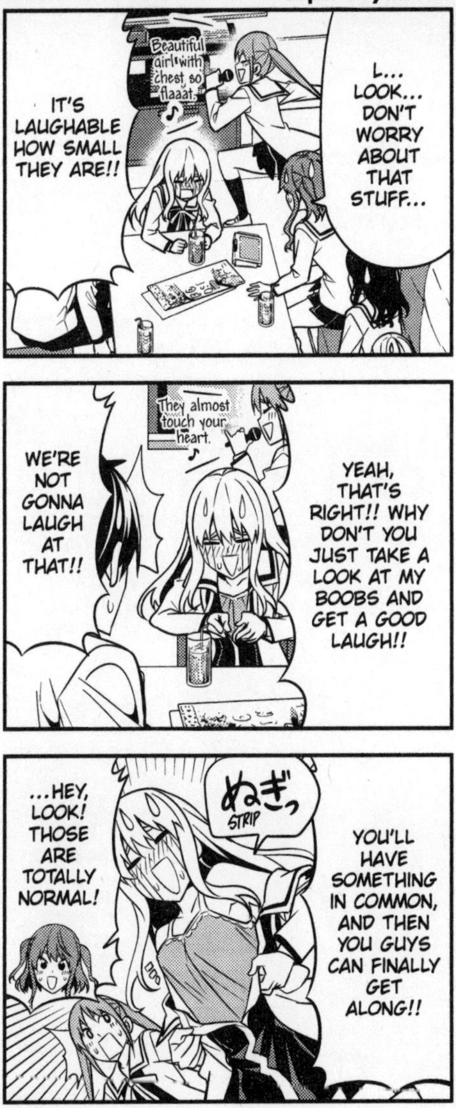
L... LOOK... DON'T WORRY ABOUT THAT STUFF...
Beautiful girl with chest so flaaat.
IT'S LAUGHABLE HOW SMALL THEY ARE!!
YEAH, THAT'S RIGHT!! WHY DON'T YOU JUST TAKE A LOOK AT MY BOOBS AND GET A GOOD LAUGH!!
They almost touch your heart.
WE'RE NOT GONNA LAUGH AT THAT!!
YOU'LL HAVE SOMETHING IN COMMON, AND THEN YOU GUYS CAN FINALLY GET ALONG!!
ぬぎっ
STRIP
...HEY, LOOK! THOSE ARE TOTALLY NORMAL!
IT'S ALL FAKE!!
HOW CAN I EVEN LAUGH AT THAT...?
pad
DEFLATE
There it is...

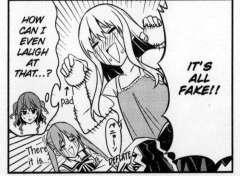

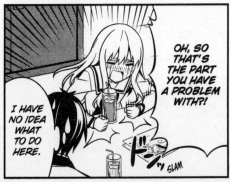

Full Body Flat

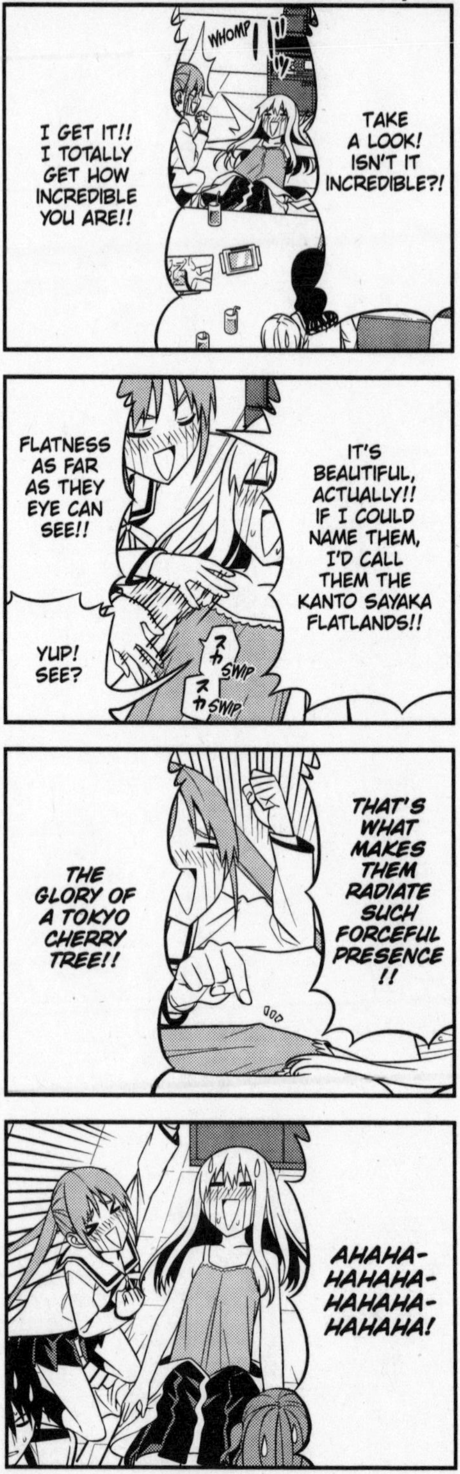
TAKE A LOOK! ISN'T IT INCREDIBLE?!
WHOMP
I GET IT!! I TOTALLY GET HOW INCREDIBLE YOU ARE!!
IT'S BEAUTIFUL, ACTUALLY!! IF I COULD NAME THEM, I'D CALL THEM THE KANTO SAYAKA FLATLANDS!!
FLATNESS AS FAR AS THEY EYE CAN SEE!!
スカ SWIP
スカ SWIP
YUP! SEE?
THAT'S WHAT MAKES THEM RADIATE SUCH FORCEFUL PRESENCE!!
THE GLORY OF A TOKYO CHERRY TREE!!
AHAHA-HAHAHA-HAHAHA-HAHAHA!

Super Sayaka #3

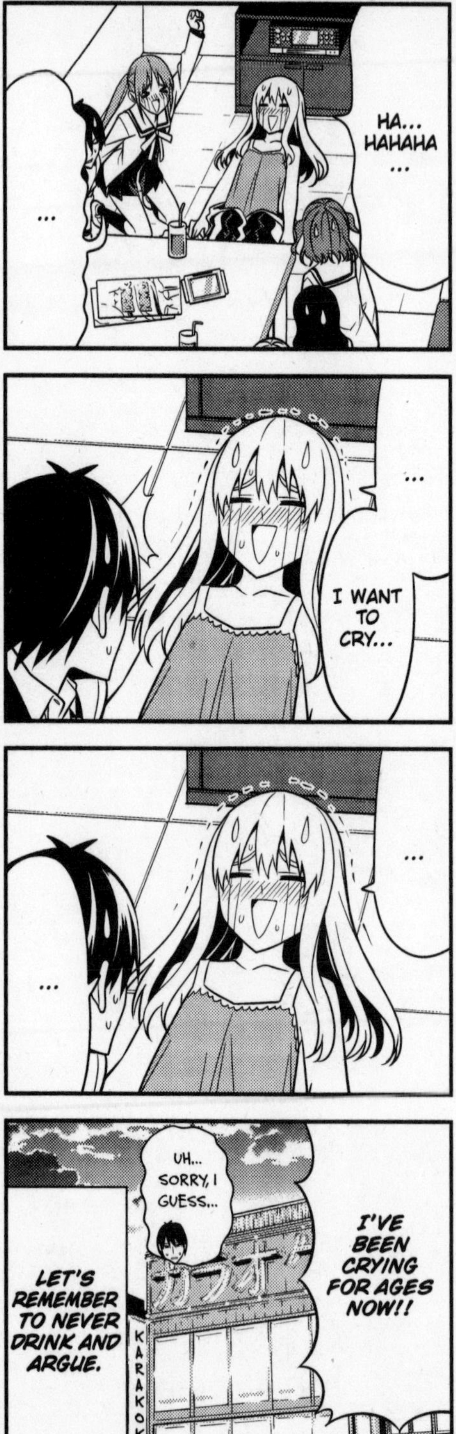
HA... HAHAHA ...
...
...
I WANT TO CRY...
...
...
I'VE BEEN CRYING FOR AGES NOW!!
UH... SORRY, I GUESS...
KARAKOKE
LET'S REMEMBER TO NEVER DRINK AND ARGUE.

The Eternal Light of Super Sayaka

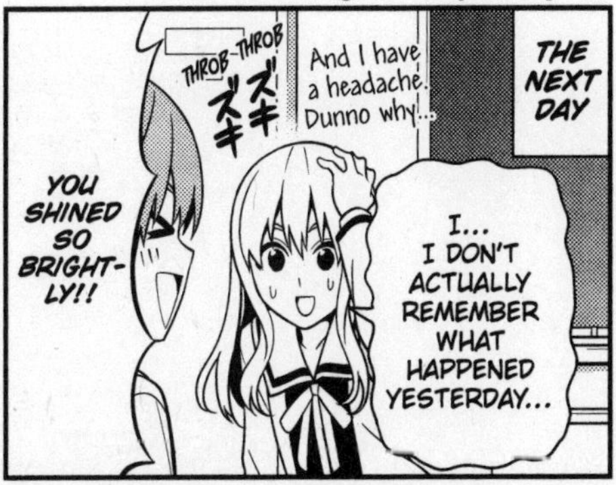
THE NEXT DAY
And I have a headache. Dunno why...
THROB-THROB
I... I DON'T ACTUALLY REMEMBER WHAT HAPPENED YESTERDAY...
YOU SHINED SO BRIGHTLY!!

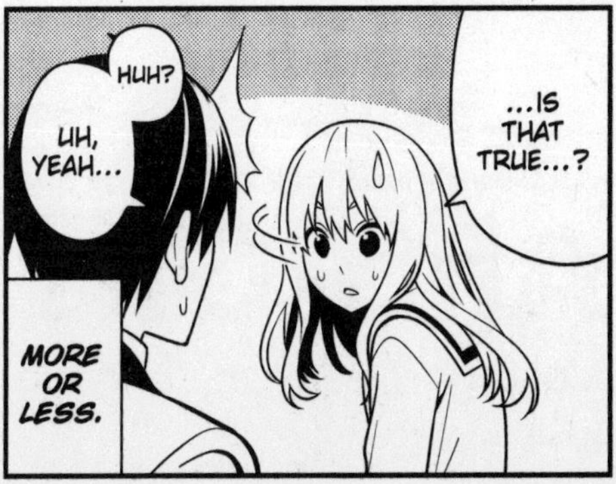
...IS THAT TRUE...?
HUH?
UH, YEAH...
MORE OR LESS.

(We drink, drinking it in, and drinking it in, we drink)

Aho-Girl

\ˈahô͵gərl \ *Japanese, noun.*
A clueless girl.

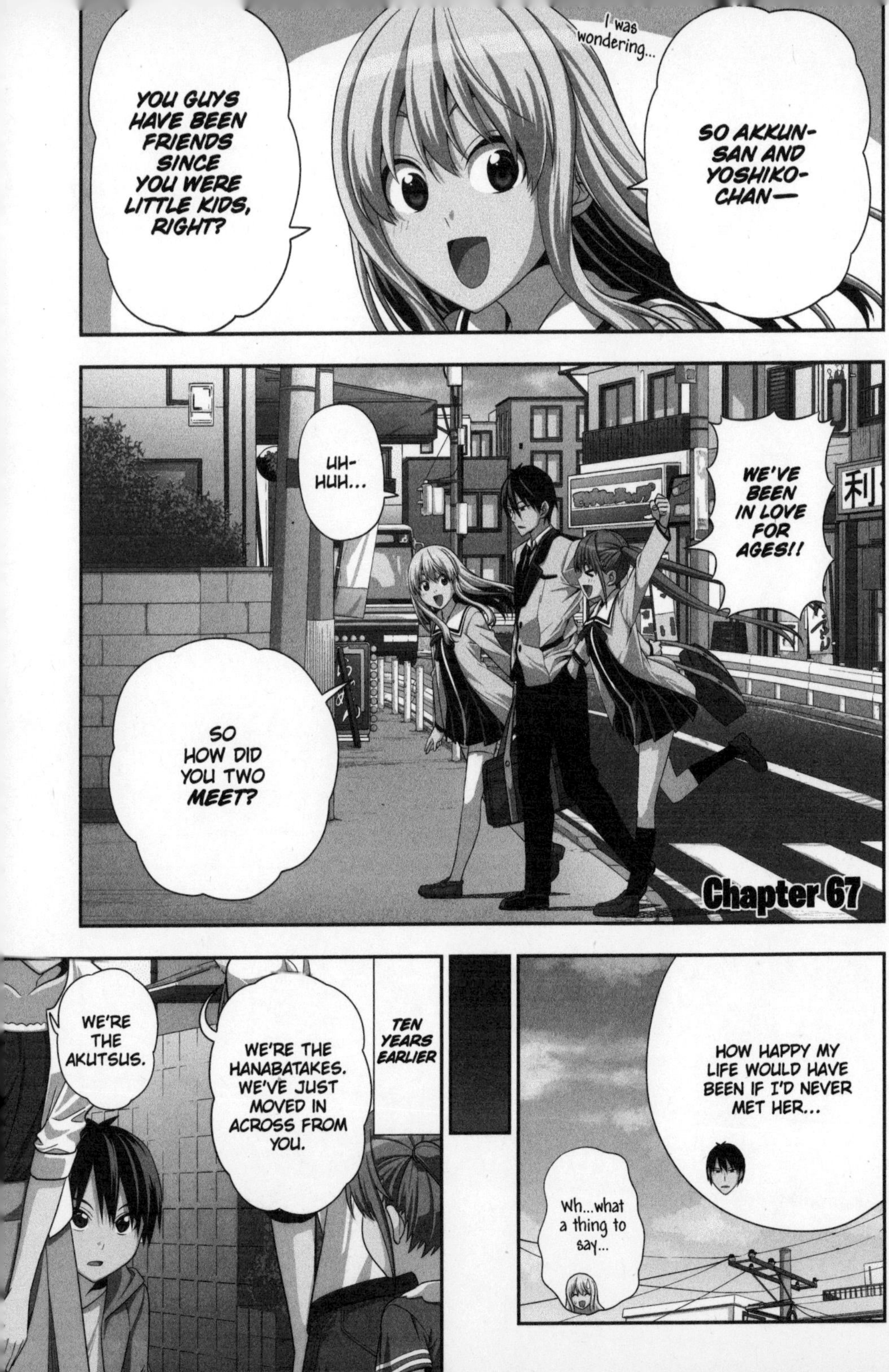
I was wondering...
SO AKKUN-SAN AND YOSHIKO-CHAN—
YOU GUYS HAVE BEEN FRIENDS SINCE YOU WERE LITTLE KIDS, RIGHT?
WE'VE BEEN IN LOVE FOR AGES!!
UH-HUH...
SO HOW DID YOU TWO MEET?
Chapter 67
HOW HAPPY MY LIFE WOULD HAVE BEEN IF I'D NEVER MET HER...
Wh...what a thing to say...
TEN YEARS EARLIER
WE'RE THE HANABATAKES. WE'VE JUST MOVED IN ACROSS FROM YOU.
WE'RE THE AKUTSUS.

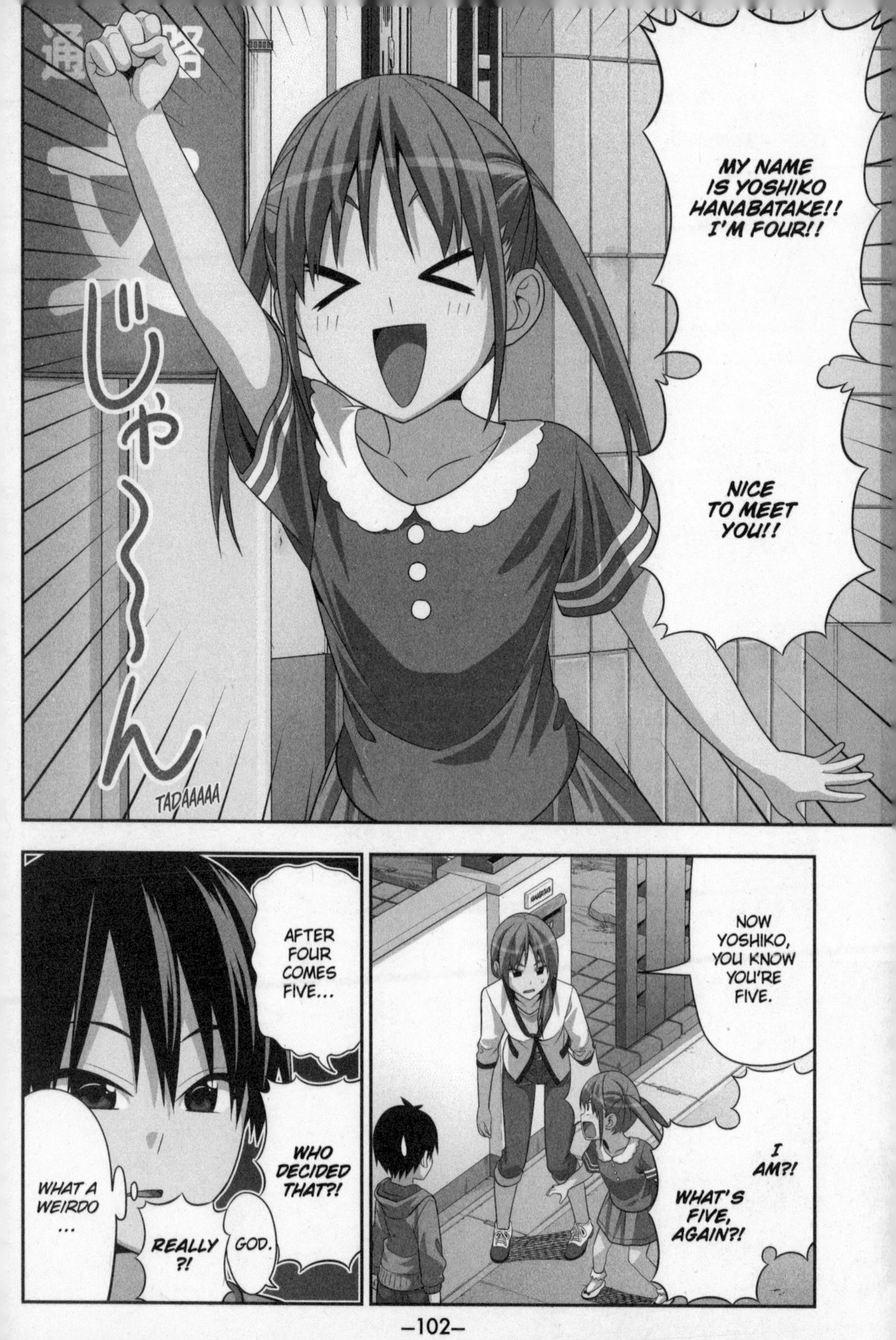
じゃ〜〜ん
TADAAAAA
MY NAME IS YOSHIKO HANABATAKE!! I'M FOUR!!
NICE TO MEET YOU!!
NOW YOSHIKO, YOU KNOW YOU'RE FIVE.
I AM?!
WHAT'S FIVE, AGAIN?!
AFTER FOUR COMES FIVE...
WHO DECIDED THAT?!
GOD.
REALLY?!
WHAT A WEIRDO...

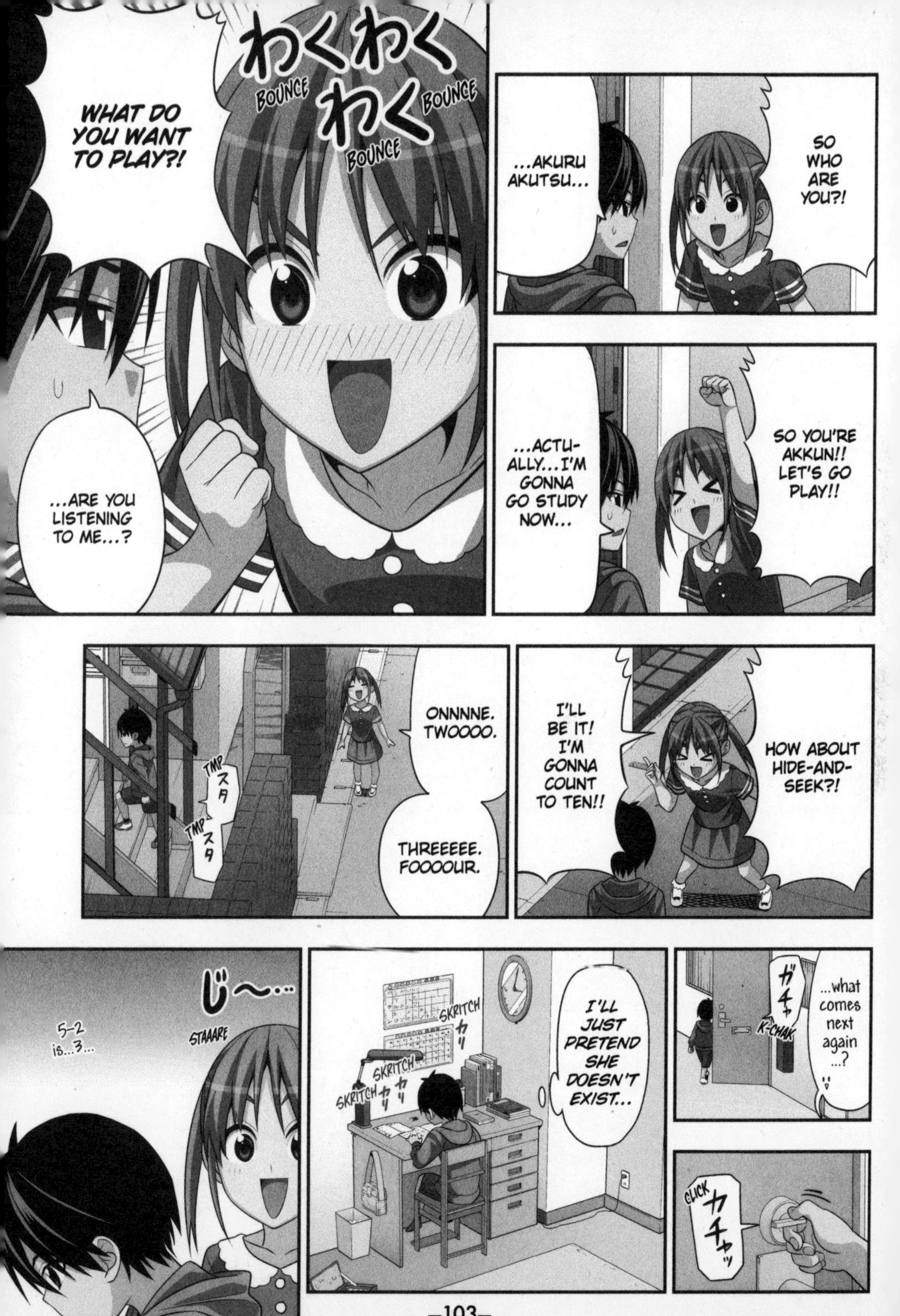
SO WHO ARE YOU?!
...AKURU AKUTSU...
SO YOU'RE AKKUN!! LET'S GO PLAY!!
...ACTU-ALLY...I'M GONNA GO STUDY NOW...
わくわく わく
BOUNCE BOUNCE BOUNCE
WHAT DO YOU WANT TO PLAY?!
...ARE YOU LISTENING TO ME...?
HOW ABOUT HIDE-AND-SEEK?!
I'LL BE IT! I'M GONNA COUNT TO TEN!!
ONNNNE. TWOOOO.
THREEEEE. FOOOOUR.
TMP スタ
TMP スタ
...what comes next again ...?
ガチャ
K-CHAK
カチャッ
CLICK
I'LL JUST PRETEND SHE DOESN'T EXIST...
SKRITCH カリ
SKRITCH カリ
SKRITCH カリ
じ～…
STAAARE
5-2 is...3...

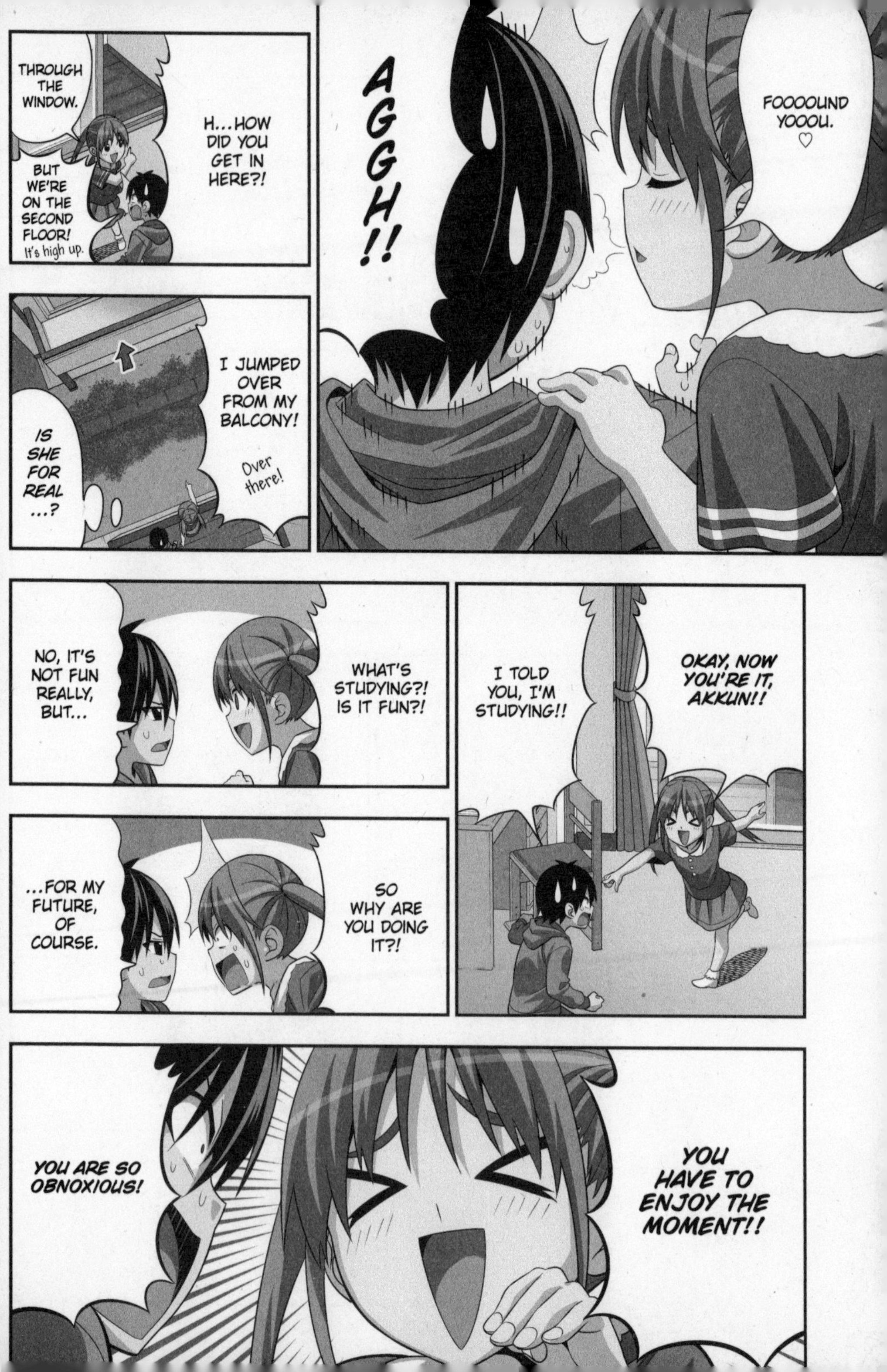
FOOOOUND YOOOU. ♡
AGGH!!
H...HOW DID YOU GET IN HERE?!
THROUGH THE WINDOW.
BUT WE'RE ON THE SECOND FLOOR!
It's high up.
I JUMPED OVER FROM MY BALCONY!
Over there!
IS SHE FOR REAL...?
OKAY, NOW YOU'RE IT, AKKUN!!
I TOLD YOU, I'M STUDYING!!
WHAT'S STUDYING?! IS IT FUN?!
NO, IT'S NOT FUN REALLY, BUT...
SO WHY ARE YOU DOING IT?!
...FOR MY FUTURE, OF COURSE.
YOU HAVE TO ENJOY THE MOMENT!!
YOU ARE SO OBNOXIOUS!

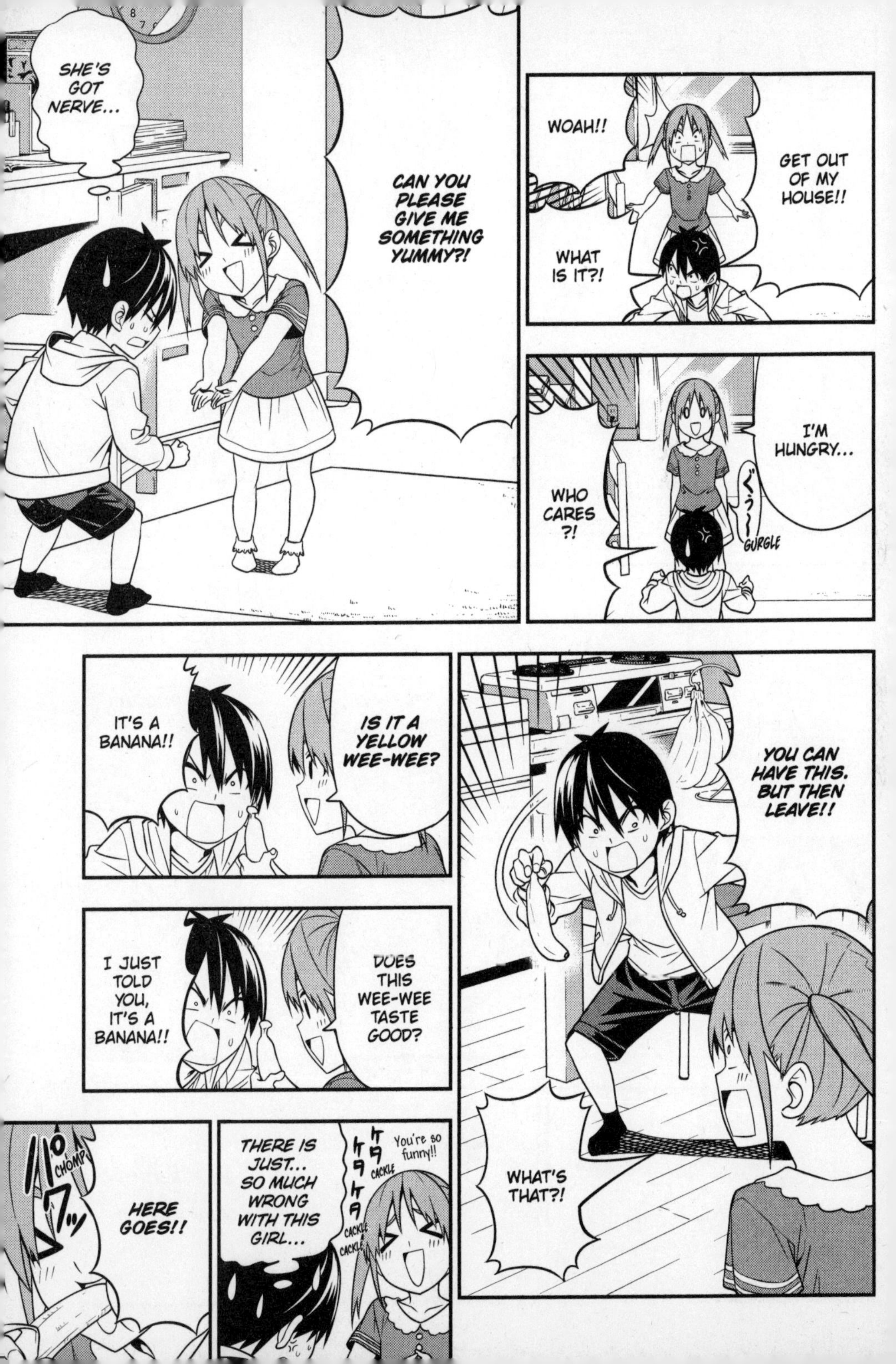
GET OUT OF MY HOUSE!!
WOAH!!
WHAT IS IT?!
I'M HUNGRY...
ぐぅ~ GURGLE
WHO CARES?!
CAN YOU PLEASE GIVE ME SOMETHING YUMMY?!
SHE'S GOT NERVE...
YOU CAN HAVE THIS. BUT THEN LEAVE!!
WHAT'S THAT?!
IS IT A YELLOW WEE-WEE?
IT'S A BANANA!!
DOES THIS WEE-WEE TASTE GOOD?
I JUST TOLD YOU, IT'S A BANANA!!
ケタケタケタ CACKLE CACKLE CACKLE
You're so funny!!
THERE IS JUST... SO MUCH WRONG WITH THIS GIRL...
パクッ CHOMP
HERE GOES!!

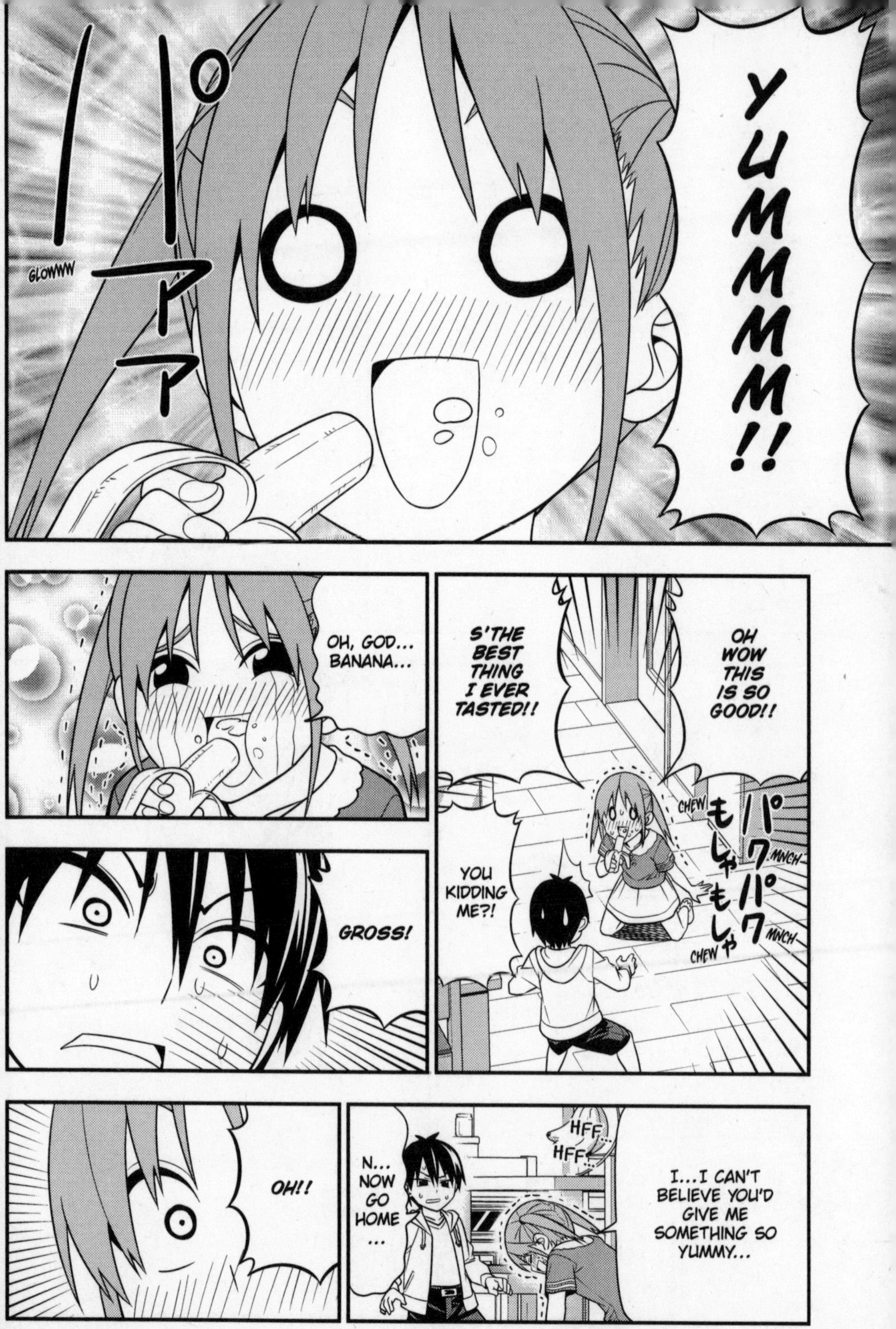
YUMMMMM!!
パーアア
GLOWWW
OH WOW THIS IS SO GOOD!!
S'THE BEST THING I EVER TASTED!!
パクパク
MNCH MNCH
もしゃもしゃ
CHEW CHEW
YOU KIDDING ME?!
OH, GOD... BANANA...
GROSS!
I...I CAN'T BELIEVE YOU'D GIVE ME SOMETHING SO YUMMY...
HFF... HFF...
N... NOW GO HOME ...
OH!!

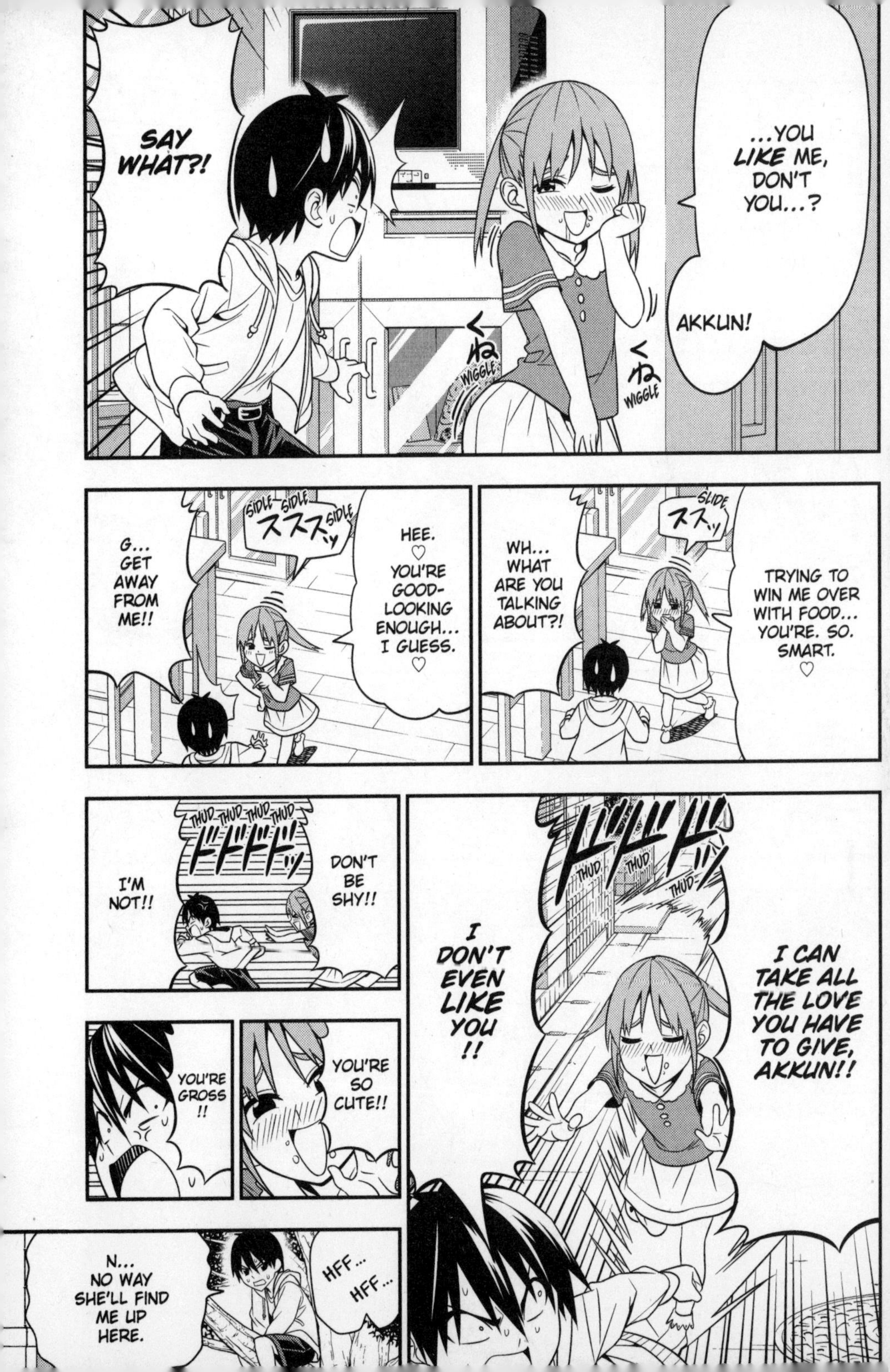

...YOU LIKE ME, DON'T YOU...?
AKKUN!
くね WIGGLE
くね WIGGLE
SAY WHAT?!
TRYING TO WIN ME OVER WITH FOOD... YOU'RE. SO. SMART. ♡
ススッ SLIDE
WH... WHAT ARE YOU TALKING ABOUT?!
HEE. ♡ YOU'RE GOOD-LOOKING ENOUGH... I GUESS. ♡
SIDLE SIDLE SIDLE スススッ
G... GET AWAY FROM ME!!
ドドドドッ THUD THUD THUD
I CAN TAKE ALL THE LOVE YOU HAVE TO GIVE, AKKUN!!
I DON'T EVEN LIKE YOU!!
DON'T BE SHY!!
THUD THUD THUD THUD ドドドドッ
I'M NOT!!
YOU'RE SO CUTE!!
YOU'RE GROSS!!
HFF... HFF...
N... NO WAY SHE'LL FIND ME UP HERE.

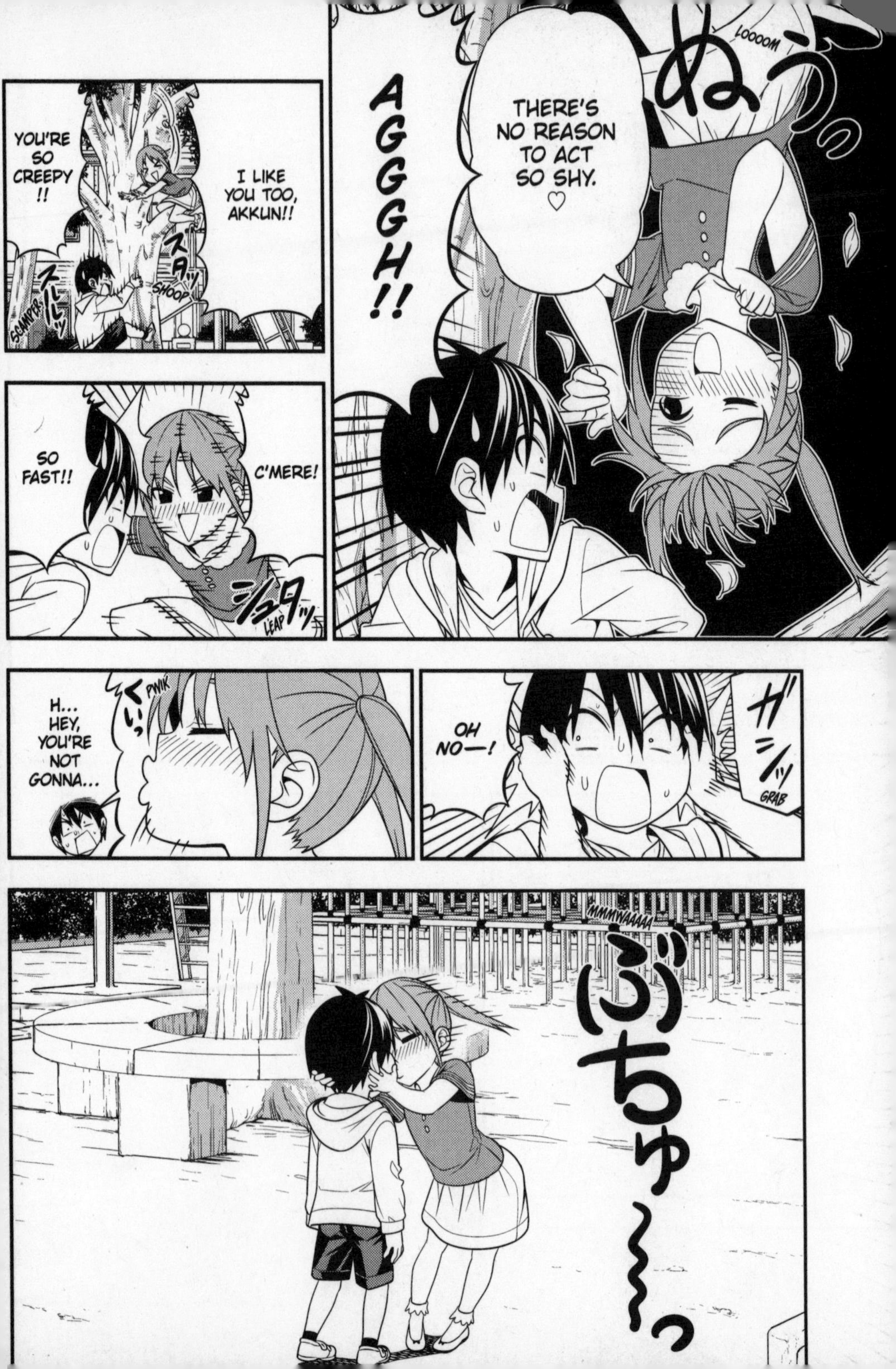

ぬう
LOOOM
THERE'S NO REASON TO ACT SO SHY. ♡
AGGGH!!
I LIKE YOU TOO, AKKUN!!
YOU'RE SO CREEPY!!
スタッ
SHOOP
スルルッ
SCAMPER
C'MERE!
SO FAST!!
シュタッ
LEAP
ガシッ
GRAB
OH NO—!
くいっ
PWIK
H... HEY, YOU'RE NOT GONNA...
MMMWAAAAA
ぶちゅ～～ッ

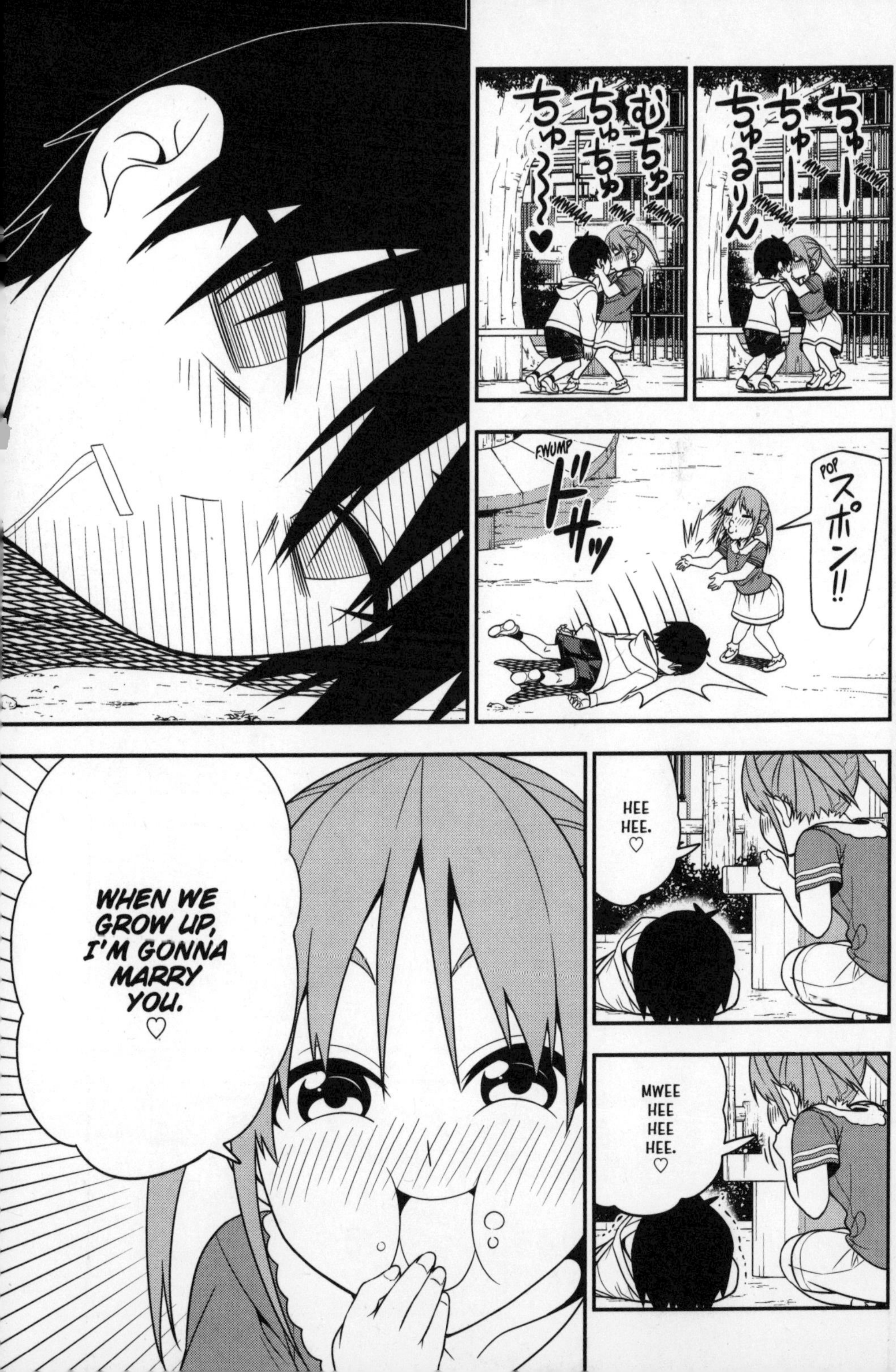
ちゅーちゅーちゅるりん
むちゅちゅちゅちゅ〜♥
POP
スポン!!
FWUMP
ドサッ
HEE HEE. ♡
MWEE HEE HEE HEE. ♡
WHEN WE GROW UP, I'M GONNA MARRY YOU. ♡

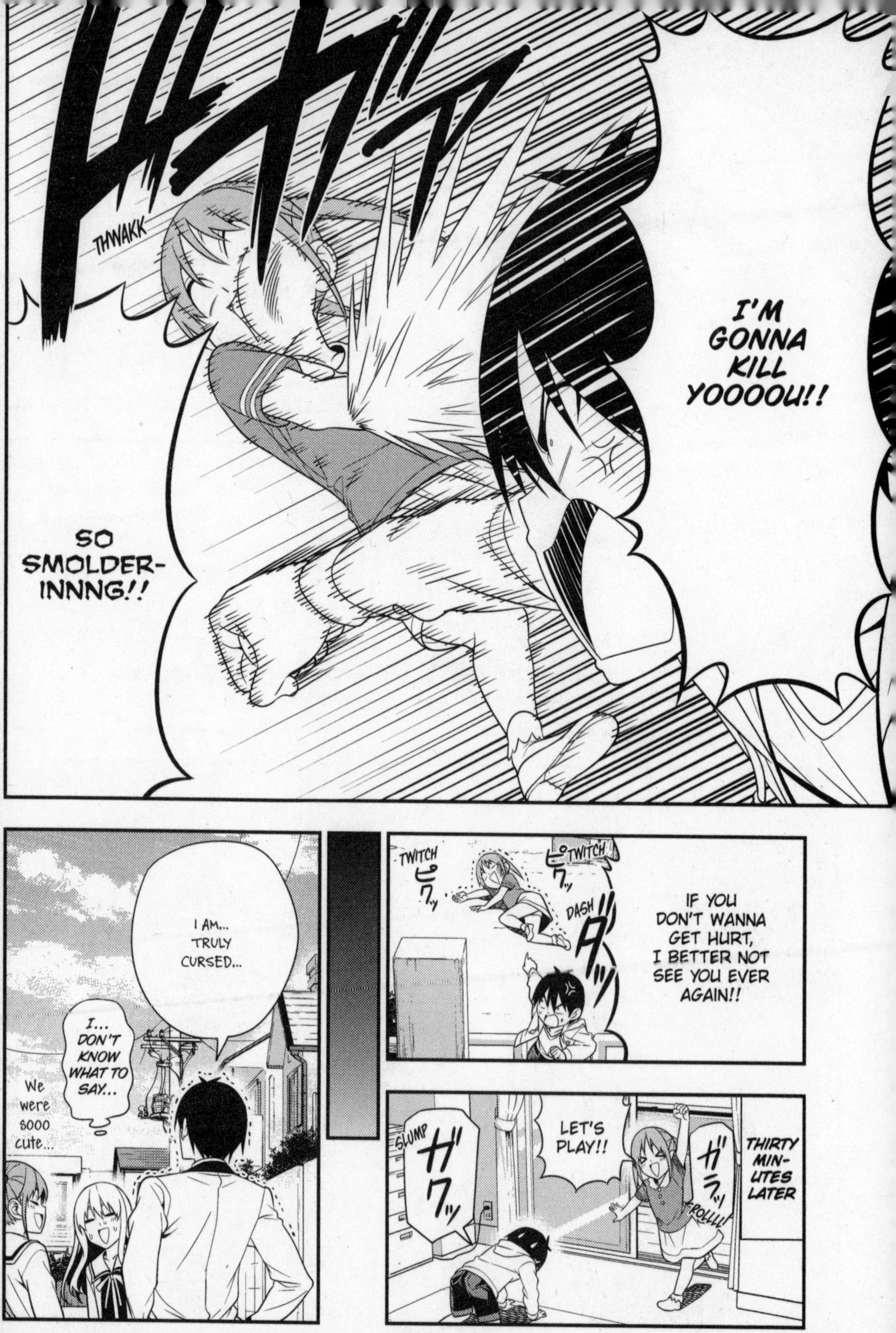
I'M GONNA KILL YOOOOU!!
THWAKK
SO SMOLDER-INNNG!!
IF YOU DON'T WANNA GET HURT, I BETTER NOT SEE YOU EVER AGAIN!!
TWITCH
TWITCH
DASH
THIRTY MIN-UTES LATER
LET'S PLAY!!
ROLLLL
SLUMP
I AM... TRULY CURSED...
I... DON'T KNOW WHAT TO SAY...
We were sooo cute...

So Basically Nothing

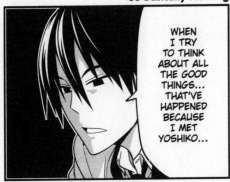

WHEN I TRY TO THINK ABOUT ALL THE GOOD THINGS... THAT'VE HAPPENED BECAUSE I MET YOSHIKO...
MEETING YOU IS THE ONLY THING I CAN THINK OF...
WHINE. WHIIINE.

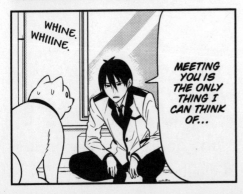

(4000 6000 6000 2000)

Aho-Girl

\\'ahô͵gərl\\ *Japanese, noun.*
A clueless girl.

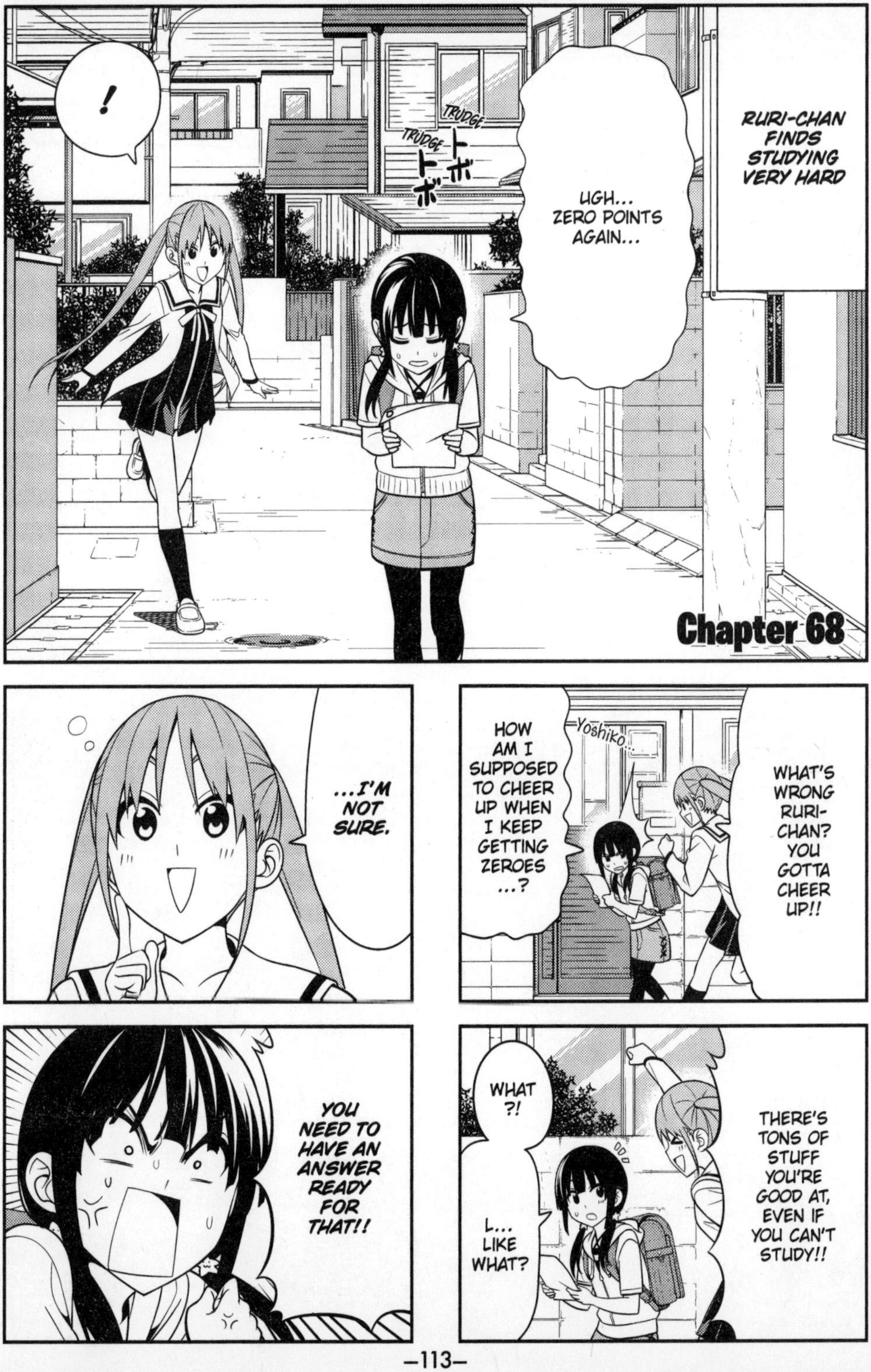

RURI-CHAN FINDS STUDYING VERY HARD
UGH... ZERO POINTS AGAIN...
TRUDGE トボ
TRUDGE トボ
!
Chapter 68
WHAT'S WRONG RURI-CHAN? YOU GOTTA CHEER UP!!
Yoshiko...
HOW AM I SUPPOSED TO CHEER UP WHEN I KEEP GETTING ZEROES ...?
...I'M NOT SURE.
THERE'S TONS OF STUFF YOU'RE GOOD AT, EVEN IF YOU CAN'T STUDY!!
WHAT ?!
I... LIKE WHAT?
YOU NEED TO HAVE AN ANSWER READY FOR THAT!!

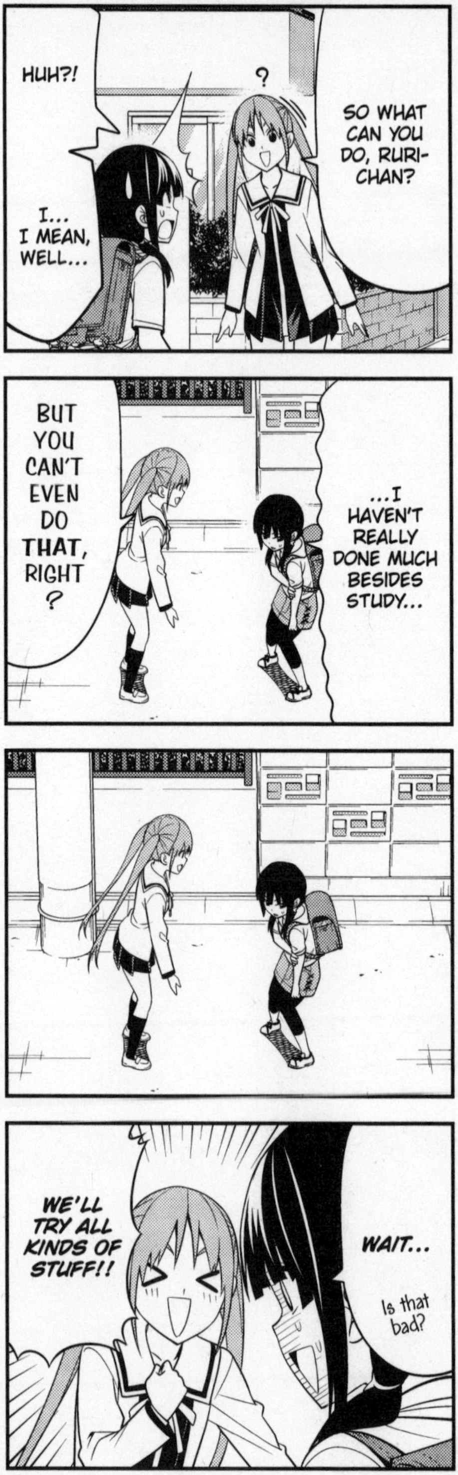
SO WHAT CAN YOU DO, RURI-CHAN?
?
HUH?!
I... I MEAN, WELL...
...I HAVEN'T REALLY DONE MUCH BESIDES STUDY...
BUT YOU CAN'T EVEN DO THAT, RIGHT?
WAIT...
Is that bad?
WE'LL TRY ALL KINDS OF STUFF!!

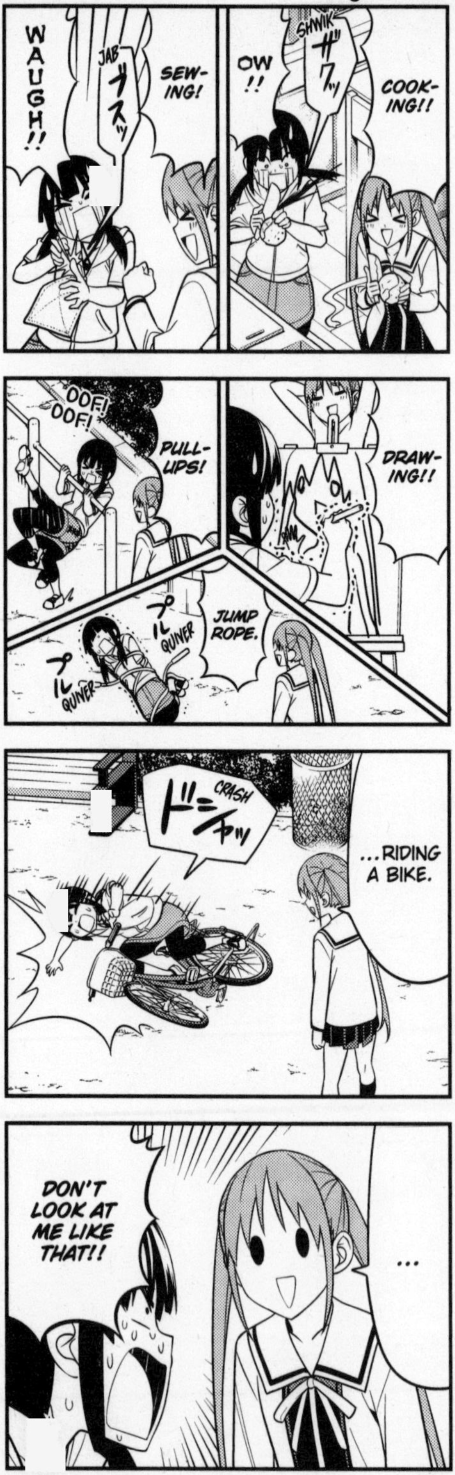
COOKING!!
ザクッ SHWIK
OW!!
SEWING!
ブスッ JAB
WAUGH!!
DRAWING!!
PULL-UPS!
OOF! OOF!
JUMP ROPE.
プル QUIVER
プル QUIVER
...RIDING A BIKE.
ドシャッ CRASH
...
DON'T LOOK AT ME LIKE THAT!!

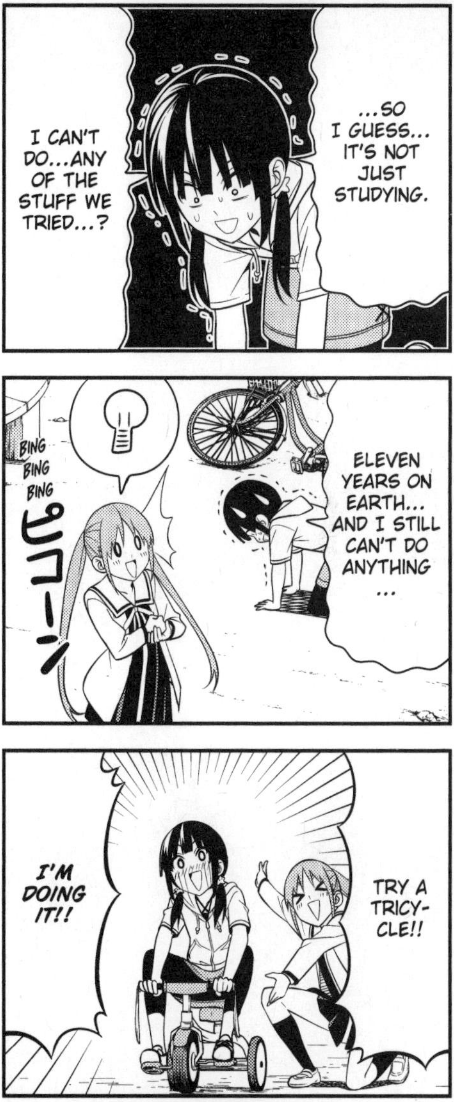
...SO I GUESS... IT'S NOT JUST STUDYING.
I CAN'T DO...ANY OF THE STUFF WE TRIED...?
ELEVEN YEARS ON EARTH... AND I STILL CAN'T DO ANYTHING ...
BING BING BING
TRY A TRICY-CLE!!
I'M DOING IT!!
ANYONE CAN DO THIS!!

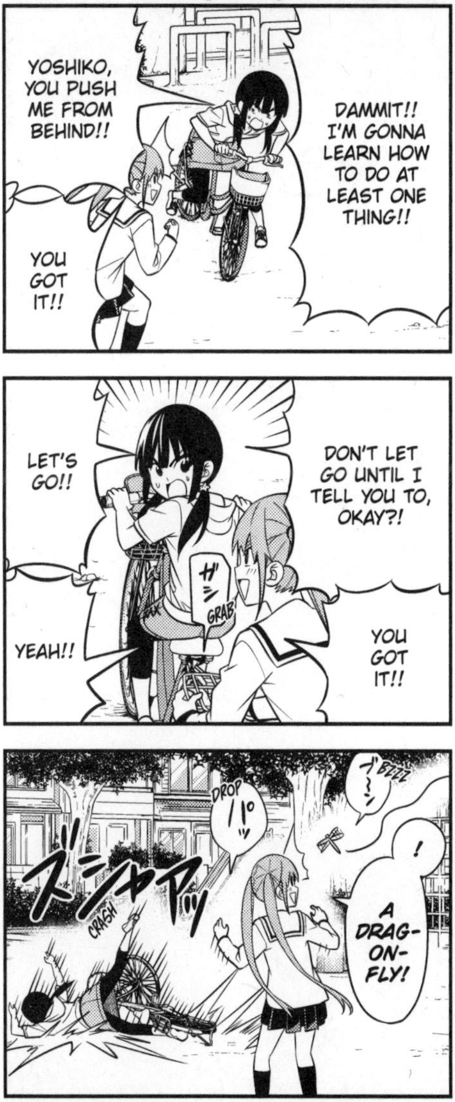
DAMMIT!! I'M GONNA LEARN HOW TO DO AT LEAST ONE THING!!
YOSHIKO, YOU PUSH ME FROM BEHIND!!
YOU GOT IT!!
DON'T LET GO UNTIL I TELL YOU TO, OKAY?!
LET'S GO!!
GRAB
YOU GOT IT!!
YEAH!!
BZZZ
!
A DRAG-ON-FLY!
DROP
CRASH
Wait for meee!
TP TP TP
QUIVER QUIVER

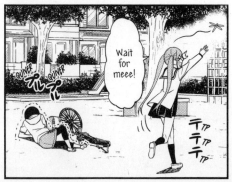

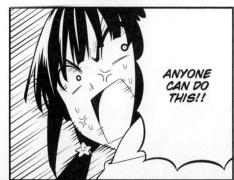

They Really Are Bewitching

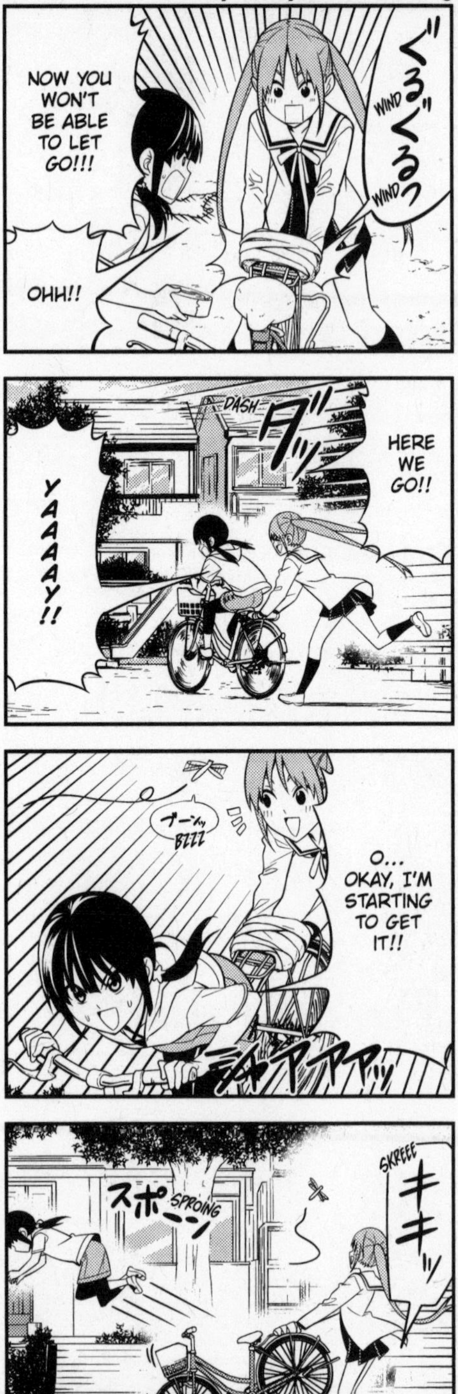

ぐるぐるっ
WIND
WIND
NOW YOU WON'T BE ABLE TO LET GO!!!
OHH!!
ダッ
DASH
HERE WE GO!!
YAAAAAY!!
O... OKAY, I'M STARTING TO GET IT!!
ブーンッ
BZZZ
シャアアアッ
キキッ
SKREEE
スポーン
SPROING

A Heavy Air of Exhaustion

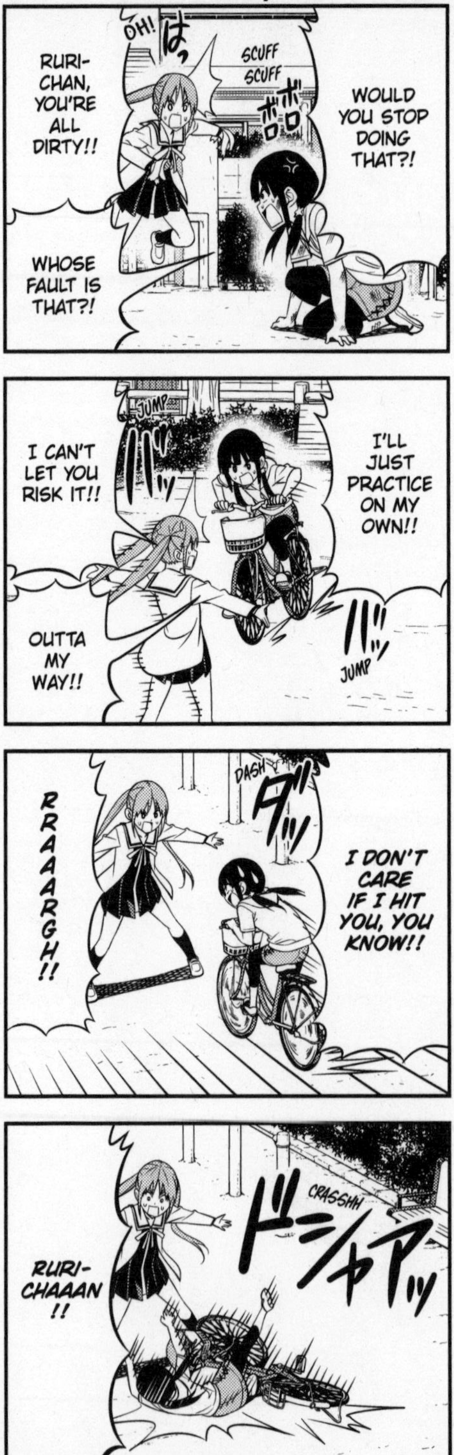

WOULD YOU STOP DOING THAT?!
ボロボロ
SCUFF SCUFF
はっ
OH!
RURI-CHAN, YOU'RE ALL DIRTY!!
WHOSE FAULT IS THAT?!
I'LL JUST PRACTICE ON MY OWN!!
バッ
JUMP
I CAN'T LET YOU RISK IT!!
バッ
JUMP
OUTTA MY WAY!!
ダッ
DASH
I DON'T CARE IF I HIT YOU, YOU KNOW!!
RRAAAARGH!!
ドシャアッ
CRASSHH
RURI-CHAAAN!!

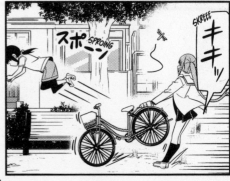

Get up, Ruri-chan!

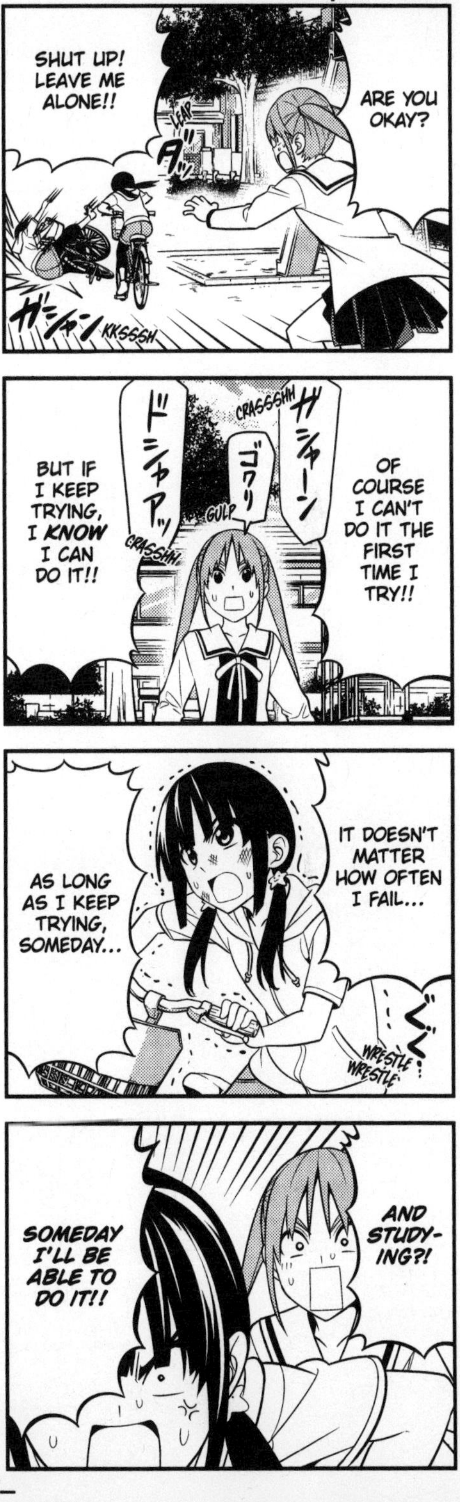
ARE YOU OKAY?
SHUT UP! LEAVE ME ALONE!!
LEAP
KKSSSH
OF COURSE I CAN'T DO IT THE FIRST TIME I TRY!!
CRASSSHH
GULP
BUT IF I KEEP TRYING, I *KNOW* I CAN DO IT!!
CRASSHH
IT DOESN'T MATTER HOW OFTEN I FAIL...
AS LONG AS I KEEP TRYING, SOMEDAY...
WRESTLE WRESTLE
AND STUDYING?!
SOMEDAY I'LL BE ABLE TO DO IT!!

You Can't Start Yet, Dummy

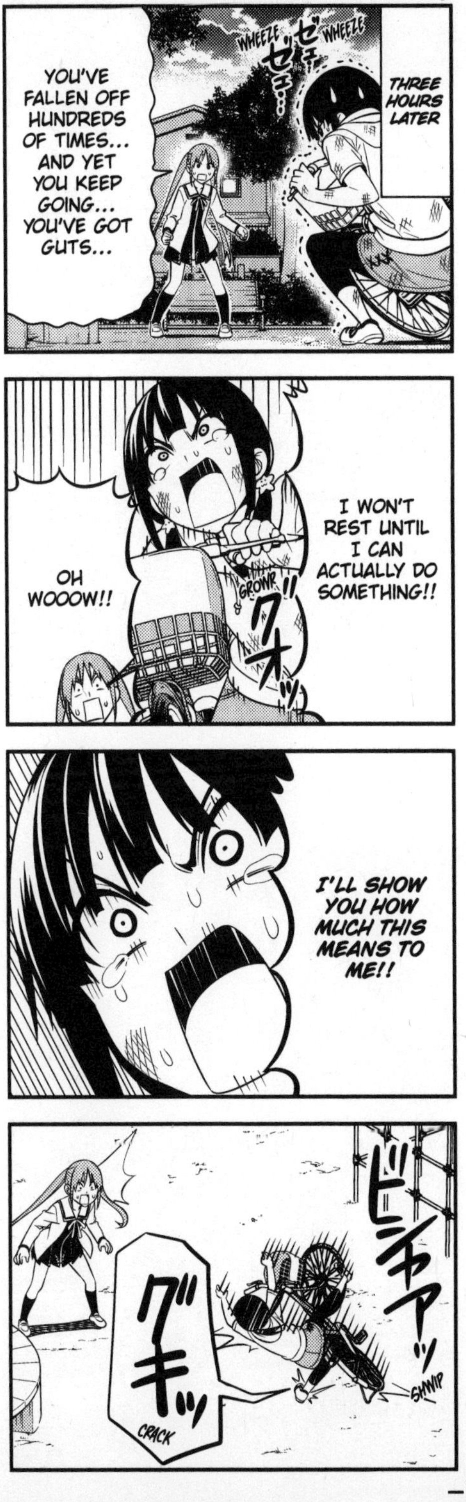
THREE HOURS LATER
WHEEZE WHEEZE
YOU'VE FALLEN OFF HUNDREDS OF TIMES... AND YET YOU KEEP GOING... YOU'VE GOT GUTS...
I WON'T REST UNTIL I CAN ACTUALLY DO SOMETHING!!
GROWR
OH WOOOW!!
I'LL SHOW YOU HOW MUCH THIS MEANS TO ME!!
SHNIP
CRACK

Oh Nooo

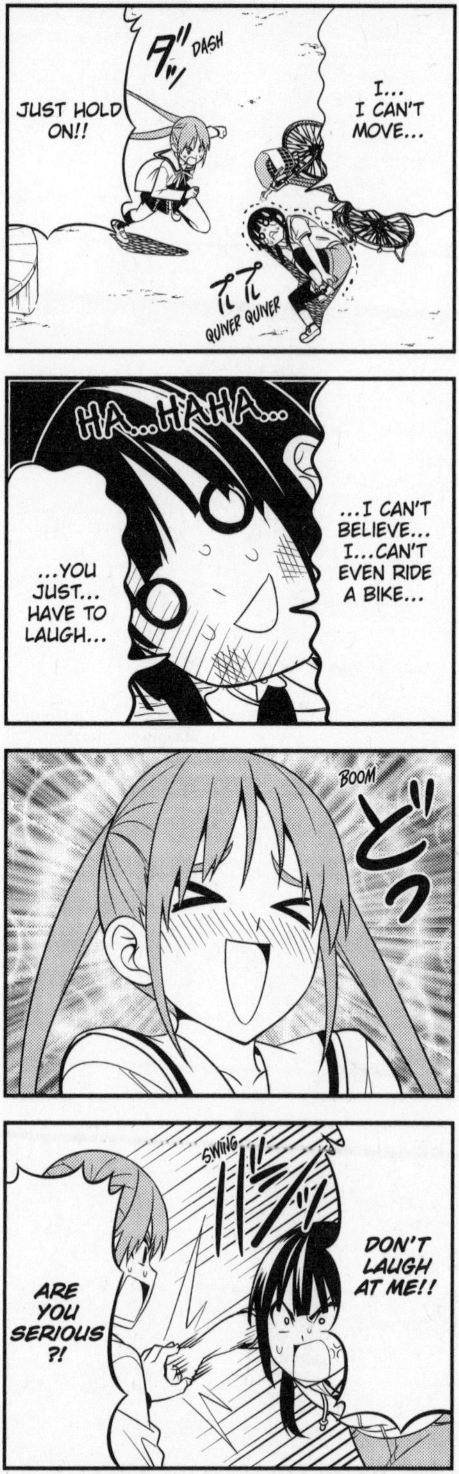
I... I CAN'T MOVE...
DASH
JUST HOLD ON!!
QUIVER QUIVER
HA...HAHA...
...I CAN'T BELIEVE... I...CAN'T EVEN RIDE A BIKE...
...YOU JUST... HAVE TO LAUGH...
BOOM
SWING
DON'T LAUGH AT ME!!
ARE YOU SERIOUS?!

We Found It

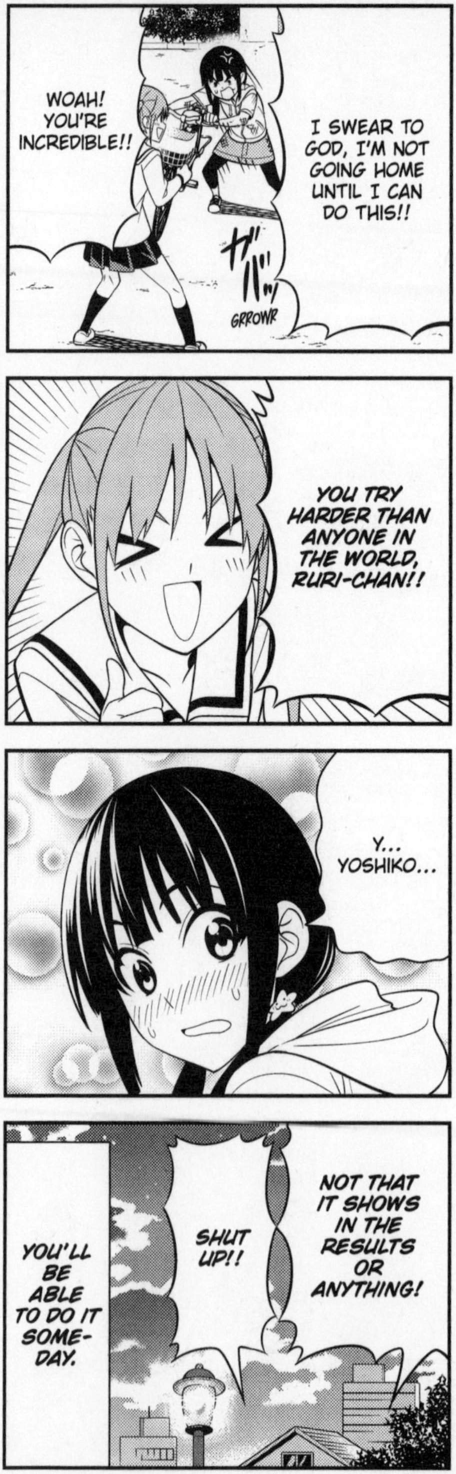
I SWEAR TO GOD, I'M NOT GOING HOME UNTIL I CAN DO THIS!!
WOAH! YOU'RE INCREDIBLE!!
GRROWR
YOU TRY HARDER THAN ANYONE IN THE WORLD, RURI-CHAN!!
Y... YOSHIKO...
NOT THAT IT SHOWS IN THE RESULTS OR ANYTHING!
SHUT UP!!
YOU'LL BE ABLE TO DO IT SOME-DAY.

It Requires Technique

I KNOW!

WOOF!

YOU CAN RIDE THE DOG UNTIL YOU LEARN HOW TO RIDE THE BIKE!!

BONK

DASH

(I want to ride my)

Aho-Girl

\'ahô,gərl\ *Japanese, noun.*

A clueless girl.

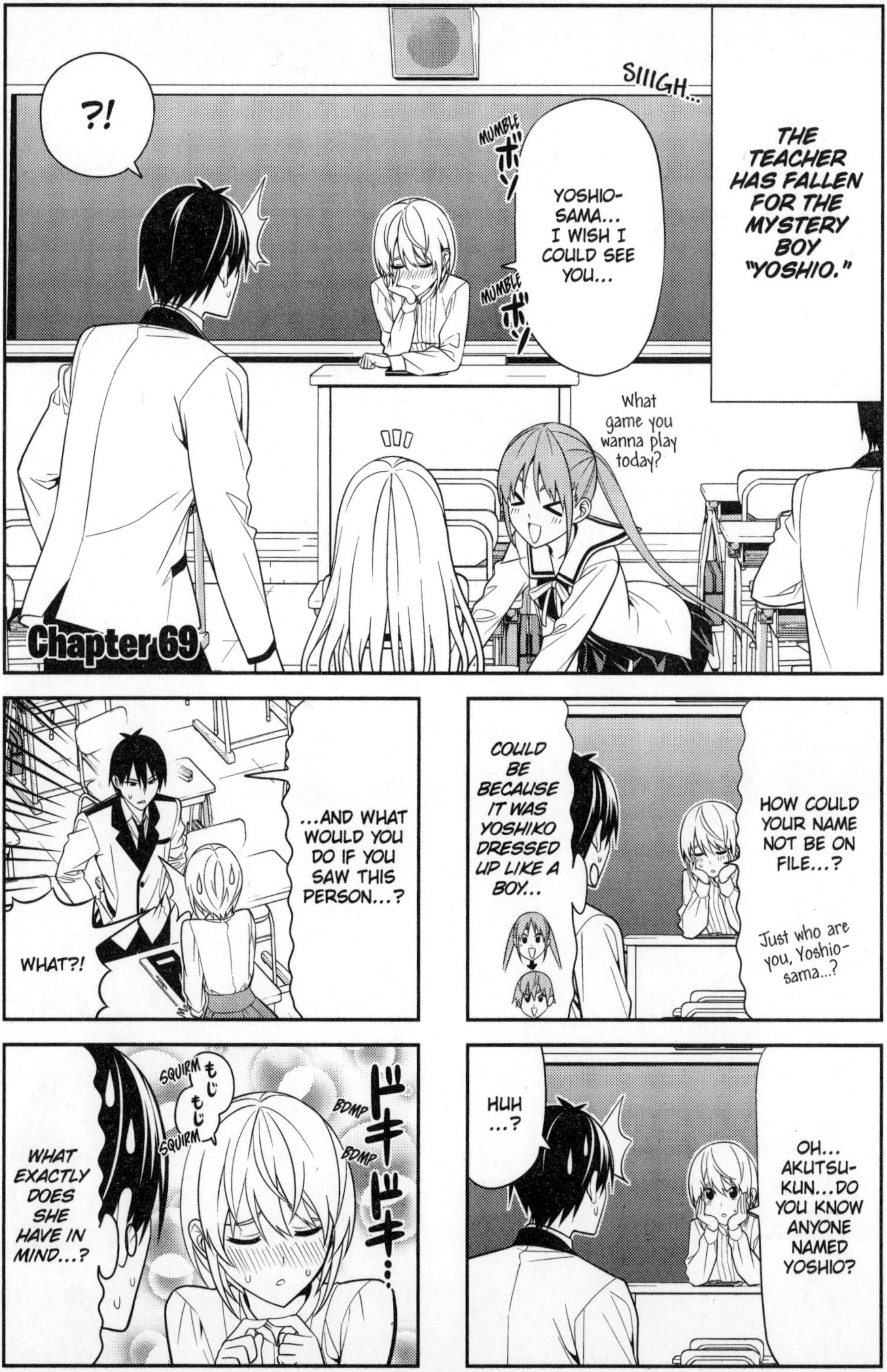
THE TEACHER HAS FALLEN FOR THE MYSTERY BOY "YOSHIO."
SIIIGH...
MUMBLE ボソ
YOSHIO-SAMA... I WISH I COULD SEE YOU...
MUMBLE ボソ
?!
What game you wanna play today?
Chapter 69
HOW COULD YOUR NAME NOT BE ON FILE...?
Just who are you, Yoshio-sama...?
COULD BE BECAUSE IT WAS YOSHIKO DRESSED UP LIKE A BOY...
...AND WHAT WOULD YOU DO IF YOU SAW THIS PERSON...?
WHAT?!
OH... AKUTSU-KUN...DO YOU KNOW ANYONE NAMED YOSHIO?
HUH ...?
BDMP BDMP ドキドキ...
SQUIRM もじもじ SQUIRM
WHAT EXACTLY DOES SHE HAVE IN MIND...?

Details in Aho-Girl Vol. 3

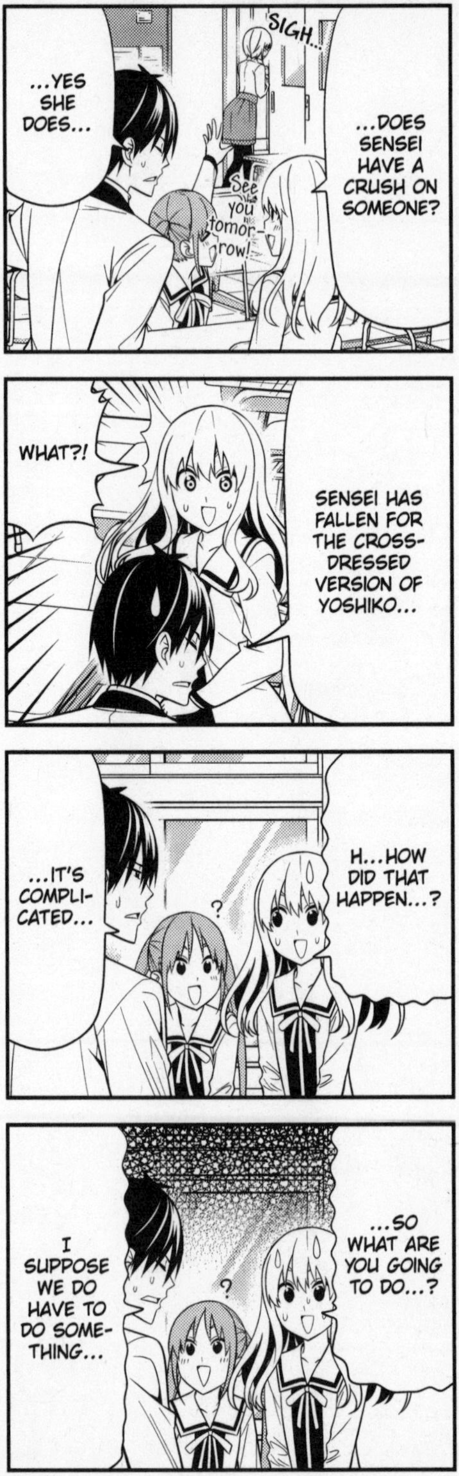
SIGH...
...DOES SENSEI HAVE A CRUSH ON SOMEONE?
See you tomor-row!
...YES SHE DOES...
SENSEI HAS FALLEN FOR THE CROSS-DRESSED VERSION OF YOSHIKO...
WHAT?!
H...HOW DID THAT HAPPEN...?
...IT'S COMPLICATED...
...SO WHAT ARE YOU GOING TO DO...?
I SUPPOSE WE DO HAVE TO DO SOME-THING...

What a Nasty Thing You Are!

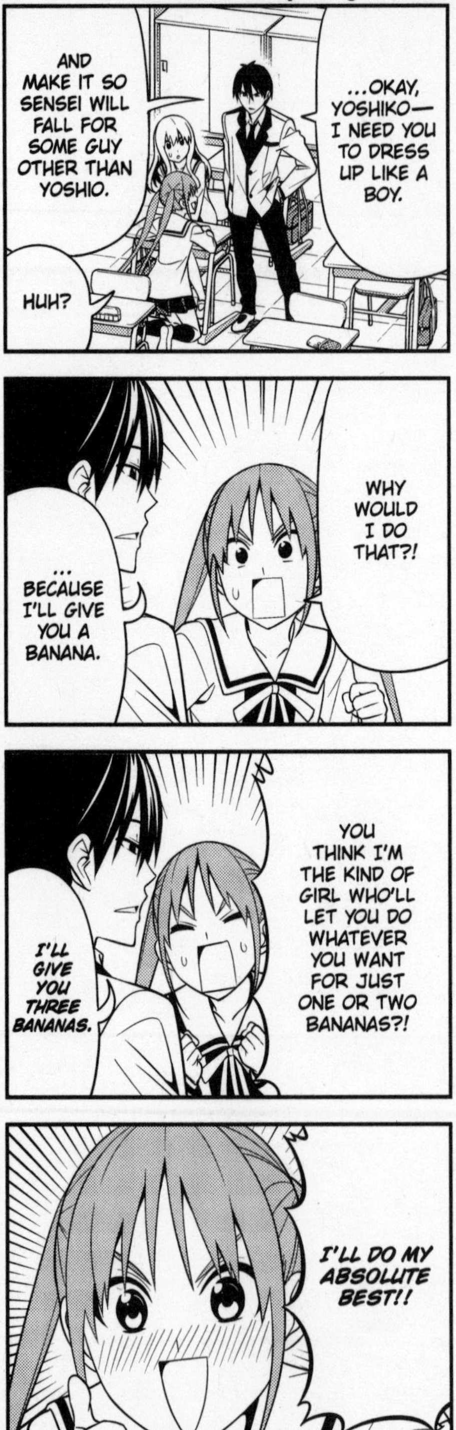
...OKAY, YOSHIKO— I NEED YOU TO DRESS UP LIKE A BOY.
AND MAKE IT SO SENSEI WILL FALL FOR SOME GUY OTHER THAN YOSHIO.
HUH?
WHY WOULD I DO THAT?!
... BECAUSE I'LL GIVE YOU A BANANA.
YOU THINK I'M THE KIND OF GIRL WHO'LL LET YOU DO WHATEVER YOU WANT FOR JUST ONE OR TWO BANANAS?!
I'LL GIVE YOU THREE BANANAS.
I'LL DO MY ABSOLUTE BEST!!

At a Loss for Words

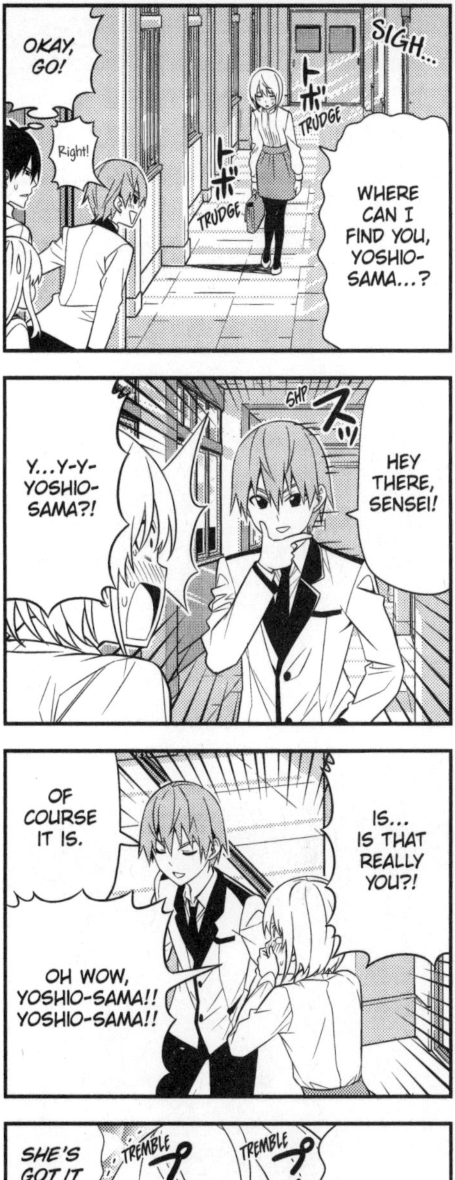
SIGH...
トボ
TRUDGE
WHERE CAN I FIND YOU, YOSHIO-SAMA...?
OKAY, GO!
Right!
トボ
TRUDGE
スッ
SHP
HEY THERE, SENSEI!
Y...Y-Y-YOSHIO-SAMA?!
IS... IS THAT REALLY YOU?!
OF COURSE IT IS.
OH WOW, YOSHIO-SAMA!! YOSHIO-SAMA!!
プル
TREMBLE
YOSHIO... SAMA...
プル
TREMBLE
SHE'S GOT IT BAD...
プル
TREMBLE
S... SURE DOES...

Yoshio's Strategy

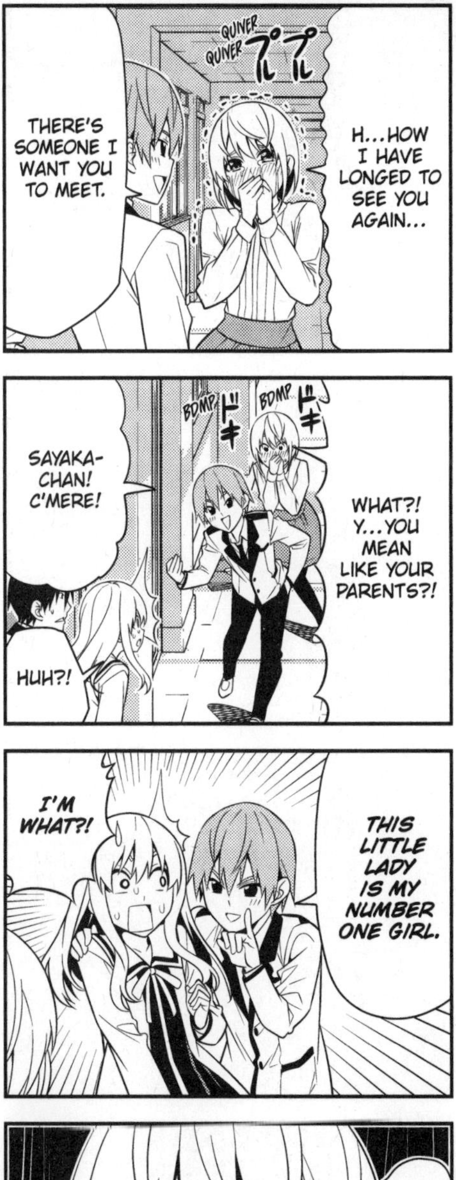
H...HOW I HAVE LONGED TO SEE YOU AGAIN...
プルプル
QUIVER QUIVER
THERE'S SOMEONE I WANT YOU TO MEET.
ドキ
BDMP
WHAT?! Y...YOU MEAN LIKE YOUR PARENTS?!
ドキ
BDMP
SAYAKA-CHAN! C'MERE!
HUH?!
THIS LITTLE LADY IS MY NUMBER ONE GIRL.
I'M WHAT?!
...SHE'S WHAT...?

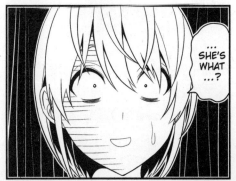

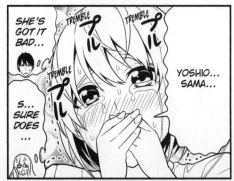

Yoshio, You Scoundrel

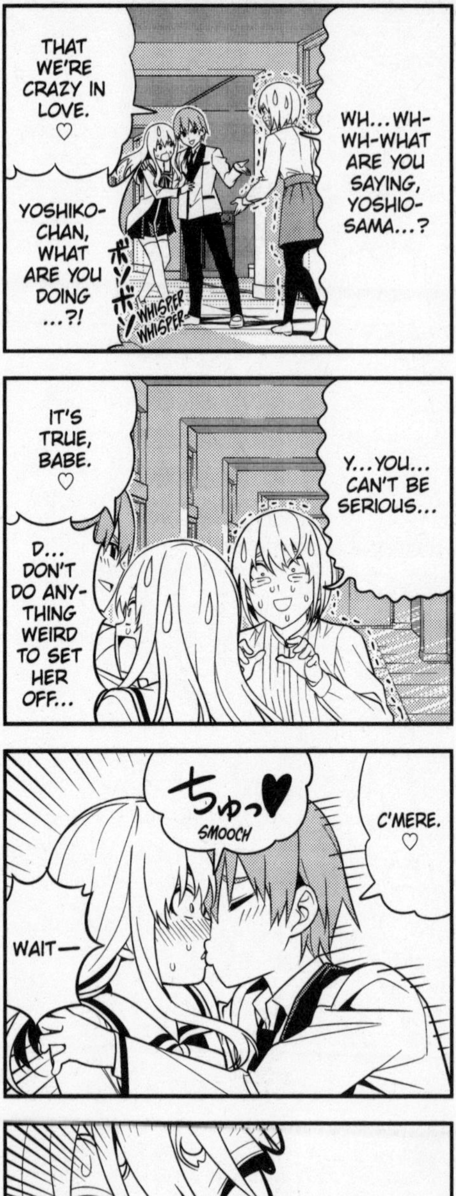
WH...WH-WH-WHAT ARE YOU SAYING, YOSHIO-SAMA...?
THAT WE'RE CRAZY IN LOVE. ♡
YOSHIKO-CHAN, WHAT ARE YOU DOING...?!
ボソボソ WHISPER WHISPER
Y...YOU... CAN'T BE SERIOUS...
IT'S TRUE, BABE. ♡
D... DON'T DO ANY-THING WEIRD TO SET HER OFF...
C'MERE. ♡
ちゅっ♥ SMOOCH
WAIT—
WHY WON'T IT END?!

Yoshio's Activities

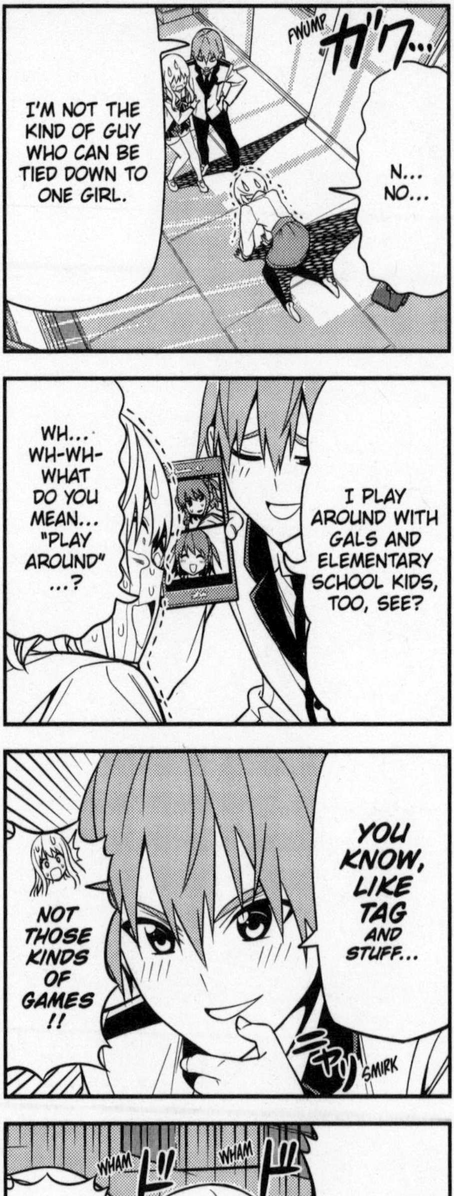
FWUMP ガク...
N... NO...
I'M NOT THE KIND OF GUY WHO CAN BE TIED DOWN TO ONE GIRL.
I PLAY AROUND WITH GALS AND ELEMENTARY SCHOOL KIDS, TOO, SEE?
WH... WH-WH-WHAT DO YOU MEAN... "PLAY AROUND"...?
YOU KNOW, LIKE TAG AND STUFF...
ニヤリ SMIRK
NOT THOSE KINDS OF GAMES!!
WHAM ド WHAM ド
WAAAAAH!
Wait for meee!
Ah ha ha ha!
But...it's working...!!

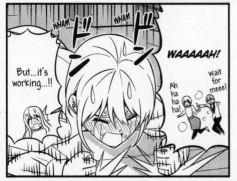

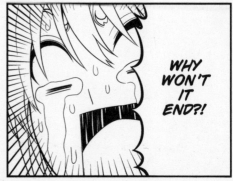

Taking the Brunt

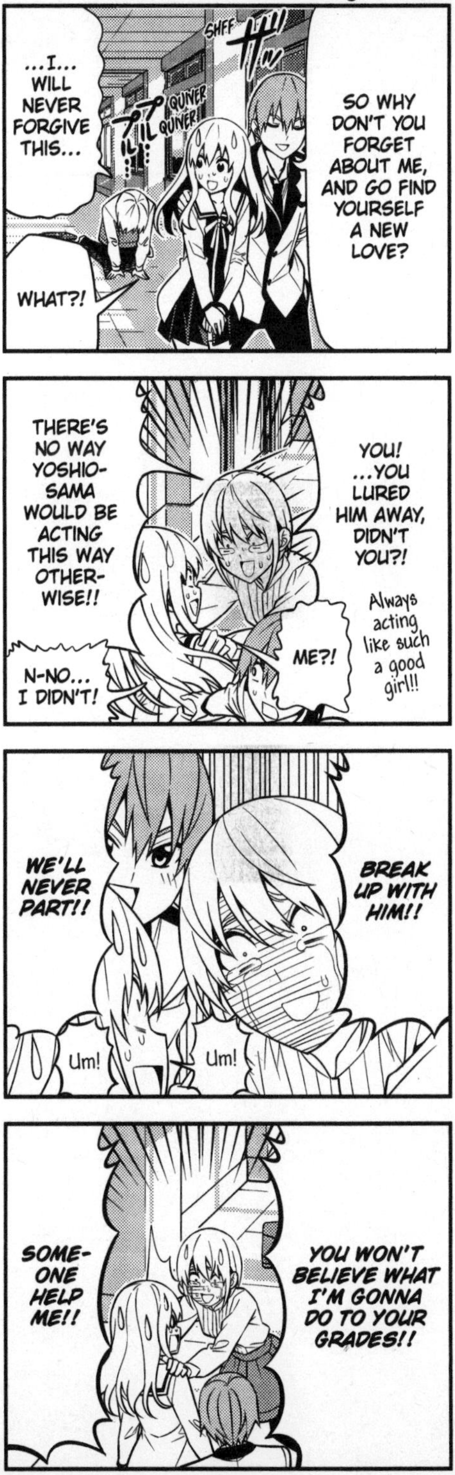
SO WHY DON'T YOU FORGET ABOUT ME, AND GO FIND YOURSELF A NEW LOVE?
SHFF
QUIVER QUIVER
...I... WILL NEVER FORGIVE THIS...
WHAT?!
YOU! ...YOU LURED HIM AWAY, DIDN'T YOU?!
Always acting like such a good girl!!
ME?!
THERE'S NO WAY YOSHIO-SAMA WOULD BE ACTING THIS WAY OTHERWISE!!
N-NO... I DIDN'T!
BREAK UP WITH HIM!!
Um!
WE'LL NEVER PART!!
Um!
YOU WON'T BELIEVE WHAT I'M GONNA DO TO YOUR GRADES!!
SOME-ONE HELP ME!!

Proof that She's Serious

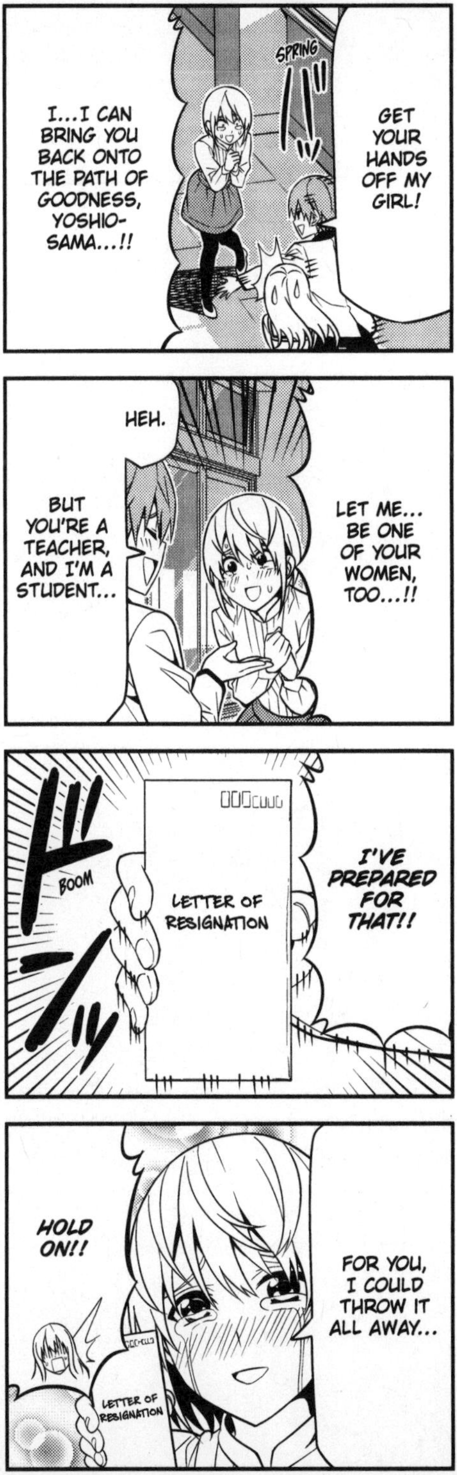
GET YOUR HANDS OFF MY GIRL!
SPRING
I...I CAN BRING YOU BACK ONTO THE PATH OF GOODNESS, YOSHIO-SAMA...!!
LET ME... BE ONE OF YOUR WOMEN, TOO...!!
HEH.
BUT YOU'RE A TEACHER, AND I'M A STUDENT...
I'VE PREPARED FOR THAT!!
LETTER OF RESIGNATION
BOOM
FOR YOU, I COULD THROW IT ALL AWAY...
HOLD ON!!
LETTER OF RESIGNATION

An Educator on the Edge

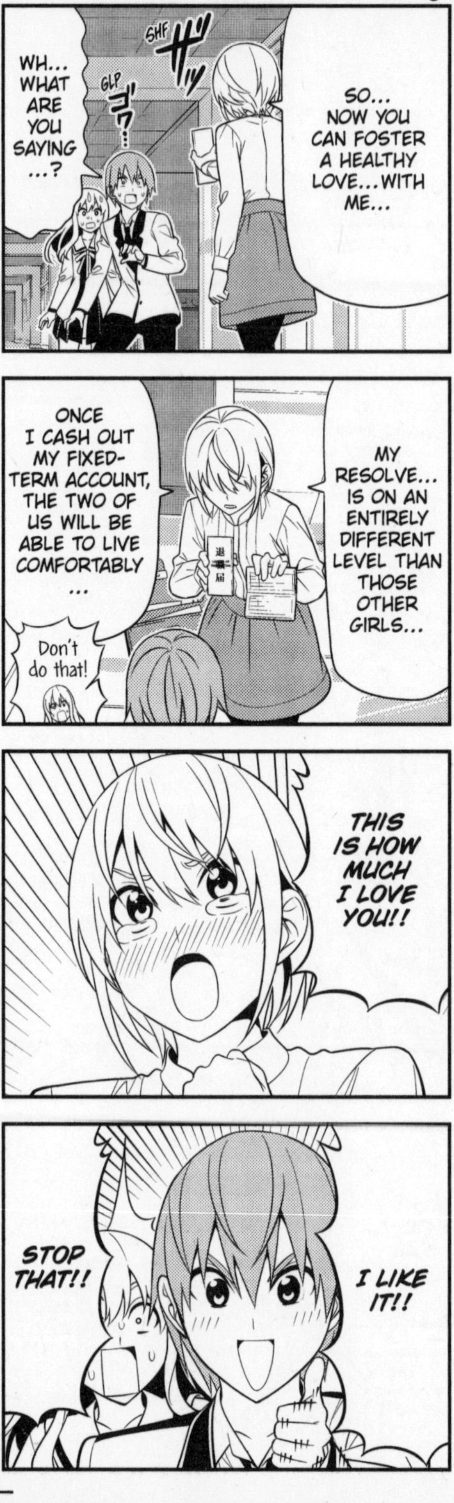
SO... NOW YOU CAN FOSTER A HEALTHY LOVE... WITH ME...
SHF
WH... WHAT ARE YOU SAYING ...?
GLP
MY RESOLVE... IS ON AN ENTIRELY DIFFERENT LEVEL THAN THOSE OTHER GIRLS...
ONCE I CASH OUT MY FIXED-TERM ACCOUNT, THE TWO OF US WILL BE ABLE TO LIVE COMFORTABLY ...
Don't do that!
THIS IS HOW MUCH I LOVE YOU!!
I LIKE IT!!
STOP THAT!!

No Way...to Earn a Living?!

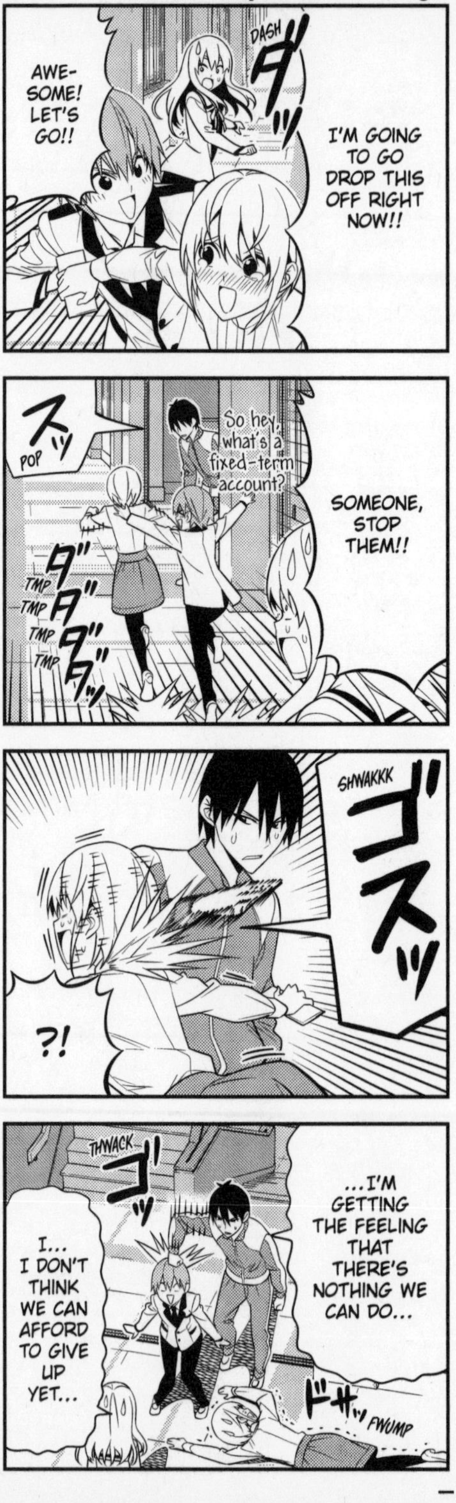
I'M GOING TO GO DROP THIS OFF RIGHT NOW!!
DASH
AWE-SOME! LET'S GO!!
SOMEONE, STOP THEM!!
So hey, what's a fixed-term account?
POP
TMP TMP TMP TMP
SHWAKKK
?!
...I'M GETTING THE FEELING THAT THERE'S NOTHING WE CAN DO...
THWACK
I... I DON'T THINK WE CAN AFFORD TO GIVE UP YET...
FWUMP

Subliminal Messaging

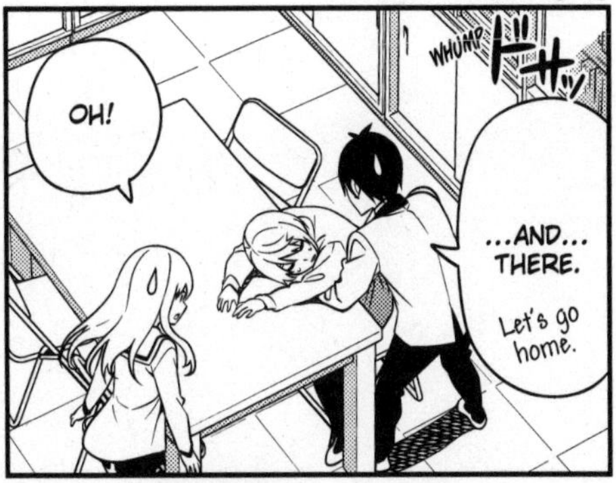
WHUMP
...AND... THERE.
Let's go home.
OH!

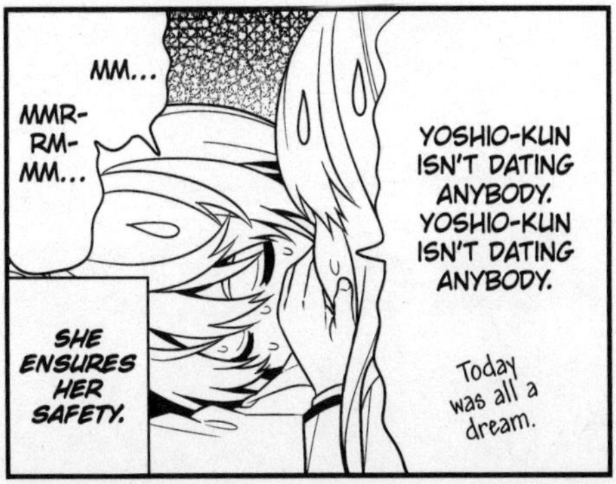
YOSHIO-KUN ISN'T DATING ANYBODY. YOSHIO-KUN ISN'T DATING ANYBODY.
Today was all a dream.
MM...
MMR-RM-MM...
SHE ENSURES HER SAFETY.

Aho-Girl

\\'ahô͵gərl\\ *Japanese, noun.*
A clueless girl.

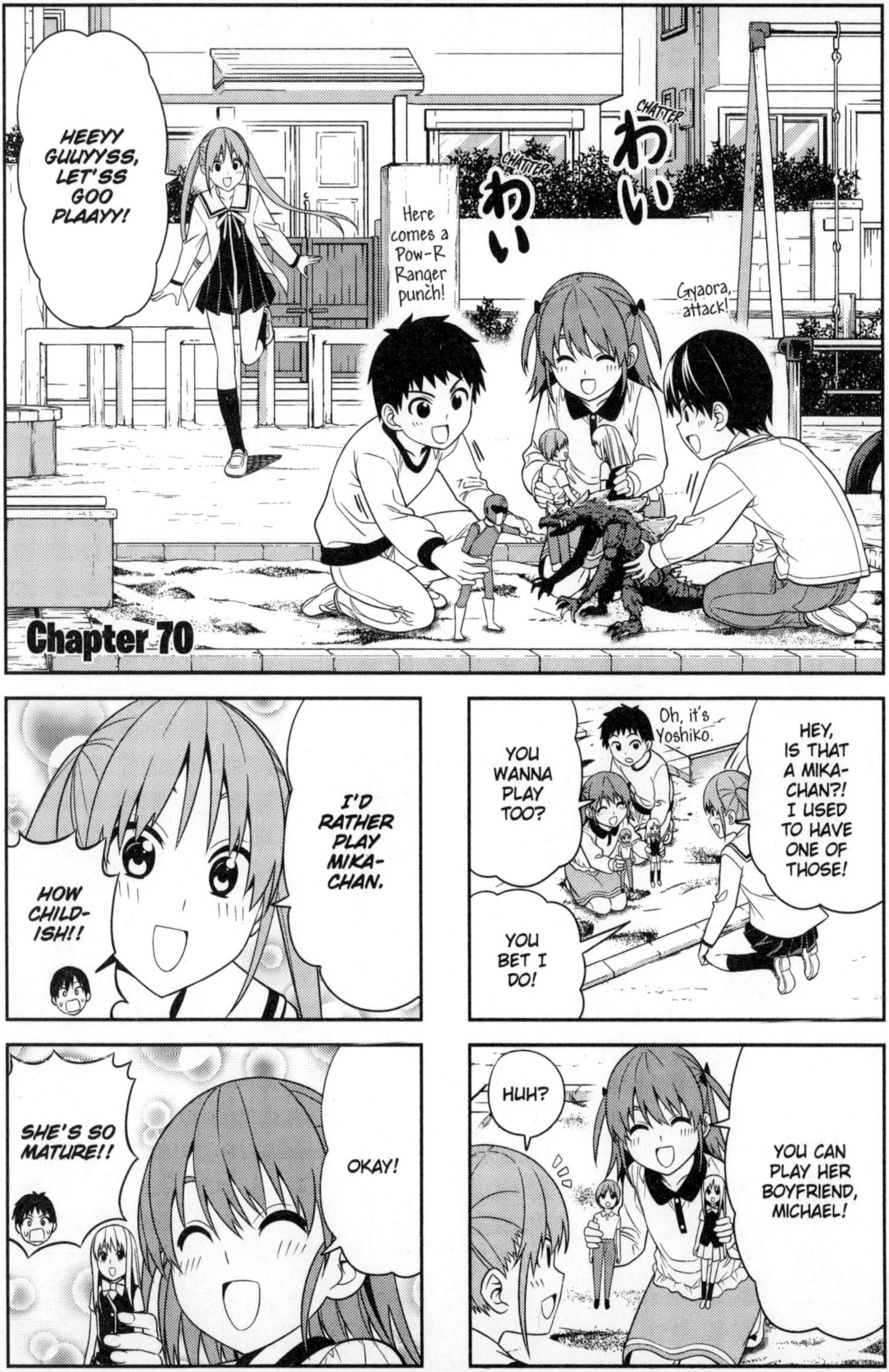
Gyaora, attack!
CHATTER
わい
CHATTER
わい
Here comes a Pow-R Ranger punch!
HEEYY GUUYYSS, LET'SS GOO PLAAYY!
Chapter 70
HEY, IS THAT A MIKA-CHAN?! I USED TO HAVE ONE OF THOSE!
Oh, it's Yoshiko.
YOU WANNA PLAY TOO?
YOU BET I DO!
I'D RATHER PLAY MIKA-CHAN.
HOW CHILD-ISH!!
YOU CAN PLAY HER BOYFRIEND, MICHAEL!
HUH?
OKAY!
SHE'S SO MATURE!!

You're the Only Thing I Want

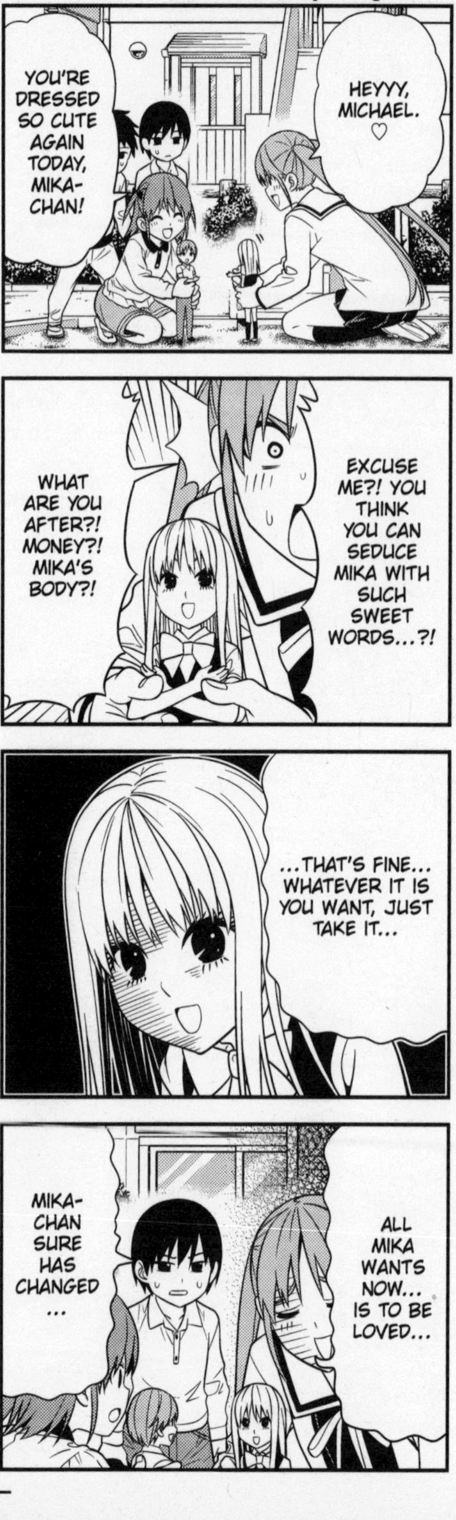
HEYYY, MICHAEL. ♡
YOU'RE DRESSED SO CUTE AGAIN TODAY, MIKA-CHAN!
EXCUSE ME?! YOU THINK YOU CAN SEDUCE MIKA WITH SUCH SWEET WORDS...?!
WHAT ARE YOU AFTER?! MONEY?! MIKA'S BODY?!
...THAT'S FINE... WHATEVER IT IS YOU WANT, JUST TAKE IT...
ALL MIKA WANTS NOW... IS TO BE LOVED...
MIKA-CHAN SURE HAS CHANGED...

He's So Big...Hearted

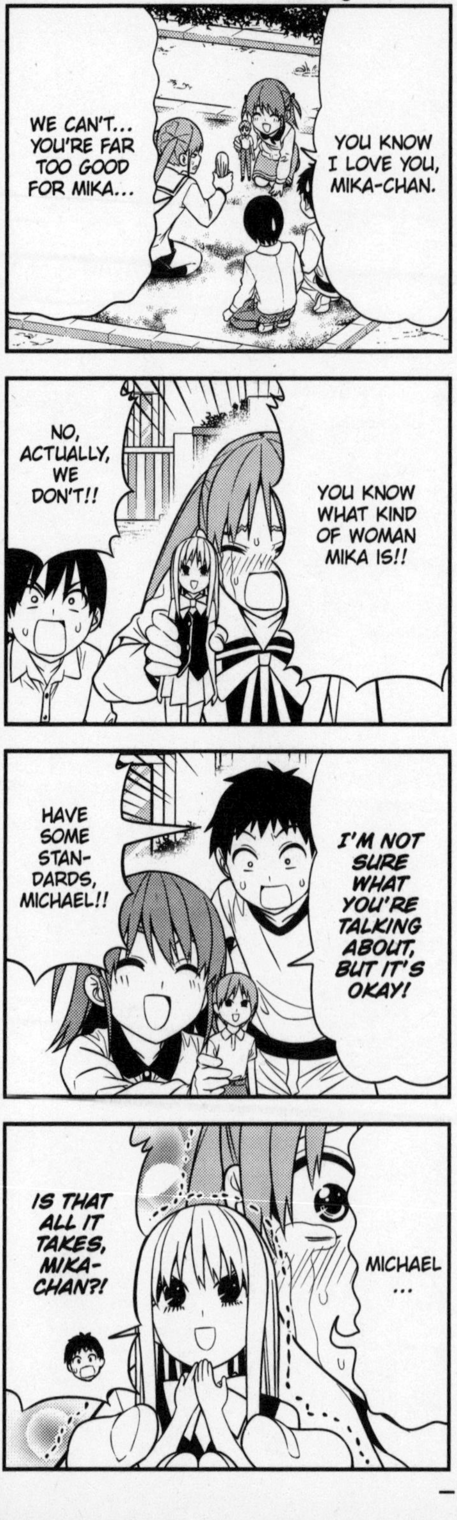
YOU KNOW I LOVE YOU, MIKA-CHAN.
WE CAN'T... YOU'RE FAR TOO GOOD FOR MIKA...
YOU KNOW WHAT KIND OF WOMAN MIKA IS!!
NO, ACTUALLY, WE DON'T!!
I'M NOT SURE WHAT YOU'RE TALKING ABOUT, BUT IT'S OKAY!
HAVE SOME STANDARDS, MICHAEL!!
MICHAEL...
IS THAT ALL IT TAKES, MIKA-CHAN?!

Out of Nowhere, a Tragedy

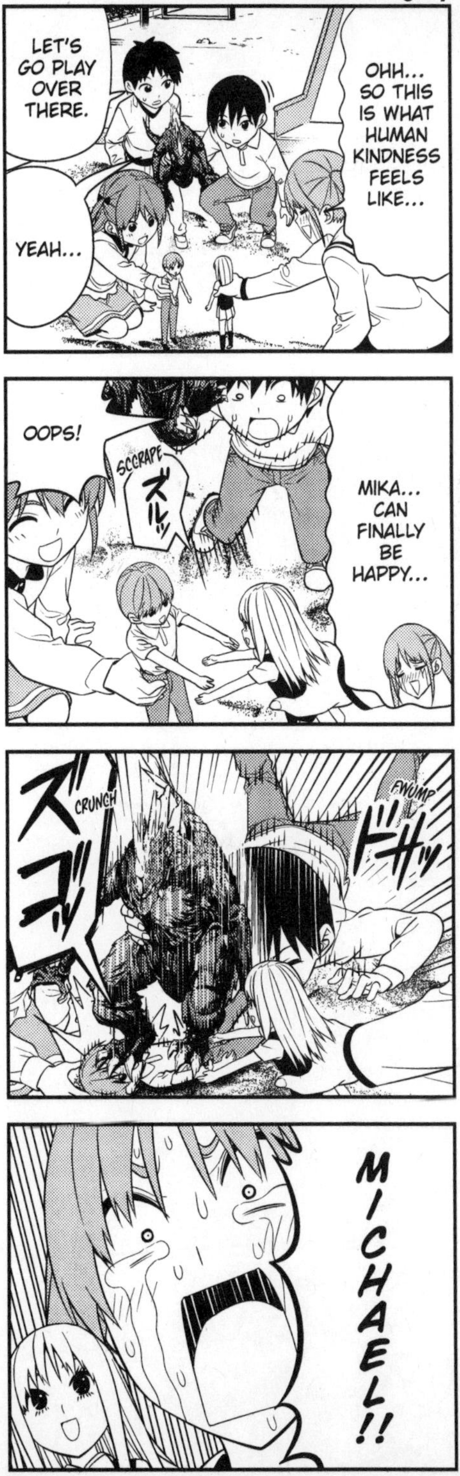
OHH... SO THIS IS WHAT HUMAN KINDNESS FEELS LIKE...
LET'S GO PLAY OVER THERE.
YEAH...
MIKA... CAN FINALLY BE HAPPY...
OOPS!
SCCRAPE ズルッ
FWUMP ドサッ
CRUNCH ズゴッ
MICHAEL!!

M...Mika-chan?!

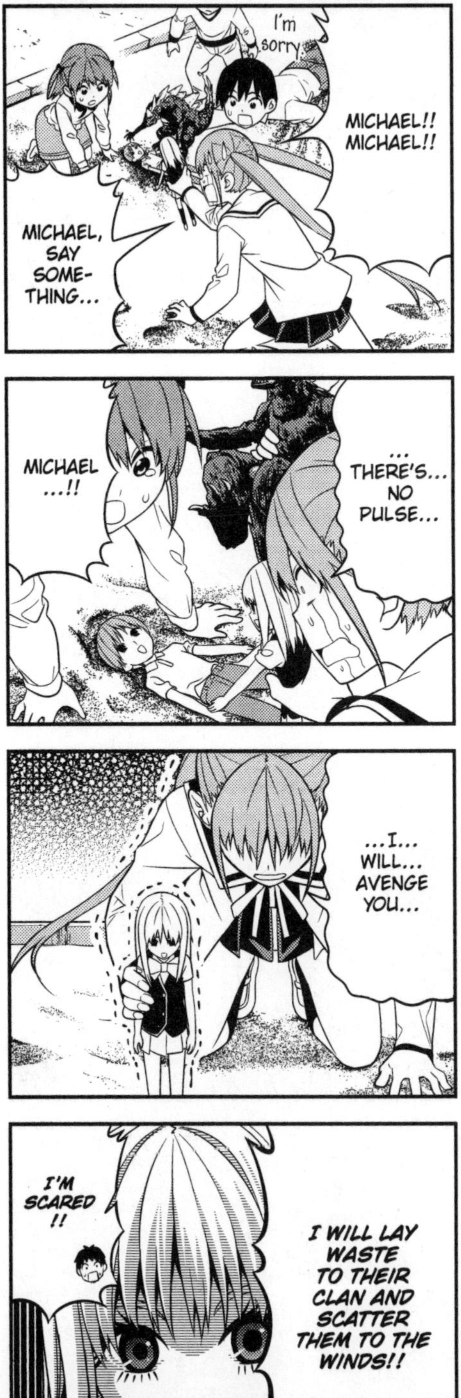
I'm sorry
MICHAEL!! MICHAEL!!
MICHAEL, SAY SOME-THING...
... THERE'S... NO PULSE...
MICHAEL ...!!
...I... WILL... AVENGE YOU...
I WILL LAY WASTE TO THEIR CLAN AND SCATTER THEM TO THE WINDS!!
I'M SCARED!!

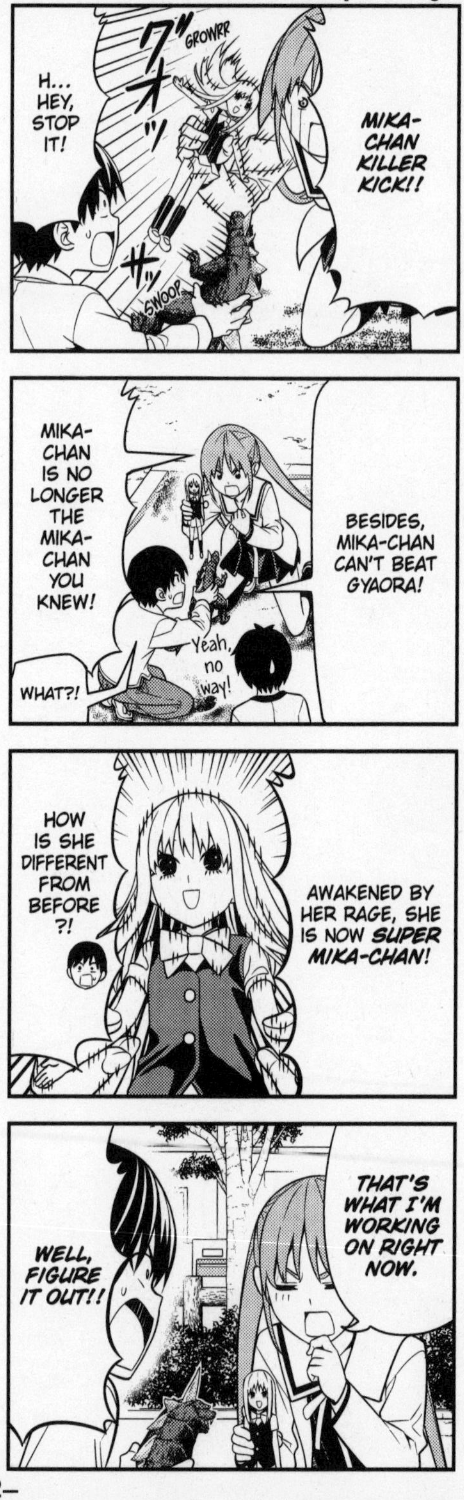
MIKA-CHAN KILLER KICK!!
GROWRR
H... HEY, STOP IT!
SWOOP
BESIDES, MIKA-CHAN CAN'T BEAT GYAORA!
MIKA-CHAN IS NO LONGER THE MIKA-CHAN YOU KNEW!
Yeah, no way!
WHAT?!
AWAKENED BY HER RAGE, SHE IS NOW SUPER MIKA-CHAN!
HOW IS SHE DIFFERENT FROM BEFORE?!
THAT'S WHAT I'M WORKING ON RIGHT NOW.
WELL, FIGURE IT OUT!!

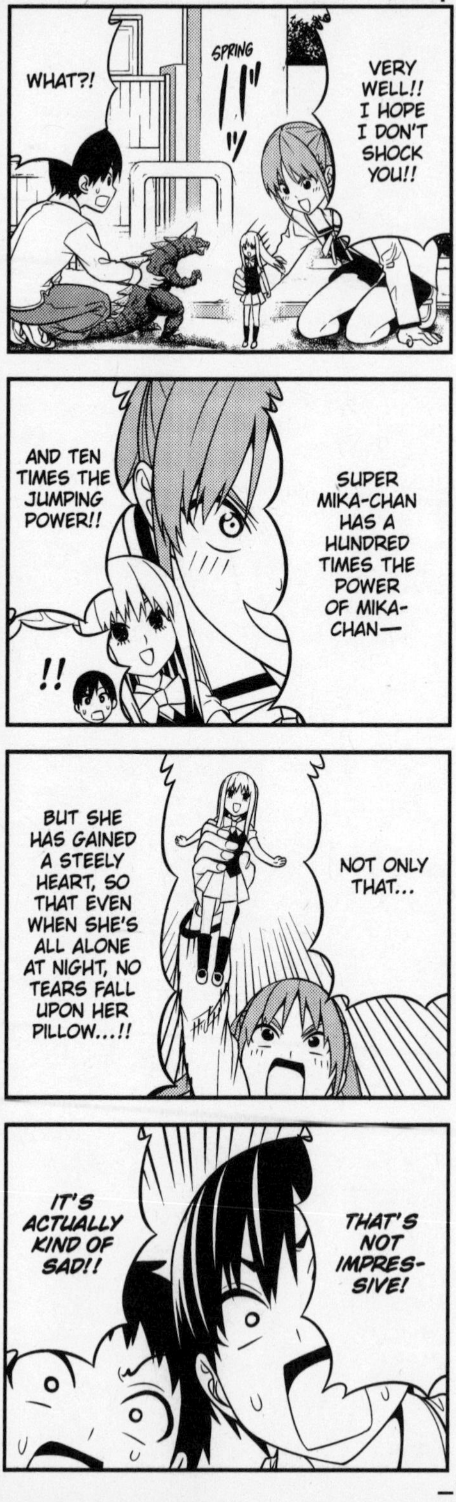
VERY WELL!! I HOPE I DON'T SHOCK YOU!!
SPRING
WHAT?!
SUPER MIKA-CHAN HAS A HUNDRED TIMES THE POWER OF MIKA-CHAN—
AND TEN TIMES THE JUMPING POWER!!
!!
NOT ONLY THAT...
BUT SHE HAS GAINED A STEELY HEART, SO THAT EVEN WHEN SHE'S ALL ALONE AT NIGHT, NO TEARS FALL UPON HER PILLOW...!!
THAT'S NOT IMPRESSIVE!
IT'S ACTUALLY KIND OF SAD!!

Damage Effect

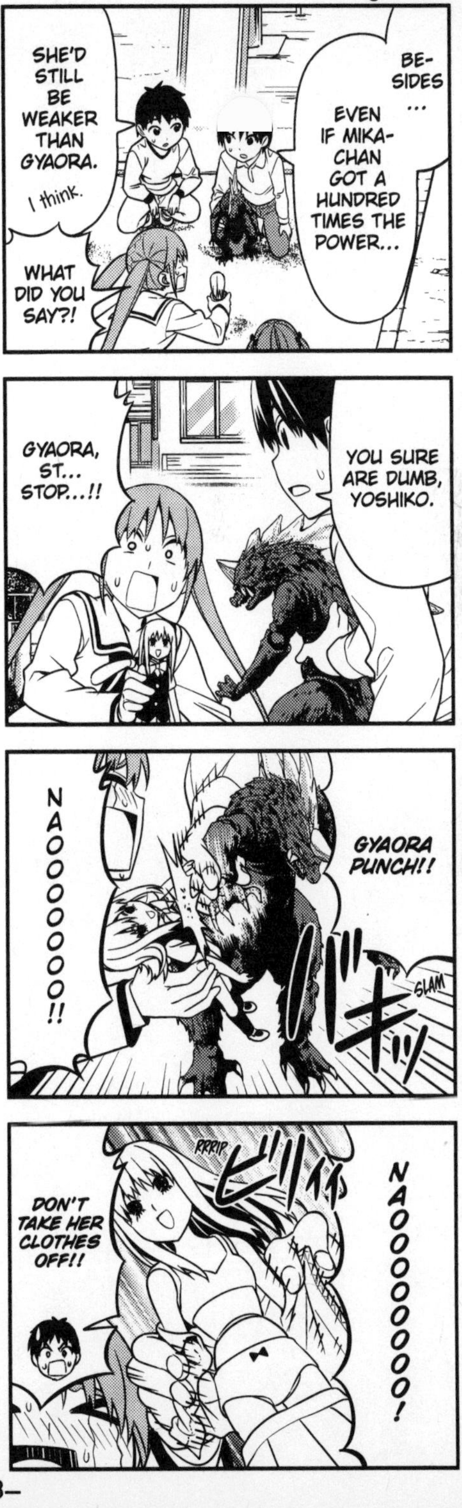
BESIDES... EVEN IF MIKA-CHAN GOT A HUNDRED TIMES THE POWER...
SHE'D STILL BE WEAKER THAN GYAORA.
I think.
WHAT DID YOU SAY?!
YOU SURE ARE DUMB, YOSHIKO.
GYAORA, ST... STOP...!!
GYAORA PUNCH!!
SLAM
NAOOOOOOOOO!!
NAOOOOOOOOOO!
RRRIP
DON'T TAKE HER CLOTHES OFF!!

A Pure Love

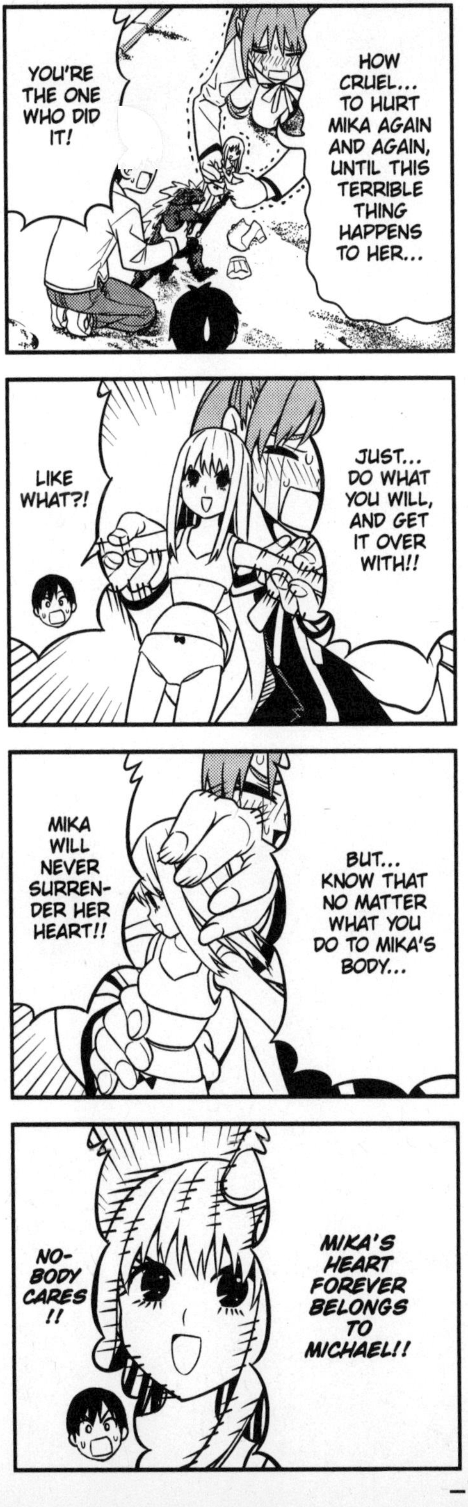
HOW CRUEL... TO HURT MIKA AGAIN AND AGAIN, UNTIL THIS TERRIBLE THING HAPPENS TO HER...
YOU'RE THE ONE WHO DID IT!
JUST... DO WHAT YOU WILL, AND GET IT OVER WITH!!
LIKE WHAT?!
BUT... KNOW THAT NO MATTER WHAT YOU DO TO MIKA'S BODY...
MIKA WILL NEVER SURRENDER HER HEART!!
MIKA'S HEART FOREVER BELONGS TO MICHAEL!!
NOBODY CARES!!

He Is BACK

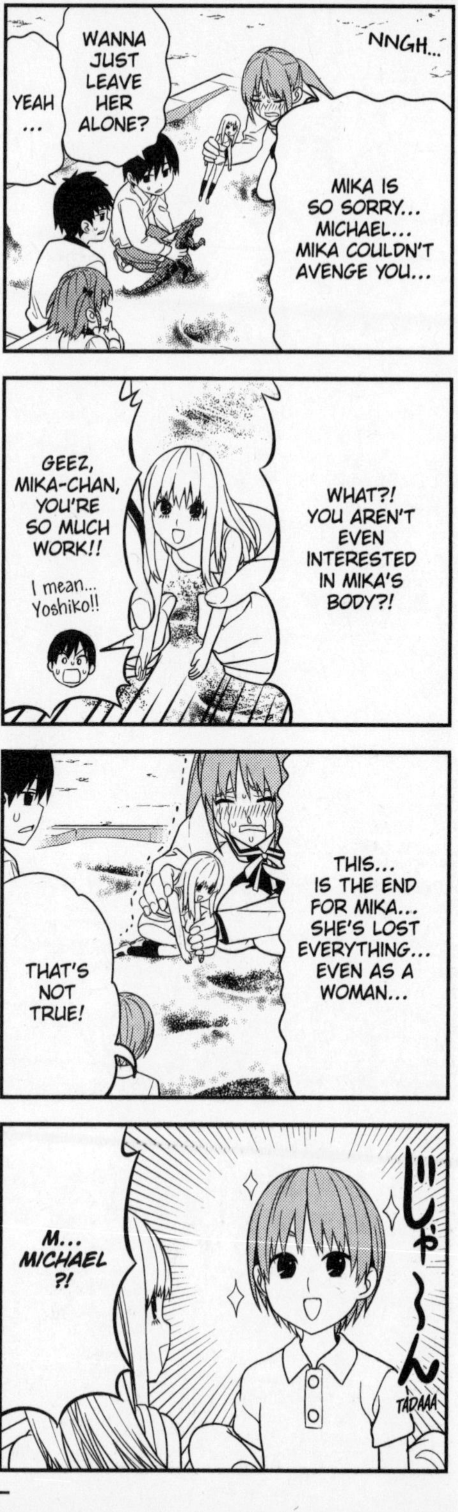
NNGH...
MIKA IS SO SORRY... MICHAEL... MIKA COULDN'T AVENGE YOU...
WANNA JUST LEAVE HER ALONE?
YEAH ...
WHAT?! YOU AREN'T EVEN INTERESTED IN MIKA'S BODY?!
GEEZ, MIKA-CHAN, YOU'RE SO MUCH WORK!!
I mean... Yoshiko!!
THIS... IS THE END FOR MIKA... SHE'S LOST EVERYTHING... EVEN AS A WOMAN...
THAT'S NOT TRUE!
じゃ～ん
TADAAA
M... MICHAEL ?!

Miracle of Love

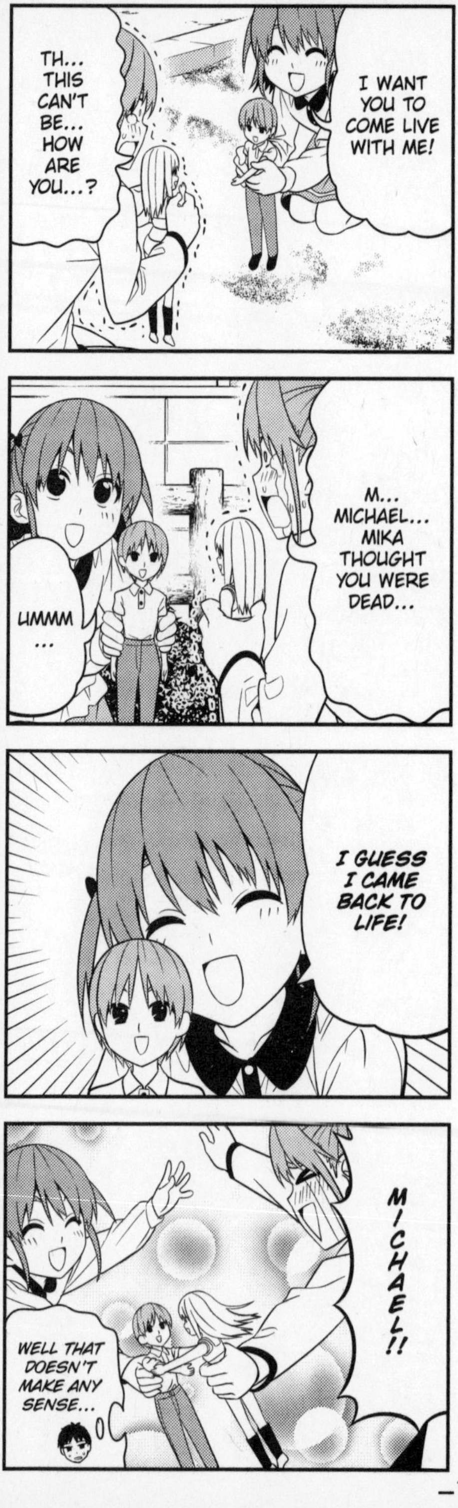
I WANT YOU TO COME LIVE WITH ME!
TH... THIS CAN'T BE... HOW ARE YOU...?
M... MICHAEL... MIKA THOUGHT YOU WERE DEAD...
UMMM ...
I GUESS I CAME BACK TO LIFE!
MICHAEL!!
WELL THAT DOESN'T MAKE ANY SENSE...

Happy Ending

MICHAEL
...
MIKA-
CHAN...
SMOOCH
ちゅっ

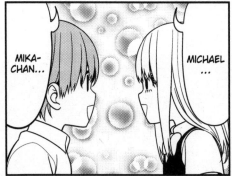

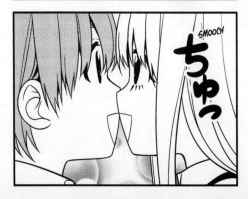

(The Giants, the Great Bird, and)

Aho-Girl

\'ahô͵gərl\ *Japanese, noun*.

A clueless girl.

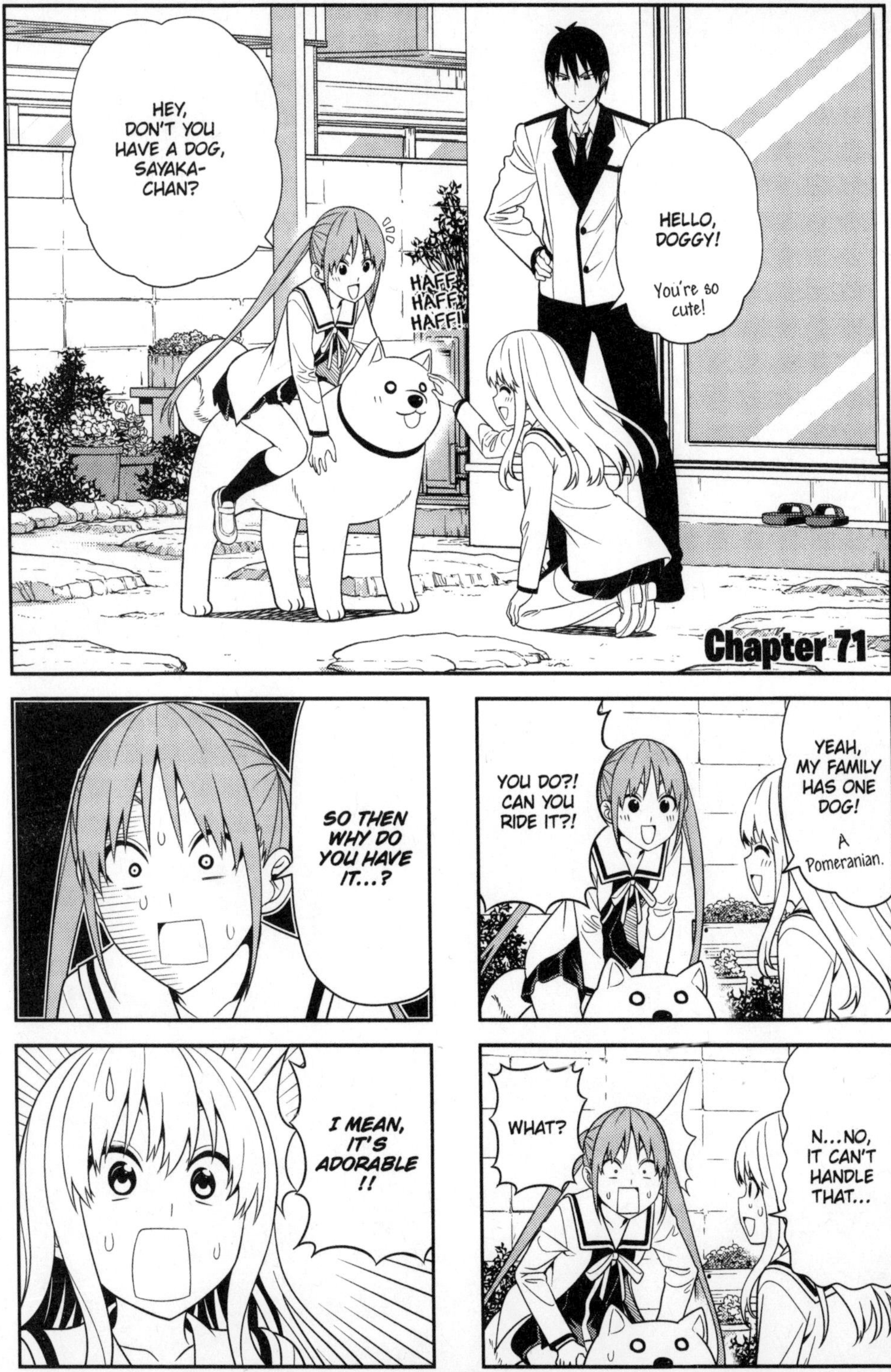
HELLO, DOGGY!
You're so cute!
HAFF HAFF HAFF!!
HEY, DON'T YOU HAVE A DOG, SAYAKA-CHAN?
Chapter 71
YEAH, MY FAMILY HAS ONE DOG!
A Pomeranian.
YOU DO?! CAN YOU RIDE IT?!
SO THEN WHY DO YOU HAVE IT...?
N...NO, IT CAN'T HANDLE THAT...
WHAT?
I MEAN, IT'S ADORABLE !!

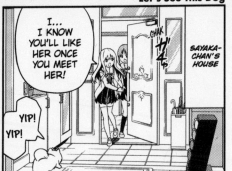

Akkun's Read on the Dog

CUTE? IS THAT ALL?
IT...IT'S REALLY SOOTHING!
BUT MY DOG IS CUTE, AND I CAN RIDE HIM, AND HE'S STRONG AND SMART.
DO YOU UNDERSTAND ANYTHING?
ALL OTHER DOGS ARE A WASTE OF TIME COMPARED TO THIS GUY.
HEY!!
YOU HAVE A POINT...
MY DOG IS VERY SOOTHING!!

Let's See This Dog

SAYAKA-CHAN'S HOUSE
CHAK
I... I KNOW YOU'LL LIKE HER ONCE YOU MEET HER!
YIP! YIP!
SAY HELLO, POMÉ-CHAN!
HIFF HIFF!
POMÉ-CHAN!!
WIIIII?
ISN'T SHE ADORABLE?!
...SHE LOOKS SO WEAK...
I SAID, ISN'T SHE ADORABLE?!

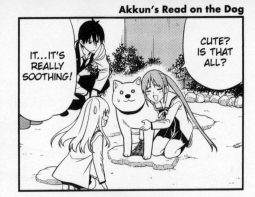

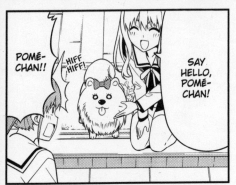

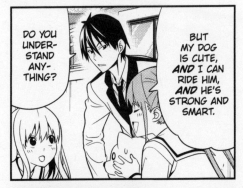

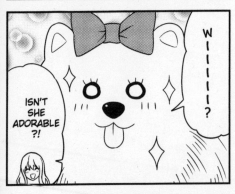

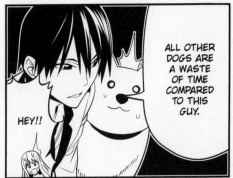

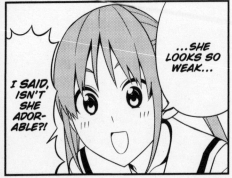

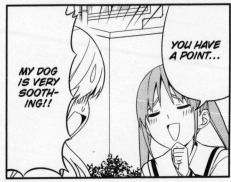

Love at First Sight

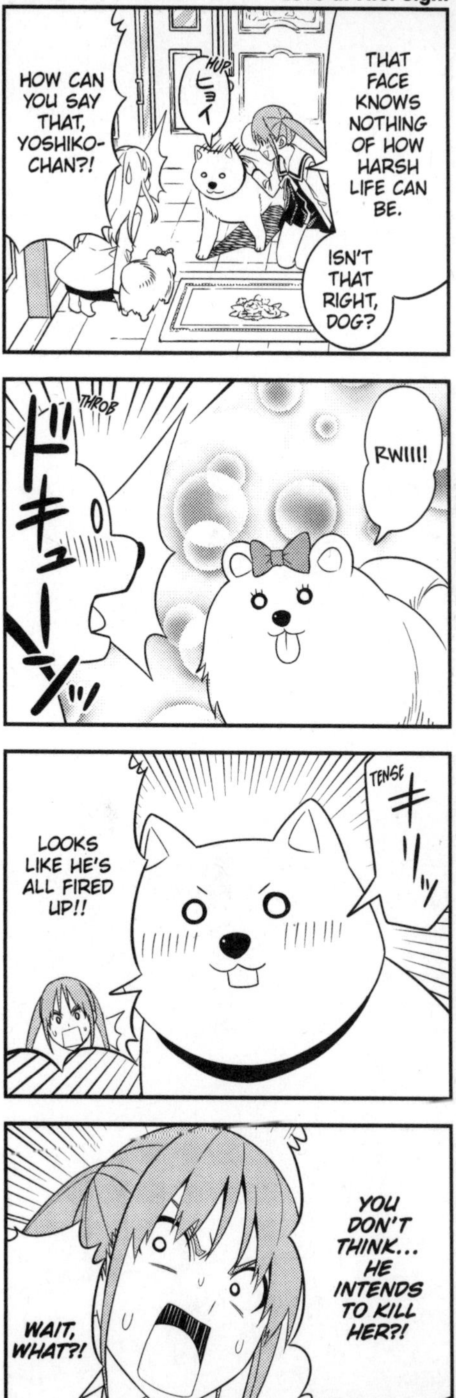
THAT FACE KNOWS NOTHING OF HOW HARSH LIFE CAN BE.
HUP ヒョイ
HOW CAN YOU SAY THAT, YOSHIKO-CHAN?!
ISN'T THAT RIGHT, DOG?
RWIII!
THROB ドキューンッ
TENSE キリッ
LOOKS LIKE HE'S ALL FIRED UP!!
YOU DON'T THINK... HE INTENDS TO KILL HER?!
WAIT, WHAT?!

Flinch

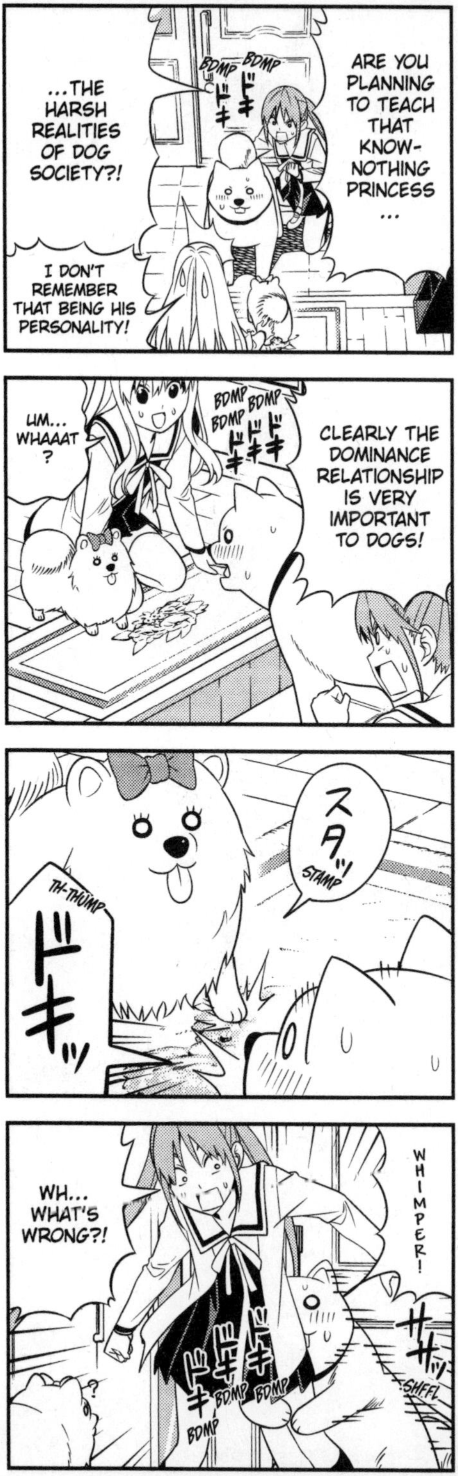
ARE YOU PLANNING TO TEACH THAT KNOW-NOTHING PRINCESS...
BDMP BDMP ドキドキ
...THE HARSH REALITIES OF DOG SOCIETY?!
I DON'T REMEMBER THAT BEING HIS PERSONALITY!
CLEARLY THE DOMINANCE RELATIONSHIP IS VERY IMPORTANT TO DOGS!
BDMP BDMP BDMP ドキドキドキ
UM... WHAAAT?
スタッ STAMP
TH-THUMP ドキッ
WHIMPER!
サッ SHFFL
ドキドキドキ BDMP BDMP BDMP
WH... WHAT'S WRONG?!

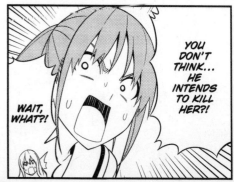

Love Can't Be Stopped

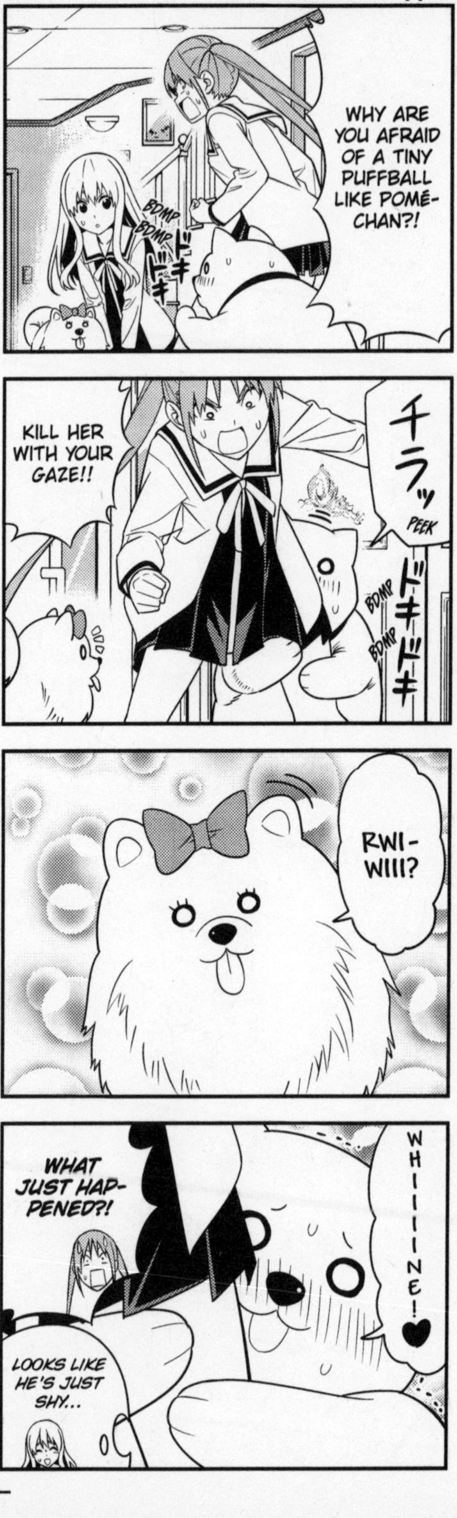
WHY ARE YOU AFRAID OF A TINY PUFFBALL LIKE POMÉ-CHAN?!
BDMP BDMP ドキドキ
KILL HER WITH YOUR GAZE!!
チラッ PEEK
ドキドキ BDMP BDMP
RWI-WIII?
WHIIIINE!♥
WHAT JUST HAP-PENED?!
LOOKS LIKE HE'S JUST SHY...

Misread

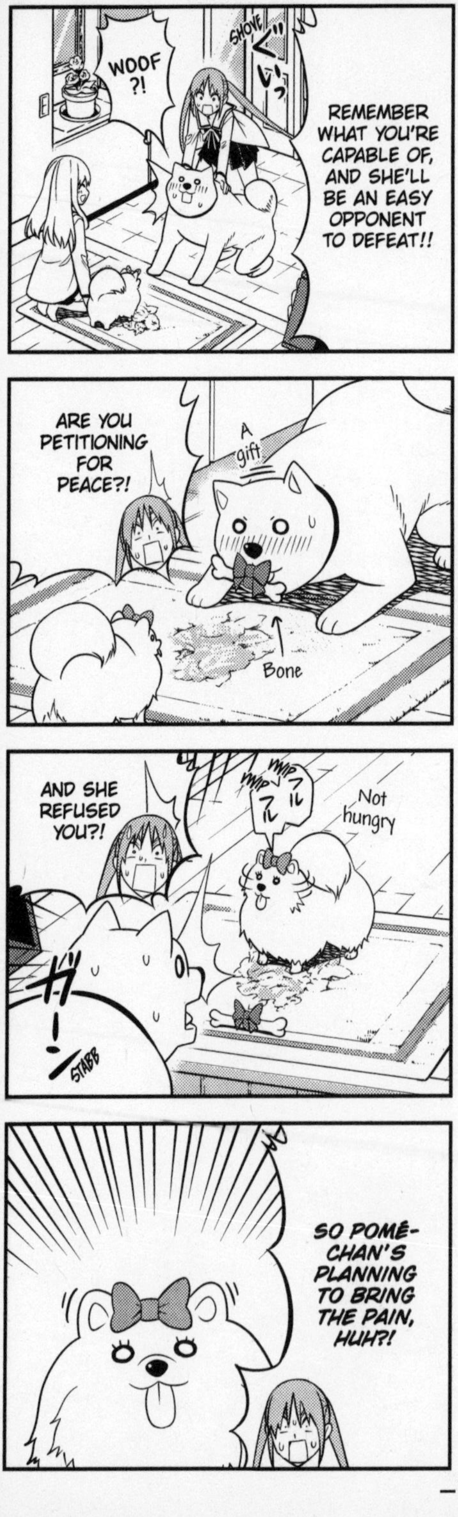
REMEMBER WHAT YOU'RE CAPABLE OF, AND SHE'LL BE AN EASY OPPONENT TO DEFEAT!!
SHOVE ぐいっ
WOOF?!
A gift
ARE YOU PETITIONING FOR PEACE?!
Bone
Not hungry
WHIP WHIP フルフル
AND SHE REFUSED YOU?!
ガーン STABB
SO POMÉ-CHAN'S PLANNING TO BRING THE PAIN, HUH?!

Communication

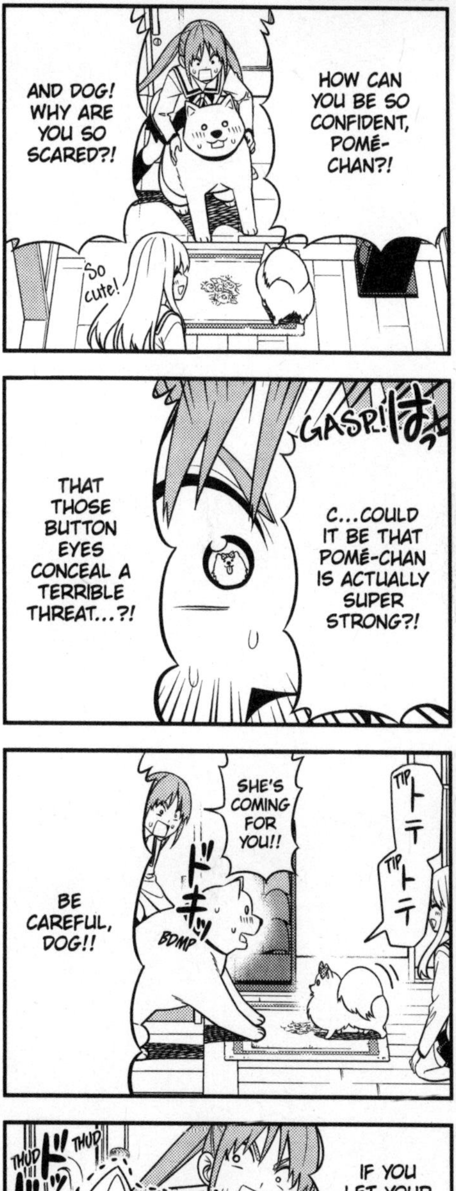
HOW CAN YOU BE SO CONFIDENT, POMÉ-CHAN?!
AND DOG! WHY ARE YOU SO SCARED?!
So cute!
GASP!! はっ
C...COULD IT BE THAT POMÉ-CHAN IS ACTUALLY SUPER STRONG?!
THAT THOSE BUTTON EYES CONCEAL A TERRIBLE THREAT...?!
TIP トテ
TIP トテ
SHE'S COMING FOR YOU!!
ドキッ BDMP
BE CAREFUL, DOG!!
IF YOU LET YOUR GUARD DOWN, SHE'LL MURDER YOU!!
ドッ THUD
ドッ THUD
ドッ THUD
ドッ THUD
ドッ THUD
ドッ
じ～… STAAARE

Breakdown

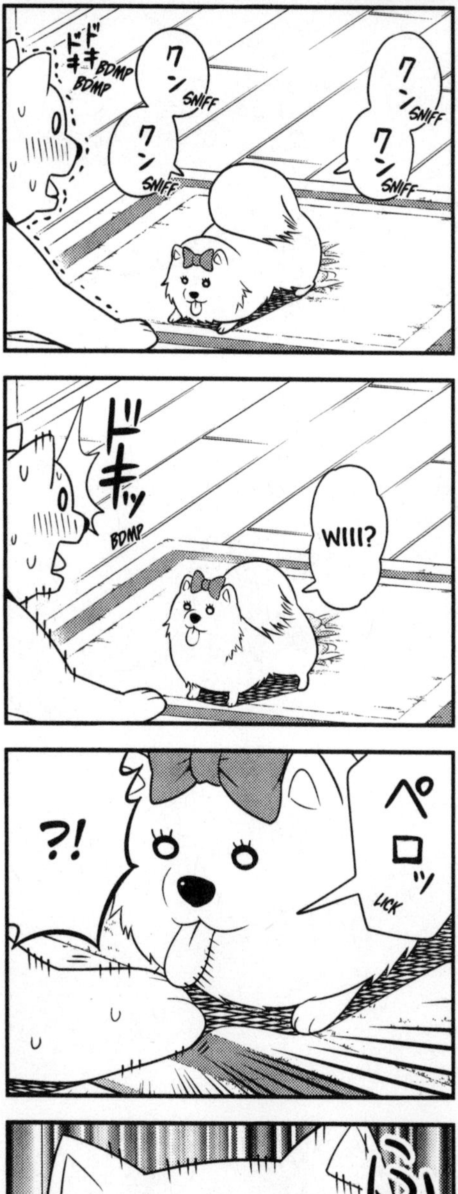
ワン SNIFF ワン SNIFF
ワン SNIFF ワン SNIFF
ドキ ドキ BDMP BDMP
WIII?
ドキッ BDMP
ペロッ LICK
?!
ふにゃ～ん MELLLLT

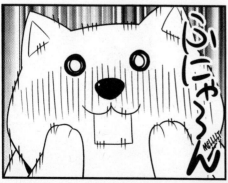

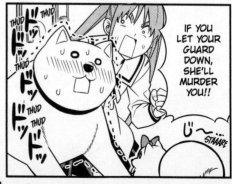

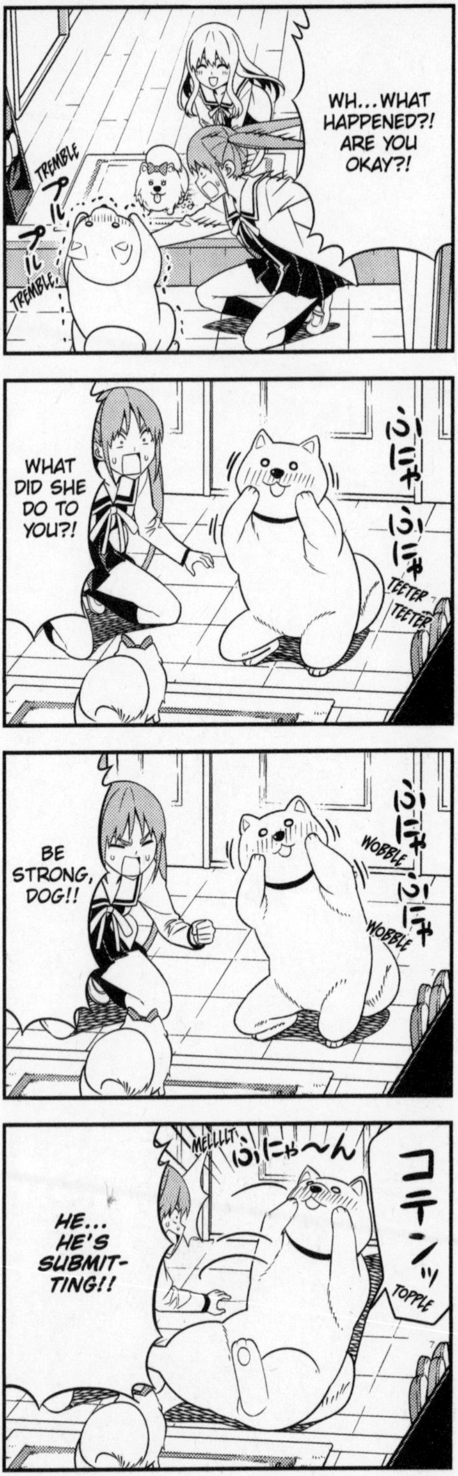
WH...WHAT HAPPENED?! ARE YOU OKAY?!
TREMBLE
プル
プル
TREMBLE
ふにゃ
ふにゃ
TEETER
TEETER
WHAT DID SHE DO TO YOU?!
ふにゃ
WOBBLE
ふにゃ
WOBBLE
BE STRONG, DOG!!
コテンッ
TOPPLE
ふにゃ〜ん
MELLLLT
HE... HE'S SUBMITTING!!

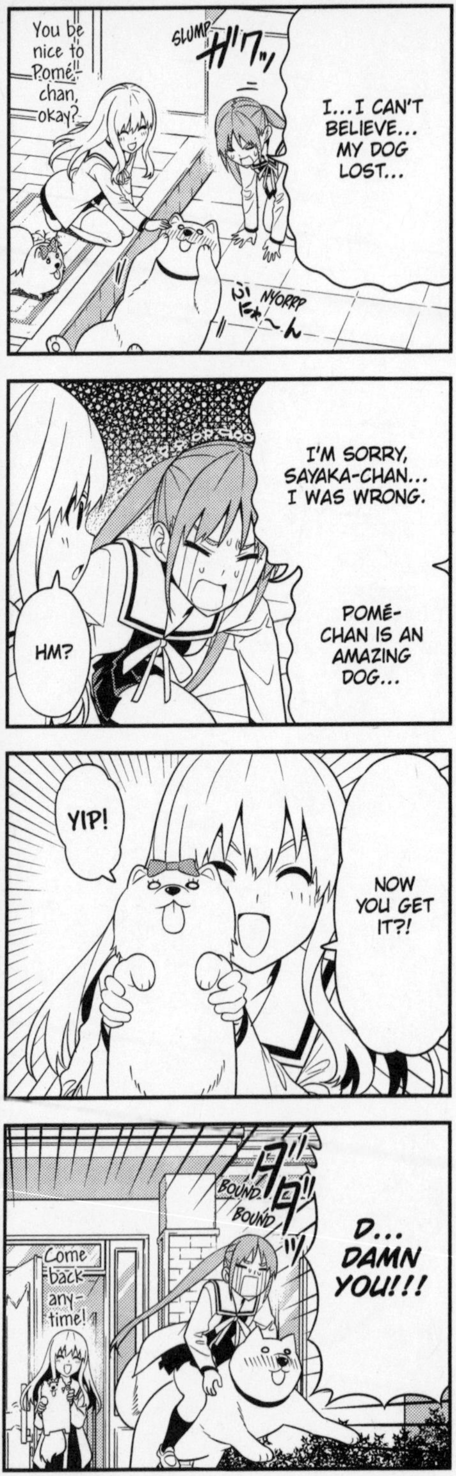
I...I CAN'T BELIEVE... MY DOG LOST...
SLUMP
ガクッ
You be nice to Pomé-chan, okay?
NYORRP
ふにゃ〜ん
I'M SORRY, SAYAKA-CHAN... I WAS WRONG.
POMÉ-CHAN IS AN AMAZING DOG...
HM?
NOW YOU GET IT?!
YIP!
D... DAMN YOU!!!
ダダッ
BOUND
BOUND
Come back any-time!

Akkun Is Shocked, Too

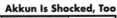

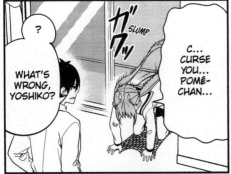

C... CURSE YOU... POMÉ-CHAN...
SLUMP
?
WHAT'S WRONG, YOSHIKO?
DOG... WAS DEFEAT-ED...
TH... THAT'S NOT POSSI-BLE...!!
What dog could have managed that...?!

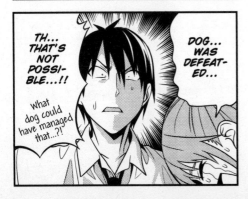

Aho-Girl

\\'ahô͵gərl\\ *Japanese, noun.*
A clueless girl.

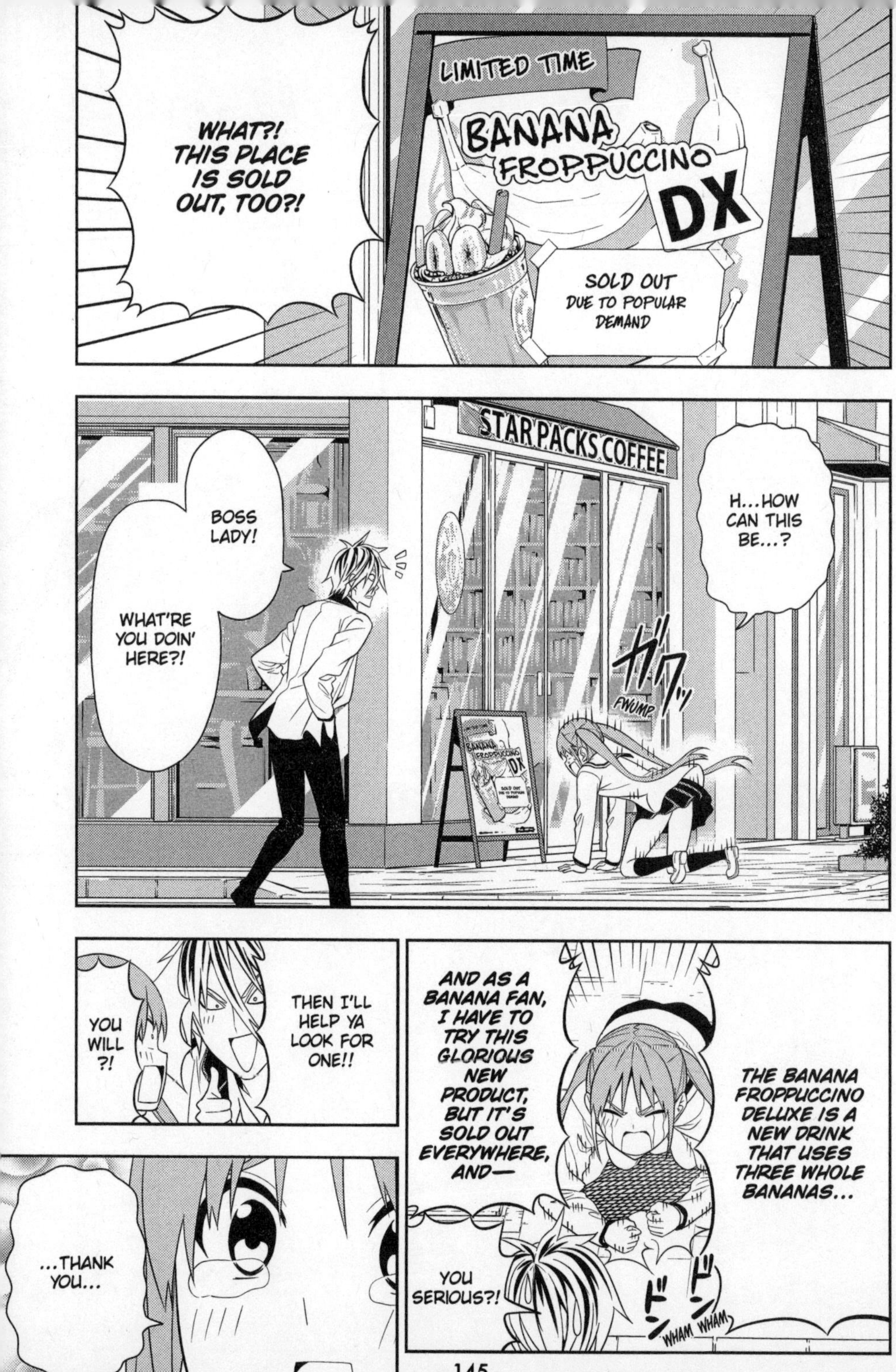
LIMITED TIME
BANANA FROPPUCCINO
DX
SOLD OUT DUE TO POPULAR DEMAND
WHAT?! THIS PLACE IS SOLD OUT, TOO?!
H...HOW CAN THIS BE...?
FWUMP
BOSS LADY!
WHAT'RE YOU DOIN' HERE?!
THE BANANA FROPPUCCINO DELUXE IS A NEW DRINK THAT USES THREE WHOLE BANANAS...
AND AS A BANANA FAN, I HAVE TO TRY THIS GLORIOUS NEW PRODUCT, BUT IT'S SOLD OUT EVERYWHERE, AND—
YOU SERIOUS?!
WHAM WHAM
THEN I'LL HELP YA LOOK FOR ONE!!
YOU WILL ?!
...THANK YOU...

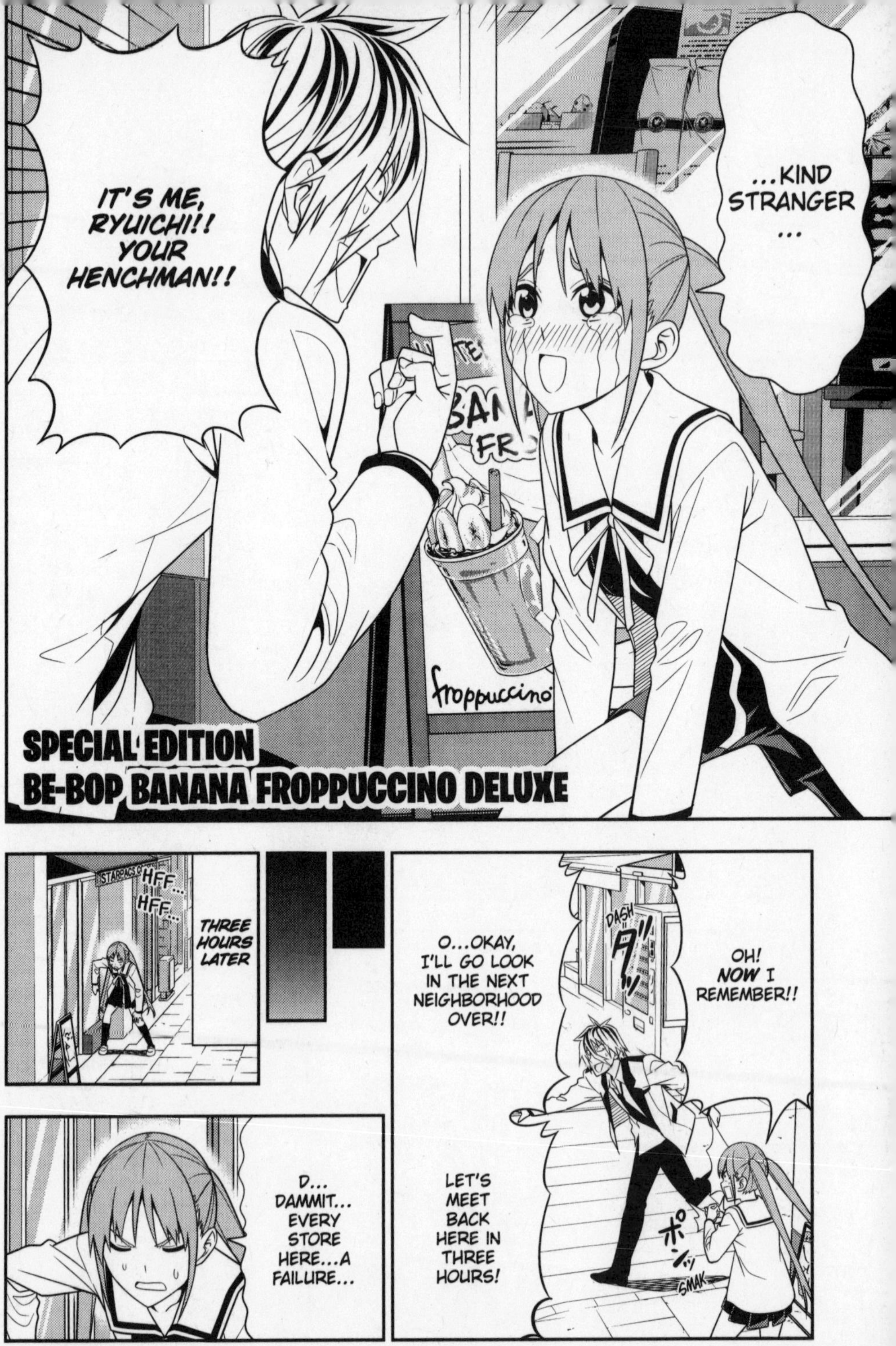
...KIND STRANGER ...
IT'S ME, RYUICHI!! YOUR HENCHMAN!!
froppuccino
SPECIAL EDITION
BE-BOP BANANA FROPPUCCINO DELUXE
OH! NOW I REMEMBER!!
DASH
O...OKAY, I'LL GO LOOK IN THE NEXT NEIGHBORHOOD OVER!!
LET'S MEET BACK HERE IN THREE HOURS!
SMAK
THREE HOURS LATER
HFF... HFF...
D... DAMMIT... EVERY STORE HERE...A FAILURE...

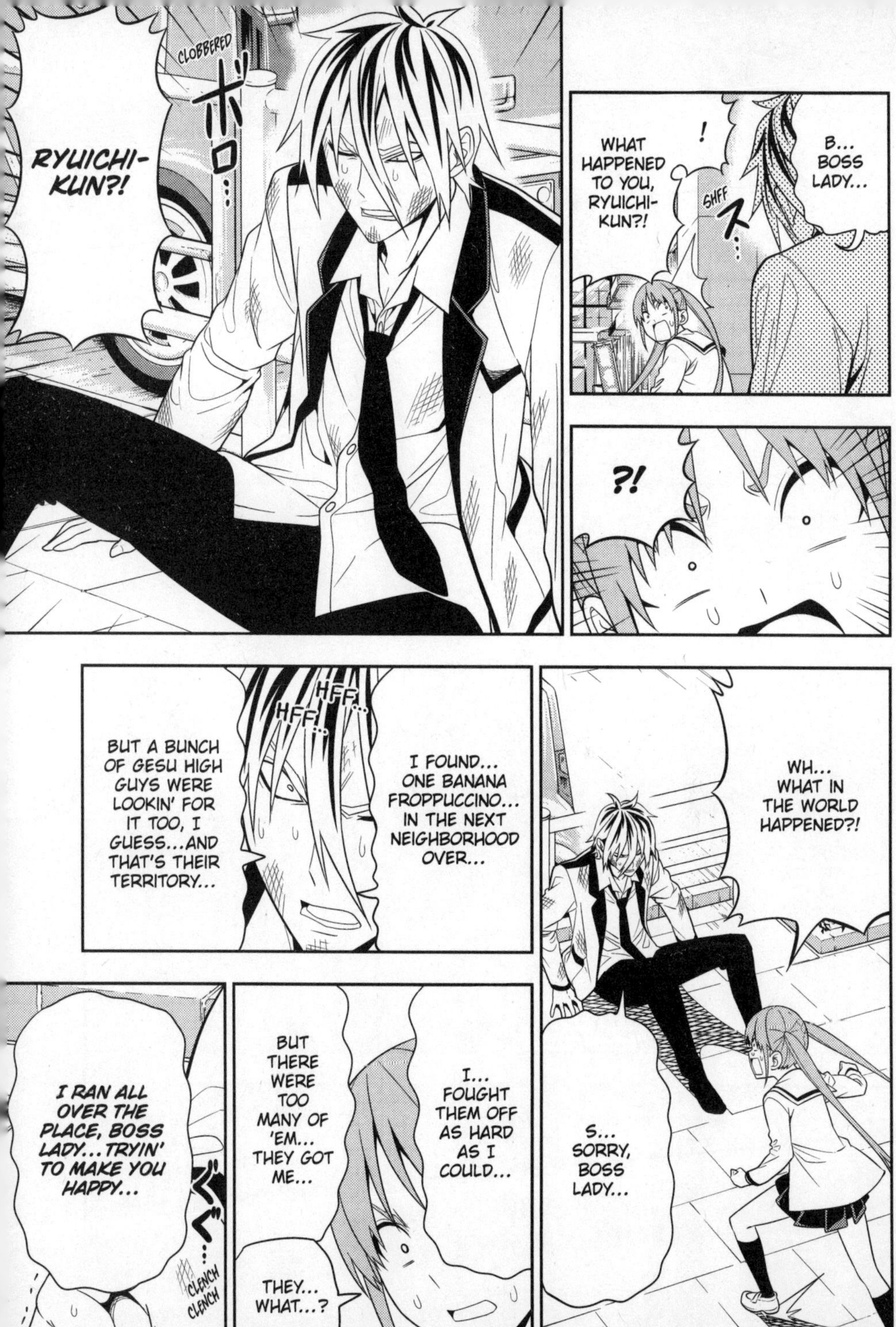
B... BOSS LADY...
!
SHFF
WHAT HAPPENED TO YOU, RYUICHI-KUN?!
?!
CLOBBERED
RYUICHI-KUN?!
WH... WHAT IN THE WORLD HAPPENED?!
S... SORRY, BOSS LADY...
HFF... HFF...
I FOUND... ONE BANANA FROPPUCCINO... IN THE NEXT NEIGHBORHOOD OVER...
BUT A BUNCH OF GESU HIGH GUYS WERE LOOKIN' FOR IT TOO, I GUESS...AND THAT'S THEIR TERRITORY...
I... FOUGHT THEM OFF AS HARD AS I COULD...
BUT THERE WERE TOO MANY OF 'EM... THEY GOT ME...
THEY... WHAT...?
I RAN ALL OVER THE PLACE, BOSS LADY...TRYIN' TO MAKE YOU HAPPY...
CLENCH CLENCH

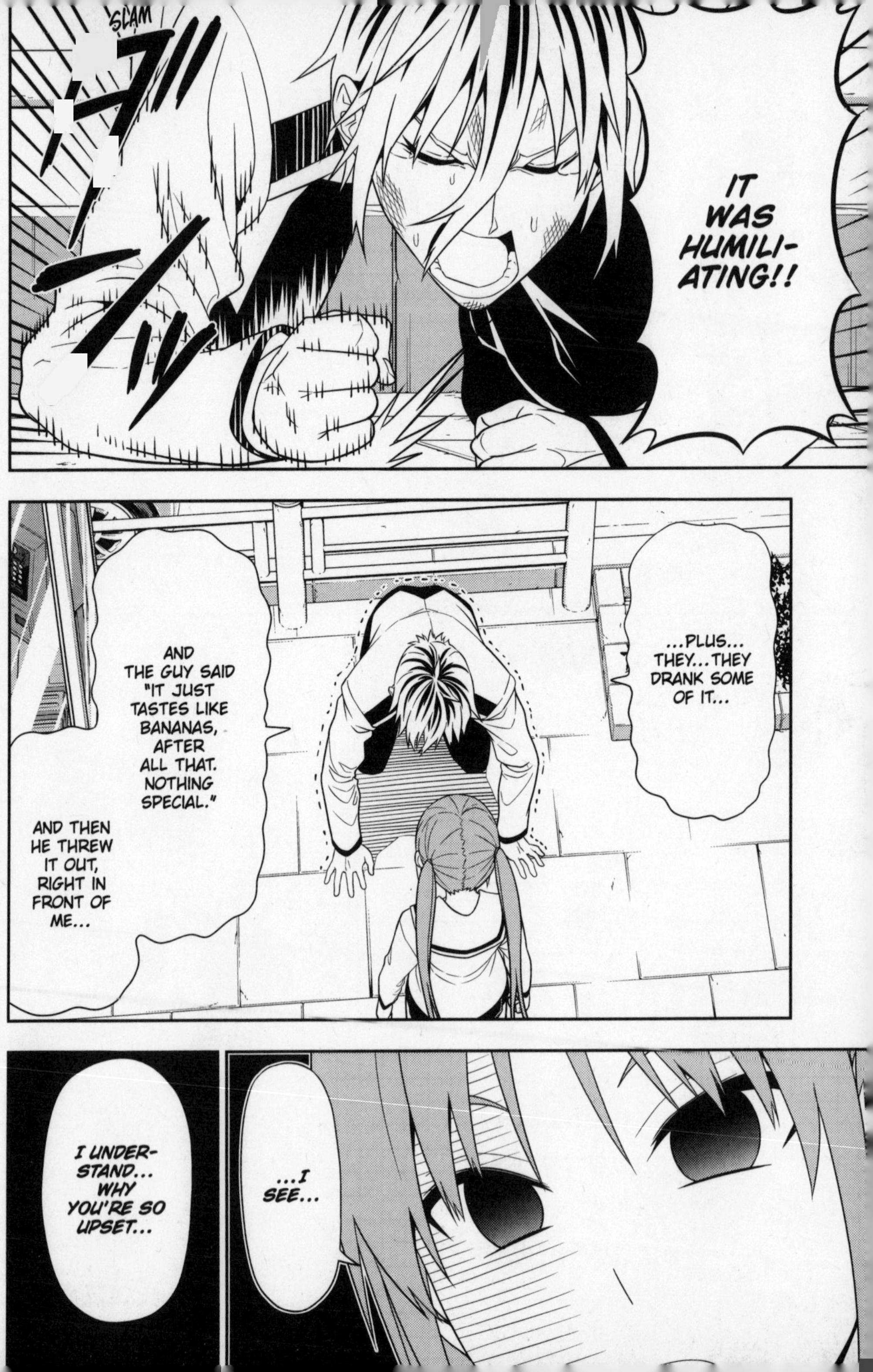
IT WAS HUMILI-ATING!!
SLAM
...PLUS... THEY...THEY DRANK SOME OF IT...
AND THE GUY SAID "IT JUST TASTES LIKE BANANAS, AFTER ALL THAT. NOTHING SPECIAL."
AND THEN HE THREW IT OUT, RIGHT IN FRONT OF ME...
...I SEE...
I UNDER-STAND... WHY YOU'RE SO UPSET...

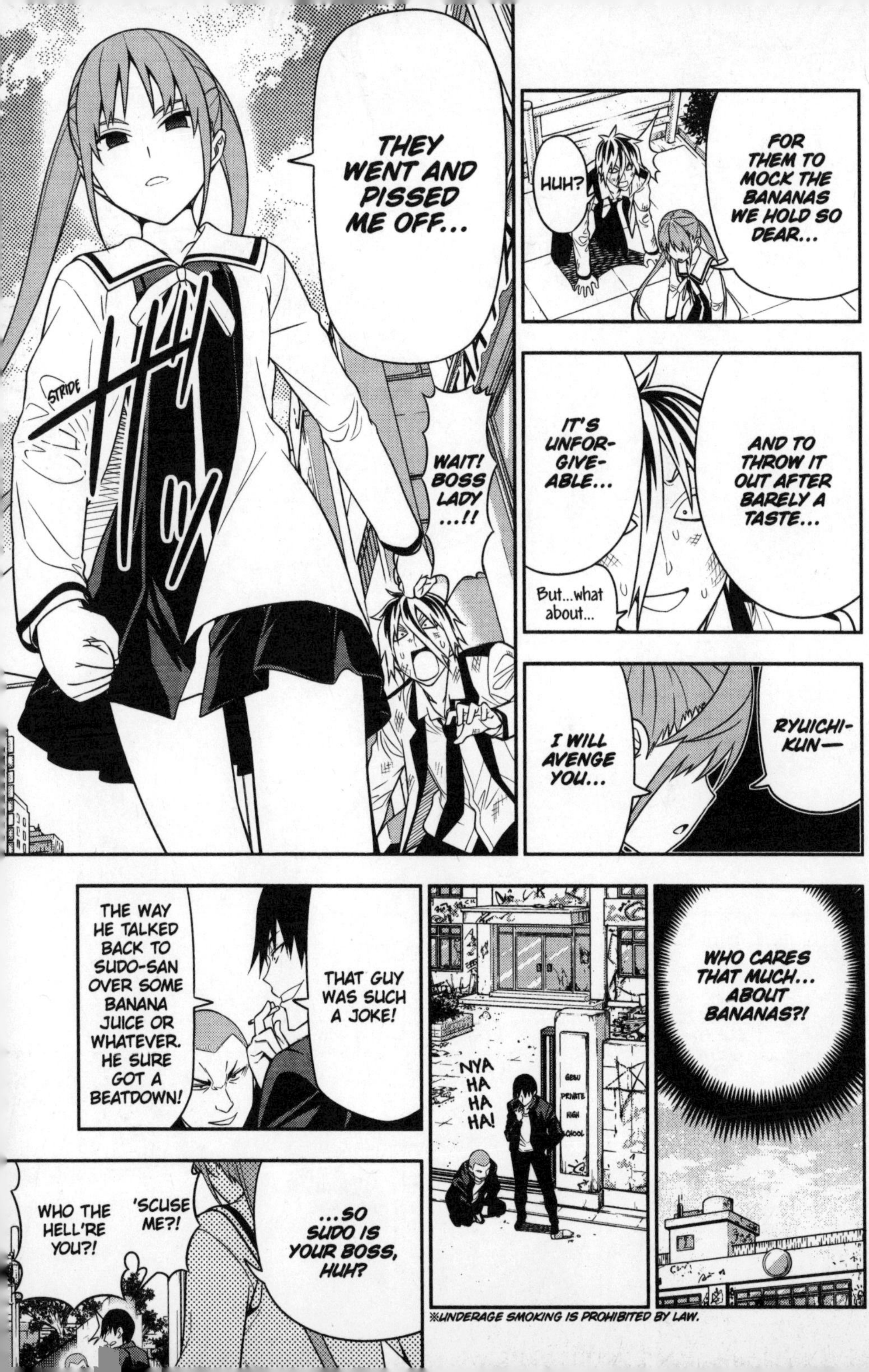
FOR THEM TO MOCK THE BANANAS WE HOLD SO DEAR...
HUH?
AND TO THROW IT OUT AFTER BARELY A TASTE...
IT'S UNFORGIVE-ABLE...
But...what about...
RYUICHI-KUN—
I WILL AVENGE YOU...
THEY WENT AND PISSED ME OFF...
WAIT! BOSS LADY ...!!
STRIDE
WHO CARES THAT MUCH... ABOUT BANANAS?!
GEBU PRIVATE HIGH SCHOOL
NYA HA HA HA HA!
THAT GUY WAS SUCH A JOKE!
THE WAY HE TALKED BACK TO SUDO-SAN OVER SOME BANANA JUICE OR WHATEVER. HE SURE GOT A BEATDOWN!
...SO SUDO IS YOUR BOSS, HUH?
'SCUSE ME?!
WHO THE HELL'RE YOU?!
※UNDERAGE SMOKING IS PROHIBITED BY LAW.

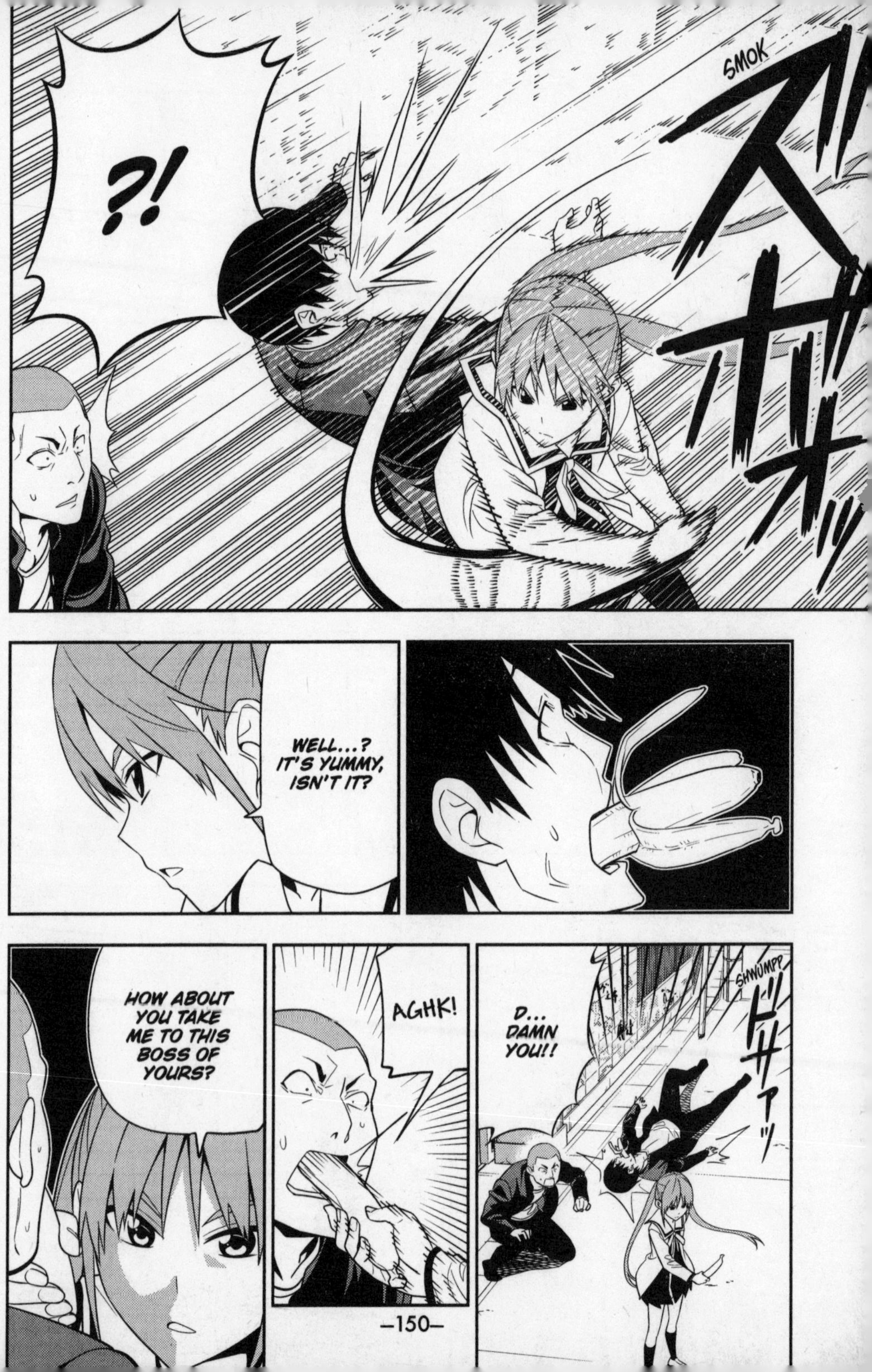
SMOK
?!
WELL...? IT'S YUMMY, ISN'T IT?
SHWUMPP
D... DAMN YOU!!
AGHK!
HOW ABOUT YOU TAKE ME TO THIS BOSS OF YOURS?

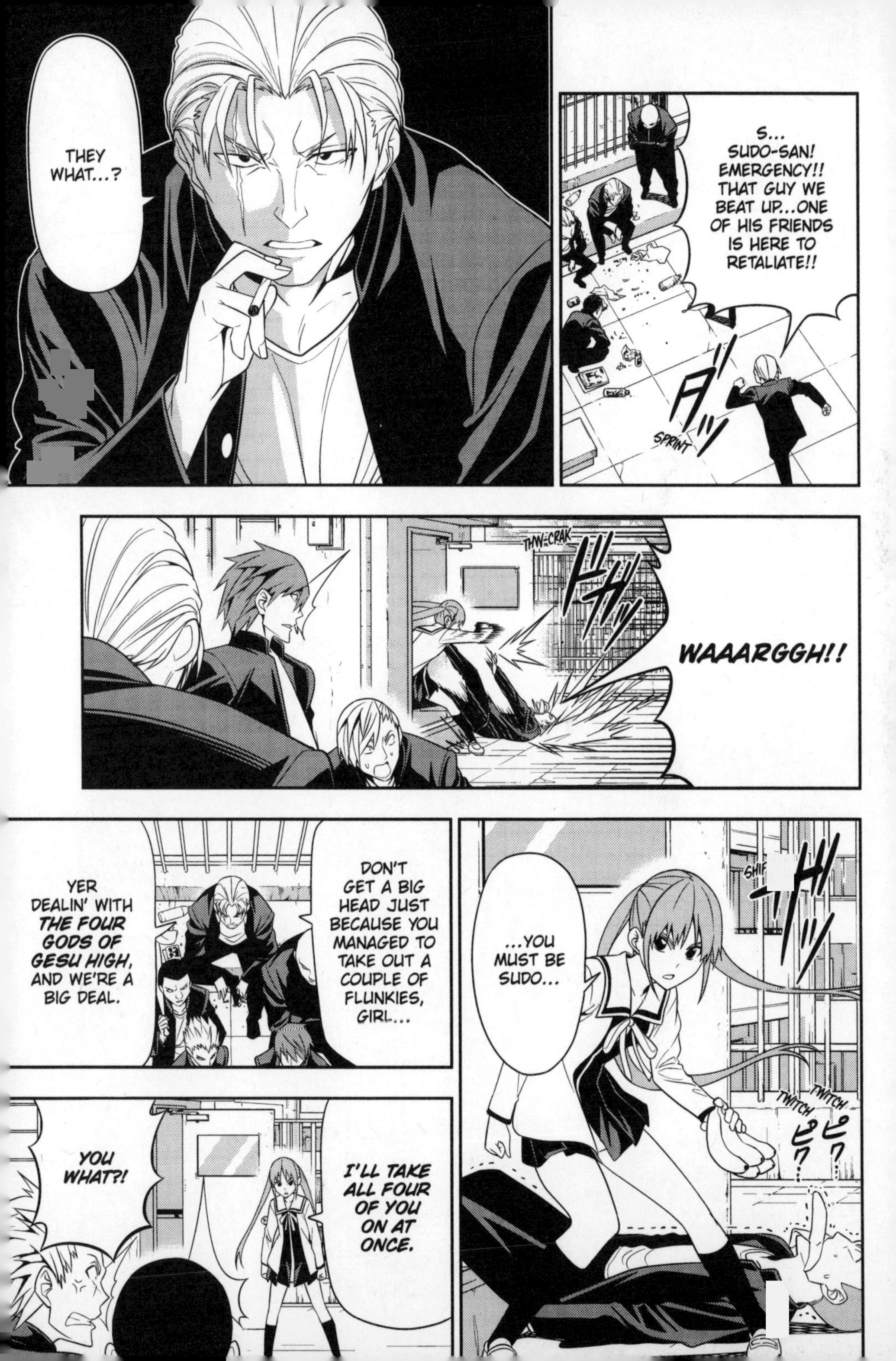
S... SUDO-SAN! EMERGENCY!! THAT GUY WE BEAT UP...ONE OF HIS FRIENDS IS HERE TO RETALIATE!!
SPRINT
THEY WHAT...?
THW-CRAK
WAAARGGH!!
...YOU MUST BE SUDO...
SHIF
TWITCH
TWITCH
DON'T GET A BIG HEAD JUST BECAUSE YOU MANAGED TO TAKE OUT A COUPLE OF FLUNKIES, GIRL...
YER DEALIN' WITH THE FOUR GODS OF GESU HIGH, AND WE'RE A BIG DEAL.
I'LL TAKE ALL FOUR OF YOU ON AT ONCE.
YOU WHAT?!

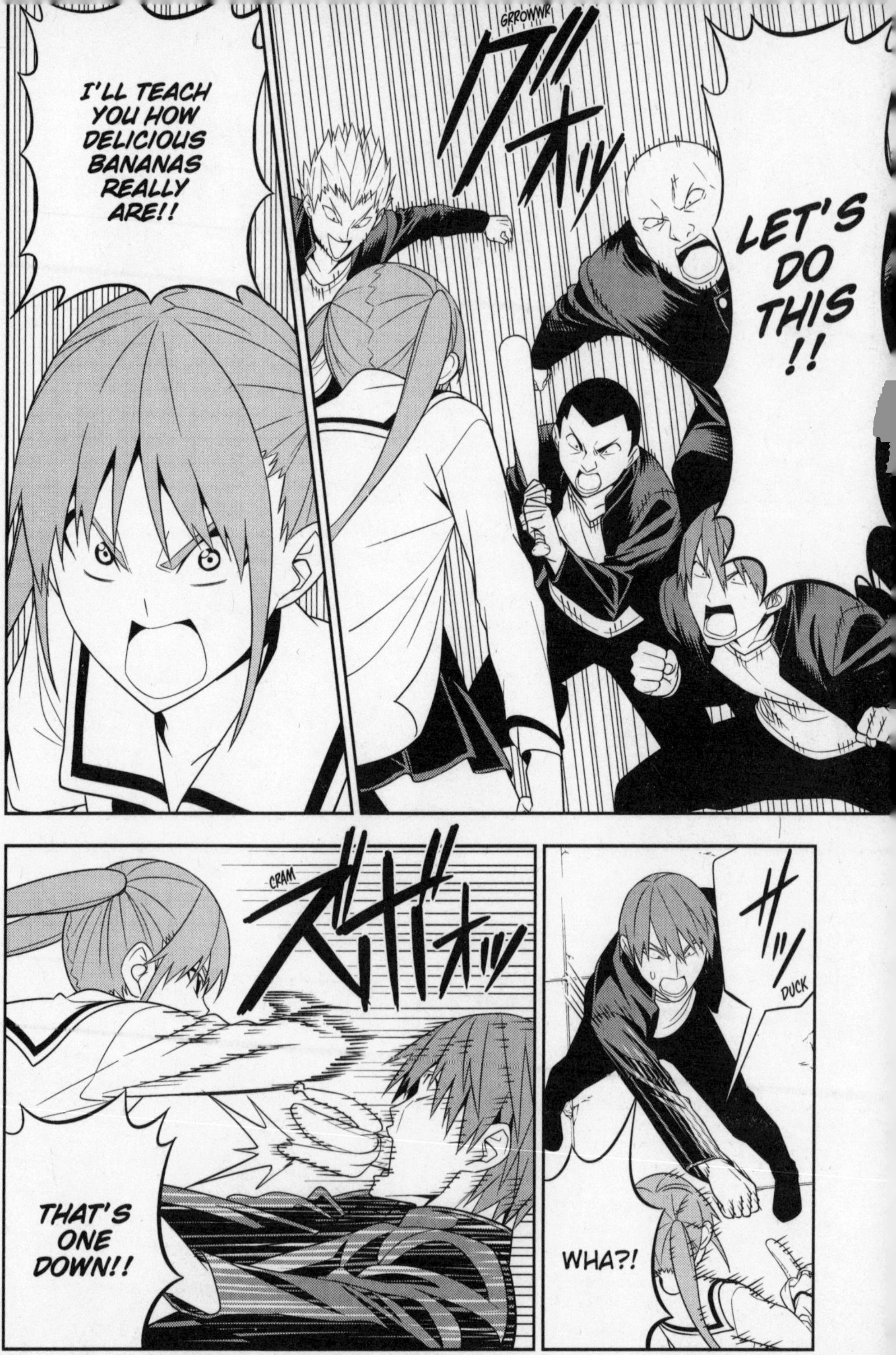
GRROWWR
LET'S DO THIS!!
I'LL TEACH YOU HOW DELICIOUS BANANAS REALLY ARE!!
DUCK
WHA?!
CRAM
THAT'S ONE DOWN!!

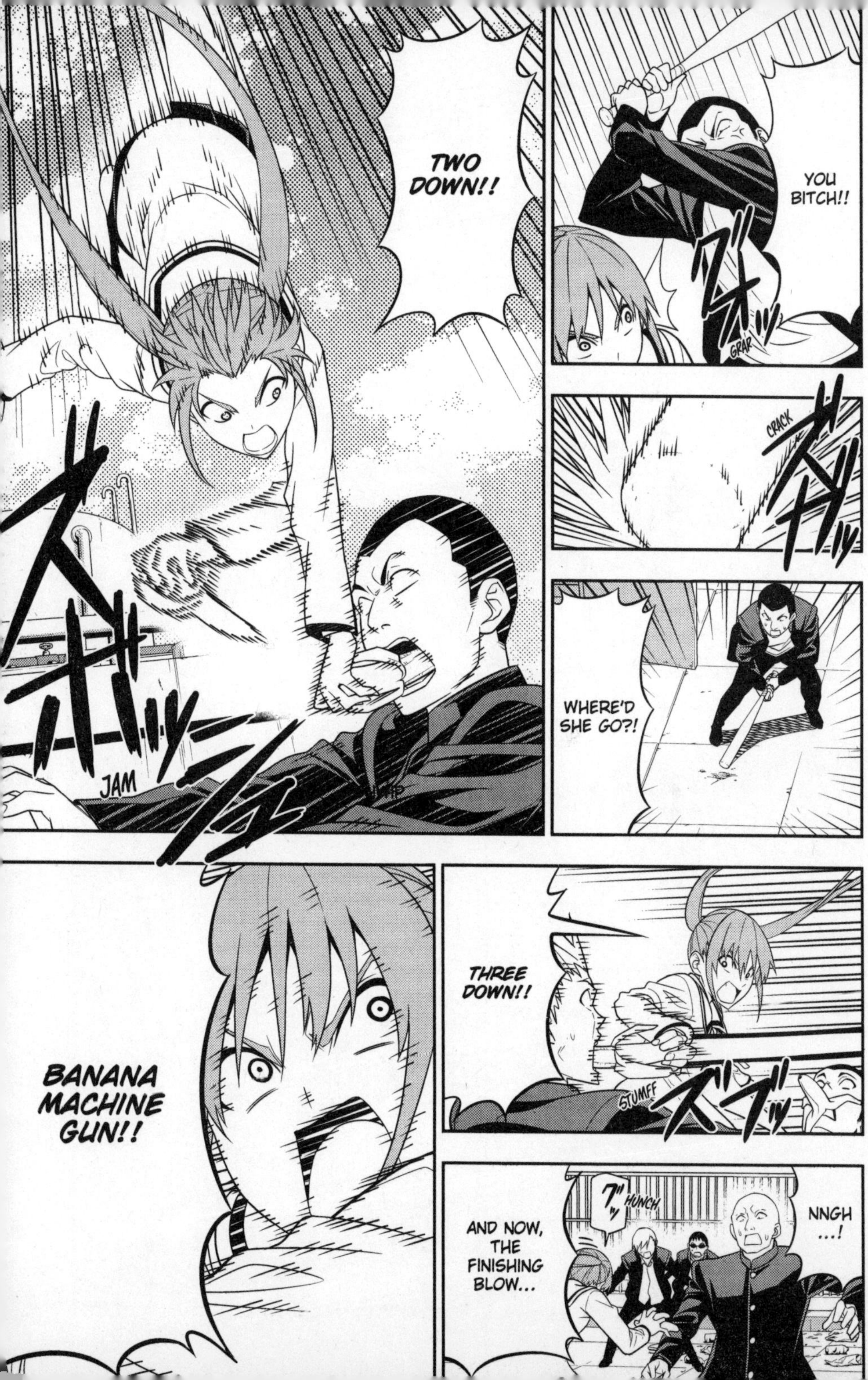
YOU BITCH!!
GRAR
CRACK
WHERE'D SHE GO?!
TWO DOWN!!
JAM
THREE DOWN!!
STUMFF
NNGH ...!
HUNCH
AND NOW, THE FINISHING BLOW...
BANANA MACHINE GUN!!

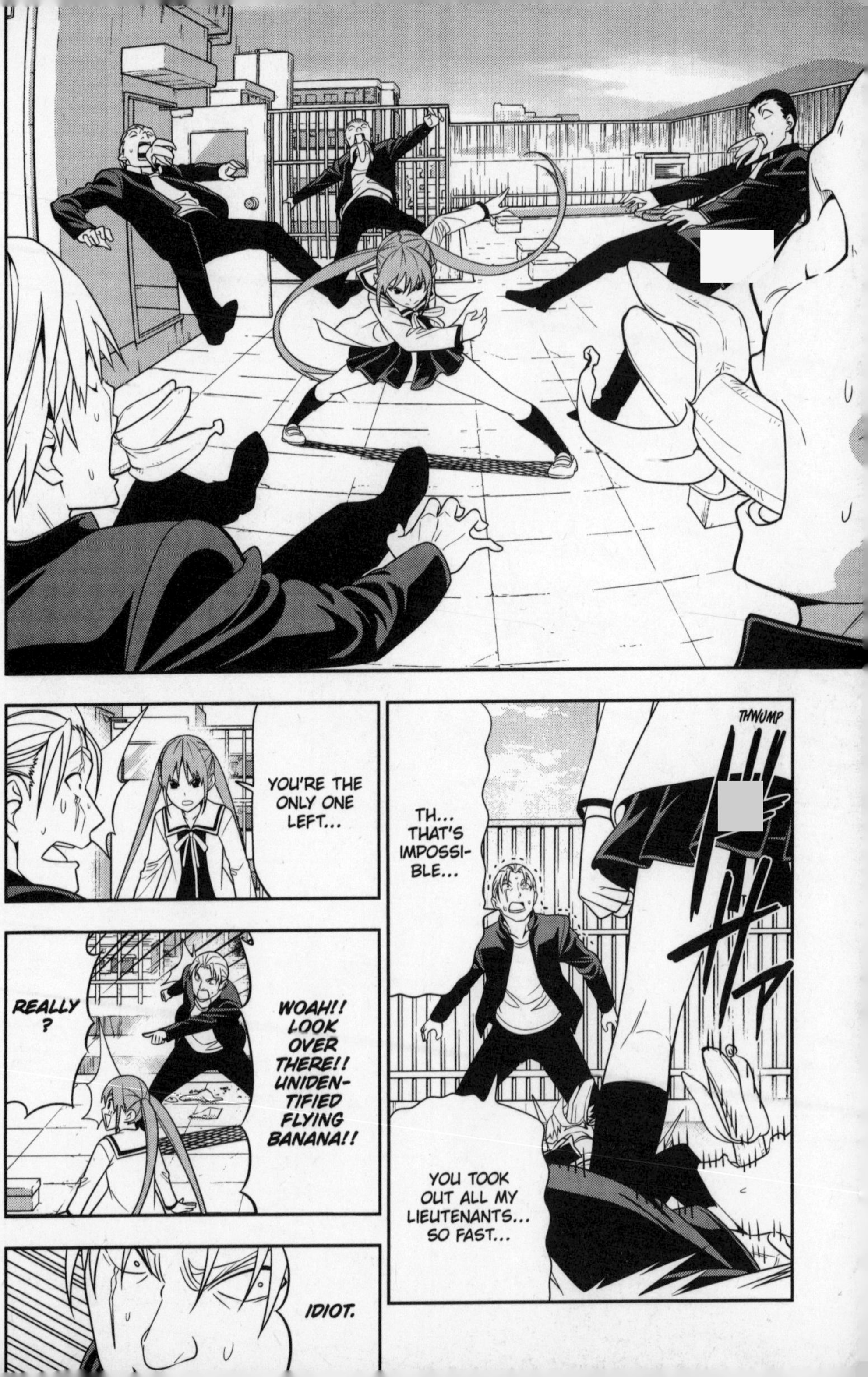
THWUMP
TH... THAT'S IMPOSSIBLE...
YOU TOOK OUT ALL MY LIEUTENANTS... SO FAST...
YOU'RE THE ONLY ONE LEFT...
WOAH!! LOOK OVER THERE!! UNIDENTIFIED FLYING BANANA!!
REALLY?
IDIOT.

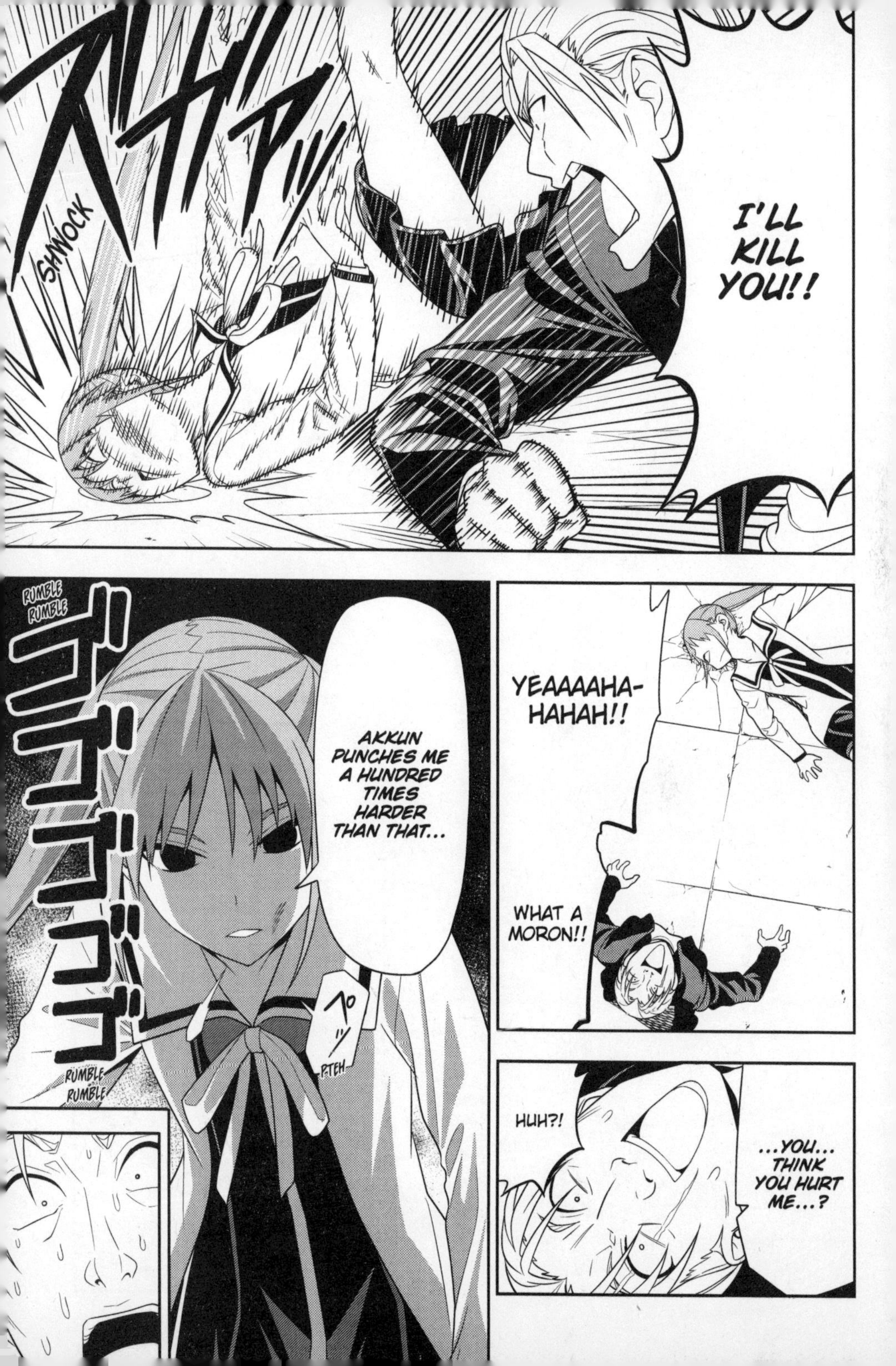
I'LL KILL YOU!!
SHWOCK
YEAAAAHA-HAHAH!!
WHAT A MORON!!
HUH?!
...YOU... THINK YOU HURT ME...?
RUMBLE RUMBLE
AKKUN PUNCHES ME A HUNDRED TIMES HARDER THAN THAT...
PTEH
RUMBLE RUMBLE

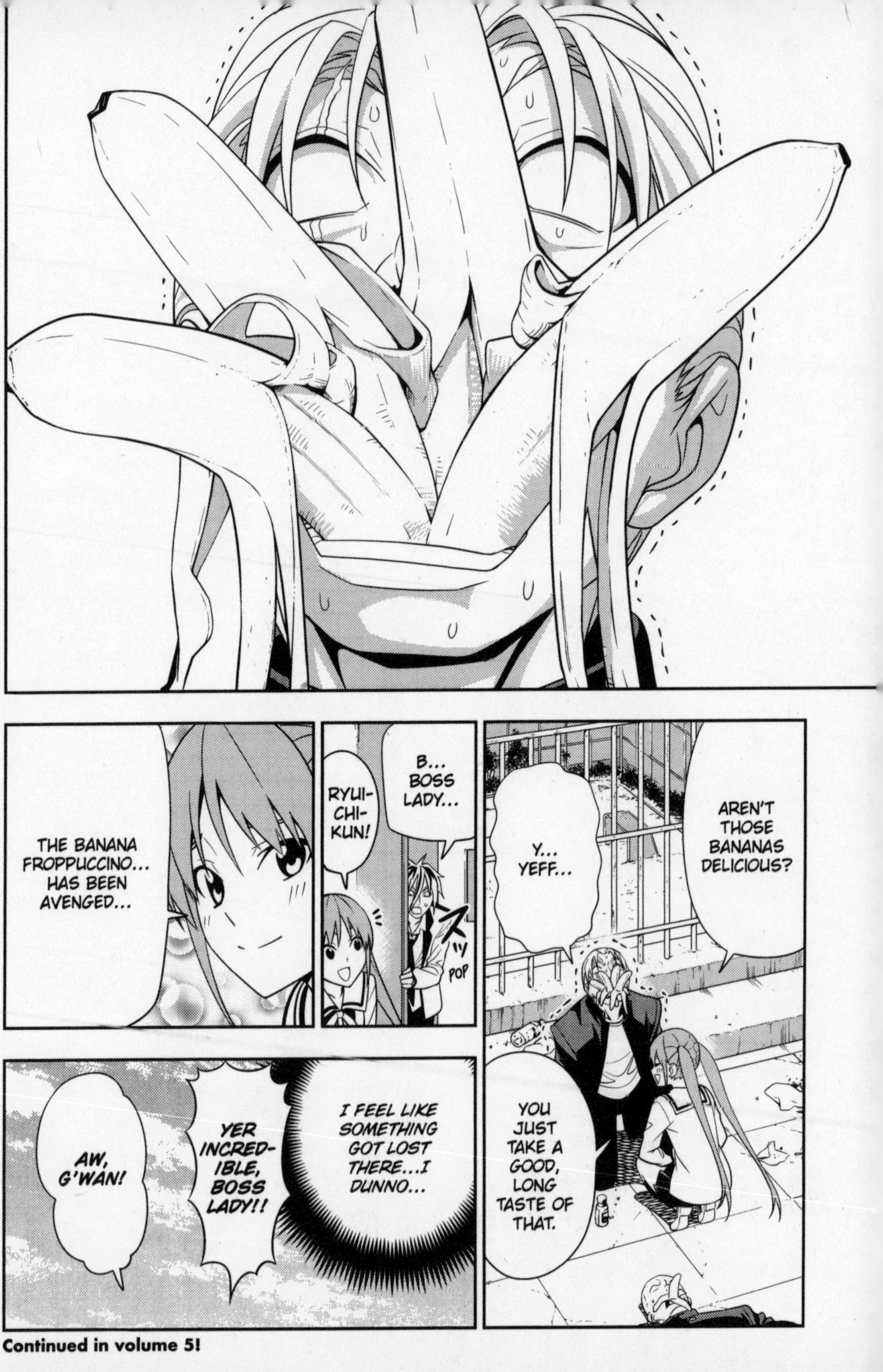
AREN'T THOSE BANANAS DELICIOUS?
Y... YEFF...
YOU JUST TAKE A GOOD, LONG TASTE OF THAT.
B... BOSS LADY...
RYUICHI-KUN!
ッ POP
THE BANANA FROPPUCCINO... HAS BEEN AVENGED...
I FEEL LIKE SOMETHING GOT LOST THERE...I DUNNO...
YER INCREDIBLE, BOSS LADY!!
AW, G'WAN!

Continued in volume 5!

(Come back and see us in volume 5)

Aho-Girl

\\'ahô͵gərl\\ *Japanese, noun.*

A clueless girl.

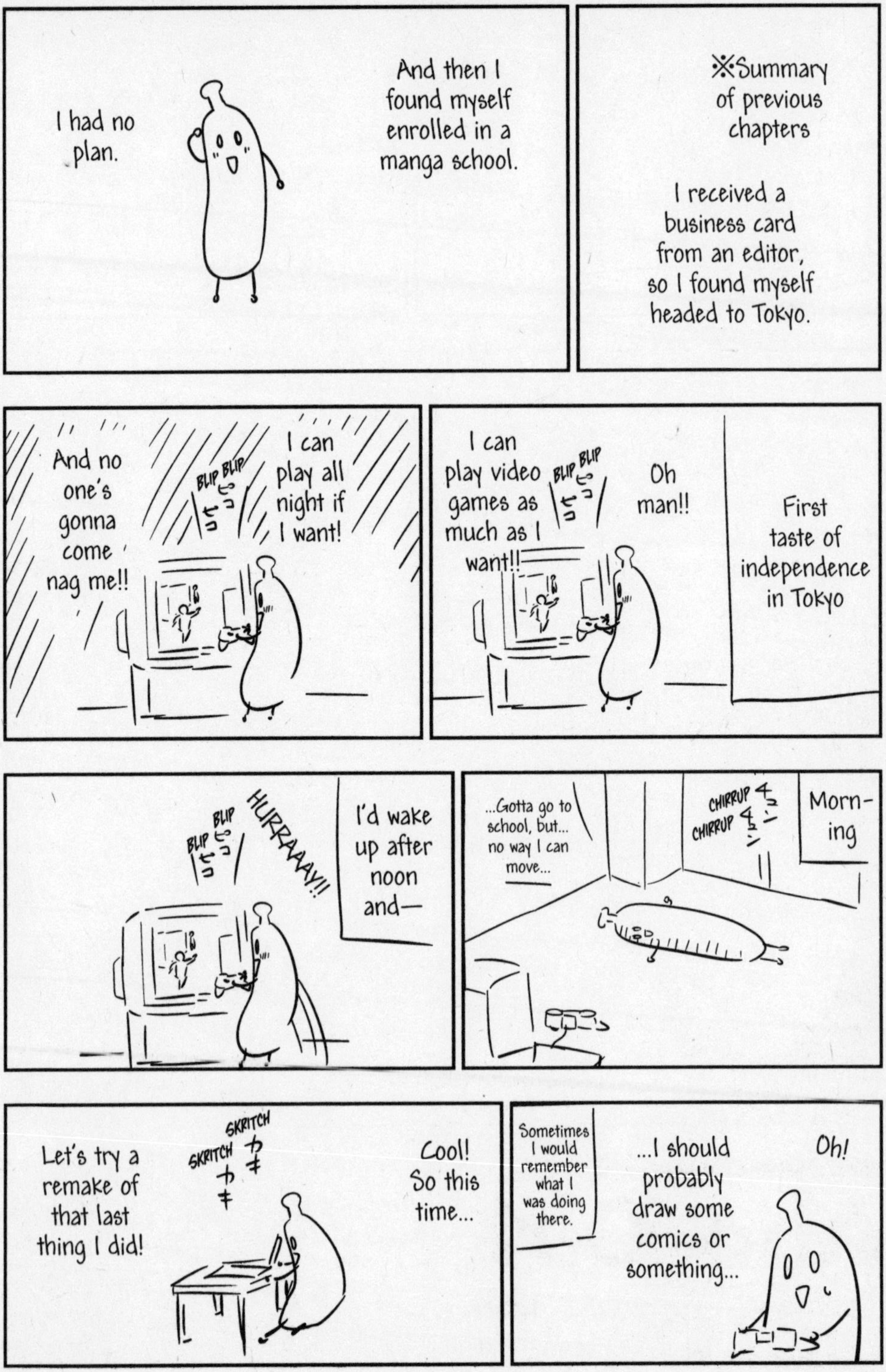
※Summary of previous chapters
I received a business card from an editor, so I found myself headed to Tokyo.
And then I found myself enrolled in a manga school.
I had no plan.
First taste of independence in Tokyo
Oh man!!
BLIP BLIP
I can play video games as much as I want!!
I can play all night if I want!
BLIP BLIP
And no one's gonna come nag me!!
Morn-ing
CHIRRUP CHIRRUP
...Gotta go to school, but... no way I can move...
I'd wake up after noon and—
HURRAAAY!!
BLIP BLIP
Oh!
...I should probably draw some comics or something...
Sometimes I would remember what I was doing there.
Cool! So this time...
SKRITCH SKRITCH
Let's try a remake of that last thing I did!

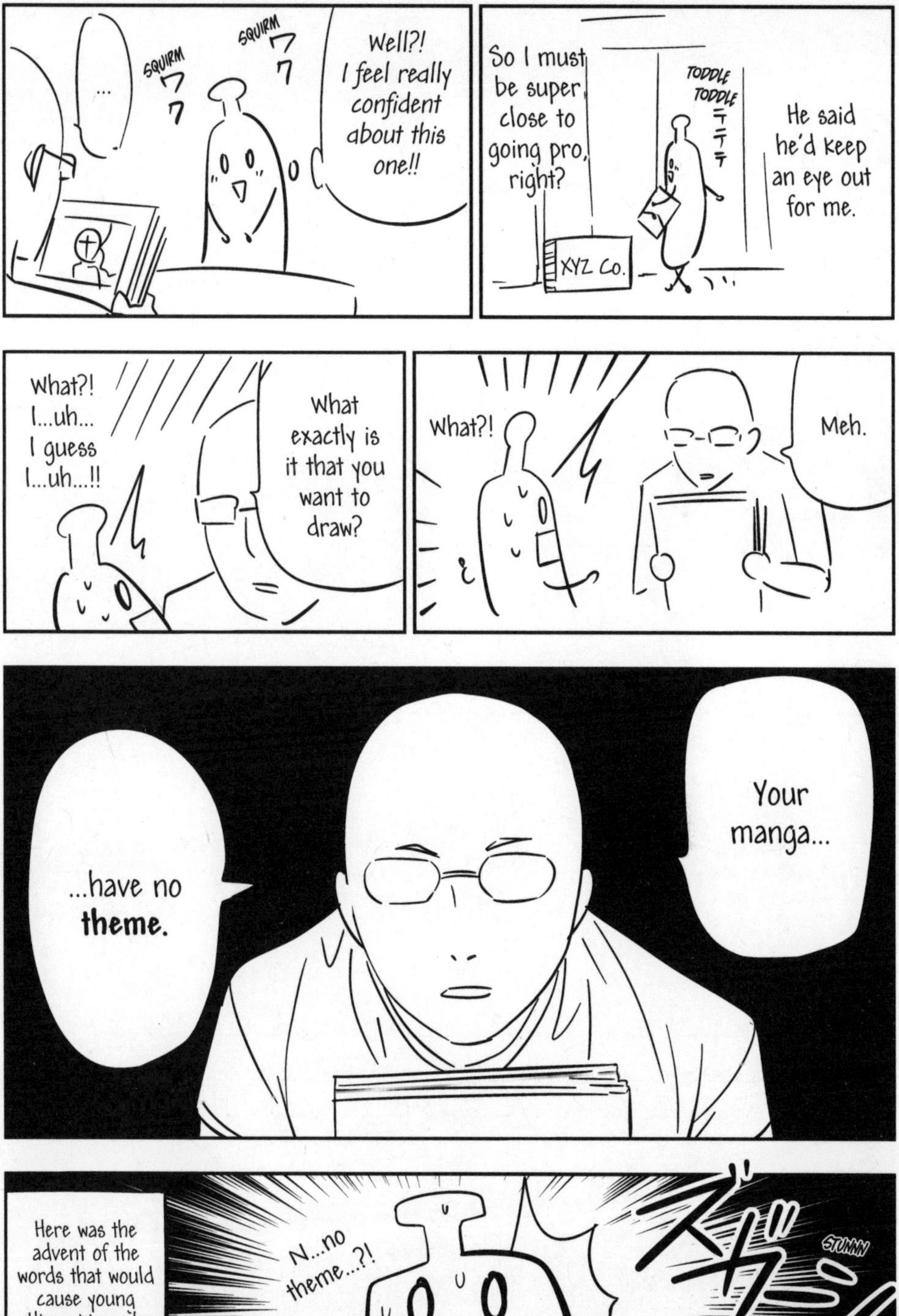
TODDLE TODDLE
He said he'd keep an eye out for me.
So I must be super close to going pro, right?
XYZ Co.
Well?! I feel really confident about this one!!
SQUIRM
SQUIRM
...
Meh.
What?!
What exactly is it that you want to draw?
What?! I...uh... I guess I...uh...!!
Your manga...
...have no **theme.**
STUNNN
N...no theme...?!
Here was the advent of the words that would cause young Hiroyuki much suffering.

To be continued

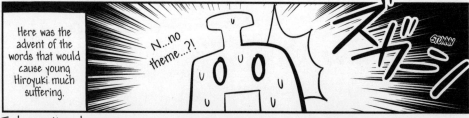

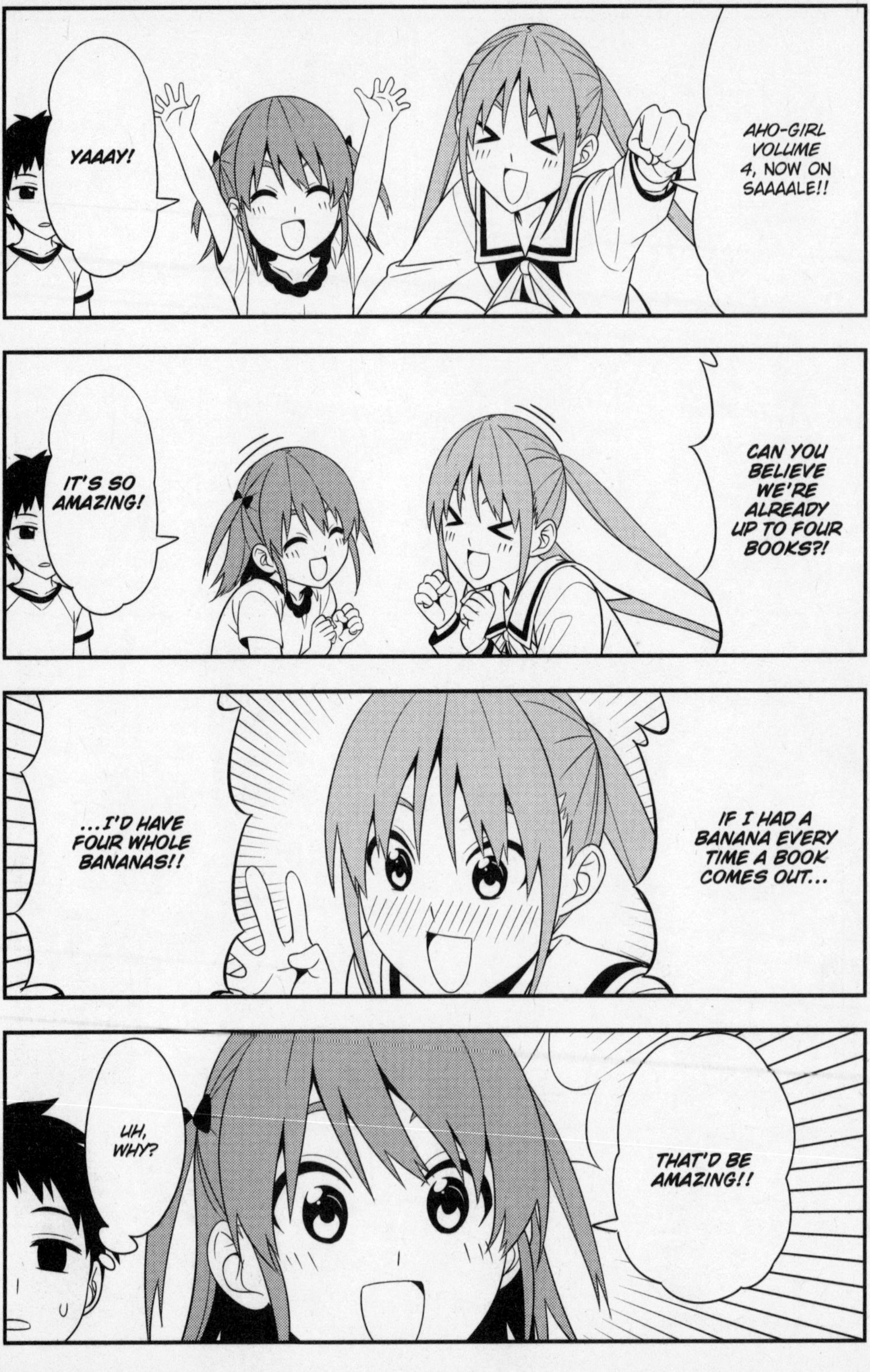
AHO-GIRL VOLUME 4, NOW ON SAAAALE!!
YAAAY!
CAN YOU BELIEVE WE'RE ALREADY UP TO FOUR BOOKS?!
IT'S SO AMAZING!
IF I HAD A BANANA EVERY TIME A BOOK COMES OUT...
...I'D HAVE FOUR WHOLE BANANAS!!
THAT'D BE AMAZING!!
UH, WHY?

Translation Notes

Page 2
"Aggravated straight man"
This is an explanatory gloss of the Japanese term "tsukkomi." The tsukkomi and boke duo are a common trope in manzai-style stand-up comedy routines. The boke, like Yoshiko, draws over-the-top and just plain stupid conclusions to the tsukkomi's set-ups. The tsukkomi tries to remain calm and reasonable during the act, but is invariably pushed into extreme and sometimes violent reactions out of his frustration.

Page 3
"Head Monitor"
The head monitor's title in Japanese includes the word fuuki, which roughly translates to "moral order" or "discipline." She would not be merely checking for hall passes the way a hall monitor in a Western school might, and would be more broadly responsible for reporting anything in violation of the moral standards of the institution.

Page 5
"Kanto region"
This is the region of Japan where Tokyo is located. In addition to Tokyo, the region also encompasses six other prefectures (Gunma, Tochigi, Ibaraki, Saitama, Chiba, and Kanagawa).

Page 10
"Double Peace"
Flashing the double peace sign in pictures is a common pose for photos. Where in America we would say "cheese" and everyone smiles and picks their pose, in Japan it's common for people to put up a peace sign. The double peace sign is also great to express your enthusiasm... except when you're holding onto an umbrella in midair.

Page 12
"Ah! Ah! Arashiii! Game Center"
This quote is from the opening theme song to the 1982 anime series Game Center Arashi, which was based on a manga running from 1978 to 1984. The series followed the protagonist, a boy named Arashi (meaning "storm"), who was an early video game enthusiast, spending all his time at arcades and challenging others to achieve new high scores. The series was perhaps the earliest to deal with competitive video game players, and helped to popularize video games when they were still a new innovation.

Page 14
"Sayaka's Leveling up Her Straight Man Skills!"
See the discussion of tsukkomi above, regarding Akkun's character memo on page 2.

Page 14
"What about Dogs A through D⁈"
This joke has been localized. In the original Japanese, the joke hinges on a cute word for a dog: wan-chan. The word is derived from the onomatopoeia for barking (wan wan) and the diminutive name suffix -chan. Coincidentally, this Japanese word sounds a lot like a Chinese name as pronounced in Japanese, where the name Wang is pronounced "Wan." Therefore, Yoshiko seems ignorant of the common word "wan-chan" (analogous to puppy) and instead thinks she's hearing a Chinese name along the lines of "Chen Wang." Yoshiko being ignorant of the word "wan-chan" is roughly as ridiculous as not knowing the word "doggy."

Page 20
"Nyan to Wonderful"
The name of a series of video games that began on PlayStation 1, *Nyan to Wonderful* is a pet care simulator released in 1996. The name is a partial pun on the Japanese onomatopoeia for a cat's meow (nyan) and a dog's barking (wan wan), and the Japanese pronunciation of the English word "wonderful" (wandafuru).

Page 21
"Gals"
The term "gal" (Japanese: "gyaru") refers to a broad segment of popular youth culture in Japan that began in the mid-1990s. The term encompasses many distinct subcultures with different stereotyped behaviors (such as extreme tanning, bleached-white hair, or casual dating in exchange for spending money) that are considered contrary to prevailing Japanese morality. In general, though, most people who are labeled by the term "gal" merely subscribe to a particular fashion aesthetic characterized by loose socks (the familiar slouchy socks that hang loose around the ankles), lightly bleached hair, extensive nail art or cell phone bangles, and—of particular relevance here—school uniform skirts that are rolled up at the waist to be scandalously short.

Page 28
"Mash! Ortega!"
These are the names of a team of three elite Zeon pilots in the *Mobile Suit Gundam* universe, who comprise a team called the Black Tri-Stars. Mash and Ortega are joined in their daring flights not by *Aho-Girl*, but by Gaia.

Japanese culture, he is pursued by the child oni (monster or demon) trio who are trying to retrieve an artifact the prince stole from King Enma, the Buddhist judge of the dead and ruler of the underworld.

Page 38
"The Real—Really Real—"
This title refers to a song titled "Maji Sunshine" by Hey! Say! JUMP, released in 2016. The song title takes advantage of Japanese furigana, which is usually a sort of pronunciation guide written in smaller characters above the main text. The more ordinary word "real" is provided a furigana reading of a slang term for "real." Because the furigana is the pronunciation guide, the title of the song in Japanese ends up being romanized as "Maji Sunshine."

Page 40
"Sure Death: The Professional"
This is the title of a jidaigeki (period piece, usually featuring samurai) TV series that ran from 1979 to 1981. The series follows the adventures of the assassin Mondo Nakamura and his colleagues in Edo-era (1603 to 1868) Tokyo. Several movie adaptations of the Sure Death series are available in English, the first under the title Hissatsu: Sure Death.

"Sneaking in to visit my husband at night"
The term used here (yobai, literally "night crawling") enjoys a storied history in Japanese literature and culture. Made most famous in the West by the classical Japanese masterwork The Tale of Genji, yobai is a romantic practice in which a man sneaks into the bedroom of his intended at night, after the rest of her household has gone to sleep, so that the two may enjoy a tryst presumably unbeknownst to her family. The relationship may or may not progress to marriage, but in the rigid formality of pre-industrial Japanese society where public displays of affection were extremely frowned-upon, yobai was one of the only avenues of romance available. Given this cultural context, the practice would be considered ludicrously old-fashioned for someone in modern Japan to be engaged in.

Page 41
"Obasan"
This is a respectful form of address for an older (but not old) woman, meaning "aunt." Contrast to obaasan for "grandmother" and babaa for a more disrespectful term along the lines of "hag."

Page 46
"Umeebo"
This is a riff on a staple Japanese candy, "Umaibo." The candy's name more or less means "delicious stick," but

Page 30
"Is This... Time for Girl-talk?!"
The original title refers to a joshikai (literally "girl meeting"), which is somewhat like a "girls' night out" in English, but can refer to any get-together intended only for the ladies.

Page 31
"Thanks for That!"
This is a play on the Japanese phrase conventionally used after finishing a meal. However, the phrase is derived from a Japanese verb meaning "to humbly receive" and can be used as such, sarcastically or not.

"Well That's No Good"
The titles along this line are based in the Japanese title, ダメ出し (damedashi), which more literally means "finding fault with something" and especially pointing it out for attention. The word is also a homophone for ダメ だし (damedashi), which would translate into the "Well That's No Good" of the English title. Since saying "that's no good" is an act of finding fault, we decided to go with that.

Page 32
"You Have to Tell Him"
The Japanese phrase used for the title (kuchi ni dashite) is translated here in accordance with its meaning, "to communicate something verbally." However, as those with more familiarity with Japanese may have noticed, the phrase could be more literally, but artificially, translated as "use your mouth." No doubt this particular gal wouldn't pick up on the more suggestive implication, since she's so shy about just talking.

Page 34
"Can You Hear Me Now?"
The Japanese gag here is a reference to the 1997 song "Calling" by the Japanese rock band B'z. A refrain in the song asks "Can you hear this (my) voice?" Given the obscurity of this reference to a North American audience, we massaged the joke into a more contemporary reference to an ad slogan you may recognize.

Page 36
"Aobee, Kisuke,"
This is a reference to Ojarumaru, a yonkoma (i.e., four-panel, the same format as Aho-Girl) manga series, which features a group of characters called "the child oni trio" composed of Aobee, Kisuke, and Akane. The series began in 1998, and has been adapted into an anime series which is still being aired. The story follows the titular Ojarumaru, a 5 year-old prince from the Heian era (794 to 1185 CE), who is somehow time-warped to modern Japan. As the young prince navigates modern

Page 76
"Just Like James Dean"
This is a reference to a 1983 hit song that launched the career of Itsumi Osawa, "A Girl Like James Dean." The grammatical structure of Japanese puts "a girl" at the end of the clause, where "Aho-Girl" appears in these interstitial gags. Thus, if the format allowed, a better translation would be "Aho-Girl Like James Dean."

Page 84
"The Comic Artist and His"
This is a reference to another series by Hiroyuki, *The Comic Artist and His Assistants*, which ran from 2008 to 2012 in Square Enix's seinen (roughly equivalent to "men aged 18 to 35") manga magazine, *Young Gangan*. An anime adaptation aired in 2014.

Page 90
"Hurricanrana"
The title is the name of a wrestling move in which one wrestler wraps his or her legs around the neck of another, flipping their opponent into a pile driver.

Page 92
"La'cryma"
This refers to a Japanese visual kei rock band named La'cryma Christi (Latin for "the tears of Christ"), which was active from 1991 to 2007.

Page 95
"Super Sayaka Appears on the Scene"
This title, and the subsequent "Super Sayaka 2" and "3" titles, refer to the *Dragon Ball Heroes* video game, in which different Super Saiyan characters appear in numbered installments. These titles therefore mirror a player's progress through the game, encountering different boss characters.

Page 95
"Alcohol isn't for minors, kids!"
The legal drinking age in Japan is 20, which is considered the overall age of adulthood, with some exceptions. A national holiday, Coming of Age Day (Seinen no Hi), celebrates everyone who has turned 20 in the past year.

Page 98
"Full Body Flat"
The Japanese term used here, literally "full-flat body," originates in terminology for cars. Specifically, the term refers to any car where the seats can go into a fully flat position, allowing a person to sleep flat inside the car. Through usage, the term also came to be applied to aircraft carriers (i.e., ships with a flat surface on top). With the release of the *Kantai Collection* ("Fleet Collection" or "Combined Fleet Girls Collection") game in 2013, vari-

the word umai or "delicious" is often pronounced with a coarser accent as "umee." Yoshiko using the word "Umeebo" barely disguises the actual product to avoid any copyright issues, since some consumers may actually pronounce it that way themselves. For the curious, the candy is sold in the form of a tube containing small corn puffs, and is said to have a consistency somewhat similar to Cheetos.

Page 49
"Takenoko no Mura"
This candy name is an only-barely-disguised reference to another famous Japanese candy, "Takenoko no Sato" ("Bamboo Shoot Village"). Both mura and sato translate to "village," so this is somewhat like the candy in the manga being named "Bamboo Shoot Hamlet." The candy itself is approximately the size of a pencil-topper eraser, and is a conical biscuit shaped like a bamboo shoot and partially dipped in chocolate.

Page 56
"Shove It"
The Japanese title makes a pun on two separate meanings of the word nejikomu: "protest/complain" and "ram in."

Page 60
"Priority one: sleep. Priority two:"
This is a saying used as a rule of thumb for healthy living. The full saying reads "Priority one: sleep. Priority two: food. Priority three: exercise," although the order of the three elements seems to be up for debate in other versions.

Page 61
"Cultural festival"
A common feature of manga and anime, the school cultural festival is something like an open house at U.S. schools with a more carnival or street fair atmosphere. The various homeroom classes and extracurricular clubs organize exhibits to display their achievements and the atmosphere of the school for visitors. Often, these festivals are open not just to the students' families, but also to the general public, allowing the entire community to see what the school is like and how the students spend their time.

Page 68
"Pure LOVE Academy: Maiden Heart"
This is the name of an imaginary, self-published manga series featured within a live-action TV sitcom called *Urero ☆ Mikansei Shojo*, which deals with a low-tier talent agency trying to make it big by landing a great client.

Page 123
In Japanese culture, a raised pinky finger implies a woman, especially a woman of romantic interest such as a girlfriend, wife, or mistress. The male equivalent is a raised thumb, though since Japan also uses the Western-style "thumbs up" gesture, context is important.

Page 125
"Your grades"
The term glossed here as "grades" is more literally translated "confidential ranking." Confidential ranking is a somewhat arbitrary system of scoring students within a school. Each school determines what subjects are scored and what grading scale is used. A student's performance in the main school subjects like math or history typically factors into the calculation of the confidential ranking, but school activities or other special achievements (like captain of the basketball team) may also be included. Due to this lack of uniformity, these scores do not have any official use, but can influence the academic standing of the student within the school. For example, if her homeroom teacher is sabotaging her, Sayaka could somehow get 100% on all her academic grades and still not be considered the top student in her class, and could be passed over for recommendations or recognitions analogous to valedictorian.

Page 126
"Fixed-term account"
This is something like an IRA or other retirement savings account in the US, where the financial institution offers better interest rates on the understanding that there will be severe penalties for making withdrawals from the account before an agreed-upon date.

Page 128
"Etchy sketchy"
This is part of a nonsense rhyming chant used in some children's games such as tag.

Page 129
"Gyaora"
The Japanese uses the disguised name "Gyaora" for the kaiju (giant monster) toy. This appears to be a reference to a 1967 film called variously *Return of the Giant Monsters*, *Gamera vs. Gyaos*, and *Gamera vs. Gaos*, which features two kaiju doing battle against each other: Gamera, a testudine monster, and Gyaos, a pterodactyl-like beast.

"Mika-chan"
"Mika-chan" is a disguised reference to the highly popular "Licca" or "Licca-chan" line of Japanese dress-up dolls, which debuted in 1967. Licca-chan occupies the

ous types of Japanese battleships were imagined as cute anime girls. Ryujo, one of the aircraft carrier characters, was drawn as particularly flat-chested and underdeveloped in comparison to the other girls, and was therefore teasingly called "full-flat body." Obviously, there is no English equivalent to this particular term.

Page 98
"Kanto"
See the note for page 5 above.

Page 100
"We drink, drinking it in, and drinking it in, we drink"
This is a lyric in Eigo Kawashima's 1975 song "Drinks, Tears, a Man, and a Woman."

Page 112
"4000 6000 6000 2000"
In the web-based *Kantai Collection* game (see note for page 98 above), these numbers refer to the combination of ingredient settings for "fuel," "steel," "ammunition," and "bauxite" needed to unlock the battleship character Yamato, who is then built from these materials in the player's dry-dock.

Page 121
"Yoshio-sama"
As in most cultures, teachers in Japan are considered socially superior to their students and deserving of respect. Therefore, within the Japanese framework of honorific suffixes, teachers have a wide latitude to use any of the suffixes denoting equality or social superiority when addressing their students, or to omit any suffix at all (this is most common with male teachers). This would mean that Oshieda-sensei would, in a typical student-teacher relationship, refer to her students by their last names as "Akutsu-kun" or "Hanabatake-san," as she has done in the past. However, here she is dreamily reminiscing about Yoshio, the boy who stole her heart. Contrary to her usual pattern for addressing students, she uses his first name and the reverential -sama suffix. Such a form of address is typical of swooning tween girls admiring an unattainable heartthrob, and shows that Oshieda-sensei has abandoned any thought of her superior, authoritative role as teacher when it comes to this particular student.

Page 122
"What a Nasty Thing You Are!"
This is a reference to a line in *Jojo's Bizarre Adventure*, where the minor antagonist Cioccolata exclaims "Three?! You want three sweets? Three... what a nasty thing you are!"

game adaptations.

Page 151
"Four Gods of Gesu High"
"The Four Gods" is a common term used to refer to groups of powerful people in manga and anime. The term originally referred to a famous group of four intensely loyal and effective generals who served under Ieyasu Tokugawa, who in turn were named after the Four Heavenly Kings, also known as guardian kings, who in Buddhist tradition are said to each watch over one of the four cardinal directions.

same toy niche as Barbie dolls do in the United States, but her more childish appearance and canonical age of 11 has led to a much larger market share in Japan, where Barbie dolls are also available.

Page 130
"Mika"
While Yoshiko plays as Mika-chan, she refers to herself exclusively as "Mika," never using first person pronouns such as "I," "me," or "my." In English this may sound very imperious and self-absorbed, but in Japanese such a habit is not unusual for children, young women, or in close relationships. For these people, referring to oneself by name may sound cutesy. One theory is that using one's name instead of a proper pronoun shows a lack of awareness of one's relative place in society that may come across as vulnerable or pleasantly naïve. This impression may derive from the fact that, in general, the Japanese language does not require pronouns to fully convey concepts. Instead, pronouns such as "I" can be expressed by a wide variety of words that convey certain assumptions about oneself and one's listeners. For example, a man using "watashi" conveys a very different impression from a man using "ore". Therefore, aspiring Japanese speakers are urged to use caution when departing from the neutral norm in referring to themselves.

Page 133
"Damage Effect"
This refers to a trope in various media featuring fight scenes, where the shot focuses on a person receiving a special attack and lingers (often in slow motion) to show the incredible effects of the attack.

Page 136
"The Giants, the Great Bird, and"
This is a phrase used as a byline for 1960s Japan, which was a particularly prosperous era for the country overall. The phrase distills three touchstones of the time: the highly successful and popular baseball team, the Yomiuri Giants; the reigning sumo champion, Koki Taiho (the characters in "Taiho" literally mean "Great Bird"); and tamagoyaki (rolled omelet), which was offered as emblematic of the increased affordability of quality foods after the privations of World War II and the subsequent economic and social recovery.

Page 146
"Be-Bop"
This refers to the classic manga Be-Bop High School, which features two ruffian high school boys who frequently get into fights with rivals and face other coming-of-age adversities. The manga series ran from 1983 to 2003 and led to several anime, live action, and video

Aho-Girl

\\'ahô͵gərl\\ *Japanese, noun.*
A clueless girl.

KODANSHA COMICS

FIRE SOLDIER
8
TOKYO

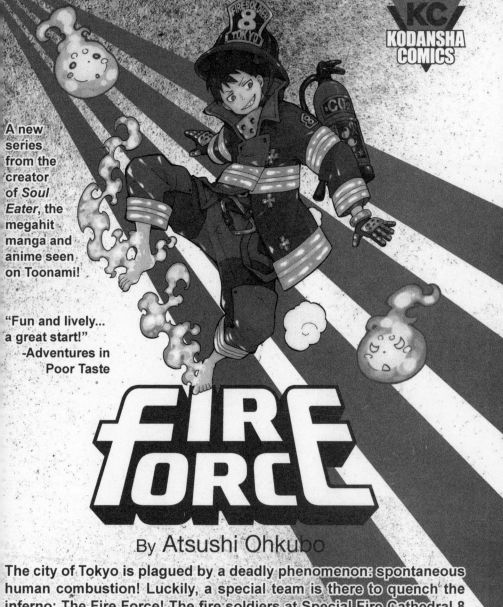

A new series from the creator of *Soul Eater*, the megahit manga and anime seen on Toonami!

"Fun and lively... a great start!"
-Adventures in Poor Taste

FIRE FORCE

By Atsushi Ohkubo

The city of Tokyo is plagued by a deadly phenomenon: spontaneous human combustion! Luckily, a special team is there to quench the inferno: The Fire Force! The fire soldiers at Special Fire Cathedral 8 are about to get a unique addition. Enter Shinra, a boy who possesses the power to run at the speed of a rocket, leaving behind the famous "devil's footprints" (and destroying his shoes in the process). Can Shinra and his colleagues discover the source of this strange epidemic before the city burns to ashes?

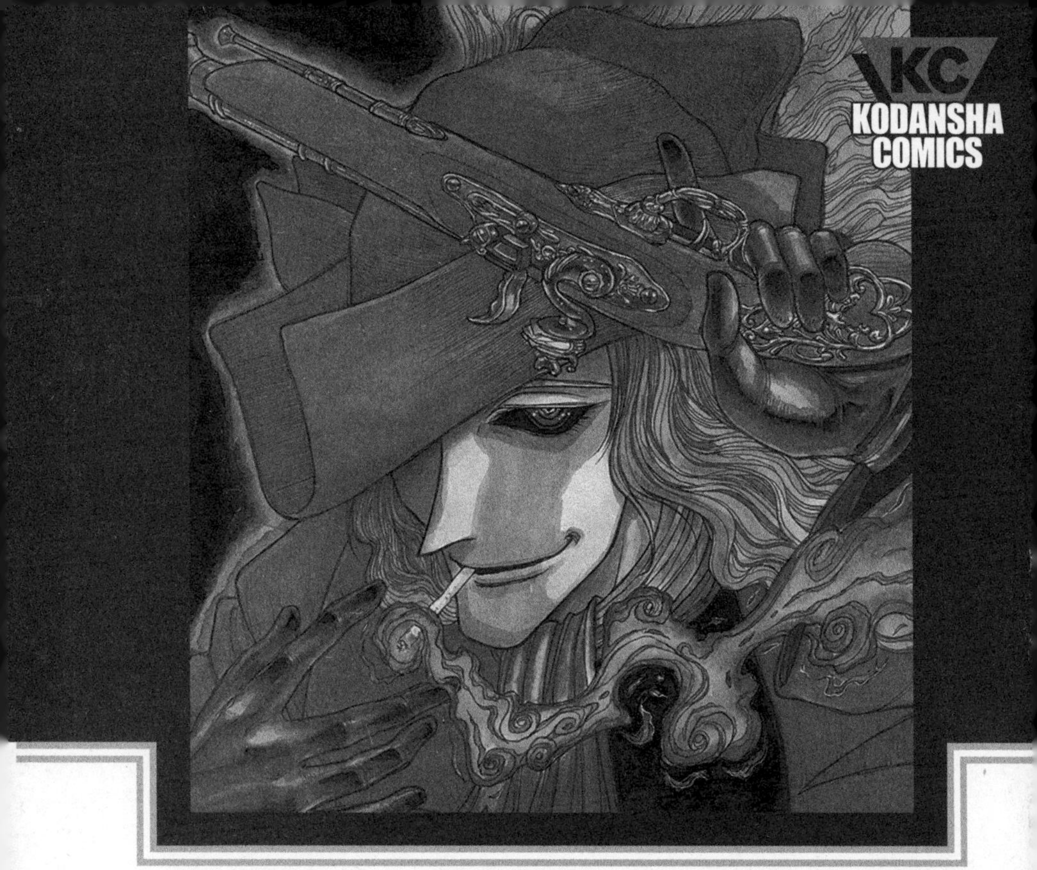
KODANSHA COMICS

The Black Museum: The Ghost and the Lady

By Kazuhiro Fujita

Deep in Scotland Yard in London sits an evidence room dedicated to the greatest mysteries of British history. In this “Black Museum” sits a misshapen hunk of lead—two bullets fused together—the key to a wartime encounter between Florence Nightingale, the mother of modern nursing, and a supernatural Man in Grey. This story is unknown to most scholars of history, but a special guest of the museum will tell the tale of The Ghost and the Lady...

Praise for Kazuhiro Fujita’s *Ushio and Tora*

“A charming revival that combines a classic look with modern depth and pacing... **Essential viewing both for curmudgeons and new fans alike.**” — Anime News Network

“**GREAT!** The first episode of Ushio and Tora captures the essence of '90s anime.” — IGN

KC KODANSHA COMICS

Japan's most powerful spirit medium delves into the ghost world's greatest mysteries!

Story by Kyo Shirodaira, famed author of mystery fiction and creator of *Spiral*, *Blast of Tempest*, and *The Record of a Fallen Vampire*.

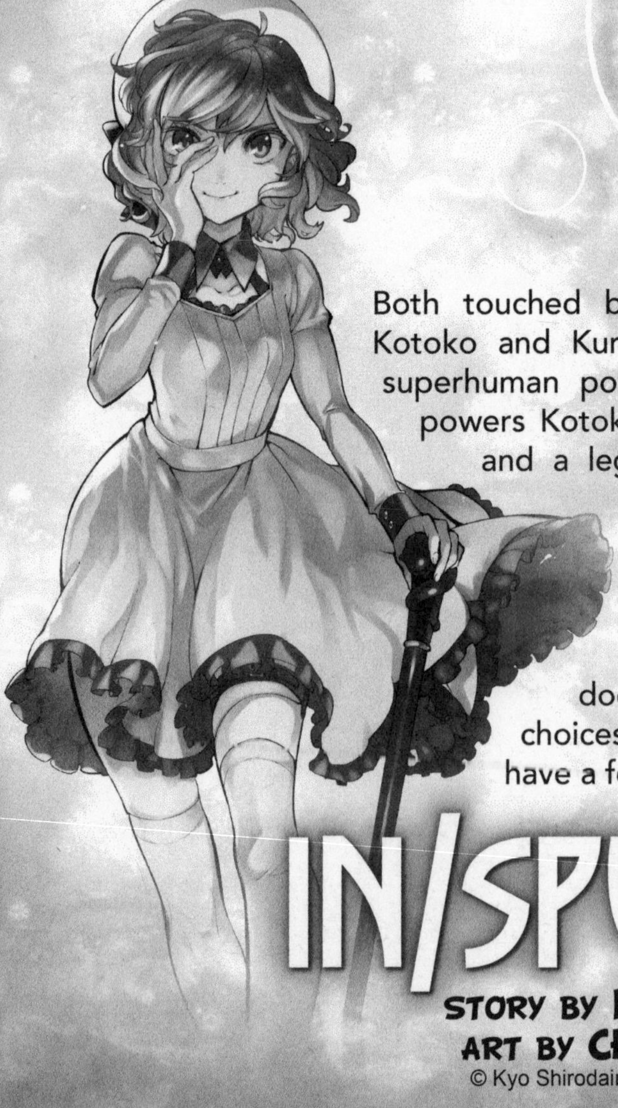

Both touched by spirits called yôkai, Kotoko and Kurô have gained unique superhuman powers. But to gain her powers Kotoko has given up an eye and a leg, and Kurô's personal life is in shambles. So when Kotoko suggests they team up to deal with renegades from the spirit world, Kurô doesn't have many other choices, but Kotoko might just have a few ulterior motives...

IN/SPECTRE

STORY BY KYO SHIRODAIRA
ART BY CHASHIBA KATASE

H A P·P·I N E S S

ーハピネスー

By Shuzo Oshimi

From the creator of *The Flowers of Evil*

Nothing interesting is happening in Makoto Ozaki's first year of high school. His life is a series of quiet humiliations: low-grade bullies, unreliable friends, and the constant frustration of his adolescent lust. But one night, a pale, thin girl knocks him to the ground in an alley and offers him a choice. Now everything is different. Daylight is searingly bright. Food tastes awful. And worse than anything is the terrible, consuming thirst...

Praise for Shuzo Oshimi's *The Flowers of Evil*

"A shockingly readable story that vividly—one might even say queasily—evokes the fear and confusion of discovering one's own sexuality. Recommended." —The Manga Critic

"A page-turning tale of sordid middle school blackmail." —Otaku USA Magazine

"A stunning new horror manga." —Third Eye Comics

KC
KODANSHA COMICS

Based on the critically acclaimed classic horror manga

The first new *Parasyte* manga in over 20 years!

NEO
PARASYTE f

BY ASUMIKO NAKAMURA, EMA TOYAMA, MIKI RINNO, LALAKO KOJIMA, KAORI YUKI, BANKO KUZE, YUUKI OBATA, KASHIO, YUI KUROE, ASIA WATANABE, MIKIMAKI, HIKARU SURUGA, HAJIME SHINJO, RENJURO KINDAICHI, AND YURI NARUSHIMA

A collection of chilling new *Parasyte* stories from Japan's top shojo artists!

Parasites: shape-shifting aliens whose only purpose is to assimilate with and consume the human race... but do these monsters have a different side? A parasite becomes a prince to save his romance-obsessed female host from a dangerous stalker. Another hosts a cooking show, in which the real monsters are revealed. These and 13 more stories, from some of the greatest shojo manga artists alive today, together make up a chilling, funny, and entertaining tribute to one of manga's horror classics!

New action series from Hiroyuki Takei, creator of the classic shonen franchise Shaman King!

In medieval Japan, a bell hanging on the collar is a sign that a ca has a master. Norachiyo's bell hangs from his katana sheath, but he nonetheless a stray — a ronin. This one-eyed cat samurai travels across dishonest world, cutting through pretense and deception with his blade

By
Hiroyuki Takei

Having lost his wife, high school teacher Kōhei Inuzuka is doing his best to raise his young daughter Tsumugi as a single father. He's pretty bad at cooking and doesn't have a huge appetite to begin with, but chance brings his little family together with one of his students, the lonely Kotori. The three of them are anything but comfortable in the kitchen, but the healing power of home cooking might just work on their grieving hearts.

"This season's number-one feel-good anime!" —Anime News Network

"A beautifully-drawn story about comfort food and family and grief. Recommended." —Otaku USA Magazine

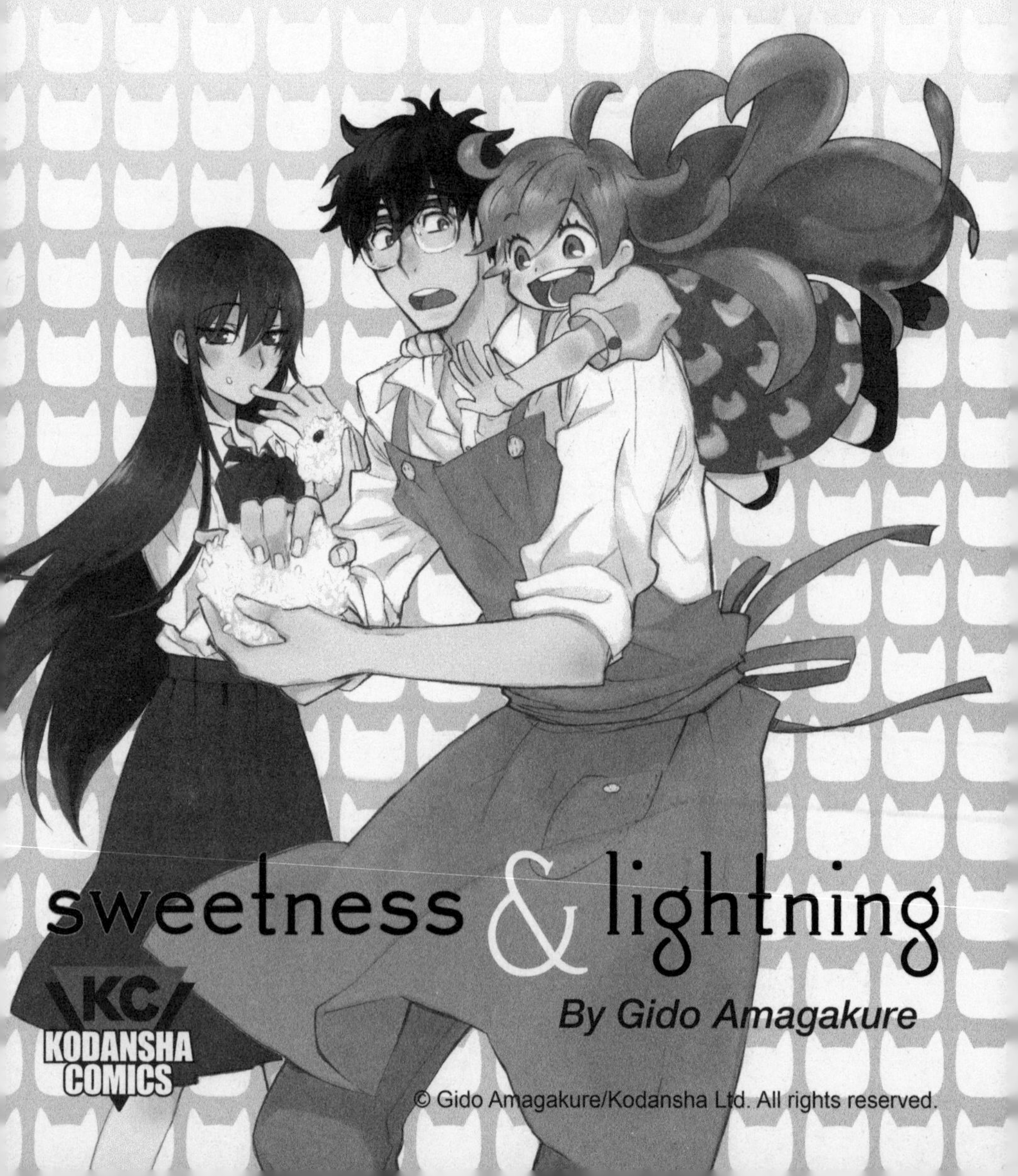

sweetness & lightning
By Gido Amagakure
KC
KODANSHA COMICS

The award-winning manga about what happens inside you!

"Far more entertaining than it ought to be... what kid doesn't want to think that every time they sneeze a torpedo shoots out their nose?"
–Anime News Network

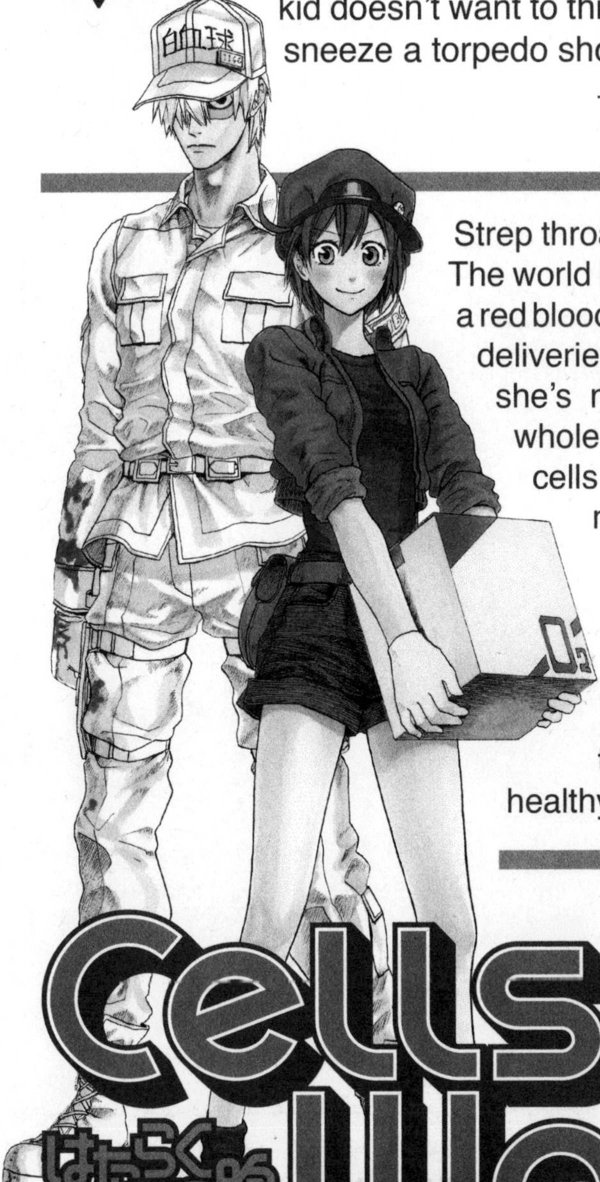

白血球

Strep throat! Hay fever! Influenza! The world is a dangerous place for a red blood cell just trying to get her deliveries finished. Fortunately, she's not alone...she's got a whole human body's worth of cells ready to help out! The mysterious white blood cells, the buff and brash killer T cells, even the cute little platelets—everyone's got to come together if they want to keep you healthy!

Cells at Work!

はたらく細胞

By Akane Shimizu

Aho-Girl volume 4 is a work of fiction. Names, characters, places, and incidents are the products of the author's imagination or are used fictitiously. Any resemblance to actual events, locales, or persons, living or dead, is entirely coincidental.

A Kodansha Comics Trade Paperback Original.

Published in the United States by Kodansha Comics, an imprint of Kodansha USA Publishing, LLC, New York.

Publication rights for this English edition arranged through Kodansha Ltd., Tokyo.

First published in Japan in 2014 by Kodansha Ltd., Tokyo, as *Aho Gaaru* volume 4.

ISBN 978-1-63236-460-9

Printed in the United States of America.

www.kodanshacomics.com

9 8 7 6 5 4 3 2 1

Translator: Karen McGillicuddy
Lettering: S. Lee
Editing: Paul Starr
Kodansha Comics edition cover design by Phil Balsman